OS X® Mountain Lion FOR DUMMIES®

by Bob "Dr. Mac" LeVitus

WILEY

John Wiley & Sons, Inc.

OS X® Mountain Lion For Dummies®

Published by
John Wiley & Sons, Inc.
111 River Street
Hoboken, NJ 07030-5774

www.wiley.com

Copyright © 2012 by John Wiley & Sons, Inc., Hoboken, New Jersey

Published by John Wiley & Sons, Inc., Hoboken, New Jersey

Published simultaneously in Canada

For general information on our other products and services, please contact our Customer Care Department within the U.S. at 877-762-2974, outside the U.S. at 317-572-3993, or fax 317-572-4002.

For technical support, please visit www.wiley.com/techsupport.

Wiley publishes in a variety of print and electronic formats and by print-on-demand. Some material included with standard print versions of this book may not be included in e-books or in print-on-demand. If this book refers to media such as a CD or DVD that is not included in the version you purchased, you may download this material at http://booksupport.wiley.com. For more information about Wiley products, visit www.wiley.com.

Library of Congress Control Number is available from the Publisher upon request.

ISBN 978-1-118-39418-2 (pbk); ISBN 978-1-118-46199-0 (ebk); ISBN 978-1-118-48698-6 (ebk); ISBN 978-1-118-48697-9 (ebk)

Manufactured in the United States of America

10 9 8 7 6 5 4 3 2 1

WILEY

About the Author

Bob LeVitus, often referred to as "Dr. Mac," has written or co-written more than 60 popular computer books, including *iPhone For Dummies, iPad For Dummies, Incredible iPad Apps For Dummies, Incredible iPhone Apps For Dummies, OS X For Dummies* for every version of OS X for John Wiley & Sons, Inc.; *Stupid Mac Tricks* and *Dr. Macintosh* for Addison-Wesley; and *The Little iTunes Book* and *The Little iDVD Book* for Peachpit Press. His books have sold more than a million copies worldwide.

Bob has penned the popular Dr. Mac column for the *Houston Chronicle* since 1996 and has been published in dozens of computer magazines over the past 25 years. His achievements have been documented in major media around the world. (Yes, that was him juggling a keyboard in *USA Today* a few years back!)

Bob is known for his expertise, trademark humorous style, and ability to translate techie jargon into usable and fun advice for regular folks. Bob is also a prolific public speaker, presenting more than 100 Macworld Expo training sessions in the U.S. and abroad, keynote addresses in three countries, and Macintosh training seminars in many U.S. cities. (He also won the Macworld Expo MacJeopardy World Championship three times before retiring his crown.)

Bob is considered a leading authority on Apple technology. From 1989 to 1997, he was a contributing editor/columnist for *MacUser* magazine, writing the Help Folder, Beating the System, Personal Best, and Game Room columns at various times.

In his copious spare time, Bob heads up a team of expert technical consultants who do nothing but provide technical help and training to Mac, iPhone, and iPad users via telephone, e-mail, and/or a unique Internet-enabled remote control software, which allows the team to see and control your Mac no matter where in the world you may be.

If you're having problems with your Mac, you ought to give them a try. You'll find them at www.boblevitus.com or 408-627-7577.

Prior to giving his life over to computers, LeVitus spent years at Kresser/Craig/D.I.K. (a Los Angeles advertising agency and marketing consultancy) and its subsidiary, L & J Research. He holds a B.S. in marketing from California State University.

Dedication

For the sixty-fourth time, this book is dedicated to the love of my life, my wife and best friend, Lisa, who taught me almost everything I know about almost everything I know except computers.

And, again for the sixth-fourth time, this book is also dedicated to my kids, Allison and Jacob, who love their Apple gadgets almost as much as I love them (the kids, not the Apple gadgets).

Author's Acknowledgments

Thanks to my super-agent, Carole "Swifty" McClendon. We've been together more than 20 years and you're *still* the greatest.

Special thanks to everyone at Apple who helped me turn this book around in record time: Keri Walker, Monica Sarkar, Janette Barrios, Greg (Joz) Joswiak, Teresa Brewer, and all the rest. I couldn't have done it without you.

Big-time thanks to the gang at Wiley: Bob "Is it done yet?" Woerner, Jean "Queen of the Editors" Nelson, Andy "Big Boss Man" Cummings, Barry "Still No Humorous Nickname" Pruett, my longtime technical editor Dennis R. Cohen, who (as usual) did a rocking job, and all the others.

Thanks also to my family and friends for putting up with me during my all-too-lengthy absences during this book's gestation. And thanks to Saccone's Pizza, Sodastream, The Garden Spot Café & Catering, The Noble Pig, and J. Mueller BBQ for sustenance.

And finally, thanks to you, gentle reader, for buying this book.

Publisher's Acknowledgments

We're proud of this book; please send us your comments at `http://dummies.custhelp.com`. For other comments, please contact our Customer Care Department within the U.S. at 877-762-2974, outside the U.S. at 317-572-3993, or fax 317-572-4002.

Some of the people who helped bring this book to market include the following:

Acquisitions and Editorial

Project Editor: Jean Nelson

Executive Editor: Bob Woerner

Copy Editor: Jean Nelson

Technical Editor: Dennis R. Cohen

Editorial Manager: Jodi Jensen

Editorial Assistant: Leslie Saxman

Sr. Editorial Assistant: Cherie Case

Cover Photo: © iStockphoto.com / Cary Westfall

Cartoons: Rich Tennant
(`www.the5thwave.com`)

Composition Services

Project Coordinator: Sheree Montgomery

Layout and Graphics: Carl Byers, Joyce Haughey, Christin Swinford

Proofreader: Dwight Ramsey

Indexer: BIM Indexing & Proofreading Services

Publishing and Editorial for Technology Dummies

    Richard Swadley, Vice President and Executive Group Publisher

    Andy Cummings, Vice President and Publisher

    Mary Bednarek, Executive Acquisitions Director

    Mary C. Corder, Editorial Director

Publishing for Consumer Dummies

    Kathleen Nebenhaus, Vice President and Executive Publisher

Composition Services

    Debbie Stailey, Director of Composition Services

Contents at a Glance

Introduction *1*

Part I: Introducing OS X Mountain Lion: The Basics *7*

Chapter 1: OS X Mountain Lion 101 (Prerequisites: None) 9
Chapter 2: The Desktop and Windows and Menus (Oh My)! 25
Chapter 3: Have It Your Way 47
Chapter 4: What's Up, Dock? 69
Chapter 5: The Finder and Its Desktop 87

*Part II: Mountain Lion Taming (Or "Organization
for Smart People")* *119*

Chapter 6: The Care and Feeding of Files and Folders..121
Chapter 7: Four Terrific Timesaving Tools 163
Chapter 8: Dealing with Disks 183
Chapter 9: Organizing Your Life 193

*Part III: Do Unto Mountain Lion: Getting
Things Done* *209*

Chapter 10: Internet-Working...211
Chapter 11: Communications Made Easy 227
Chapter 12: The Musical Mac 257
Chapter 13: The Multimedia Mac 273
Chapter 14: Words and Letters 285

Part IV: Making This Mountain Lion Your Very Own ... *295*

Chapter 15: Publish or Perish: The Fail-Safe Guide to Printing...........................297
Chapter 16: Sharing Your Mac and Liking It..313
Chapter 17: Features for the Way You Work..347

Part V: The Care and Feeding of Your Mountain Lion.... *369*

Chapter 18: Safety First: Backups and Other Security Issues 371
Chapter 19: Utility Chest..387
Chapter 20: Troubleshooting OS X...399

Part VI: The Part of Tens **409**

Chapter 21: Almost Ten Ways to Speed Up Your Mac Experience 411

Chapter 22: Ten Ways to Make Your Mac Better by Throwing Money at It.......... 421

Chapter 23: Ten (Or So) Great Websites for Mac Freaks............................ 427

Appendix: Installing or Reinstalling OS X Mountain Lion
(Only If You Have To) 435

Index **441**

Table of Contents

Introduction 1

About This Book 1
What You Won't Find in This Book 2
Conventions Used in This Book 2
Foolish Assumptions 3
How This Book Is Organized 3
Icons Used in This Book 5
Where to Go from Here 5

Part 1: Introducing OS X Mountain Lion: The Basics 7

Chapter 1: OS X Mountain Lion 101 (Prerequisites: None) 9

Gnawing to the Core of OS X 10
A Safety Net for the Absolute Beginner (Or Any User) 12
    Turning the dang thing on 12
    What you should see on startup 12
    Shutting down properly 16
    A few things you should definitely NOT do with your Mac 17
    Point-and-click boot camp 19
Not Just a Beatles Movie: Help and the Help Menu 20

Chapter 2: The Desktop and Windows and Menus (Oh My)! 25

Touring the Finder and Its Desktop 26
Anatomy of a Window 27
    Top o' the window to ya! 30
    A scroll new world 31
    (Hyper)Active windows 32
Dialog Dealie-Boppers 33
Working with Windows 35
    Opening and closing windows 35
    Resizing windows and window panes 36
    Moving windows 36
    Shuffling windows 37
Menu Basics 38
    The ever-changing menu bar 38
    Shortcut menus: They're sooo contextual 39

Recognizing disabled options 40
Navigating submenus 41
Underneath the Apple menu tree 42
Using keyboard shortcut commands 44

Chapter 3: Have It Your Way...47
Introducing System Preferences.. 47
Putting a Picture on the Desktop.. 50
Setting Up a Screen Saver.. 51
Putting Widgets on the Dashboard 53
Translation.. 56
Flight Tracker 56
Giving Buttons, Menus, and Windows a Makeover 57
Adjusting the Keyboard, Mouse, Trackpad, and Other Hardware.......... 60
Keyboard.. 60
Mouse 64
Bluetooth 65
Trackpad (notebooks and desktops with a Magic Trackpad) 66
Styling Your Sound 67
Changing sound effects 68
Choosing output and input options 68

Chapter 4: What's Up, Dock?...69
A Quick Introduction to Your Dock... 70
The default icons of the Dock 70
Trash talkin'.. 73
Opening application menus in the Dock............................ 75
Reading Dock icon body language...................................... 77
Opening files from the Dock 78
Customizing Your Dock 78
Adding Dock icons 78
Removing an icon from the Dock.. 81
Resizing the Dock.. 82
What should you put in YOUR Dock?................................. 82
Setting your Dock preferences 83

Chapter 5: The Finder and Its Desktop 87
Introducing the Finder and Its Minions: The Desktop and Icons 87
Introducing the Desktop 88
Bellying up to the toolbar 90
Figuring out what an icon is 93
Identifying your Finder icons in the wild.......................... 93
Aliases: Greatest Thing since Sliced Bread 95
Creating aliases 97
Deleting aliases 98
Hunting down an alias's parent... 98

The View(s) from a Window..99
    Moving through folders fast in Column view 99
    Perusing in Icon view 100
    Listless? Try touring folders in List view...............102
    You gotta go with the flow..................................104
Finder on the Menu 105
    The actual Finder menu 105
    Like a road map: The current folder's pop-up menu 107
    Going places with the Go menu 108
Customizing Finder Windows 111
    Adding folders to the Sidebar 111
    Setting Finder preferences..................................112
Digging for Icon Data in the Info Window................................114

Part II: Mountain Lion Taming (Or "Organization for Smart People")..................................... 119

Chapter 6: The Care and Feeding of Files and Folders 121

Understanding the OS X Folder Structure...............................122
    Understanding nested folders...............................123
    From the top: The Computer folder 124
    Peeking into the Applications folder 125
    Finding fonts (and more) in the public Library folder.................125
    Let it be: The System folder...............................127
    The usability of the Users folder 128
    There's no place like Home 128
    Your personal Library card 130
Saving Your Document before It's Too Late 132
    Stepping through a basic Save..............................133
    Save As versus Duplicate: Different names for same result........138
Open Sez Me..141
    With drag-and-drop 143
    With a Quick Look..143
    When your Mac can't open a file............................144
    With the application of your choice........................145
Organizing Your Stuff in Folders.......................................147
    Files versus folders.......................................147
    Organizing your stuff with subfolders......................148
    Creating new folders.......................................150
    Navigating with spring-loaded folders 151
    Smart Folders 152
Shuffling Around Files and Folders 155
    Comprehending the Clipboard................................155
    Copying files and folders 156
    Pasting from the Clipboard 157
    Moving files and folders...................................158

Selecting multiple icons 159
Playing the icon name game: Renaming icons 160
Compressing files.. 161
Getting rid of icons 161

Chapter 7: Four Terrific Timesaving Tools........................163

With a Quick Look 163
Share and share alike with the Share menu 165
Slide into Slideshow (full-screen) mode 166
Spotlight on Finding Files and Folders Faster............................. 167
Using the Search box in Finder windows................................... 167
Using the Spotlight menu and window 169
Finding files by other attributes... 170
Exposé Yourself to Mission Control's Spaces.............................. 172
The painless Mission Control pane 172
Hot corners!.. 175
Spaces from 30,000 feet (An overview)..................................... 175
Getting around in space(s) 179
Launchpad: The Place for Applications... 181
Customizing Your Launchpad.. 182

Chapter 8: Dealing with Disks 183

Comprehending Disks... 184
Some disks need to be formatted first 184
Moving and copying between disks 185
Surprise: Your PC Disks Work, Too!.. 185
Burning CDs and DVDs 186
Burning on the fly 187
Creating a burn folder 191
Getting Disks out of Your Mac 191

Chapter 9: Organizing Your Life..193

Keeping Track with Calendar.. 194
Navigating Calendar views... 194
Creating calendars... 195
Grouping calendars 197
Deleting a calendar or group.. 198
Creating and managing events 199
Are you available?.. 201
Reminders: Protection Against Forgetting 202
Getting started with Reminders 202
To do or not to do: Setting reminders...................................... 203
Everything you need to know about the Notification Center....... 205
Use Notes for Making Notes 206

Part III: Do Unto Mountain Lion: Getting Things Done 209

Chapter 10: Internet-Working. 211
Getting Connected to the Internet...212
   Setting up your modem...212
   Your Internet service provider and you 213
   Plugging in your Internet-connection settings 213
Browsing the Web with Safari...215
   Navigating with the toolbar buttons 215
   Bookmarking your favorite pages...217
   What's on your reading list?...219
   Using the terrific Top Sites page...220
   Searching with Google...222
   Checking out Help Center 224
Video Calls with FaceTime 224

Chapter 11: Communications Made Easy. 227
Collecting Your Contacts...227
   Adding contacts 228
   Importing contacts from other programs.............................230
   Creating a basic group 230
   Setting up a Smart Group (based on contact criteria)................231
   The Views are lovely 232
   iCloud + Contacts = Your contacts everywhere 233
   Sending e-mail to a contact or group 234
Sending and Receiving E-Mail with Mail 235
   Setting up Mail...235
   Composing a new message...236
   A quick overview of the toolbar...238
   Working with stationery 240
   Checking your mail...241
   Dealing with spam...241
   Changing your preferences 242
   Mail rules rule...243
   Mailboxes smart and plain 244
   Sign here, please 246
   Take a (Quick) look and (Slide) show me some photos 247
Communicating with Messages 249
   What the heck is an iMessage?...250
   Chit-chatting with Messages...250
   Chatting with audio and video 252
   Remote Screen Sharing: Remarkable and superbly satisfying.....253

Chapter 12: The Musical Mac 257

Introducing iTunes 257
Working with Media 260
    Adding songs 261
    Adding movies and videos 263
    Adding podcasts 263
    Learning from iTunes U 264
    Listening to Internet radio 265
All about Playlists 266
    Creating a regular playlist 266
    Working with smart playlists 267
    Burning a playlist to CD 268
    Looking at two specific playlists 269

Chapter 13: The Multimedia Mac 273

Watching Movies with DVD Player 273
Playing Movies and Music in QuickTime Player 276
You're the Star with Photo Booth 277
Viewing and Converting Images and PDFs in Preview ... 279
Importing Media 281
    Downloading photos from a camera 281
    Downloading DV video from a camcorder 283

Chapter 14: Words and Letters 285

Processing Words with TextEdit 285
    Creating and composing a document 286
    Working with text 288
    Adding graphics to documents 290
Font Mania 292
    Types of fonts 292
    Managing your fonts with Font Book 293
    Installing fonts manually 294

Part IV: Making This Mountain Lion Your Very Own.... 295

Chapter 15: Publish or Perish: The Fail-Safe Guide to Printing 297

Before Diving In 297
Ready: Connecting and Adding Your Printer 298
    Connecting your printer 298
    Setting up a printer for the first time 300
    One last thing: Printer sharing 302
Set: Setting Up Your Document with Page Setup 302
Print: Printing with the Print Sheet 304
    Printing a document 304
    Choosing among different printers 305

Choosing custom settings...306
Saving custom settings..309
Preview and PDF Options 309
Just the Fax 311

Chapter 16: Sharing Your Mac and Liking It **313**
Introducing Networks and File Sharing 314
Portrait of home-office networking...............................315
Three ways to build a network 317
Setting Up File Sharing..318
Access and Permissions: Who Can Do What 320
Users and groups and guests 320
Creating users 321
OS X knows best: Folders shared by default................328
Sharing a folder or disk by setting permissions 329
Useful settings for permissions...................................334
Unsharing a folder 336
Connecting to a Shared Disk or Folder on a Remote Mac.......337
Changing Your Password 341
Changing your account password on your Mac 341
Changing the password of any account but your own
on your Mac 341
Changing the password for your account
on someone else's Mac..342
More Types of Sharing...343
Screen Sharing..343
Web Sharing..344
Internet Sharing..345
And yet more ways to share...346

Chapter 17: Features for the Way You Work **347**
Talking and Listening to Your Mac 347
Dictation: You talk and your Mac types........................348
Commanding your Mac by voice 349
Listening to your Mac read for you 354
Automatic Automation..356
AppleScript..357
Automator..358
A Few More Useful Goodies..360
App Store 361
Accessibility 361
Energy Saver 363
Bluetooth 364
Ink 364
Automatic Login (Users & Groups System Preferences pane) 365
Boot Camp 365
AirPlay Mirroring...366

Part V: The Care and Feeding of Your Mountain Lion... 369

Chapter 18: Safety First: Backups and Other Security Issues 371
Backing Up Is (Not) Hard to Do 372
    Backing up with Mountain Lion's excellent Time Machine.........372
    Backing up by using the manual, brute-force method..................375
    Backing up by using commercial backup software.......................376
Why You Need Two Sets of Backups 376
Non-Backup Security Concerns 378
    About viruses and other malware 378
    Firewall: Yea or nay?...380
    Install recommended software updates 381
Protecting Your Data from Prying Eyes...382
    Blocking or limiting connections 383
    Locking down files with FileVault 383
    Setting other options for security...384

Chapter 19: Utility Chest 387
Calculator 387
Activity Monitor...388
AirPort Utility 390
ColorSync Utility..390
DigitalColor Meter 391
Disk Utility 391
    First Aid tab 391
    Erase tab 391
    Partition tab...392
    RAID tab 393
    Restore tab 393
Grab...394
Grapher...394
Keychain Access 395
Migration Assistant 396
System Information 397
Terminal..397

Chapter 20: Troubleshooting OS X. 399
About Startup Disks and Booting 399
    Finding or creating a startup disk..400
    They call it a prohibitory sign for a reason 400
Recovering with Recovery HD 402
    Step 1: Run First Aid 403
    Step 2: Safe Boot into Safe Mode..405
    Step 3: Zapping the PRAM/NVRAM..406
    Step 4: Reinstalling OS X 407
    Step 5: Things to try before taking your Mac in for repair 407
If Your Mac Crashes at Startup...408

Part VI: The Part of Tens... *409*

Chapter 21: Almost Ten Ways to Speed Up Your Mac Experience **411**

Use Those Keyboard Shortcuts 411
Improve Your Typing Skills 413
Resolution: It's Not Just for New Year's Anymore 413
A Mac with a View — and Preferences, Too 415
Get a New, Faster Model 416
You Can Never Have Too Much RAM! 417
Get an Accelerated Graphics Card 417
Get a New Hard Drive..418
Get a Solid State Drive (SSD) 419

Chapter 22: Ten Ways to Make Your Mac Better
by Throwing Money at It **421**

RAM 421
Backup Software and/or Hardware 422
A Better Monitor (Or a Second One)..422
A Fast Internet Connection...423
Games...423
Multimedia Titles...424
Some Big Honking Speakers with a Subwoofer...........................424
A New Mouse and/or Keyboard...424
A MacBook Air or MacBook Pro 425

Chapter 23: Ten (Or So) Great Websites for Mac Freaks **427**

MacFixIt...427
Macworld..428
The Mac Observer..428
CNET Downloads (formerly VersionTracker)..............................429
MacInTouch...429
Alltop...429
Apple Support and Knowledge Base 431
Ramseeker 431
Other World Computing 432
EveryMac.com..432
dealmac..433
Dr. Mac Consulting 433

Appendix: Installing or Reinstalling OS X Mountain Lion
(Only If You Have To) **435**

How to Install (or Reinstall) OS X...436
Getting Set Up with Setup Assistant...437

Index.. *441*

Introduction

*Y*ou made the right choice twice: OS X Mountain Lion and this book. Take a deep breath, and get ready to have a rollicking good time. That's right. This is a computer book, but it's fun. What a concept! Whether you're brand spanking new to the Mac or a grizzled Mac vet, I guarantee that reading this book to discover the ins and outs of OS X Mountain Lion will make everything easier. The publisher couldn't say as much on the cover if it weren't true!

About This Book

This book's roots lie with my international best seller *Macintosh System 7.5 For Dummies,* an award-winning book so good that now-deceased Mac cloner Power Computing gave away a copy with every Mac clone it sold. *OS X Mountain Lion For Dummies* is the latest revision and has been, once again, completely updated to include all the OS X goodness in Mountain Lion. In other words, this edition combines all the old, familiar features of previous editions — but is once again updated to reflect the latest and greatest offering from Apple as well as feedback from readers.

Why write a *For Dummies* book about Mountain Lion? Well, Mountain Lion is a big, somewhat complicated personal-computer operating system. So I made *OS X Mountain Lion For Dummies* a not-so-big, not-very-complicated book that shows you what Mountain Lion is all about without boring you to tears, confusing you, or poking you with sharp objects.

In fact, I think you'll be so darned comfortable that I wanted the title to be *OS X Mountain Lion Without Discomfort,* but the publishers wouldn't let me. Apparently, we *For Dummies* authors have to follow some rules and using *For Dummies* and *OS X Mountain Lion* in this book's title are among them.

And speaking of *dummies,* remember that's just a word. I don't think you're dumb — quite the opposite! My second choice for this book's title was *OS X Mountain Lion For People Smart Enough to Know They Need Help with It,* but you can just imagine what Wiley thought of that. ("C'mon, that's the whole point of the name!" they insisted. "Besides, it's shorter our way.")

The book is chock-full of information and advice, explaining everything you need to know about OS X in language you can understand — along with time-saving tips, tricks, techniques, and step-by-step instructions, all served up in generous quantities.

What You Won't Find in This Book

Another rule we *For Dummies* authors must follow is that our books cannot exceed a certain number of pages. (Brevity is the soul of wit, and all that.) So I wish I could have included some things, but they didn't fit. Although I feel confident you'll find everything you need to know about OS X Mountain Lion in this book, some things bear further looking into, including these:

✔ **Information about some of the applications (programs) that come with OS X Mountain Lion:** An installation of OS X Mountain Lion includes roughly 50 separate applications, mostly located in the Applications folder and the Utilities folder within it. I'd love to walk you through each one of them, but that would have required a book a whole lot bigger, heavier, and more expensive than this one.

I brief you on the small handful of bundled applications essential to using OS X Mountain Lion and keep the focus there — namely, Calendar, Contacts, Messages, Mail, Safari, TextEdit, and the like, as well as important utilities you may need to know how to use someday.

For what it's worth, many books cover the applications that come with OS X Mountain Lion, as well as applications commonly bundled with Mountain Lion on a new Mac, such as iLife; the one my publisher suggested I recommend is *OS X Mountain Lion All-in-One For Dummies,* written by Mark L. Chambers, which is (of course) also published by Wiley.

✔ **Information about Microsoft Office, iLife, iWork, Adobe Photoshop, Quicken, and most other third-party applications:** Okay, if all the gory details of all the bundled (read: *free*) OS X Mountain Lion applications don't fit here, I think you'll understand why digging into third-party applications that cost extra was out of the question.

✔ **Information about programming for the Mac:** This book is about *using* OS X Mountain Lion, not writing code for it. Dozens of books cover programming on the Mac, most of which are two or three times the size of this book.

Conventions Used in This Book

To get the most out of this book, you need to know how I do things and why. Here are a few conventions I use in this book to make your life easier:

✔ When I want you to open an item in a menu, I write something like "Choose File⇨Open," which means, "Pull down the File menu and choose the Open command."

✔ Stuff you're supposed to type appears in bold type, **like this**.

- ✓ **Sometimes an entire a sentence is in boldface, as you see when I present a numbered list of steps. In those cases, I leave the bold off what you're supposed to type,** like this.

- ✓ Web addresses, programming code (not much in this book), and things that appear on-screen are shown in a special monofont typeface, `like this`. (If you're reading an ebook version of this book, web addresses are clickable links.)

- ✓ For keyboard shortcuts, I write something like ⌘+A, which means to hold down the ⌘ key (the one with the little pretzel and/or symbol on it) and then press the A key on the keyboard. If you see something like ⌘+Shift+A, that means to hold down the ⌘ and Shift keys while pressing the A key. Again, for clarity, I never refer to the ⌘ key with the symbol. I reserve that symbol for the menu (Apple menu). For the Command key, I use only the ⌘ symbol. Got it? Very cool.

Foolish Assumptions

Although I know what happens when you make assumptions, I've made a few anyway. First, I assume that you, gentle reader, know nothing about using OS X — beyond knowing what a Mac is, that you want to use OS X, that you want to understand OS X without having to digest an incomprehensible technical manual, and that you made the right choice by selecting this particular book. And so I do my best to explain each new concept in full and loving detail. Maybe that's foolish, but . . . oh well.

Oh, and I also assume that you can read. If you can't, ignore this paragraph.

How This Book Is Organized

OS X Mountain Lion For Dummies is divided into six logical parts, numbered (surprisingly enough) 1 through 6. By no fault of mine, they're numbered using those stuffy old Roman numerals, so you see I–VI where you (in my humble opinion) ought to see Arabic numbers 1–6. It's another rule that _For Dummies_ authors have to follow, I think.

Anyway, it's better if you read the parts in order, but if you already know a lot — or think you know a lot — feel free to skip around and read the parts that interest you most.

Part I: Introducing OS X Mountain Lion: The Basics: This first part is very, very basic training. From the mouse to the Desktop, from menus, windows, and icons to the snazzy-but-helpful Dock, it's all here. A lot of what you need to know to navigate the depths of OS X safely (and sanely) and perform basic tasks can be found in this part. And although old-timers might just want to skim it, newcomers should probably read every word. Twice.

Part II: Mountain Lion Taming (Or "Organization for Smart People"): In this part, I build on the basics of Part I and really get you revving with your Mac. Here, I cover additional topics that every Mac user needs to know, coupled with some hands-on, step-by-step instructions. The part starts with a closer look at ways you can organize your files and folders, followed by a chapter about using removable media (which means *ejectable discs* — mostly CDs and DVDs). Last, but certainly not least, is a chapter about all the Mountain Lion applications (such as Calendar, Contacts, Messages, and Mail) that help you keep your digital life organized.

Part III: Do Unto Mountain Lion: Getting Things Done: This part is chock-full of ways to do productive stuff with your Mac. You discover the Internet — or at least how to get it working on your Mac and what to do with it after you do. Next, you look at the digital-media side of things with chapters about music, video, games, and digital photos. Finally, you look at Mountain Lion's built-in tools for writing — namely, TextEdit and fonts.

Part IV: Making This Mountain Lion Your Very Own: Here, I get into the nitty-gritty underbelly of making OS X Mountain Lion work the way you want it to work. I start with the ins and outs of printing under OS X. Then I move on to somewhat more advanced topics, such as file sharing, creating and using multiple user accounts (and why you might want to), and the lowdown on numerous OS X Mountain Lion features — Text to Speech, speech recognition, automation, and more — that can make your computing experience even more pleasant.

Part V: The Care and Feeding of Your Mountain Lion: This part starts with a chapter about backups and security, which not only stresses the importance of backing up your data, but also shows you how to do it almost painlessly. I introduce you to a handful of useful utilities included with Mountain Lion, and explain when and how to use them. Finally, I tell you how to avoid most disasters, as well as what to do in the event that a major mishap does occur.

Part VI: The Part of Tens: Finally, it's The Part of Tens, which might have started life as a Letterman rip-off but does include heaping helpings of tips, optional software, great Mac websites, and hardware ideas.

Appendix: Last, but certainly not least, I cover installing or reinstalling OS X Mountain Lion in the Appendix. The whole process has become quite easy with this version of the system software, but if you have to install Mountain Lion yourself, it would behoove you to read this helpful Appendix first.

Icons Used in This Book

Little round pictures (icons) appear off to the left side of the text throughout this book. Consider these icons miniature road signs, telling you a little something extra about the topic at hand. Here's what the different icons look like and what they all mean.

Look for Tip icons to find the juiciest morsels: shortcuts, tips, and undocumented secrets about Mountain Lion. Try them all; impress your friends!

When you see this icon, it means that this particular morsel is something that I think you should memorize (or at least write on your shirt cuff).

Put on your propeller-beanie hat and pocket protector; these parts include the truly geeky stuff. It's certainly not required reading, but it must be interesting or informative, or I wouldn't have wasted your time with it.

Read these notes very, very, very carefully. (Did I say *very?*) Warning icons flag important cautionary information. The author and publisher won't be responsible if your Mac explodes or spews flaming parts because you ignored a Warning icon. Just kidding. Macs don't explode or spew (with the exception of a few choice PowerBook 5300s, which won't run Mountain Lion anyway). But I got your attention, didn't I?

These icons represent my ranting or raving about something that either bugs me or makes me smile. When I'm ranting, imagine foam coming from my mouth. Rants are required to be irreverent, irrelevant, or both. I try to keep them short, for your sake.

Well, now, what could this icon possibly be about? Named by famous editorial consultant Mr. Obvious, this icon highlights all things new and different in OS X Mountain Lion.

Where to Go from Here

The first few chapters of this book are where I describe the basic things that you need to understand to operate your Mac effectively. If you're new to Macs and OS X Mountain Lion, start there.

Even though OS X Mountain Lion is somewhat different from previous Mac operating systems, the first part of the book is so basic that if you've been using a Mac for long, you might think you know it all — and okay, you might know most of it. But hey! Not-so-old-timers need a solid foundation. So here's my advice: Skip the stuff you know; you'll get to the better stuff faster.

I would love to hear how this book worked for you. So please send me your thoughts, platitudes, likes and dislikes, and any other comments. Did this book work for you? What did you like? What didn't you like? What questions were unanswered? Did you want to know more (or less) about something? Tell me! I have received more than 100 suggestions about previous editions, most of which are incorporated here. So keep up the good work! E-mail me at `MountainLion4Dummies@boblevitus.com`. I appreciate your feedback, and I *try* to respond to all reasonably polite e-mail within a few days.

So what are you waiting for? Go — enjoy the book!

Part I
Introducing OS X Mountain Lion: The Basics

The 5th Wave   By Rich Tennant

AFTER INSTALLING OS X, NED AND LORETTA SELECT THE COMPUTER'S BACKGROUND

"Oh — I like this background much better than the basement."

In this part . . .

Because I believe it's important to crawl before you walk, in this part, you get a look at the most basic of basics — such as how to turn on your Mac. Next, I acquaint you with the OS X Finder, with its Desktop, windows, icons, and menus (oh my)! Then you find out how to make this cat your own by customizing your work environment to suit your style. After that is a date with the Dock. And last but certainly not least, you discover ways you can use the Finder to make life with Mountain Lion ever so much easier.

So get comfortable, roll up your sleeves, fire up your Mac if you like, and settle down with Part I, a delightful little section I like to think of as "The Hassle-Free Way to Get Started with OS X Mountain Lion."

OS X Mountain Lion 101 (Prerequisites: None)

In This Chapter

▶ Understanding what an operating system is and is not

▶ Turning on your Mac

▶ Getting to know the startup process

▶ Turning off your Mac

▶ Avoiding major Mac mistakes

▶ Pointing, clicking, dragging, and other uses for your mouse

▶ Getting help from your Mac

C ongratulate yourself on choosing OS X, which stands for *Macintosh Operating System X* — that's the Roman numeral *ten,* not the letter *X* (pronounced *ten,* not *ex).* You made a smart move because you scored more than just an operating-system upgrade. OS X Mountain Lion includes several new features that make using your Mac easier and dozens of improvements that help you do more work in less time.

In this chapter, I start at the very beginning and talk about OS X in mostly abstract terms; then I move on to explain what you need to know to use OS X Mountain Lion successfully.

If you've been using OS X for a while, some of the information in this chapter might seem hauntingly familiar; some features that I describe haven't changed from earlier versions of OS X. But if you decide to skip this chapter because you think you have all the new stuff figured out, I assure you that you'll miss at least a couple of things that Apple didn't bother to tell you (as if you read every word in OS X Help — the only user manual Apple provides — anyway!).

Tantalized? Let's rock.

There is one last thing: If you're about to upgrade to Mountain Lion from an earlier version of OS X, you might want to peruse the Appendix first. It describes the process of installing or reinstalling Mountain Lion in full and loving detail, and has other useful information about installing Mountain Lion. 'Nuff said.

Gnawing to the Core of OS X

The operating system (that is, the *OS* in *OS X)* is what makes a Mac a Mac. Without it, your Mac is a pile of silicon and circuits — no smarter than a toaster.

"So what does an operating system do?" you ask. Good question. The short answer is that an operating system controls the basic and most important functions of your computer. In the case of OS X and your Mac, the operating system

- ✓ Manages memory
- ✓ Controls how windows, icons, and menus work
- ✓ Keeps track of files
- ✓ Manages networking
- ✓ Does housekeeping (No kidding!)

Other forms of software, such as word processors and web browsers, rely on the operating system to create and maintain the environment in which they work their magic. When you create a memo, for example, the word processor provides the tools for you to type and format the information. In the background, the operating system is the muscle for the word processor, performing crucial functions such as the following:

- ✓ Providing the mechanism for drawing and moving the on-screen window in which you write the memo
- ✓ Keeping track of a file when you save it
- ✓ Helping the word processor create drop-down menus and dialogs for you to interact with

- ✐ Communicating with other programs
- ✐ And much, much more (stuff that only geeks could care about)

So, armed with a little background in operating systems, take a gander at the next section before you do anything else with your Mac.

One last thing: As I mention in the introduction (I'm repeating it here only in case you normally don't read introductions), OS X Mountain Lion comes with more than 50 applications. Although I'd love to tell you all about each and every one, I have only so many pages at my disposal. If you need more info on the programs I don't cover, may I (again) recommend *OS X Mountain Lion All-in-One For Dummies,* written by Mark L. Chambers, or *iLife For Dummies,* written by my old friends Tony Bove and Cheryl Rhodes (both published by John Wiley & Sons, Inc.).

The Mac advantage

Most of the world's personal computers use Microsoft Windows (though more and more people are switching to the Mac these days). But you're among the lucky few to have a computer with an operating system that's intuitive, easy to use, and (dare I say?) fun. If you don't believe me, try using Windows for a day or two. Go ahead. You probably won't suffer any permanent damage. In fact, you'll really begin to appreciate how good you have it. Feel free to hug your Mac. Or give it a peck on the disc-drive slot (assuming your Mac has one; some, like the MacBook Air and Mac Mini, don't.). Just try not to get your tongue caught.

As someone once told me, "Claiming that the Macintosh is inferior to Windows because most people use Windows is like saying that all other restaurants serve food that's inferior to McDonald's."

We might be a minority, but Mac users have the best, most stable, most modern all-purpose operating system in the world, and here's why: Unix, on which OS X is based, is widely regarded as the best industrial-strength operating system

on the planet. For now, just know that being based on Unix means that a Mac running OS X will crash less often than an older Mac or a Windows machine, which means less downtime. Being Unix-based also means far fewer viruses and malicious software. But perhaps the biggest advantage OS X has is that when an application crashes, it doesn't crash your entire computer, and you don't have to restart the whole computer to continue working.

By the way, with the advent of Intel-powered Macs a few years ago, you can now run Windows natively. That's right — you can now install and run Microsoft Windows on any Mac powered by an Intel processor, as described in Chapter 17. Don't let that Unix stuff scare you. It's there if you want it, but if you don't want it or don't care (like most of us), you'll rarely even know it's there. In fact, you'll rarely (if ever) see the word *Unix* again in this book. As far as you're concerned, Unix under the hood means your Mac will just run and run and run without crashing and crashing and crashing.

A Safety Net for the Absolute Beginner (Or Any User)

In the following sections, I deal with the stuff that OS X Help doesn't cover — or doesn't cover in nearly enough detail. If you're a first-time Macintosh user, please, *please* read this section of the book carefully; it could save your life. Okay, okay, perhaps I'm being overly dramatic. What I mean to say is that reading this section could save your *Mac* or your sanity. Even if you're an experienced Mac user, you might want to read this section. Chances are you'll see at least a few things you might have forgotten that will come in handy now that you've been reminded of them.

Turning the dang thing on

Okay. This is the big moment — turning on your Mac! Gaze at it longingly first, and say something cheesy, such as "You're the most awesome computer I've ever known." If that doesn't turn on your Mac (and it probably won't), keep reading.

Apple, in its infinite wisdom, has manufactured Macs with power buttons on every conceivable surface: on the front, side, and back of the computer itself and even on the keyboard or monitor.

So if you don't know how to turn on your Mac, don't feel bad; just look in the manual or booklet that came with your Mac. It's at least one thing that the documentation *always* covers.

 These days, most Macs have a power-on button near the keyboard (notebooks) or the back (iMacs). It usually looks like the little circle thingie you see in the margin.

 Don't bother choosing Help⇨Mac Help, which opens the Help Viewer program. It can't tell you where the switch is. Although the Help program is good for finding out a lot of things, the location of the power switch isn't among them. If you haven't found the switch and turned on the Mac, of course, you can't access Help anyway. (D'oh!)

What you should see on startup

When you finally do turn on your Macintosh, you set in motion a sophisticated and complex series of events that culminates in the loading of OS X and the appearance of the OS X Desktop. After a small bit of whirring, buzzing, and flashing (meaning that the operating system is loading), OS X first tests all your hardware — slots, ports, disks, random-access memory (RAM), and so on. If everything passes, you hear a pleasing musical tone and see the tasteful gray Apple logo in the middle of your screen, along with a small spinning-pinwheel cursor somewhere on the screen. Both are shown in Figure 1-1.

Figure 1-1: This is what you'll see if everything is fine and dandy when you turn on your Mac.

Here are the things that might happen when you power up your Mac:

✔ **Fine and dandy:** Next, you might or might not see the OS X login screen, where you enter your name and password. If you do, press Return or Enter (after you type your name and password, of course), and away you go.

If you don't want to have to type your name and password every time you start or restart your Mac (or even if you do), check out Chapter 17 for the scoop on how to turn the login screen on or off.

Either way, the Desktop soon materializes before your eyes. If you haven't customized, configured, or tinkered with your Desktop, it should look pretty much like Figure 1-2. Now is a good time to take a moment for positive thoughts about the person who convinced you that you wanted a Mac. That person was right!

Figure 1-2: The OS X Mountain Lion Desktop after a brand-spanking-new installation of OS X.

The legend of boot

Boot this. *Boot* that. "I *booted* my Mac and. . . ." or "Did it *boot?*" and so on. Talking about computers for long without hearing the *boot* word is nearly impossible. But why *boot?* Why not *shoe* or *shirt* or even *shazam?*

Back in the very olden days — say, 1958 or a little earlier — starting a computer required you to toggle little manual switches on the front panel, which began an internal process that loaded the operating system. The process became known as *bootstrapping* because if you toggled the right switches, the computer would "pull itself up by its bootstraps." This phrase didn't take long to transmogrify into *booting* and finally to *boot.*

Over the years, *booting* has come to mean turning on almost any computer or even a peripheral device, such as a printer. Some people also use it to refer to launching an application ("I booted Excel").

So the next time one of your gearhead friends says the b-word, ask whether he knows where the term comes from. Then dazzle him with the depth and breadth of your (not-quite-useful) knowledge!

✏ **Blue/black/gray screen of death:** If any of your hardware fails when it's tested, you might see a blue, black, or gray screen.

Some older Macs played the sound of a horrible car wreck instead of the chimes, complete with crying tires and busting glass. It was exceptionally unnerving, which might be why Apple doesn't use it anymore.

The fact that something went wrong is no reflection on your prowess as a Macintosh user. Something is broken, and your Mac may need repairs. If this is happening to you right now, check out Chapter 20 to try to get your Mac well again.

If your computer is under warranty, dial 1-800-SOS-APPL, and a customer-service person can tell you what to do. Before you do anything, though, skip ahead to Chapter 20. It's entirely possible that one of the suggestions there can get you back on track without your having to spend even a moment on hold.

 ✏ **Prohibitory sign (formerly known as the flashing-question-mark disk):** Most users eventually encounter the prohibitory sign shown in the left margin (which replaced the flashing question-mark-on-a-disk icon and flashing folder icon back in OS X Jaguar). This icon means that your Mac can't find a startup disk, hard drive, network server, or DVD-ROM containing a valid Macintosh operating system. See Chapter 20 for ways to ease your Mac's ills.

✏ **Kernel panic:** You shouldn't see this very often, but you might occasionally see a block of text in four languages, including English, as shown in Figure 1-3. This means that your Mac has experienced a *kernel panic,* the most severe type of system crash. If you restart your Mac and see this message again, look in Chapter 20 for a myriad of possible cures for all kinds of ailments, including this one.

You need to restart your computer. Hold down the Power button for several seconds or press the Restart button.

Veuillez redémarrer votre ordinateur. Maintenez la touche de démarrage enfoncée pendant plusieurs secondes ou bien appuyez sur le bouton de réinitialisation.

Sie müssen Ihren Computer neu starten. Halten Sie dazu die Einschalttaste einige Sekunden gedrückt oder drücken Sie die Neustart-Taste.

コンピュータを再起動する必要があります。パワーボタンを数秒間押し続けるか、リセットボタンを押してください。

Figure 1-3: If this is what you're seeing, things are definitely *not* fine and dandy.

How do you know which version of the Mac OS your computer has? Simple:

1. **Choose About This Mac from the menu (the menu with the symbol in the top-left corner of the menu bar).**

   The About This Mac window pops up on your screen, as shown in Figure 1-4. The version you're running appears just below *OS X* in the center of the window. Version 10.8 is the release we know as *Mountain Lion.*

   If you're curious or just want to impress your friends, OS X version 10.7 was known as Lion; 10.6 as Snow Leopard; 10.5 as Leopard; 10.4 as Tiger; 10.3 as Panther; 10.2 as Jaguar; 10.1 as Puma; and 10.0 as Cheetah.

2. **Click the More Info button to launch the System Information application.**

   This app shows you much more information, including bus speed, number of processors, caches, installed memory, networking, storage devices, and much more. You can find more about this useful program in Chapter 19.

Figure 1-4: See which version of OS X you're running.

Shutting down properly

Turning off the power without shutting down your Mac properly is one of the worst things you can do to your poor Mac. Shutting down your Mac improperly can really screw up your hard drive, scramble the contents of your most important files, or both.

If a thunderstorm is rumbling nearby, or you're unfortunate enough to have rolling blackouts where you live, you might really want to shut down your Mac. (See the next section, where I briefly discuss lightning and your Mac.)

To turn off your Mac, always use the Shut Down command on the menu or shut down in one of these kind-and-gentle ways:

- Press the Power key once and then click the Shut Down button in the Are You Sure You Want To Shut Down Your Computer Now? dialog.

- On keyboards that don't have a Power key, press Control+Eject instead — and then click the Shut Down button that appears in the Are You Sure You Want To Shut Down Your Computer Now? dialog.

  You can use a handy keyboard shortcut when the Shut Down button (or any button, for that matter) is highlighted in blue and pulsating slightly. Pressing the Return or Enter key is the same as clicking that button.

Eternally yours . . . *now*

OS X is designed so that you never have to shut it down. You can configure it to sleep after a specified period of inactivity. (See Chapter 17 for more info on the Energy Saver features of OS X.) If you do so, your Mac will consume very little electricity when it's sleeping and will usually be ready to use (when you press any key or click the mouse) in less than a minute. On the other hand, if you're not going to be using it for a few days, you might want to shut it down anyway.

Note: If you leave your Mac on constantly, and you're gone when a lightning storm or rolling blackout hits, your Mac might get wasted. So be sure you have adequate protection — say, a decent surge protector designed specifically for computers — if you decide to leave your Mac on and unattended for long periods. See the section "A few things you should definitely NOT do with your Mac," elsewhere in this chapter, for more info on lightning and your Mac. Often as not, I leave it on when I'm on the road so that I can access it from my laptop via remote screen sharing. So because OS X is designed to run 24/7, I don't shut it down at night unless the night happens to be dark and stormy.

The Are You Sure You Want To Shut Down Your Computer Now? dialog sports a check-box option in OS X Mountain Lion: Reopen Windows When Logging Back In. If you check this box, your Mac will start back up with the same windows (and applications) that were open when you shut down or restarted. I think it's pretty darn sweet! I'm happy to report that Mountain Lion is full of such nice little improvements.

Most Mac users have been forced to shut down improperly more than once without anything horrible happening, of course — but don't be lulled into a false sense of security. Break the rules one time too many (or under the wrong circumstances), and your most important files *will* be toast. The *only* time you should turn off your Mac without shutting down properly is when your screen is completely frozen or when your system crashed due to a kernel panic and you've already tried everything else. (See Chapter 20 for what those "everything else"s are.) A really stubborn crash doesn't happen often — and less often under OS X than ever before — but when it does, forcing your Mac to turn off and then back on might be the only solution.

A few things you should definitely NOT do with your Mac

In this section, I cover the bad stuff that can happen to your computer if you do the wrong things with it. If something bad has already happened to you — I know . . . I'm beginning to sound like a broken record — see Chapter 20.

✔ **Don't unplug your Mac when it's turned on.** Very bad things can happen, such as having your operating system break. See the preceding section, where I discuss shutting down your system properly.

Note that this warning doesn't apply to laptops as long as their battery is at least partially charged. As long as there's enough juice in the battery to power your Mac, you can connect and disconnect its power adapter to your heart's content.

✔ **Don't use your Mac when lightning is near.** Here's a simple life equation for you: Mac + lightning = dead Mac. 'Nuff said. Oh, and don't place much faith in inexpensive surge protectors. A good jolt of lightning will fry the surge protector and your computer — as well as possibly frying your modem, printer, and anything else plugged into the surge protector. Some surge protectors can withstand most lightning strikes, but those warriors aren't the cheapies that you buy at your local computer emporium. Unplugging your Mac from the wall during electrical storms is safer and less expensive. (Don't forget to unplug your external modem, network hubs, printers, and other hardware that plugs into the wall as well; lightning can fry them, too.)

For laptops, disconnect the power adapter and all other cables (because whatever those cables are connected to could fry, and fry your laptop right along with it). That said, you could use your laptop during a storm, if you like. Just make sure that it's 100 percent wireless and cableless if you do.

✔ **Don't jostle, bump, shake, kick, throw, dribble, or punt your Mac, especially while it's running.** Most Macs contain a hard drive that spins at 4,200 revolutions per minute (rpm) or more. A jolt to a hard drive while it's reading or writing a file can cause the head to crash into the disk, which can render many — or all — files on it unrecoverable. Ouch!

✔ **Don't forget to back up your data!** If the stuff on your hard drive means anything to you, you must back it up. Not *maybe*. *Must*. Even if your most important file is your last saved game of Bejeweled, you still need to back up your files. Fortunately, OS X Mountain Lion includes an awesome backup utility called Time Machine. (Unfortunately, you need either an external hard drive or an Apple Time Capsule device to take advantage of it.) So I beg you: Please read Chapter 18 now, and find out how to back up before something horrible happens to your valuable data!

I *strongly* recommend that you read Chapter 18 sooner rather than later — preferably before you do any significant work on your Mac. Dr. Macintosh says, "There are only two kinds of Mac users: Those who have lost data and those who will." Which kind do you want to be?

✔ **Don't kiss your monitor while wearing stuff on your lips.** For obvious reasons! Use a clean, soft cloth and/or OmniCleanz display cleaning solution (I love the stuff, made by RadTech; www.radtech.us) to clean your display.

Don't use household window cleaners or paper towels. Either one can harm your display. Use a soft clean cloth, and if you're going to use a cleaner, make sure it's specifically designed not to harm computer displays. (And spray it on the *cloth,* not the screen.)

Point-and-click boot camp

Are you new to the Mac? Just figuring out how to move the mouse around? Now is a good time to go over some fundamental stuff that you need to know for just about everything you'll be doing on the Mac. Spend a few minutes reading this section, and soon you'll be clicking, double-clicking, pressing, and pointing all over the place. If you think you have the whole mousing thing pretty much figured out, feel free to skip this section. I'll catch you on the other side.

Still with me? Good. Now for some basic terminology:

✔ **Point:** Before you can click or press anything, you have to *point* to it. Place your hand on your mouse, and move it so that the cursor arrow is over the object you want — like on top of an icon or a button.

✔ **Click:** Also called *single click.* Use your index finger to push the mouse button all the way down and then let go so the button produces a satisfying clicking sound. (If you have one of the new optical Apple Pro mice, you push down the whole thing to click.) Use a single-click to highlight an icon, press a button, or activate a check box or window.

In other words, first you point and then you click — *point and click,* in computer lingo.

✔ **Double-click:** *Click twice* in rapid succession. With a little practice, you can perfect this technique in no time. Use a double-click to open a folder or to launch a file or application.

✔ **Control-click:** Hold down the Control key while single-clicking. Control-clicking is the same as right-clicking a Windows system and displays a menu (called a *contextual menu*) where you Control-clicked. In fact, if you're blessed with a two-or-more-button mouse such as the Apple Magic Mouse, you can right-click and avoid having to hold down the Control key. (You may have to enable this feature in the Mouse System Preference pane.)

If you have a Mac with a built-in trackpad or Apple Magic Trackpad, you can configure it to recognize a two-fingered tap as a right-click. (You may have to enable this feature in the Trackpad System Preference pane.)

✓ **Drag:** *Dragging* something usually means you have to click it first and hold down the mouse button. Then you move the mouse on your desk or mouse pad so that the cursor and whatever you select moves across the screen. The combination of holding down the button and dragging the mouse is usually referred to as *clicking and dragging.*

✓ **Choosing an item from a menu:** To get to Mac OS menu commands, you must first open a menu and then pick the option you want. Point at the name of the menu you want with your cursor, press the mouse button down, and then drag downward until you select the command you want. When the command is highlighted, finish selecting by letting go of the mouse button.

If you're a longtime Mac user, you probably hold down the mouse button the whole time between clicking the name of the menu and selecting the command you want. You can still do it that way, but you can also click the menu name to open it, release the mouse button, drag down to the item you want to select, *and then click again.* In other words, OS X menus stay open after you click them, even if you're not holding down the mouse button. After you click a menu to open it, you can even type the first letter (or letters) of the item to select it and then execute that item by pressing the spacebar or the Return or Enter key.

A menu remains open until you click something else. Go ahead and give it a try . . . I'll wait.

The terms given in the preceding list apply to all Mac laptop, desktop, and tower systems. If you use a MacBook, MacBook Pro, or Apple Magic Trackpad, however, there are a few more terms — such as *tap*, *swipe*, *rotate*, *pinch*, and *spread* — you'll want to add to your lexicon. You can read all about them in full and loving detail in Chapter 3.

Not Just a Beatles Movie: Help and the Help Menu

One of the best features about all Macs is the excellent built-in help, and OS X Mountain Lion doesn't cheat you on that legacy: This system has online help in abundance. When you have a question about how to do something, the Help Center is the first place you should visit (after this book, of course).

Clicking the Help menu reveals the Search Help field at the top of the menu and the Mac Help item, which opens the Mac Help window, as shown in Figure 1-5.

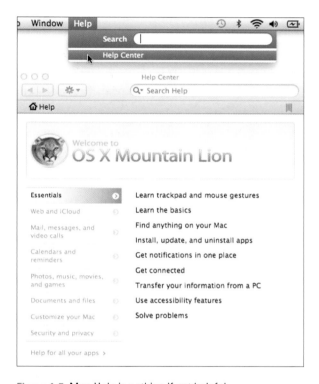

Figure 1-5: Mac Help is nothing if not helpful.

The keyboard shortcut for Help appears on the Help menu as ⌘+?, but you really need to press Shift+⌘+? to open Help using the keyboard.

Just so you know, this is the only shortcut I can think of in which the menu doesn't display an up arrow (Shift+⌘+?) to let you know that you need to press Shift.

You can find out much more about keyboard shortcuts in Chapter 3.

To use Mac Help, simply type a word or phrase in either Search field — the one in the Help menu itself or the one near the top of the Help window on the right side — and then press Return or Enter. In a few seconds, your Mac provides you one or more articles to read, which (theoretically) are related to your question. Usually. If you type **menus** and press Return, for example, you get 17 help topics, as shown in Figure 1-6.

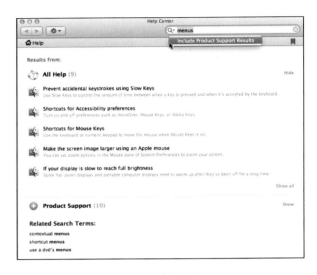

Figure 1-6: You have questions? Mac has answers.

As long as your Mac is connected to the Internet, search results include articles from Apple's online support database by default. Click the magnifying-glass icon to the left of the Search field, as shown in Figure 1-6, if you want to disable this feature.

I can't think of any reason why you'd want to disable this useful feature, but I want you to know that you can if you like.

Although you don't have to be connected to the Internet to use Mac Help, you do need an Internet connection to get the most out of it. (Chapter 10 can help you set up an Internet connection, if you don't have one.) That's because OS X installs only certain help articles on your hard drive. If you ask a question that those articles don't answer, Mac Help connects to Apple's website and downloads the answer (assuming that you have an active Internet connection). These answers are the Support Articles, denoted by a plus sign (as shown at the bottom of the window in Figure 1-6, earlier in this chapter). Click one of these entries, and Help Viewer retrieves the text over the Internet. Although this can sometimes be inconvenient, it's also quite smart. This way, Apple can update the Help system at any time without requiring any action from you.

Furthermore, after you've asked a question and Mac Help has grabbed the answer from the Apple website, the answer remains on your hard drive forever. If you ask for it again — even at a later date — your computer won't have to download it from the Apple website again.

Finally, here's a cool feature I like to call *automatic visual help cues.* Here's how they work:

1. **Type a word or phrase in the Help menu's Search field.**

2. **Select any item that has a menu icon to its left (such as the Secure Empty Trash item in Figure 1-7).**

Figure 1-7: If you choose an item with a menu icon, an arrow points to that item in context.

The automatic visual cue — an arrow — appears, pointing at that command in the appropriate menu.

The Desktop and Windows and Menus (Oh My)!

In This Chapter

▶ Checking out the parts of a window

▶ Dealing with dealie-boppers in windows

▶ Resizing, moving, and closing windows

▶ Getting comfortable with menu basics

This chapter introduces important features of OS X, starting with the first thing you see when you log in: the Finder and its Desktop. After a quick look around the Desktop, you get a look into two of its most useful features: windows and menus.

Windows are (and have always been) an integral part of Macintosh computing. Windows in the Finder (or, as a PC user would say, "on the Desktop") show you the contents of the hard drive, optical drive, flash (thumb) drive, network drive, disk image, and folder icons; windows in applications do many things. The point is that windows are part of what makes your Mac a Mac; knowing how they work — and how to use them — is essential.

OS X

Version 10.8

Software Update...

Processor 2 GHz Intel Core i7

Memory 8 GB 1333 MHz DDR3

Startup Disk Macintosh HD

More Info...

Menus are another quintessential part of the Macintosh experience. The latter part of this chapter starts you out with a few menu basics. As needed, I direct you to other parts of the book for greater detail. So relax and don't worry. By the end of this chapter, you'll be ready to work with windows and menus in any application that uses them (and most applications, games excluded, do).

Touring the Finder and Its Desktop

The Finder is the program that creates the Desktop, keeps track of your files and folders, and is always running. Just about everything you do on your Mac begins and ends with the Finder. It's where you manage files, store documents, launch programs, and much more. If you ever expect to master your Mac, the first step is to master the Finder and its Desktop. Check out the default Mac Finder and Desktop for OS X Mountain Lion in Figure 2-1.

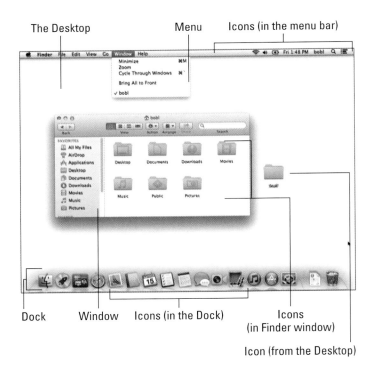

Figure 2-1: The default Mountain Lion Finder and Desktop.

The Finder is the center of your Mac OS experience, so before I go any further, here's a quick description of its most prominent features:

- **Desktop:** The Desktop is the area behind the windows and the Dock, where your hard-drive icon (ordinarily) lives. The Desktop isn't a window, yet it acts like one. Like a folder window or drive window, the Desktop can contain icons. But unlike most windows, which require a bit of navigation to get to, the Desktop is a great place for things you use a lot, such as folders, applications, or particular documents.

Some folks use the terms *Desktop* and *Finder* interchangeably to refer to the total Macintosh environment you see after you log in — the icons, windows, menus, and all that other cool stuff. Just to make things confusing, the background you see on your screen — the picture behind your hard-drive icon and your open windows — is *also* called the Desktop. In this book, I refer to the application you use when the Desktop is showing as the *Finder.* When I say *Desktop,* I'm talking about the picture background behind your windows and the Dock, which you can use as a storage place for icons if you want.

To make things even more confusing, the Desktop is a full-screen representation of the icons in the Desktop folder inside your Home folder. Don't panic — this is all explained in more detail in Chapter 6.

- **Dock:** The Dock is the Finder's main navigation shortcut tool. It makes getting to frequently used icons easy, even when you have a screen full of windows. Like the Desktop, the Dock is a great place for the folders, applications, and specific documents you use most. Besides putting your frequently used icons at your fingertips, it's extremely customizable; read more about it in Chapter 4.

- **Icons:** Icons are the little pictures you see in your windows and even on your Desktop. Icons represent the things you work with on your Mac, such as applications (programs), documents, folders, utilities, and more.

- **Windows:** Opening most icons (by double-clicking them) makes a window appear. Windows in the Finder show you the contents of hard-drive and folder icons, and windows in applications usually show you the contents of your documents. In the sections that follow, you can find the full scoop on Mountain Lion windows, which may be different from Mac windows in previous OS releases.

- **Menus:** Menus let you choose to do things, such as create new folders; duplicate files; cut, copy, or paste text; and so on. I introduce menu basics later in this chapter in the "Menu Basics" section; you find details about working with menus for specific tasks throughout this book.

Whereas this section offers a basic introduction to the Finder and Desktop, Chapter 5 explains in detail how to navigate and manage your files in the Finder. You find out how to use the Finder toolbar, navigate folders and subfolders, and switch among views, among other things. But before you start using the Finder, it helps to know the basics of working with windows and menus; if these Mac features are new to you, I suggest that you read this entire chapter and pay special attention to Chapter 5 later.

Anatomy of a Window

Windows are a ubiquitous part of using a Mac. When you open a folder, you see a window. When you write a letter, the document that you're working on appears in a window. When you browse the Internet, web pages appear in a window . . . and so on.

For the most part, windows are windows from program to program. You'll probably notice that some programs (Adobe Photoshop or Microsoft Word, for example) take liberties with windows by adding features (such as pop-up menus) or textual information (such as zoom percentage or file size) in the scroll-bar area of a document window.

Don't let it bug you; that extra fluff is just window dressing (pun intended). Maintaining the window metaphor, many information windows display different kinds of information in different *panes,* or discrete sections within the window.

And so, without further ado, the following list gives you a look at the main features of a typical Finder window (as shown in Figure 2-2). I discuss these features in greater detail in later sections of this chapter.

Figure 2-2: A typical Finder window in OS X Mountain Lion.

If your windows don't look exactly like the one shown in Figure 2-2, don't be concerned. You can make your windows look and feel any way you like. As I explain later in the "Working with Windows" section, moving and resizing windows are easy tasks. Chapter 3 explains how to customize certain window features. Chapter 5 focuses on ways you can change a window's view, specifically when you're using the Finder.

Meanwhile, here's what you see (clockwise from top left):

- **Close, Minimize, and Zoom (gumdrop) buttons:** Shut 'em, shrink and place 'em in the Dock, and make 'em grow.

- **View buttons:** Choose among four exciting views of your window: Icon, List, Column, and Cover Flow. Find out more about views in Chapter 5.

- **Arrange menu:** Click this little doohickey to arrange this window's icons by Kind, Application, Date Modified, Date Created, Date Last Opened, Date Added, Size, or Label. Or, of course, by None.

- **Action button:** This button is really a pop-up menu of commands you can apply to currently selected items in the Finder window or on the Desktop. (These are generally the same commands you'd see in the shortcut menu if you right-clicked or Control-clicked the same items.)

- **Window title:** Shows the name of the window.

⌘-click the name of the window to see a pop-up menu with the complete path to this folder (try it). This tip applies to most windows you'll encounter, not just Finder windows. So ⌘-click a window's title and you'll usually see the path to it's enclosing folder on your disk.

You can also have the path displayed at the bottom of every Finder window by choosing View⟳Show Path Bar, as shown in the active window (Applications) in Figure 2-4.

- **Search field:** Type a string of characters here, and OS X Mountain Lion digs into your system to find items that match by filename or document contents (yes, words within documents).

- **Toolbar:** Buttons for frequently used commands and actions.

- **Icon Resizer:** Use this slider control to change the size of the icons in this window. (Note that this control appears on windows only in the Icon view, which you find out all about in Chapter 5.)

- **Scroll bars:** Use the scroll bars for moving around a window.

- **Sidebar:** Frequently used items live here.

- **Forward and Back buttons:** These buttons take you to the next or previous folder displayed in this particular window.

If you're familiar with web browsers, the Forward and Back buttons in the Finder work the same way. The first time you open a window, neither button is active. But as you navigate from folder to folder, these buttons remember your breadcrumb trail so you can quickly traverse backward or forward, window by window. You can even navigate this way from the keyboard by using the shortcuts ⌘+[for Back and ⌘+] for Forward.

The Forward and Back buttons remember only the other folders you've visited that appear in *that* open window. If you've set a Finder Preference so that a folder always opens in a new window — or if you forced a folder to open in a new window, which I describe in a bit — the Forward and Back buttons won't work. You have to use the modern, OS X–style window option, which uses a single window, or the buttons are useless.

Kudos to Apple for fixing something I ranted about in earlier editions of this book. In Snow Leopard and earlier releases of OS X, if you hid the toolbar, the Sidebar was also hidden, whether you liked it or not. Conversely, if you wanted to see the toolbar, you'd have to see the Sidebar as well. Mountain Lion gives you the flexibility to show or hide them independently in its View menu, as you see in Chapter 5.

Top o' the window to ya!

Take a gander at the top of a window — any window. You see three buttons in the top-left corner and the name of the window in the top center. The three buttons (called *gumdrop buttons* by some folks because they look like, well, gumdrops) are officially known as Close, Minimize, and Zoom, and their colors (red, yellow, and green, respectively) pop off the screen. Here's what they do:

- **Close (red):** Click this button to close the window.

- **Minimize (yellow):** Click this button to minimize the window. Clicking Minimize appears to close the window, but instead of making it disappear, Minimize adds an icon for the window in the Dock.

  See the section about minimizing windows into application icons in Chapter 4 if a document icon doesn't appear in your Dock when you minimize its window.

  To view the window again, click the Dock icon for the window that you minimized. If the window happens to be a QuickTime movie, the movie continues to play, albeit at postage-stamp size, in its icon in the Dock. (I discuss the Dock in detail in Chapter 4.)

- **Zoom (green):** Click this button to make the window larger or smaller, depending on its current size. If you're looking at a standard-size window, clicking Zoom *usually* makes it bigger. (I say *usually* because if the window is larger than its contents, clicking this button shrinks the window to the smallest size that can completely enclose the contents without scrolling.) Click the Zoom button again to return the window to its previous size.

A scroll new world

Yet another way to see more of what's in a window or pane is to scroll through it. Scroll bars appear at the bottom and right sides of any window or pane that contains more stuff — icons, text, pixels, or whatever — than you can see in the window. Figure 2-3, for example, shows two instances of the same window: Dragging the scroll bar on the right side of the front window reveals the items above DVD Player and FaceTime and below iDVD and Image Capture, which you see in the expanded window in the background. Dragging the scroll bar on the bottom of the window reveals items to the left and right, such as Dictionary, iChat, GarageBand, and iPhoto.

Simply click and drag a scroll bar to move it up or down or side to side.

Figure 2-3: The same window twice; in the front window, you use the scroll bars to see the hidden icons that are visible in the back window.

If your scroll bars don't look exactly like the ones in Figure 2-3 or work as described in the following list, don't worry. These are System Preferences you can configure to your heart's desire, but you'll have to wait until Chapter 3 to find out how.

Here are some ways you can scroll in a window:

 ✔ **Click a scroll bar and drag.** The content of the window scrolls proportionally to how far you drag the scroll bar.

✔ **Click in the scroll bar area but don't click the scroll bar itself.** The window scrolls either one page up (if you click above the scroll bar) or down (if you click below the scroll bar). You can change a setting in your General System Preferences pane to cause the window to scroll proportionally to where you click.

For what it's worth, the Page Up and Page Down keys on your keyboard function the same way as clicking the grayish scroll bar area (the vertical scroll bar only) in the Finder and many applications. But these keys don't work in every program; don't become too dependent on them. Also, if you've purchased a mouse, trackball, or other pointing device that has a scroll wheel, you can scroll vertically in the active (front) window with the scroll wheel or press and hold the Shift key to scroll horizontally. Alas, this horizontal scrolling-with-the-Shift-key works in Finder windows, but not in all applications. For example, it works in Apple's TextEdit application, but not in Microsoft Word.

✔ **Use the keyboard.** In the Finder, first click an icon in the window and then use the arrow keys to move up, down, left, or right. Using an arrow key selects the next icon in the direction it indicates — and automatically scrolls the window, if necessary. In other programs, you might or might not be able to use the keyboard to scroll. The best advice I can give you is to try it — either it'll work or it won't.

✔ **Use a two-finger swipe (on a trackpad).** If you have a notebook with a trackpad or use a Magic Trackpad or Magic Mouse, just swipe the pad with two fingers to scroll in a window.

(Hyper)Active windows

To work within a window, the window must be *active*. The active window is always the frontmost window, and inactive windows always appear behind the active window. Only one window can be active at a time. To make a window active, click it anywhere — in the middle, on the title bar, or on a scroll bar. It doesn't matter where; just click anywhere to activate it.

Look at Figure 2-4 for an example of an active window in front of an inactive window (the Applications window and the Utilities window, respectively).

The following is a list of the major visual cues that distinguish active from inactive windows:

✔ **The active window's title bar:** The Close, Minimize, and Zoom buttons are red, yellow, and green. The inactive windows' buttons are not.

This is a nice visual cue — colored items are active, and gray ones are inactive. Better still, if you move your mouse over an inactive window's gumdrop buttons, they light up in their usual colors so you can close, minimize, or zoom an inactive window without first making it active. Neat!

 ✓ **Other buttons and scroll bars in an active window:** They're bright. In an inactive window, these features are grayed out and more subdued.

 ✓ **Bigger and darker drop shadows in an active window:** They grab your attention more than those of inactive windows.

Inactive window

Active window

Figure 2-4: An active window in front of an inactive window.

Dialog Dealie-Boppers

Dialogs are special windows that pop up over the active window. You generally see them when you select a menu item that ends in an ellipsis (...).

Dialogs can contain a number of standard Macintosh features (I call them *dealie-boppers*), such as radio buttons, pop-up menus, tabs, text-entry fields, and check boxes. You see these features again and again in dialogs. Take a moment to look at each of these dealie-boppers in Figure 2-5.

 ✓ **Radio buttons:** *Radio buttons* are so named because, like the buttons on your car radio (if you have a very old car), only one at a time can be active. (When they're active, they appear to be pushed in, just like the old radio buttons.) Radio buttons always appear in a group of two or more; when you select one, all the others are automatically deselected.

 Here's a nifty and undocumented shortcut: You can usually select check boxes and radio buttons by clicking their names (instead of the buttons or boxes).

 ✓ **Tabs:** When a dialog contains more information than can fit in a single window the info may be divided among panes denoted by tabs. In Figure 2-5, the New Document tab is selected on the left, and the Open and Save tab is selected on the right.

✔ **Pop-up menus:** These menus are appropriately named because that's what they do: They pop up when you click them. In Figure 2-5, the Document Type menu has been clicked and is popped up; the other pop-up menus — Opening Files, Saving Files (mostly obscured by the popped-up Document Type menu), Styling, and Encoding — are unclicked and unpopped.

You can always recognize a pop-up menu because it appears in a slightly rounded rectangle and has a double-ended arrow symbol (or a pair of triangles, if you like) on the right.

Have you figured out yet what radio buttons, tabs, and pop-up menus have in common? *Hint:* All three enable you to make a single selection from a group of options. (Well, okay, that was more of an answer than a hint.)

✔ **Text-entry fields:** In text-entry fields, you type text (including numbers) from the keyboard. In Figure 2-5, the Width, Height, Author, Organization, and Copyright options are text-entry fields.

✔ **Check boxes:** The last dealie-bopper that you see frequently is the check box. In a group of check boxes, you can select as many options as you like. Check boxes are selected when they contain a check mark, and they're deselected when they're empty, as shown in Figure 2-5.

Some applications have *tri-state* check boxes (and no, I'm not talking geography here). These special check boxes are empty when nothing in the group is selected, sport an x when everything in the group is selected, and sport a minus sign (–) when some items in the group are selected and some are not. This type of check box is often used for the Custom Install screen of OS X installers.

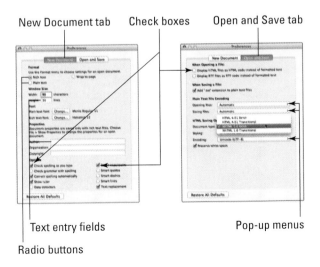

New Document tab Check boxes Open and Save tab

Text entry fields Pop-up menus

Radio buttons

Figure 2-5: This window offers most dealie-boppers you're ever likely to encounter.

Working with Windows

In the following sections, I give you a closer look at windows themselves: how you move them, size them, and use them. And although Mountain Lion windows are similar to windows you've used in other versions of Mac OS (and even, dare I say it, Windows), you may just discover a new wrinkle or two.

If you're relatively new to the Mac, you might want to read this section while sitting at your computer, trying the techniques as you read them. You might find it easier to remember something you read if you actually do it. If you've been using your Mac for a while, you've probably figured out how windows work by now.

Opening and closing windows

To start peering into windows on your Mac, first you need to know how to open and close them. When you're working in the Finder, you can choose the following commands from the File menu. Note that you'll probably find similar commands on the File menu of programs other than the Finder.

You'll use many of these commands frequently, so it would behoove you to memorize the keyboard shortcuts. If you're not sure how keyboard shortcuts work, check out "Using keyboard shortcut commands," later in this chapter.

- **New Finder Window (⌘+N):** Opens a new Finder window. In other programs, ⌘+N might open a new document, project, or whatever that program helps you create.

- **Open (⌘+O):** Opens the selected item, be it an icon, a window, or a folder.

- **Close Window (⌘+W):** Closes the active window. If no windows are open or if no window is selected, the Close Window command is grayed out and can't be chosen. Or if you prefer, you can close a window by clicking the red Close button in the top-left corner.

If you hold down the Option key with the File menu open, the Close Window command changes to Close All. This very useful command enables you to close all open Finder windows. But it shows up only when you press the Option key; otherwise, it remains hidden.

Note that several other commands in the File menu transmogrify when you press the Option key. It would be off topic to get into them here, but here's a tip: Press the Option key, and browse all the Finder menus. At least a dozen useful commands appear only if the Option key is pressed. Press it early and often for hidden (often time-saving) commands.

Resizing windows and window panes

If you want to see more (or less) of what's in a window, just hover the pointer over any edge or corner and drag. When the cursor turns into a little double-headed arrow, as shown in Figure 2-6, click and drag to resize the window.

Figure 2-6: Hover over any corner or edge; when the arrow cursor appears, click and drag to resize the window.

Display windows, like those in the Finder, frequently consist of multiple panes. If you look at Figure 2-6, the line divides the blue Sidebar to the left of it and the actual contents of the window to the right. When your mouse pointer hovers over the resizing area of this bar, the cursor changes to a vertical bar (or it could be horizontal if the panes are one above the other) with little arrows pointing out of both sides, as shown in the margin and Figure 2-6.

When you see this cursor, you can click and drag anywhere in the dividing line that separates the Sidebar from the rest of the window. Doing so resizes the two panes relative to each other; one gets larger and one gets smaller.

Moving windows

To move a window, click anywhere in a window's title bar (or anywhere in the gray part of a display window, except on a button, menu, search field, or scroll bar) and drag the window to wherever you want it. The window moves wherever you move the mouse, stopping dead in its tracks when you release the mouse button.

Shuffling windows

I've already spent plenty of pages giving you the scoop on how to work with windows. But wait; there's more . . . the commands on the Window menu provide tools you can use to manage your windows. (Refer to Figure 2-1.) Here is a brief look at each of the items on the Window menu (and if you're unfamiliar with menus and keyboard shortcuts, I explain how they work later in this chapter):

- **Minimize (⌘+M):** Use this command to minimize the active Finder window to the Dock and unclutter your Desktop. It's the same as clicking the yellow gumdrop button.

- **Zoom:** This command does the same thing as the green gumdrop button. If you've forgotten what the green gumdrop does already, just turn back a few pages to the "Top o' the window to ya!" section and read it again.

- **Cycle Through Windows (⌘+`):** Each time you choose this command or use the keyboard shortcut for it, a different window becomes active. So if you have three windows — call 'em Window 1, Window 2, and Window 3 — and you're using Window 1, this command deactivates Window 1 and activates Window 2. If you choose it again, the command deactivates Window 2 and activates Window 3. Choose it one more time, and it deactivates Window 3 and reactivates Window 1.

- **Bring All to Front:** In OS X Mountain Lion, windows from different applications interleave. For example, you can have (from front to back) a Finder window, a Microsoft Word window, an Adobe Photoshop window, another Microsoft Word window, and another Finder window. Choosing Bring All to Front while the Finder is the active application enables you to have both of the Finder windows in this example move in front of those belonging to Word and Photoshop.

    If you want to bring all the windows belonging to the Finder (or any other program, for that matter) to the front at the same time, you can also click the appropriate Dock icon (the Finder, in this case).

    If you hold down the Option key when you click the Window menu, Minimize Window changes to Minimize All, and the Zoom command changes to Zoom All.

- **Other items:** The remaining items on the Window menu are the names of all currently open Finder windows. Click a window's name to bring it to the front.

Menu Basics

Mac menus are often referred to as *pull-down menus.* To check out the OS X menus, click the Finder button in the Dock to activate the Finder and then look at the top of your screen. From left to right, you see the Apple menu, the Finder menu, and six other menus. To use an OS X menu, click its name to make the menu appear and then pull (drag) down to select a menu item. Piece of cake!

Ever since Mac OS 8, menus stay down after you click their names until you either select an item or click outside the menu's boundaries.

The ever-changing menu bar

Before you start working with OS X menus, you really, really should know this about menus in general: *They can change unexpectedly.* Why? Well, the menus you see on the menu bar at the top of the screen always reflect the program that's active at the time. When you switch from the Finder to a particular program — or from one program to another — the menus change immediately to match whatever program you switched to.

Figure 2-7 shows the menu bars for the Finder, TextEdit, and Preview applications.

Figure 2-7: Menu bars change to reflect the active application.

An easy way to tell which program is active is to look at the application menu — it's the leftmost menu with a name, just to the right of the menu. When you're in the Finder, of course, the application menu reads *Finder.* But if you switch to another program (by clicking its icon in the Dock or by clicking any window associated with the program) or launch a new program, that menu changes to the name of the active program.

When you have an application open, the commands on the menu change, too — but just a little bit. What makes this cool is that you have access to some standard application menu items whether you're running Mail or Safari. For example, most (but not all) applications have Cut, Copy, and Paste commands in their Edit menus, and Open, Save, and Print commands in their File menus. You can find much more about commands for applications in Part III, which explains how applications that come with OS X Mountain Lion can help you get things you want to do done.

Shortcut menus: They're sooo contextual . . .

Shortcut menus, sometimes called contextual menus, list commands that apply only to the item that is currently selected. Shortcut menus might be available in windows, on icons, and in most places on the Desktop.

To use them, you either hold down the Control key and click — which you can call a *Control-click* to sound cool to your Mac friends — or, if your mouse has two or more buttons, *right-click.*

Most Mac laptops (as well as the Magic Trackpad and the Magic Mouse) let you click the trackpad using two fingers to simulate a right-click or Control-click. If this doesn't work for you, make sure the Secondary Click check box is enabled in the Two Fingers section of the Trackpad System Preference pane.

Actions appear in shortcut menus only if they make sense for the item that you Control-click or right-click. (That's why people call 'em *shortcut!* They stick to the immediate context.) Figure 2-8 shows the shortcut menu that appears when you Control-click (or right-click) a document icon on the left and the shortcut menu for the Desktop on the right.

Figure 2-8: Only relevant items appear in a shortcut menu.

Shortcut menus are also available in most applications. Open your favorite app and try Control-clicking to find out whether those menus are there. In most cases, using a shortcut menu is a quick way to avoid going to the menu bar to choose a command. In some programs — such as iMovie, iTunes, and many more — shortcut menus are the *only* way to access some commands.

To make the Finder-related shortcut menus available to users who didn't have the foresight to purchase this book, Apple added the Actions button to the toolbar. As a result, people who don't know about Control-clicking or right-clicking (or have only one free hand) can access most shortcut menus by clicking the Actions button and displaying its shortcut menu. You, on the other hand, gentle reader, know how to get at these commands without having to run your mouse all the way up to the Action button in the toolbar, plus a handful of commands appear in the Control-click/right-click shortcut menu that don't appear in the Actions button/menu.

I'm a big fan of multibutton mice, and shortcut menus are a huge reason for this preference. Fortunately, Apple now includes multibutton mice with all its desktop computers (except the Mac Mini, which doesn't include a mouse, keyboard, or monitor). You may have to enable it. If you have an older Mac with a single-button mouse, you might want to replace that mouse with one that offers you at least two buttons. With a multibutton mouse, you need only one hand to access these beautiful little shortcut menus.

Get in the habit of Control-clicking (or right-clicking or two-finger clicking) items on your screen. Before you know it, using shortcut menus will become second nature to you.

Recognizing disabled options

Menu items that appear in black on a menu are currently available. Menu items that aren't currently available are grayed out, meaning that they're disabled for the time being. You can't select a disabled menu item.

In Figure 2-9, the File menu on the left is pulled down while nothing is selected in the Finder; this is why many of the menu items are disabled (in gray). These items are disabled because an item (such as a window or icon) must be selected for you to use one of these menu items. For example, the Show Original command is grayed out because it works only if the selected item is an alias. On the right side of Figure 2-9, I selected a document before I pulled down the menu; notice that many of the formerly disabled commands are enabled when an icon is selected.

Finally, notice that items that end in an ellipsis (...), such as the Burn "I Am A Document" To Disc command in Figure 2-9, will open a dialog with additional options.

Figure 2-9: File menu with nothing selected (left) and with a document icon selected (right); the disabled items are grayed out.

Navigating submenus

Some menu items have more menus attached to them, and these are called *submenus* — menus that are subordinate to a menu item. If a menu has a black triangle to the right of its name, it has a submenu.

To use a submenu, click a menu name once (to drop the menu down) and then slide your cursor down to any item with a black triangle. When the item is highlighted, move your mouse to the right just slightly. The submenu should pop out of the original menu's item, as shown in Figure 2-10.

Figure 2-10: The Apple menu's Recent Items selection, with its submenu popped out.

Underneath the Apple menu tree

On the far-left side of the menu bar sits a little , which, if you click it, actually displays a menu. No matter what application is active, the menu is always available in the top-left corner of your menu bar.

The menu bar is always available, even with apps that hide it in full-screen mode. To make it reappear, move your cursor to the top of the screen, wait a second or two, and watch the menu bar magically reappear.

From top to bottom, the menu gives you a number of options, including the following:

- **About This Mac:** Choose this item to see what version of OS X you're running, what kind of Mac and processor you're using, how much memory your Mac has, and the name of your Startup Disk. The window that appears also sports a Get Info button that will launch the Apple System Information utility; there, you can find out more than you'll probably ever want or need to know about your Mac's hardware and software.

If you click the version number in this window, it changes to the *build number* (Apple's internal tracking number for versions). If you click the build number in this window, it changes to the serial number of your Mac. Finally, if you click the serial number of your Mac in this window, it changes to the version number again. This interesting effect is shown in Figure 2-11.

Figure 2-11: Click the Version, build, or serial number to cycle through these three informative items in this window.

- **Software Update:** If you're connected to the Internet, choose this item to have your Mac check with the mothership (Apple) to see whether any updates are available for OS X, its included applications, other Apple-branded applications such as iPhoto, Final Cut Pro, Pages, or even Apple-branded peripheral devices, such as the iPod or iPhone.

✔ **System Preferences:** Choose this item to open the System Preferences window (which I discuss further in Chapter 3 and elsewhere).

✔ **Dock (submenu):** This lets you mess with options for the Dock. Scour Chapter 4 for more info on the Dock.

✔ **Recent Items:** This lets you quickly access applications, documents, and servers you've used recently, as shown in Figure 2-10.

✔ **Force Quit:** Use this option only in emergencies. What's an emergency? Use it when an application becomes recalcitrant or otherwise misbehaves, or refuses to quit when you say Quit.

Memorize the keyboard shortcut for Force Quit (⌘+Option+power button). Sometimes a program gets so badly hosed that you can't click anywhere and other keyboard shortcuts won't do anything at all. It doesn't happen often, nor does it happen to everyone. If it should happen to you, calmly press the magic key combo you memorized (⌘+Option+power button), and the Force Quit Applications dialog (usually) appears. Click the name of the program that's acting up and then click the Force Quit button or press the Return or Enter key to make the balky application stop balking.

The reason Force Quit should be used only in an emergency is that if you use it on an application that's working fine and have any unsaved documents, your work since the last time you saved the file will be blown away.

Or not. The Auto Save and Versions features, which first appeared in Lion, are still the default for Apple's own applications. You'll hear more about these features in Chapter 6; if the app you're using supports Auto Save features, you shouldn't lose any (or at least not much) of your work regardless of when you last saved.

✔ **Shut Down options:** These four commands do exactly what their names imply:

- *Sleep:* Puts your Mac into an energy-efficient state of suspended animation. See the section about Energy Saver in Chapter 17 for details on the Energy Saver System Preference pane and sleeping.

- *Restart:* Quits all open programs and restarts your Mac. It's quite polite about this task, asking if you want to save any unsaved changes in open documents before complying.

- *Shut Down:* Turns off your Mac. See Chapter 1 for details.

- *Log Out:* Quits all open programs and logs you out. Again, your Mac will be ever so polite, asking if you want to save unsaved changes in open documents before complying. When it's done, the login screen appears.

Using keyboard shortcut commands

Most menu items, or at least the most common ones, have *keyboard shortcuts* to help you quickly navigate your Mac without having to haggle so much with the mouse. Using these key combinations activates menu items without using the mouse; to use them, you press the Command (⌘) key and then press another key (or keys) without releasing the ⌘ key. Memorize the shortcuts that you use often.

Some people refer to the Command key as the *Apple key.* That's because on many keyboards, that key has both the pretzel-like Command-key symbol (⌘) and an Apple logo () on it. To avoid confusion, I always refer to ⌘ as the Command key.

Here are five things to know that will give you a handle on keyboard shortcuts:

- ✔ **Keyboard shortcuts are shown in menus.** For example, Figure 2-9 shows that the keyboard shortcut for the Print command appears on the menu after the words Print: ⌘+P. Any menu item with one of these pretzel-symbol+letter combinations after its name can be executed with that keyboard shortcut. Just hold down the ⌘ key and press the letter shown in the menu — N for New Finder Window, F for Find, and so on — and the appropriate command executes.

- ✔ **Capital letters don't mean that you have to press Shift as part of the shortcut.** Although the letters next to the ⌘ symbol in the Finder menus are indeed capitals, they just identify the letter on the keyboard. For example, if you see ⌘+P, just hold down the ⌘ key and then press P. Some programs have keyboard combinations that require the use of ⌘ and the Shift key, but those programs tell you so by calling the key combination something like ⇧+⌘+S or ⇧+⌘+O. (Look at the Empty Trash shortcut in Figure 2-12 to see one of these up-facing arrows in its natural environment.)

- ✔ **Recognize the funky-looking Option-key symbol.** You'll see one other symbol sometimes used in keyboard shortcuts: It represents the Option key (sometimes abbreviated in keyboard shortcuts as *Opt* and, on some keyboards, also labeled *Alt*). Check it out next to the Hide Others command, shown in Figure 2-12.

  What this freakish symbol means in the Finder menu item (Hide Others in Figure 2-12) is that if you hold down both the Option and ⌘ keys as you press the H key, all applications other than the Finder will be hidden.

Figure 2-12: Some keyboard shortcuts, such as Hide Others, use the Option (⌥) key in combination with the Command (⌘) key.

🖛 **Okay, there was more than one more symbol.** Occasionally, you'll see a caret (^) used as the symbol for the Control key.

🖛 **If it makes sense, it's probably a shortcut.** Most keyboard shortcuts have a mnemonic relationship with their names. For example, here are some of the most basic keyboard shortcuts:

Command	*Mnemonic Keyboard Shortcut*
New Finder Window	⌘+N
New Folder	Shift+⌘+N
Open	⌘+O
Get Info	⌘+I
Select All	⌘+A
Copy	⌘+C
Duplicate	⌘+D

More menus 4 U

If you like the menus you've seen so far, have I got a treat for you: OS X Mountain Lion includes 24 additional special-purpose menus, known as Menu Extras, that you can install if you like. Some — including Sound, Displays, Battery, and others — can be enabled from the appropriate System Preferences pane. But the easiest way is to open the Menu Extras folder (System/Library/CoreServices/Menu Extras) and double-click each Menu Extra you want to install.

The following figure shows a handful of the Menu Extras installed in the menu bar.

If you install a Menu Extra and later decide that you don't need or want it in your menu bar, hold down the ⌘ key and drag it off the menu bar; it disappears with a satisfying poof.

3

Have It Your Way

In This Chapter

▶ Making it just the way you like it with System Preferences

▶ Beautifying your Mountain Lion with a Desktop background and screen saver

▶ Working with those wonderful Dashboard widgets

▶ Customizing hardware and keyboard shortcuts

▶ Setting up for superb sound

*E*veryone works a bit differently, and everyone likes to use the Mac in a particular way. In this chapter, you find out how to tweak various options so everything is just the way you like it. The first things most people like to do are set their background and screen saver and populate the Dashboard with handy widgets. You can begin with that stuff, but keep in mind that you can do much more.

You can change the colors in windows, the standard font, and more if you like. Your Mac lets you choose how on-screen elements behave and how your hardware — such as the keyboard, mouse, and any wireless Bluetooth gadgets — interacts with your Mac.

Introducing System Preferences

You should start by becoming familiar with System Preferences, which appears on the Apple (🍎) menu and in the Dock.

The following steps explain how to move around the System Preferences window, no matter what you're trying to tweak:

1. **Open the System Preferences window, shown in Figure 3-1.**

Figure 3-1: The System Preferences window is where you change your on-screen world.

You can do this in at least four ways: Choose **⌘**⟳System Preferences, open the System Preferences icon in your Applications folder, click the System Preferences icon in Launchpad, or click the System Preferences icon on your Dock.

2. **Click any of the icons in the System Preferences window.**

The bottom part of the window changes to reflect the options for whichever icon you click. When this happens, I call the bottom part of the window a *pane*. So, for example, when you click the General icon in the System Preferences window, the bottom part of the window becomes the General System Preference pane.

When you finish working with a System Preference pane, you can, of course, choose System Preferences⟳Quit System Preferences (shortcut: ⌘+Q).

3. **To work with a different System Preference pane, click the Show All button in the toolbar; choose View⟳Show All Preferences; or press ⌘+L to return to the window with icons for all available System Preference panes.**

Alternatively, you can choose a different System Preference pane right from the View menu, as shown in Figure 3-2. Also notice that you can navigate to the next or previous pane you've viewed with the Back and Forward buttons below the red and yellow gumdrops (shortcuts ⌘+[and ⌘+], respectively). Back and Forward commands also appear on the View menu.

Figure 3-2: The View menu and the System Preferences window, organized alphabetically.

One last general tip before you work with an actual System Preferences pane: If you press (don't click; just press and keep pressing for a couple of seconds) the System Preferences icon in the Dock, a menu that looks almost exactly like the View menu in Figure 3-2 pops up and lets you open a specific System Preferences pane without first seeing the System Preferences window. If you know which System Preferences pane you need, this shortcut is often the fastest way to get to it.

You can get rid of the categories altogether and display the icons in alphabetical order. As a bonus, it makes the System Preferences window roughly 25 percent smaller on-screen. To do so, choose View➪Organize Alphabetically. The categories disappear; the window shrinks; and the icons are alphabetized, as shown in Figure 3-2. To switch from alphabetical view back to category view, choose View➪Organize by Categories.

System Preferences is actually an application; you can find it in the Applications folder. The menu item and Dock icon are merely shortcuts that open the System Preferences application. The actual files for preferences panes are stored in the Preference Panes folder, inside the Library folder in the System folder. If you choose to install third-party preference panes, they should go either in the Preference Panes folder in the Library folder at the top level of your startup disk (if you want them to be available to all users) or in the Preference Panes folder in the (hidden) Library inside your Home folder (if you want to keep them to yourself). Don't sweat this technical stuff too much; most System Preferences panes come with an installer that puts them in the proper folder for you. (You discover the thrills and chills of that hidden Home/Library folder in Chapter 6.)

Putting a Picture on the Desktop

Figure 3-3 shows my Desktop with a portrait of my dog Zeke. (See the default Desktop background in Figure 3-2.)

Figure 3-3: My beautified Desktop.

Here's how you can change your Desktop picture if you care to:

1. **From the Desktop, choose ⇨System Preferences.**

   Or Control-click the Desktop itself and choose Change Desktop Background from the contextual menu, and skip to Step 3.

   The System Preferences window appears.

2. **Click the Desktop & Screen Saver icon.**

   When the Desktop & Screen Saver Preferences pane appears, click the Desktop tab if it's not selected already, as it is in Figure 3-4.

3. **Click a folder in the column on the left, and then click a picture in the area on the right.**

   In Figure 3-4, I clicked a picture called Pink Lotus Flowers, one of the items in the Desktop Pictures folder.

Figure 3-4: Choosing a flower as my Desktop picture.

You have at least three other ways to change your Desktop picture:

✔ Drag a picture file from the Finder onto the *image well* (the little rectangular picture to the left of the picture's name).

✔ Choose the Pictures Folder in the list of folders on the left side of the Desktop & Screen Saver System Preference pane, and then choose a folder by using the standard Open File dialog. That folder then appears in the list; you can use any picture files it contains for your Desktop picture.

✔ Click one of the iPhoto Albums items in the column on the left side of the Desktop & Screen Saver System Preferences pane.

Although I love having a beautiful Desktop picture, I use a plain white Desktop (click Solid Colors in the list, and then click the white color swatch) for most of the figures in this book so you can see fine details.

Setting Up a Screen Saver

OS X comes with several screen-saver modules. To set up your screen saver, follow these steps:

1. **Open System Preferences, click the Desktop & Screen Saver icon, and then click the Screen Saver tab to see the options shown in Figure 3-5.**

Figure 3-5: The Screen Saver tab.

2. **In the Screen Savers column on the left side of the pane, choose a screen saver that interests you.**

   Scroll down to see all of the available Slideshows and Screen Savers.

   If you can't decide, scroll to the bottom of the screen savers list and choose Random to have your Mac choose a different screen saver at random each time the screen saver kicks in.

3. **(Optional) To see what the chosen module looks like in action, click the large Preview image on the right.**

   A little Preview button appears on the image when you hover your cursor over it to remind you how to see a preview. Nice touch!

   Press any key or click anywhere to end the test.

4. **After you've chosen a screen saver, select the number of minutes you want the Mac to wait before activating the screen saver from the Start After pop-up menu.**

5. **Choose the Show with Clock check box to display a digital clock along with the screen saver.**

6. **(Optional) Click the Hot Corners button to choose which corner of your screen activates the screen saver and which disables it.**

   If you enable this option, when you move your cursor to the chosen corner of the screen, you activate or disable the screen saver until you move the cursor elsewhere. Note that hot corners are optional and are turned off by default.

7. **When you're done, close the Desktop & Screen Saver pane.**

You can require a password to wake your Mac from sleep or a screen saver. To do so, follow these steps:

1. **Open System Preferences, click the Security and Privacy icon, and then click the General tab at the top of the System Preferences pane.**

2. **Choose the Require Password after Sleep or Screen Saver Begins check box.**

3. **Choose a length of time from the pop-up menu between the words** *Password* **and** *After,* **which contains options such as Immediately, 15 minutes, and 4 hours.**

   From now on, you must supply the user account password to wake up your computer. (User accounts and passwords are discussed in Chapter 16 and the Appendix.)

Putting Widgets on the Dashboard

Dashboard offers a way-cool set of *widgets,* Apple's name for the mini-applications that live inside the Dashboard layer. You see, Dashboard takes over your screen when you invoke it (as shown in Figure 3-6) by clicking Dashboard's Dock icon or pressing its keyboard shortcut: F4 on newer Mac keyboards or F12 (or fn+F12) on almost any Mac keyboard. In Figure 3-6, Dashboard is shown with just a few of its default widgets: Calculator, Weather, World Clock, and Calendar.

Figure 3-6: Dashboard lives in its own gray overlay layer.

Widgets are small, single-function applications that work only within Dashboard. Some widgets talk to applications on your hard drive, such as Address Book and iCal. Other widgets — such as Flight Tracker, Stocks, Movies, and Weather — gather information for you via the Internet.

The following tips can help you work with widgets:

- ✔ **Each time you invoke Dashboard,** widgets that were open the last time you used it will be on your screen.

- ✔ **To close an open widget,** click the minus sign-in-a-circle in the lower-left corner of the screen and then click the encircled X in the top-left corner of the widget you wish to close. Alternatively, you can press the Option key and hover over a widget to reveal its encircled X; click the X to close the widget.

- ✔ **To configure most widgets,** move your cursor over the bottom-right corner of a widget and click the little *i*-in-a-circle that appears (as it does with the Weather widget in Figure 3-6). The widget then flips around so you can see its backside, where the configuration options reside. For example, the Weather widget gives you choices that include your City, State, or Zip Code; Fahrenheit or Celsius; and whether to include lows in the six-day forecast (as shown in Figure 3-6), and the Clock widget allows you to choose your region and city. When you finish configuring a widget, click the Done button, which is usually (but not always) in the bottom-right corner; doing so flips the widget around again.

  Not all widgets can be configured. For example, the Calendar and Calculator widgets have no options to configure. If a little *i*-in-a-circle doesn't appear when you hover over the bottom-right corner of a widget with your cursor (or hovering while pressing the Option key), that widget has no options to configure.

- ✔ **To access widgets other than the four on your screen by default,** click the Open button (the large encircled plus sign shown earlier in the bottom-left corner of Figure 3-6) to open the Widget Selection Screen, which displays your currently available widgets, as shown in Figure 3-7.

  Widget Selection Screen may sound like a mouthful, but its former moniker, The Widget Bar, made it sound like some trendy watering hole downtown.

- ✔ **To add a widget from the Widget Selection Screen to your Dashboard,** click the widget on the Widget Selection Screen.

- ✔ **To manage your widgets on the Widget Selection Screen,** click the Manage Widgets button (the large encircled minus sign visible in the bottom-left corner of Figure 3-7), and all your widgets will begin to wiggle on the screen. If you have an iPhone, iPad, or iPod touch, you'll recognize this wiggling as the "rearrange the icons dance."

Figure 3-7: The Widget Selection Screen with the default selection of widgets.

- ✔ **To close the Widget Selection Screen,** click anywhere on the gray background or click the Open button again.

- ✔ **To move a widget around on your screen,** click almost anywhere on the widget and then drag it to the appropriate location.

  At the bottom of the Widget Selection Screen is a button titled More Widgets. Clicking it launches your web browser and shows you additional widgets you can download from the Apple website.

- ✔ **To uninstall a third-party widget that you no longer want,** merely open the Widget Selection Screen and click the red minus sign next to its name. Your Mac politely asks whether you want to move this widget to the trash. You do.

Finally, to close your Dashboard, press the same key you pressed to open Dashboard (F4 on newer Mac keyboards, or F12 or fn+F12 on almost any Mac keyboard), press the Esc key, or click the encircled arrow at the bottom right corner of the screen.

If you're using a trackpad, the three-fingered swipe is your friend. Try this: Swipe right to left with three fingers and your Dashboard will magically appear. Now swipe left to right with three fingers to make it go bye-bye.

Think of your Dashboard widgets as being handy-yet-potent mini-programs available at any time with a keystroke or click. Widgets are just so danged cool that I want to give you a quick look at a couple I consider particularly useful. Read on for details.

Translation

The Translation widget could be a lifesaver. You've been able to do this trick on the web for a while, but you can also do it right on your Dashboard. This widget translates words from one language to another. It offers more than a dozen language choices — including French, German, Spanish, Russian, Dutch, Chinese, and more — and can translate in either direction. I love the Translation widget, shown in Figure 3-8, so much that sometimes it hurts.

Figure 3-8: The Translation widget is incredibly useful when you travel abroad.

It's fun at parties, too. Try this: Type a paragraph or two of your purplest prose into Translation. Now translate back and forth to any language a few times. Howl when prose written as "It was a dark and stormy night when our heroine met her untimely demise" turns into something like "It was one night dark and stormy where our heroin met an ugly transfer." It doesn't get much better than this, folks. Alternatively, you could use iTranslate or Google Translate, both free translation apps, on your iPhone or iPad.

Flight Tracker

Flight Tracker, shown in Figure 3-9, can find flights on most airlines and report the flight's status in real time — a terrific timesaver when you have to meet a flight.

When you have to meet someone's flight, this widget can be a lifesaver. Just open Dashboard every few minutes, and you know exactly what the flight's status is at that moment.

This is a really good tip for harried air travelers: You can open more than one instance of a widget. So if you're trying to track *more than one* flight, or you want to know the weather or time in *more than one city*, just click the appropriate widget on the Widget Selection Screen, and another instance of it appears.

Figure 3-9: Finding a flight (top)
and viewing its status (bottom).

Giving Buttons, Menus, and Windows a Makeover

 Computers don't care about appearances, but if you want your Mac to
look a bit more festive (or, for that matter, businesslike), you have options
in the General pane (see Figure 3-10) at your disposal. To open this pane,
choose ⬛⇨System Preferences, and then click the General icon.

Figure 3-10: The General System Preferences
pane.

First up are the general appearance options:

- **Appearance pop-up menu:** Use this menu to choose different appearances and change the overall look of buttons, such as the three gumdrop buttons in the top-left corner of most windows.

  Apple, however, in its infinite wisdom, provides only two choices: Blue and Graphite.

- **Highlight Color pop-up menu:** From here, you can choose the color that text is surrounded by when you choose it in a document or select an icon. This time, Apple isn't so restrictive: You have eight highlight colors you can choose, plus Other, which brings up a color picker from which you can choose almost any color.

- **Sidebar Icon Size pop-up menu:** Choose small, medium, or large for icons in your Finder windows' Sidebar.

The next area in the General System Preferences pane enables you to set the behavior of scroll bars and title bars:

- The Show Scroll Bars radio buttons let you choose when you wish to see scroll bars on windows. Your choices are Automatically Based on Input Device, When Scrolling, or Always.

- The Click in the Scroll Bar To radio buttons give you the option of moving your view of a window up or down by a page (the default) or to the position in the document roughly proportionate to where you clicked in the scroll bar.

An easy way to try these options is to open a Finder window and place it side by side with the General System Preferences pane, as shown in Figure 3-11, reducing the size of the window if necessary to make scroll bars appear. Select an option, observe the behavior of the scroll bars, and then select a different option and observe again.

Choose the Jump to the Spot That's Clicked radio button if you often work with long (multipage) documents. It's quite handy for navigating long documents. And don't forget — the Page Down key does the same thing as choosing the Jump to the Next Page choice, so you lose nothing by choosing Jump to the Spot That's Clicked.

It would be even nicer if all third-party apps supported this feature, but some — including Microsoft Office 2011 — don't behave properly no matter what you choose for this setting.

Scroll bars

Figure 3-11: Here's how I try different scroll-bar settings.

The first two items in the next section are a pair of check boxes:

- **Ask to Keep Changes when Closing Documents:** Like Lion before it, Mountain Lion can save versions of your documents automatically and without any action on your part. So when you quit an application or close a document, your changes are saved automatically. If you want to be able to close documents without saving your changes, enable this option.

- **Close Windows when Quitting an Application**: Your Mac's default behavior is to reopen any documents and windows that were open when you quit that app. When you launch the app again, all the windows and documents magically reappear right where you left them. So enable this option to have your apps open to a clean slate, without reopening documents or windows from the previous session.

These last two items may not work as expected with older third-party applications. As a rule of thumb, the more time it's been since a program's last update, the more likely it is that the app will ignore these two settings.

The last item in this section of the General pane controls the Number of Recent Items that are remembered and displayed in your ⌘⇨Recent Items submenu. The default is 10, but I like having access to more than 10 applications and documents in my Recent Items submenu so I crank mine up to 20, as shown in Figure 3-11.

The final area offers a few options for how your fonts look. The Use LCD Font Smoothing when Available check box makes text look better on most displays. Unless your monitor is a very old tube-type (CRT) display, you probably want to select this check box.

The Turn Off Text Smoothing for Font Sizes x and Smaller pop-up menu (where *x* is the pop-up menu setting) does just what it says. Fonts that size and smaller are no longer *antialiased* (smoothed) when displayed.

If you find that type in small font sizes is hard for you to read, try increasing or decreasing this setting.

Adjusting the Keyboard, Mouse, Trackpad, and Other Hardware

No one uses the keyboard and mouse in the same way. Some folks don't use a mouse at all. (You might not even use the keyboard much if you use voice-recognition software or other devices, as I explain in Chapter 16.) If you're using OS X on a notebook, you have a *trackpad,* that little surface where you move your finger around to control the cursor. Or perhaps you have a Bluetooth-enabled keyboard and mouse so you can hook them up wirelessly. Regardless of what you have, you should give some thought to customizing the way it works so it feels "just right" for you.

The Keyboard, Mouse, and Trackpad System Preferences panes offer several tabs to do just that: enable you to modify the behavior of your keyboard, mouse, and trackpad in a myriad of ways. So the first thing to do is open the Keyboard preferences pane by choosing ⌘➪System Preferences and clicking the Keyboard icon.

Keyboard

The Keyboard System Preferences pane has two tabs: Keyboard and Keyboard Shortcuts.

Keyboard tab

On the Keyboard tab, you can adjust your settings in the following ways:

- Drag the Key Repeat Rate slider to set how fast a key repeats when you hold it down. This feature comes into play when (for example) you hold down the hyphen (-) key to make a line or the asterisk (*) key to make a divider.

- Drag the Delay until Repeat slider to set how long you have to hold down a key before it starts repeating.

You can type in the box that says Type Here to Test Settings to test your settings before exiting this tab.

If you have a notebook Mac (such as a MacBook, MacBook Pro, or MacBook Air), you also see one or more of these additional features:

✔ **Use all F1, F2 Keys as Standard Function Keys:** If this check box is selected, the F keys at the top of your keyboard control the active software application.

To use the special hardware features printed on each F key (display brightness, screen mirroring, sound volume, mute, and so on), you have to press the Fn (Function) key before pressing the F key. If the check box is left deselected, you have to press the Fn key if you want to use the F keys with a software application. Got it? Good.

Finally, these keys may not work if you use a third-party keyboard (one not manufactured by Apple).

✔ **Adjust Keyboard Brightness in Low Light:** This check box turns your laptop's ambient keyboard lighting on and off.

✔ **Turn Off When Computer Is Not Used For:** This slide control lets you determine how long the ambient keyboard lighting remains on when your computer isn't in use.

Of course, if your notebook computer doesn't *have* ambient keyboard lighting, as many don't, you don't see the last two items.

Ambient keyboard lighting is a cool feature, but remember that it reduces battery life. My recommendation is to use it only when you really need it.

✔ **Show Keyboard & Character Viewers in the Menu Bar:** This check box adds a new menu for opening either of these useful windows, as shown in Figure 3-12.

Click Emoji in list on the left of the Character Viewer window, as shown in Figure 3-13, to insert whimsical smiley faces and hundreds of other cute images into your documents.

✔ **Input Sources button:** Switches to the Language & Text System Preferences pane's Input Sources tab, where you can display one or more foreign language keyboards in the Input menu.

The Input menu and the Keyboard and Character Viewer menu are one and the same. If you select one or more foreign keyboards, it changes from the rather tame icon shown in Figure 3-13 to the flag of the selected keyboard, as shown in the margin (it's the Lithuanian flag, by the way).

✔ **Modifier Keys button:** Lets you change the action performed by the Caps Lock, Control, Option, and Command keys. It's particularly useful if you use a non-Apple keyboard, although it works just fine on Apple keyboards too.

Character and Keyboard Viewer menu

Keyboard Viewer window   Character Viewer window

Figure 3-12: The Keyboard and Character Viewer menu, Character Viewer window, and Keyboard Viewer window in all their glory.

Figure 3-13: Click the character you want, and it instantly appears in the document.

I'm always engaging the Caps Lock key accidentally with my overactive left pinky, so I set *my* Caps Lock key to perform No Action. Now I never type half a sentence in ALL CAPS BECAUSE I ACCIDENTALLY PRESSED THE CAPS LOCK KEY.

Keyboard Shortcuts tab

TIP

If you really hate to use your mouse or if your mouse is broken, keyboard shortcuts can be really handy. I tend to use them more on my laptop because I really don't like using the built-in-touch-mouse thing (technically, it's a *trackpad,* and I talk more about it in the next section).

I introduced some commonly used keyboard shortcuts in Chapter 2. You probably don't want to mess with those, but you can assign other commands you use often to just about any key combination you like. By creating your own keyboard shortcuts, you can have whatever commands you need literally at your fingertips.

Not only can you add, delete, or change keyboard shortcuts for many operating-system functions (such as taking a picture of the screen or using the keyboard to choose menu and Dock items), but you can also add, delete, or change keyboard shortcuts for your applications.

To begin, choose the Keyboard Shortcuts tab in the Keyboard System Preferences pane. Now you can do any or all of the following:

- **To change a shortcut,** first click the appropriate application, preference, or feature in the left column. Next, double-click the shortcut you want to change on the right side of the right column (for example, F3 or ⌘+G). The old shortcut becomes highlighted; when it does, press the new shortcut keys you wish to use.

- **To add a new shortcut,** click the + button. Choose the appropriate application from the Application pop-up menu, type the exact name of the menu command you want to add in the Menu Title field, and then press the shortcut you want to assign to that command into the Keyboard Shortcut field. If the shortcut you press is in use by another application or preference, a yellow triangular caution symbol appears next to it. It really is that simple.

- **To delete a shortcut,** choose it and then click the – button.

The Keyboard Shortcuts tab also offers options for changing the Tab order. The Full Keyboard Access radio buttons control what happens when you press the Tab key in a window or dialog:

- If you choose the Text Boxes and Lists Only radio button, the Tab key moves the cursor from one text box to the next or from one list item to the next item (usually alphabetically).

- If you choose the All Controls radio button, you can avoid using the mouse for the most part, if that's your preference.

  When All Controls is selected, the Tab key moves the focus from one item to the next in a window or dialog. So (for example) every time you press the Tab key in an Open File dialog, the focus moves — say, from the Sidebar to the file list to the Cancel button to the icon view button, and so on. Each item is highlighted to show it's selected, and you can activate the highlighted item from the keyboard by pressing the spacebar.

You can toggle this setting by pressing Control+F7. And if you don't care for Control+F7 as its shortcut, you can change it by clicking Keyboard & Text Input in the left column, double-clicking the Change the Way Tab Moves Focus item in the right column, and then pressing the new shortcut.

Mouse

The Mouse System Preferences pane is where you set your mouse speed and double-click delays.

If you use a notebook Mac, you may see a Mouse icon in the System Preferences application, but unless you have a mouse connected via USB or Bluetooth, it will just sit there searching for a mouse.

Don't be sad. If you use a notebook or an Apple Magic Trackpad, you have something that most iMac, Mac Mini, and Mac Pro users don't have — namely, the System Preferences pane named Trackpad, which I tell you about in the upcoming section, "Trackpad (notebooks and desktops with a Magic Trackpad)."

The first item in this pane is a check box: Scroll Direction: Natural. If scrolling or navigating in windows feels backward to you, try unchecking this box.

Moving right along, here are the features you'll find in the Mouse System Preferences pane (if you have a mouse connected):

- Move the Tracking Speed slider to change the relationship between hand movement of the mouse and cursor movement on-screen. This slider works just like the slider for trackpads, as I explain in the upcoming section on trackpads.

- The Double-Click Speed setting determines how close together two clicks must be for the Mac to interpret them as a double-click and not as two separate clicks. Move the slider arrow to the leftmost setting, Very Slow, for the slowest. The rightmost position, Fast, is the fastest setting, which I prefer.

- If your mouse has a scroll ball or scroll wheel, you also see a Scrolling Speed slider, which lets you adjust how fast the contents of a window scroll when you use the scroll wheel or ball.

- If your mouse has more than one button, you see a pair of Primary Mouse Button radio buttons. These let you choose which button — left or right — you use to make your primary (regular) click. Conversely, the other mouse button (the one you didn't choose) becomes your secondary (Control or right) click.

This is a setting many lefties like to change. Set the primary button as the right button, and you can click with the index finger of your left hand.

Being right-handed, I've done the opposite in Figure 3-14 and set the left button as the primary and the right button as the secondary (Control or right) click.

Notice that I have the center button — the scroll ball, on this particular mouse — set to the Off position. Why? Because I find that I click that button accidentally far too often when I'm trying to scroll.

Figure 3-14: The Mouse System Preferences pane set up for a right-hander.

Changes in the Mouse System Preferences pane take place immediately, so you should definitely play around a little and see what settings feel best for you. You can test the effect of your changes to the Double-Click Speed setting in the Double-Click Here to Test text box just below the slider before you close this Preferences pane.

Bluetooth

Bluetooth is a technology that lets you make wireless connections between your Mac and devices such as Bluetooth mice and phones. You can see a Bluetooth tab in the Mouse System Preferences pane if you're using a Bluetooth mouse. Most Macs manufactured in the past few years have Bluetooth built-in; some older models don't.

You configure Bluetooth devices you wish to use with your Mac elsewhere in the Bluetooth System Preferences pane (as described in Chapter 16).

If your Mac does, the Bluetooth tab shows you the battery level of your Bluetooth mouse or keyboard. It also offers a check box to add a Bluetooth status menu to your menu bar and a check box to let Bluetooth devices wake your computer from sleep.

Trackpad (notebooks and desktops with a Magic Trackpad)

If you use a notebook Mac — a MacBook, MacBook Air, and MacBook Pro — or a Magic Trackpad, you'll have an additional System Preferences pane called Trackpad. This pane lets you configure tracking and clicking speed as well as the gesturing behavior of your Mac's built-in trackpad.

Note that in 2008, Apple began equipping all its notebooks with a new and improved Multi-Touch trackpad. These features distinguish the new model from its predecessor:

- It's 40 percent larger than the original MacBook Pro and MacBook trackpads.
- It's fabricated from some kind of high-tech glass. So it's even smoother and more touch-friendly than the original trackpads.
- The *whole trackpad* is the click button; you just tap anywhere on it to click.
- It supports multifinger gestures that use up to four fingers at once.

If your Mac doesn't have a mouse, I recommend you check out Apple's $69 Magic Trackpad. This nifty wireless device can be used with any Mac or PC that has Bluetooth. It's also the biggest glass Multi-Touch trackpad yet, nearly 80 percent larger than the MacBook Pro's built-in trackpad. Yes, you can use the Magic Trackpad with your MacBook Pro, and yes, that does mean you have dual trackpads.

I have become more of a trackpad believer since OS X 10.7 (Lion) introduced iPhone-like gestures on the Mac. I have a Magic Trackpad and a mouse and grab whichever is appropriate at the moment.

The Trackpad System Preference Pane has three tabs — Point & Click, Scroll & Zoom, and More Gestures — as shown in Figure 3-15.

If you have an older notebook with the older style of trackpad, you may not see all of the controls in Figure 3-15.

All three tabs work the same way as the Point & Click tab shown in Figure 3-15. To enable or disable a feature, click its check box. To see how a feature works, just move your cursor over it (you don't even have to click), and a movie demonstrates that gesture on the right side of the window. In Figure 3-15, I'm pointing to the Secondary Click feature on the left; how it works is demonstrated in the movie playing on the right. Pretty cool, don't you think?

Drop-down menu   Tabs   Movie

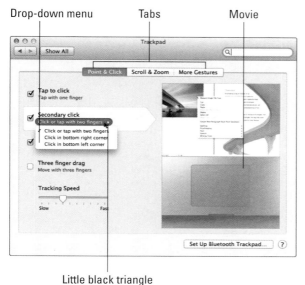

Little black triangle

Figure 3-15: The Trackpad System Preferences pane offers controls for one-finger and multifinger gestures.

There are a couple of other things you should know about the Trackpad System Preference Pane before you move on:

- ✔ If you see a little black triangle next to a feature's description, (Click or Tap with Two Fingers in Figure 3-15), there is a drop-down menu available; click near the triangle to display the options for that feature.

- ✔ The Tracking Speed slider lets you change the relationship between finger movement on the trackpad and cursor movement on-screen. A faster tracking-speed setting (moving the slider to the right) sends your cursor flying across the screen with a mere flick of the finger; slower tracking-speed settings (moving the slider to the left) make the cursor crawl across in seemingly slow motion, even when your finger is flying. Set this setting as fast as you can stand it — I like the fastest speed. Try it: You might like it.

Styling Your Sound

Out of the box, OS X Mountain Lion comes with a preset collection of beeps and controls. By using the Sound Preferences pane, however, you can change the way your Mac plays and records sound by changing settings on each of its three tabs: Sound Effects, Output, and Input.

Three items appear at the bottom of the Sound pane, no matter which of the three tabs is active:

- To make your Mac's volume louder or softer, use the Output Volume slider. You can also change or mute the volume with the designated volume and mute keys found on most Apple keyboards.

- Select the Mute check box to turn off all sound.

- Click the Show Volume in Menu Bar check box to add a volume control menu to your menu bar.

A shortcut to the Sound System Preferences pane is to press Option while pressing any of the volume keys (usually the F4 and F5 keys on older laptops and keyboards or the F11 and F12 keys on newer laptops and keyboards).

Changing sound effects

On the Sound Effects tab, choose an alert (beep) sound by clicking its name; set its volume by using the Alert Volume slider control.

You can also specify the output device through which sound effects play (if you have more than one device) by choosing it from the Play Sound Effects Through pop-up menu.

The Play User Interface Sound Effects check box turns on sound effects for actions, such as dragging a file to the Trash. The Play Feedback when Volume Is Changed check box tells your Mac to beep once for each key press to increase or decrease volume.

Choosing output and input options

If you have more than one sound-output device (in addition to the built-in speakers), you can choose it here. The Balance slider makes one stereo speaker — left or right — louder than the other.

If you have more than one sound-input device (in addition to the built-in microphone on many Macs or an iSight camera, which contains its own mic), you can choose it here. The Input Volume slider controls the Input Level (how loud input from that device will be), which is displayed as a row of blue dots. If the dots light up all the way to the right side, your input volume is too loud. Ideally, the input level should light up with about three fourths of the little blue dots — and no more.

What's Up, Dock?

In This Chapter

▶ Getting to know the Dock
▶ Discovering the default Dock icons
▶ Talkin' Trash
▶ Dock icons and their menus
▶ Delving into Dock customization

*T*he Dock appears at the bottom of your screen by default, providing quick access to your most-often-used applications, documents, and folders.

Many users prefer to have the Dock on the left or right side of the screen instead of at the bottom. You see how to do it (and more) in the coming pages.

Folder icons in the Dock are called *stacks,* and they display a fan, grid, or list of their contents when clicked. Other icons in the Dock open an application or document with one click.

The Dock is your friend. It's a great place to put files, folders, and apps you use a lot so that they're always just a click away.

A dock icon is merely a pointer (also known as an alias or shortcut) to applications, documents, and folders stored on your hard disk. So, you can add and remove icons from your Dock (as you discover shortly) without affecting the actual applications, documents, and folders. The point is that you don't need to be shy about adding or removing items from your Dock to make it more useful to you.

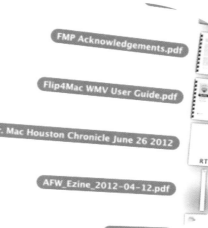

A Quick Introduction to Your Dock

Take a minute to look at the row of icons at the bottom of your display. That row, good friend, is the *Dock* (shown in Figure 4-1), and those individual pictures are known as *icons* (which I discuss in greater detail momentarily).

Figure 4-1: The Dock and all its default icons.

Dock and Launchpad (see Chapter 7) icons are odd ducks; you activate one with a single click. Most other icons in the Finder are *selected* (highlighted) when you single-click and are *opened* only when you double-click them. So Dock icons are kind of like links on a web page; you need only a single click to open them.

Here's the rundown on what happens when you click Dock icons:

- If it's **an application icon,** the application opens and becomes active. If the application is already open, it becomes active, which brings it and all its windows to the front.

- If it's **a document icon,** that document opens in its appropriate application, which becomes the active application. If that application is already open, it becomes the active application with this document in the front.

- If it's **a folder or disk icon,** a stack with its contents appears so you can pick an item. If you choose Show in Finder from this menu, the folder's window opens in the Finder.

If the item is open already when you click its Dock icon, it becomes active.

The default icons of the Dock

By default, the Dock contains a number of commonly used OS X applications, and you can also store your own applications, files, or folders there. (I show you how to do that in the "Adding Dock icons" section, later in this chapter.)

But first, look at the items you find in a standard OS X Mountain Lion Dock. If they aren't familiar to you, they certainly will be as you get to know your Mountain Lion.

I admit that I can't do justice to all the programs that come with OS X Mountain Lion that aren't, strictly speaking, part of the operating system. Alas, some of the programs in the default Dock are ones you won't be seeing much more of. But I'd hate to leave you wondering what all those icons in the Dock are, so Table 4-1 gives you a brief description of each default Dock icon (moving from left to right on-screen). If additional coverage of an item appears elsewhere in the book, the table tells you where.

To get a quick look at the name of a Dock icon, just move *(hover)* your cursor over any item in the Dock. Like magic, that item's name appears above it (like *Safari* on the left side of Figure 4-5 later in this chapter). And as I describe in the section "Resizing the Dock" (also later in this chapter), you can resize the Dock to make the icons smaller (which also makes them more difficult to see). Hovering the cursor to discover the name of a teeny icon makes this feature even more useful.

Table 4-1		Icons in the Dock	
Icon	*Name*	*What It Is*	*Go Here for More Information*
	Finder	The always-running application that manages the Desktop, files, folders, disks, and more	This chapter, and Chapters 5 and 6
	Launchpad	See all your applications arranged on a grid that looks suspiciously like an iPad or iPhone	This chapter
	Mission Control	See all your windows, applications, and spaces	Chapter 7
	Safari	A web browser	Chapter 10
	Mail	An e-mail program	Chapter 11
	Contacts	A contact manager application	Chapter 11
	Calendar	Apple's calendar program	Chapter 9

(continued)

Table 4-1 *(continued)*

Icon	Name	What It Is	Go Here for More Information
	Reminders	A to-do list and reminder application	Chapter 9
	Notes	A program for making notes	Chapter 10
	Messages	Program for sending and receiving text and multimedia messages as well as transferring files to and from and remotely controlling other Macs	Chapter 13
	FaceTime	A video chat program	Chapter 10
	Photo Booth	Program for taking photos and videos using your Mac's built-in camera	Chapter 13
	iTunes	An audio and video player and iPod manager (part of the iLife package and the only one of its apps that's free)	Chapter 12
	Mac App Store	Where you buy Mac apps from Apple	Chapter 17
	System Preferences	An application to config-ure the way many aspects of your Mac work	Chapters 3, 15, and 16
	Divider	Line that separates apps (on the left) and documents or folders (on the right)	This chapter

Icon	Name	What It Is	Go Here for More Information
	Downloads folder	This folder will contain files downloaded by Safari or Mail	Chapter 10
	Trash	Drag files and folders onto this icon to get rid of them or drag removable discs onto it to eject them.	This chapter

It's likely that your Dock won't look exactly like the one shown in Figure 4-1. If you added icons to your Dock before you upgraded to Mountain Lion, for example, you'll see those icons. If you have any of the iLife apps (such as iMovie, iPhoto, and GarageBand) installed, you may see their icons in your Dock. And if you've ever deleted one of the icons shown in Figure 4-1 from your Dock, it won't "come back" when you install Mountain Lion.

If you don't understand what I just said or want to make your Dock look exactly like the one shown in Figure 4-1, I have good news: You find out how to do that and much more before the end of this chapter.

Trash talkin'

The *Trash* is a special container where you put the icons you no longer want to hang around on your hard drive(s). Got four copies of a document named *Letter to the Editor re: Bird Waste Issue* on your hard drive? Drag three of them to the Trash. Tired of tripping over old `.pdf` and `.dmg` files you've downloaded but no longer need? Drag them to the Trash, too.

To put something in the Trash, just drag its icon onto the Trash icon and watch it disappear. As with other icons, you know that you've connected with the Trash while dragging when the icon is highlighted. And as with other Dock icons, the Trash icon's name appears when you move the cursor over the icon.

Two other ways to put items into the Trash are to select the items you want to dispose of and then choose File⇨Move to Trash or press ⌘+Delete.

If you accidentally drag something to the Trash and want it back right now, you can magically put it back where it came from — but only if the next thing you do is choose Edit⇨Undo or press ⌘+Z. Don't hesitate; the Undo command in the Finder is ephemeral and exists only until you perform another file-related activity in the Finder. In other words, as soon as you create or rename a folder, move a file from one place to another, drag a different file to the Trash, create an alias, or almost anything that affects a file or folder, choosing Edit⇨Undo or pressing ⌘+Z will undo *that* action. You'll find that some Finder actions — most of the items in the View menu, for example — don't affect Undo. So if you drag a file to the Trash and then switch views (see Chapter 5), Undo will still un-trash the file.

Files dragged to the Trash aren't deleted immediately. You know how the garbage in the can on the street curb sits there until the sanitation engineers come by and pick it up each Thursday? The OS X Trash works the same way, but without the smell. Items sit in the Trash, waiting for you to empty it. The Trash basket shows you that it has files waiting for you there. As in real life, your unemptied Trash is full of crumpled papers.

So, if you miss the window of opportunity to use the Undo command, don't worry; you can still retrieve the file from the Trash:

- **To open the Trash and see what's in there,** just click its icon in the Dock. A Finder window called Trash opens, showing you the files it contains (namely, files and folders put in the Trash since the last time it was emptied as described in the bullet after next).

- **To retrieve an item that's already in the Trash,** drag it back out, either onto the Desktop or back into the folder where it belongs.

  Or use the secret keyboard shortcut: Select the item(s) in the Trash that you wish to retrieve and press ⌘+Delete. This technique has the added benefit of magically transporting the files or folders you select from the Trash back into the folder from which they came. And, unlike Undo, the secret keyboard shortcut will work on a file or folder at any time, or at least until the next time you empty the Trash. Try it — it's sweet.

- **To empty the Trash,** choose Finder⇨Empty Trash or press Shift+⌘+Delete. If the Trash window is open, you see an Empty button just below its toolbar on the right. Clicking the button, of course, also empties the Trash.

You can also empty the Trash from the Dock by pressing the mouse button and holding it down on the Trash icon for a second or two, or right-clicking or Control-clicking the Trash icon. The Empty Trash menu item pops up like magic. Move your cursor over it to select it and then release the mouse button.

Think twice before you invoke the Empty Trash command. After you empty the Trash, the files that it contained are pretty much gone forever, or at least gone from your hard disk. My advice: Before you get too bold, read Chapter 18, and back up your hard drive at least once (several times is better). After you get proficient at backups, chances improve greatly that even though the files are technically gone forever from your hard drive, you can get them back if you really want to (at least in theory).

Finally, while you can't open a file that's in the Trash, you can select it and use QuickLook (shortcut: ⌘+Y) to see its contents before you decide to Empty Trash and permanently delete it.

And that's pretty much all there is to know about the Trash.

Opening application menus in the Dock

Single-clicking an application icon in the Dock launches that application or, if the application is already open, switches you to that application and brings forward all open windows in that application.

But application icons in the Dock — such as Calendar, Safari, iTunes, and others — also hide menus containing some handy commands. (Folder icons in the Dock have a different but no less handy menu, which I discuss in a moment.)

You can make application Dock icon menus appear in two ways:

- Press and continue to hold down the mouse button.
- Right-click or Control-click.

If you use a trackpad or a Magic Mouse, a two-finger tap will do the trick, too.

If an application isn't running, you can use either method to display a menu like the one shown in Figure 4-2.

Figure 4-2: The Options menu for an application icon (Calendar) in the Dock.

Choosing Open launches the application; choosing Show in Finder opens the enclosing folder (for example, Applications) and selects the application's icon; choosing Remove from Dock removes that application's icon from the Dock (waiting until after you quit the application if it's running); and Open at Login launches this application automatically every time you log in to this user account. If an application's icon isn't already in the Dock, you see Add to Dock rather than Remove from Dock.

Show Recents is a relatively new feature, introduced in OS X Lion. Not all applications offer this useful feature. Choose it, and icons for recently used documents appear above the Dock, as shown in Figure 4-3.

Figure 4-3: Choose Show Recents to see recently used documents.

Last but not least, if you press and hold or right-click/Control-click an open application's Dock icon, you might see a menu like the ones shown in Figure 4-4.

So there you have it: That's the default Options menu, which is what you'll see for most applications when they aren't open.

When an application *is* running, however, its Dock menu usually looks quite different, as shown in Figure 4-4 (clockwise from top left: Safari, Preview, System Preferences, Mail, and Calendar).

Figure 4-4: Press and hold or right-click/Control-click an open application's Dock icon, and menus such as these appear.

Some applications — such as Calendar, Mail, and System Preferences in Figure 4-4 — provide useful program-specific commands or options.

iTunes (not shown in the figure) has one of my favorite Dock menus, letting me control my music from the Dock with options such as Play/Pause, Next Track, Previous Track, Repeat, and Shuffle.

Other programs, including Preview and Safari in Figure 4-4, offer you a list of open windows with a check mark to indicate the active window.

Finally, the items above the list of open windows for Preview (About Downloads.pdf, Screen Shot 2011-04-11 at 11.24.33 AM, and all the rest in Figure 4-4) are recently used documents.

Reading Dock icon body language

As you use the Dock or when you're just doing regular stuff on your Mac, the Dock icons like to communicate with you. They can't talk, so they have a few moves and symbols that indicate things you might want to know. Table 4-2 clarifies what's up with your Dock icons.

Table 4-2	What Dock Icons Are Telling You
Icon Movement or Symbol	*What It Means*
The icon moves up and out of its place on the Dock for a moment, as shown in the middle of Figure 4-5.	You single-clicked a Dock icon, and it's letting you know that you activated it.
The icon does a little bouncy dance when that program is open but isn't active (that is, the menu bar isn't showing, and it isn't the frontmost program).	The program desires your attention; give its icon a click to find out what it wants.
A glowing dot appears below its Dock icon, as shown on the right side of Figure 4-5.	This application is open.
An icon that isn't ordinarily in the Dock magically appears.	You see a temporary Dock icon for every program that's currently open on the Dock until you quit that application. The icon appears because you've opened something. When you quit, its icon magically disappears.

Figure 4-5: A raised Dock icon (middle) with before (left) and after (right) shots.

Opening files from the Dock

One useful function of the Dock is that you can use it to open icons easily. The following tips explain several handy ways to open what you need from the Dock:

- **You can drag a document icon onto an application's Dock icon.** If the application knows how to handle that type of document, its Dock icon is highlighted, and the document opens in that application. If the application can't handle that particular type of document, the Dock icon isn't highlighted, and you can't drop the document on it.

  I'm getting ahead of myself here, but if the application can't handle a document, try opening the document this way: Select the icon and choose File➪Open With, or right-click/Control-click the document icon and use the Open With menu to choose the application you want to open the document with.

  If you hold down the Option key, the Open With command changes to Always Open With, which enables you to change the default application for this document permanently.

- **You can find the original icon of any item you see in the Dock by choosing Show in Finder from its Dock menu.** This trick opens the window containing the item's actual icon and thoughtfully selects that icon for you.

Customizing Your Dock

The Dock is a convenient way to get at oft-used icons. By default, the Dock comes stocked with icons that Apple thinks you'll need most frequently (refer to Table 4-1), but you can customize it to contain any icons that you choose, as you discover in the following sections. You also find out how to resize the Dock to fit your new set of icons and how to tell Dock icons what your preferences are.

Adding Dock icons

You can customize your Dock with favorite applications, a document you update daily, or maybe a folder containing your favorite recipes. Use the Dock for anything you need quick access to.

Adding an application, file, or folder to the Dock is as easy as 1-2-3:

1. **Open a Finder window that contains an application, a document file, or a folder you use frequently.**

You can also drag an icon — including a hard drive icon — from the Desktop.

2. **Click the item you want to add to the Dock.**

   As shown in Figure 4-6, I chose the TextEdit application. (It's highlighted.) I use TextEdit all the time to type and edit quick text notes to myself and others, so having its icon in the Dock is very convenient for me.

3. **Drag the icon out of the Finder window and onto the Dock.**

   An icon for this item now appears in the Dock. Note that the Dock item isn't the actual item. That item remains wherever it was — in a window or on the Desktop. The icon you see in the Dock is a shortcut that opens the item. I haven't talked about aliases (known as *shortcuts* in the Windows world) yet, but the icon in the Dock is actually an alias of the icon you dragged onto the Dock.

   Furthermore, when you remove an icon from the Dock, as you find out how to do in a moment, you aren't removing the actual application, document, or folder; you're removing only its shortcut from the Dock.

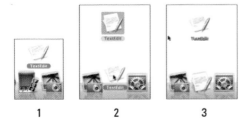

1   2   3

Figure 4-6: Adding an icon to the Dock is as easy as 1-2-3. Just drag the icon onto the Dock.

Folder, disk, document, and URL icons must be on the right side of the divider line in the Dock; Application icons must be on the left side of it. Why does the Dock force these rules upon you? I suppose that someone at Apple thinks this is what's best for you; who knows? But that's the rule: apps on the left; folders, disks, documents, and URLs on the right.

As long as you follow the rule, you can add several items to either side of the divider line at the same time by selecting them all and dragging the group to that side of the Dock. You can delete only one icon at a time from the Dock, however.

Adding a URL to the Dock works slightly differently. Here's a quick way to add a URL to the Dock:

1. **Open Safari, and go to the page with a URL that you want to save on the Dock.**

2. **Click the small icon that you find to the left of the URL in the address bar, and drag it to the right side of the dividing line in the Dock.**

3. **Release the mouse button when the icon is right where you want it.**

   The icons in the Dock slide over and make room for your URL, as shown in Figure 4-7. From now on, when you click the URL icon that you moved to your Dock, Safari opens to that page.

Figure 4-7: Drag the icon from the address bar (top) to the right side of the Dock (middle). The URL appears as a Dock icon (bottom).

If you open an icon that normally doesn't appear in the Dock, and you want to keep its temporary icon in the Dock permanently, you have two ways to tell it to stick around after you quit the program:

- Control-click (or click and hold) and choose Keep in Dock from the menu that pops up.

- Drag the icon (for an application that's currently open) off and then back to the Dock (or to a different position in the Dock) without letting go of the mouse button.

Removing an icon from the Dock

Removing an item from the Dock is as easy as 1-2 (there is no 3): Just drag its icon out of the Dock, as shown in the top part of Figure 4-8), and it disappears with a cool *poof* animation, as shown in the bottom part of Figure 4-8.

Figure 4-8: To remove an icon, drag it off the Dock, and poof — it's gone.

Choosing Remove from Dock from the item's Dock menu is another way to make the item go away.

You can't remove the icon of a program that's running from the Dock until you quit that program. Also, note that by moving an icon out of the Dock, you aren't moving, deleting, or copying the item itself; you're just removing its icon from the Dock. The item is unchanged. The icon is sort of like a library catalog card: Just because you remove the card from the card catalog doesn't mean that the book is gone from the library.

The Dock in earlier OS X releases included icons for the Documents and Applications folders; the Dock in Mountain Lion does not, at least not by default. I only mention it because having those folders in the Dock is convenient, and you should consider adding them to your Dock if they aren't already there. If you upgraded to Mountain Lion from Lion, on the other hand, the Documents and Applications folders will appear in your Mountain Lion Dock, unless you removed them prior to upgrading.

Resizing the Dock

If the default size of the Dock bugs you, you can make the Dock smaller and save yourself a lot of screen real estate. This space comes in especially handy when you add your own stuff to the Dock.

To shrink or enlarge the Dock (and its icons) without opening the Dock Preferences window, follow these steps:

1. **Make the Sizer appear (as shown in the left margin) by moving your cursor over the dotted line that you find on the right side of the Dock.**

2. **Drag the Sizer down to make the Dock smaller, holding down the mouse button until you find the size you like.**

   The more you drag this control down, the smaller the Dock gets.

3. **To enlarge the Dock again, just drag the Sizer back up.**

   Bam! Big Dock! You can enlarge the Dock until it fills your screen from side to side.

What should you put in YOUR Dock?

Put things in the Dock that you need quick access to and that you use often, or add items that aren't quickly available from menus or the Sidebar. If you like using the Dock better than the Finder window Sidebar (for example), add your Documents, Movies, Pictures, Music, or even your Home folder or hard drive to the Dock.

I suggest adding these items to your Dock:

- **A word-processing application:** Most people use word-processing software more than any other applications. Just drag the icon for yours to the left side of the Dock, and you're good to go.

  If you don't have a word processor like Microsoft Word or Apple Pages already, give TextEdit a try. It's in every OS X Applications folder, and it's more powerful than you expect from a freebie.

- **A project folder:** You know — the folder that contains all the documents for your thesis, or all the notes for the biggest project you have at work, or your massive recipe collection . . . whatever. If you add that folder to the Dock, you can access it much quicker than if you have to open several folders to find it.

- **A special utility or application:** The Preview application is an essential part of my work because I receive a lot of different image files every day. You might also want to add Internet-enabled programs you use (such as Skype, Spotify, Twitter, and so on), your favorite graphics applications (such as Adobe Photoshop or Photoshop Elements), or the game you play every afternoon when you think the boss isn't watching.

✔ **Your favorite URLs:** Save links to sites that you visit every day — the ones you use in your job, your favorite Mac news sites, or your personalized page from an Internet service provider (ISP). Sure, you can make one of these pages your browser's start page or bookmark it, but the Dock lets you add one or more additional URLs. (Refer to the "Adding Dock icons" section, earlier in this chapter, for details.)

You can add several URL icons to the Dock, but bear in mind that the Dock and its icons shrink to accommodate added icons, which makes them harder to see. Perhaps the best idea — if you want easy access to several URLs — is to create a folder full of URLs and put that folder on the Dock. Then you can just press and hold your cursor on the folder (or Control-click the folder) to pop up a menu with all your URLs.

Even though you can make the Dock smaller, you're still limited to one row of icons. The smaller you make the Dock, the larger the crowd of icons you can amass. You have to determine for yourself what's best for you: having lots of icons available in the Dock (even though they might be difficult to see because they're so tiny) or having less clutter but fewer icons in your Dock.

After you figure out which programs you use and don't use, it's a good idea to relieve overcrowding by removing the ones you never (or rarely) use from the Dock.

Setting your Dock preferences

You can change a few things about the Dock to make it look and behave just the way you want it to. First, I cover global preferences that apply to the Dock itself. After that, I discuss some preferences that apply only to folder and disk icons in the Dock.

Global Dock preferences

To change global Dock preferences, choose **🍎**⇨Dock⇨Dock Preferences. The System Preferences application opens to the Dock pane (see Figure 4-9).

You can also open the Dock Preferences by right-clicking or Control-clicking the Dock Resizer and choosing Dock Preferences from the shortcut menu.

Now you can adjust your Dock with the following preferences:

✔ **Size:** Note the slider bar here. Move this slider to the right (larger) or left (smaller) to adjust the size of the Dock in your Finder. As you move the slider, watch the Dock change size. (Now, *there's* a fun way to spend a Saturday afternoon!)

As you add items to the Dock, the icons — and the Dock itself — shrink to accommodate the new ones.

Figure 4-9: The Dock menu and the Dock System Preferences pane.

✓ **Magnification:** This slider controls how big icons grow when you pass the arrow cursor over them. Or you can deselect this check box to turn off magnification entirely.

✓ **Position on Screen:** Choose one of these three radio buttons to attach the Dock to the left side, the right side, or the bottom of your screen (the default). Personally, I prefer it on the bottom, but you should probably try all three before you decide.

✓ **Minimize Windows Using:** From this handy pop-up menu (PC users would call it a *drop-down list,* but what the heck; there's no gravity in a computer screen anyway), choose the animation that you see when you click a window's Minimize button (the yellow gumdrop). The Genie Effect is the default, but the Scale Effect seems a bit faster to me.

Want to amaze your friends? Surreptitiously hold down the Shift key when you click the Minimize button or the Dock icon of a minimized window to make the animation effect play in super slow motion.

✓ **Double-Click a Window's Title Bar to Minimize:** If you select this option, double-clicking anywhere in a window's title bar minimizes the window.

This option achieves the exact same result as clicking a window's yellow gumdrop button. The difference is that the gumdrop button is a tiny target and way over on the left side of the window, while the title bar — the gray area with the window's title (Dock in Figure 4-9) — makes a huge target the width of the window.

✓ **Minimize Windows into Application Icon:** If you select this option, when you minimize a window by clicking its yellow gumdrop button, you won't see a Dock icon for that window.

If this option isn't selected, each window you minimize gets its own personal icon on the right side of your Dock.

✔ **Animate Opening Applications:** OS X animates *(bounces)* Dock icons when you click them to open an item. If you don't like the animation, deselect (that is, uncheck) this check box, and the bouncing ceases evermore.

✔ **Automatically Hide and Show the Dock:** Don't like the Dock? Maybe you want to free the screen real estate on your monitor? Then choose the Automatically Hide and Show the Dock check box; after that, the Dock displays itself only when you move the cursor to the bottom of the screen where the Dock would ordinarily appear. It's like magic! (Okay, it's like Windows that way, but I hate to admit it.)

If the Dock isn't visible, deselect the Automatically Hide and Show the Dock check box to bring back the Dock. The option remains turned off unless you change it by checking the Automatically Hide and Show the Dock check box. Choose ➔Dock➔Turn Hiding On (or use its keyboard shortcut ⌘+Option+D).

The keyboard shortcut ⌘+Option+D is a toggle, so it reverses the state of this option each time you use it.

✔ **Show Indicator Lights for Open Applications:** Select this option if you want all open applications to display an indicator light below their Dock icons, like the Finder, Mail, Safari, Calendar, and iTunes Dock icons in Figure 4-3. Those five programs are open, whereas the others — the ones without lights — are not. If you disable this option, though I can't imagine why you'd ever want to, none of your Dock icons will ever display an indicator light.

Folder and Disk Dock Icon Menu Preferences

If you click a folder or disk icon in the Dock, its contents are displayed in a Fan, Grid, or List menu, as shown in Figure 4-10.

Figure 4-10: My Documents folder's Dock menu as Fan, Grid, and List.

If you right-click or Control-click a folder or disk icon in the Dock, its Options menu is displayed, as shown in Figure 4-11.

Figure 4-11: The Options menu
for my Documents folder.

Here are the choices on the Options menu:

- **Sort By,** which determines the order in which items in the folder or disk are displayed when you click its Dock icon.

- **Display As** determines what the Dock icon for a folder or disk looks like. If you choose Stack, as I have for the Downloads folder icon in Figure 4-11, the icon takes on the appearance of an item in the folder or disk (a picture of me in Figure 4-11). If you choose Folder, the Dock icon looks like a folder, as does the Application folder icon to the left of the Documents icon in Figure 4-11.

- **View Contents As** lets you choose Fan, Grid, or List as the menu type for the folder or disk.

  The default is Automatic, which is to say that the Dock tries to pick the menu for you. I much prefer picking the menu I consider most appropriate for a particular folder or disk. I like List menus best, especially for folders or disks with a lot of subfolders. As you can see in Figure 4-10, the List menu is the only one that lets you see and access folders inside folders (and subfolders inside other subfolders). For folders with images, I like the Grid menu because it displays easily discernible icons for the folder or disk's contents. The Fan menu is fantastic (ha!) when the folder or disk contains only a few items.

- **The Options submenu** contains the following items:

  • **Remove from Dock** removes the icon from the Dock.

  • **Show in Finder** opens the window containing the item and selects the item. So, for example, in Figures 4-10 and 4-11, my Home folder would open, and the Documents folder inside it would be selected.

The Dock is your friend. Now that you know how it works, make it work the way you want it to. Put those programs and folders you use most in the Dock, and you'll save yourself a significant amount of time and effort.

FaceTime

Font Book

Game Center

Ap

5

ɔr

Calculator

17
Calendar

Chess

Contac

The Finder and Its Desktop

In This Chapter

▶ Getting to know the Finder

▶ Using aliases: The greatest things since sliced bread

▶ View(ing) the Finder

▶ Navigating the Finder

▶ Customizing Finder windows

▶ Setting Finder preference

▶ Getting information on icons

*O*n your Mac, the Finder is your starting point — the centerpiece of your Mac experience, if you will — and it's always available. In Finder's windows or Desktop, you can double-click your way to your favorite application, your documents, or your folders. So in this chapter, I show you how to get the most from the OS X Mountain Lion Finder and its Desktop.

Introducing the Finder and Its Minions: The Desktop and Icons

The Finder is a special application unlike any other. It launches automatically as soon as you start your Mac and is always running in the background. The Desktop is a special part of the Finder unlike any other. Finally, icons and windows are the units of currency used by the Finder and Desktop.

Before I tackle any deep thoughts — such as what the Finder does or what the Desktop is — I start with a quick overview of some of the icons you're likely to encounter as you get to know the Finder and Desktop.

	Date Modified	Size
(Stills) Part 10.JPG	May 3, 2012 8:51 PM	1.4 MB
'Stills) Part 11.JPG	May 3, 2012 8:51 PM	878 KB
lls) Part 12.JPG	May 3, 2012 8:51 PM	934 KB
Part 13.JPG	May 3, 2012 8:51 PM	915 KB
14.JPG	May 3, 2012 8:51 PM	908 K
'G	May 3, 2012 8:52 PM	1
'av 3, 2012 8:52 PM		

Introducing the Desktop

The Desktop is the backdrop for the Finder — everything you see behind the Dock and any open windows. The Desktop is always available and is where you can usually find your hard drive icon(s).

This will be a whole lot easier with a picture for reference, so take a gander at Figure 5-1, which is a glorious depiction of a typical OS X Mountain Lion Finder.

Hard disk icon
in the Sidebar

Sample Folder in the Desktop folder

Users folder (inside Mountain Lion HD)

Sample File in the Desktop folder

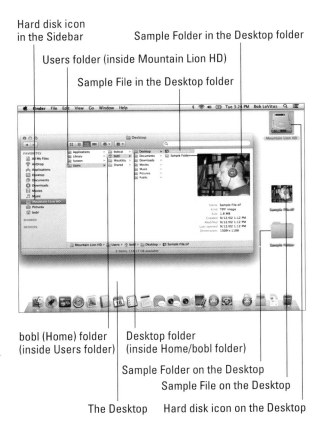

bobl (Home) folder
(inside Users folder)

Desktop folder
(inside Home/bobl folder)

Sample Folder on the Desktop

Sample File on the Desktop

The Desktop   Hard disk icon on the Desktop

Figure 5-1: A typical Finder and Desktop.

If you're not familiar with the Finder's Desktop, here are a few tips that will come in handy as you become familiar with the icons that hang out there:

✔ **Icons on the Desktop behave the same as icons in a window.** You move them and copy them just as you would icons in a window. The only difference is that icons on the Desktop aren't in a window. Because they're on the Desktop, they're more convenient to use.

✔ **The first icon you should get to know is the icon for your hard drive (see Figure 5-2).** You can usually find it on the top-right side of the Desktop. Look for the name Macintosh HD or something like that, unless you've already renamed it. (I renamed my hard drive Mountain Lion HD in Figure 5-2; see the section on renaming icons in Chapter 6 if you'd like to rename your own hard drive.) You can see how selected and deselected hard-drive icons look in Figure 5-2, too.

Mountain Lion is the first release of OS X that doesn't display your disc and hard drive icons on the Desktop by default. If you don't see your hard drive icon on the Desktop, select the check box for hard drives in Finder Preferences as described in the "Setting Finder preferences" section, later in this chapter.

Figure 5-2: Selected and deselected hard-drive icons.

✔ **Other disc or hard drive icons appear on the Desktop by default.** When you insert a CD or DVD, or connect an external hard drive, the disc or drive icon appears on the Desktop just below your startup hard-drive icon (space permitting). You can find details about working with discs and drives in Chapter 8.

✔ **You can move an item to the Desktop so you can find it right away.** Simply click its icon in any window and then, without releasing the mouse button, drag it out of the window and onto the Desktop. Then release the mouse button.

At the bottom of the Finder window in Figure 5-1 are two optional bars. The lower of the two is called the *status bar;* it tells you how many items are in each window and, if any are selected, how many you've selected out of the total, as well as how much space is available on the hard drive containing this window. And just above the status bar is the *path bar,* which shows the path from the top level of your hard drive to the selected folder (which is

`Sample File` in Figure 5-1). You can show or hide the status bar by choosing View⟹Hide/Show Status Bar and show or hide the path bar by choosing View⟹Hide/Show Path Bar. Finally, when the Toolbar is hidden (see the "Bellying up to the toolbar" section, later in this chapter) the Status Bar moves to the top of the window (the Path bar remains at the bottom of the window no matter what).

Bellying up to the toolbar

In addition to the Sidebar (mentioned in Chapter 2) and some good old-fashioned double-clicking, the OS X Finder window offers navigation aids. Several of these are on the toolbar — namely, the Back and Forward buttons, as well as the extra-helpful view buttons. You can find other handy features on the Go menu, discussed a little later in this chapter.

The toolbar, in case you didn't know, is the thick gray band right below the title bar, as shown in Figure 5-3. On it are tools and buttons that let you navigate quickly and act on selected icons. To activate a toolbar button, click it once.

You say you don't want to see the toolbar at the top of the window? Okay! Just choose View⟹Hide Toolbar or use its keyboard shortcut (⌘+Option+T), and it's gone. (If only life were always so easy!) Want it back? Choose View⟹Show Toolbar or use the same keyboard shortcut: ⌘+Option+T.

Alas, hiding the toolbar also hides the useful Sidebar and status bar. If only you could choose to hide them independently. . . . I find this fact annoying because I use the Sidebar a lot but don't use the toolbar nearly as often. To make matters worse, Mountain Lion has a new menu item — View⟹Hide Sidebar (shortcut: ⌘+Option+S) — that lets you hide the Sidebar without hiding the toolbar. For some unfathomable reason, you can't do the opposite and hide the toolbar while keeping the Sidebar visible! No, instead, if you choose View⟹Hide Toolbar (shortcut ⌘+Option+T), the Sidebar disappears along with the toolbar (and the status bar jumps to the top of the window). Boo. Hiss.

When the toolbar is hidden, opening a folder opens a *new* Finder window rather than reusing the current one (which is what happens when the toolbar is showing unless you've changed this preference in Finder preferences or are using Column view).

So here's the lowdown on the toolbar's default buttons, from left to right in Figure 5-3:

Figure 5-3: A Finder window's default toolbar.

If you've customized your toolbar by choosing View⇨Customize Toolbar, yours won't look exactly like Figure 5-3.

✏ **Forward and Back buttons:** Clicking the Forward and Back buttons displays the folders that you've viewed in this window in sequential order. If you've used a web browser, it's a lot like that.

   Here's an example of how the Back button works. Say you're in your Home folder; you click the Favorites button, and a split-second later, you realize that you actually need something in the Home folder. Just a quick click of the Back button and — *poof!* — you're back Home. As for the Forward button, well, it moves you in the opposite direction, through folders that you've visited in this window. Play around with them both; you'll find them invaluable. The keyboard shortcuts ⌘+[for Back and ⌘+] for Forward are even more useful (in my opinion) than the buttons.

✏ **View buttons:** The four view buttons change the way that the window displays its contents.

   You have four ways to view a window: Column, Icon, List, and Cover Flow. Some people like columns, some like icons, and others love lists or flows. To each her own. Play with the four Finder views to see which one works best for you. For what it's worth, I usually prefer Column view with a dash of List view thrown in when I need a folder's contents sorted by creation date or size. And the new Cover Flow view is great for folders with documents because you can see the contents of many document types right in the window, as I explain shortly.

   Don't forget that each view also has a handy keyboard shortcut: ⌘+1 for Icon view, ⌘+2 for List view, ⌘+3 for Column view, and ⌘+4 for Cover Flow view. (Views are so useful you'll find an entire section devoted to them later in this chapter.)

✏ **Action:** Click this button to see a pop-up menu of all the context-sensitive actions you can perform on selected icons, as shown in Figure 5-4.

   If you see angle brackets (>>) at the right edge of the Toolbar, as shown in Figure 5-4, one or more Toolbar items is not visible (the Search box in Figure 5-4). Click the angle brackets to select a hidden item or expand the window enough to make the angle brackets disappear.

✏ **Arrange:** Click this button to see a pop-up menu with options for displaying this window's contents, as shown in Figure 5-5, which also shows the View menu's Arrange By sub-menu, which unlike the pop-up version, includes keyboard shortcuts.

   In Figure 5-5, I selected Date Last Opened, and my Documents folder reflects that choice. While you can sort items by Date Last Opened in List view (more on that is coming up later in this chapter in the "Listless? Try touring folders in List view" section), using the Arrange menu works for all four views and offers keyboard shortcuts (look in the View menu) to boot. I use them often, and you should too!

Figure 5-4: Use the Action pop-up menu to perform common actions on selected items.

Figure 5-5: The View Menu and pop-up menu versions of Arrange By with my Documents folder arranged by Date Last Opened.

✔ **Share:** Click here to share the selected items with others. A pop-up menu lets you choose to share via Mail, Messages, or AirDrop for all files and folders, with Twitter and Flickr also appearing if the selected item happens to be an image (.jpeg, .jpg, .tiff, .tif, .png, and so on).

✔ **Search:** The toolbar's Search box is a nifty way to search for files or folders. Just type a word (or even just a few letters), and in a few seconds, the window fills with a list of files that match. You can also start a search by choosing File⇒Find (shortcut: ⌘+F). You find out about search in Chapter 7.

Figuring out what an icon is

What's an icon? Glad you asked. Each Finder icon represents an item or a container on your hard drive. Containers — hard disks, folders, CDs, DVDs, shared network volumes, and so on — can contain a virtually unlimited number of application files, document files, and folders.

Icons in the Dock and the Sidebar of Finder windows are not the same as the Finder icons I'll be discussing in this chapter — they're simply convenient pointers to actual Finder icons. Technically, Dock and Sidebar icons are aliases. (If you don't yet know what an alias is, you're going to find out long before the thrilling conclusion of this chapter.)

Anyway, working with icons is easy:

- ✒ Single-click to select.
- ✒ Double-click to open.
- ✒ Click-and-drag to move.
- ✒ Release mouse button to drop.

But enough talk. It's time to see what these puppies actually look like.

Identifying your Finder icons in the wild

Although icons all work the same, they come in different kinds, shapes, and sizes. When you've been around the Macintosh for a while, you develop a sixth sense about icons and can guess what an unfamiliar icon contains just by looking at it.

The major icons types are

- ✒ **Application icons** are *programs* — the software you use to accomplish tasks on your Mac. Mail, Safari, and iCal are applications. So are Microsoft Word and Adobe Photoshop.

  Application icons come in a variety of shapes. For example, application icons are often square-ish, diamond-shaped, rectangular, or just oddly shaped. Figure 5-6 displays application icons of various shapes.

- ✒ **Document icons** are files created by applications. Letters created with TextEdit are documents. This chapter is a document created in Microsoft Word. And my spreadsheet, PDF, video, image, and song files are all documents.

  Document icons are often reminiscent of a piece of paper, as shown in Figure 5-7.

Figure 5-6: Application icons come in many shapes.

Figure 5-7: Typical document icons.

✔ **Folder and Disk icons** are the Mac's organizational containers. You can put icons — and the applications or documents they stand for — in folders or disks. You can put folders in disks or in other folders, but you can't put a disk inside another disk.

Folders look like, well, manila folders (what a concept) and can contain just about any other icon. You use folders to organize your files and applications on your hard drive. You can have as many folders as you want, so don't be afraid to create new ones. The thought behind the whole folders thing is pretty obvious: If your hard drive is a filing cabinet, folders are its drawers and folders (duh!). Figure 5-8 shows some typical folder icons.

And while disks behave pretty much like folders, their icons often look like disks, as shown in Figure 5-9.

✔ **Alias icons** are wonderful — no, make that *fabulous* — organizational tools. I like aliases so much, in fact, that they get a whole entire section to themselves.

If you're looking for details about how to organize your icons in folders, move them around, delete them, and so on, hang in there. The next chapter (Chapter 6) is about organizing and managing files and folders.

Figure 5-8: The folders in my Home folder are pretty typical folders.

Figure 5-9: Disk icons generally look a lot like, well, disks.

Aliases: Greatest Thing since Sliced Bread

An *alias* is a tiny file that automatically opens the file, folder, disk, or network volume that it represents. Although an alias is technically an icon, it's different from other icons; it actually does nothing but open another icon automatically when you double-click. Put another way, aliases are organizational tools that let you have an icon appear in more than one place without having to create multiple copies of the file that icon represents.

An alias is very different from a duplicated file. For example, the iTunes application uses around 215 megabytes (MB) of hard-drive space. If I were to *duplicate* iTunes, I'd have two files on my hard disk, each requiring around 215MB of disk space.

An *alias* of iTunes, on the other hand, looks just like the original iTunes icon and opens iTunes when you double-click it but requires less than 1MB of hard disk space. So try placing aliases of programs and files you use most often in convenient places such as the Desktop or a folder in your Home folder.

In effect, Microsoft stole the alias feature from Apple. (If you've used Windows, you may know aliases as *shortcuts*.) But what else is new? And for what it's worth, the Mac's aliases usually don't break when you move or rename the original file; Windows shortcuts sometimes do (or at least, they used to).

Why else do I think that aliases are so great? Well, they open any file or folder on any hard drive from anywhere else on any hard drive — which is a very good trick. But there are many other reasons why I think aliases rock:

- ✔ **Convenience:** Aliases enable you to make items appear to be in more than one place, which on many occasions is exactly what you want to do. For example, keep an alias of your word processor on your Desktop and another in your Documents folder for quick access. Aliases enable you to open your word processor right away without having to navigate into the depths of your Applications folder every time you need it.

  While you're at it, you might want to put an icon for your word processor in both the Dock and the Sidebar to make it even easier to open your word processor without a lot of clicking.

- ✔ **Flexibility and organization:** You can create aliases and store them anywhere on your hard drive to represent the same document in several different folders. This is a great help when you need to file a document that can logically be stored in any of several folders. If you write a memo to Fred Smith about the Smythe Marketing Campaign to be executed in the fourth quarter, which folder does the document belong in? Smith? Smythe? Marketing? Memos? 4th Quarter? Correct answer: With aliases, it can go in every folder, if you like. Then you can find the memo wherever you look instead of guessing which folder you filed it in.

- ✔ **Integrity:** Some programs must remain in the same folder as their supporting files and folders. Some programs, for example, won't function properly unless they're in the same folder as their dictionaries, thesauruses, data files (for games), templates, and so on. Thus, you can't put the actual icon for such programs on the Desktop without impairing their functionality. An alias lets you access a program like that from anywhere on your hard drive.

I admit I'm somewhat old-school when it comes to organizing my files in the proper folders (see Chapter 6), but Mountain Lion's speedy Spotlight search mechanism along with tools like Exposé, Launchpad, and Mission Control (all, not coincidentally, discussed in Chapter 7), as well as the Sidebar's All My Files item, let you find pretty much any file on your disk in seconds.

To organize or not . . .

These days, some users prefer to have all of their files — every single one — in one folder, usually the Documents folder. There's nothing to prevent you from putting every file in one folder; OS X Mountain Lion could care less. That doesn't mean it's a good idea.

First, opening folders with thousands and thousands of files takes longer. And the more files there are, the longer it will be before you can use them. I don't know about you, but I don't like to wait, especially when I don't have to.

Second, folders with thousands of files become a nightmare in applications' Open dialogs.

The good news is that you find out how to tame the Open dialog, how to create and use subfolders, and how to organize your own stuff in Chapter 6. For those who choose to ignore the good advice in this chapter and Chapter 6, Chapter 7 introduces Spotlight, which makes it simple to find and open almost any file quickly, even files in the same folder as tens of thousands of other files. But I digress. . . .

Creating aliases

When you create an alias, its icon looks the same as the icon that it represents, but the suffix *alias* is tacked onto its name, and a tiny arrow called a *badge* (as shown in the margin) appears in the bottom-left corner of its icon. Figure 5-10 shows an alias and its *parent* icon — the icon that opens if you double-click the alias.

Alias badge

I am the parent icon.pdf

I am the parent icon's alias

Figure 5-10: An alias (right) and its parent.

To create an alias for an icon, do one of the following:

- Click the parent icon and choose File⇨Make Alias.
- Click the parent icon and press ⌘+L.
- Click the parent icon and use the Action menu's Make Alias command.
- Click an icon while holding down the Control key and then choose the Make Alias command from the contextual menu that appears. (You can explore contextual menus — which are very cool — in Chapter 2.)
- Click any file or folder, press and hold down ⌘+Option, and then drag the file or folder while continuing to hold down ⌘+Option. Presto! An alias appears where you release the mouse button.

When I first create a file, I save it in its proper folder inside the Documents folder in my Home folder. If it's a document that I plan to work on for more than a day or two (such as a magazine article or book chapter), I make an alias of the document (or folder) and plop it on my Desktop. After I finish the article or chapter and submit it to an editor, I trash the alias, leaving the original file safe and sound in its proper folder.

Deleting aliases

This is a short section because deleting an alias is such an easy chore. To delete an alias, simply drag it onto the Trash icon in the Dock. That's it! You can also Control-click it and choose Move to Trash from the contextual menu that appears, or select the icon and press ⌘+Delete.

Deleting an alias does *not* delete the parent item. (If you want to delete the parent item, you have to go hunt it down and kill it yourself.)

Hunting down an alias's parent

Suppose that you create an alias of a file, and later you want to delete both the alias and its parent file, but you can't find the parent file. What do you do? Well, you can use the Finder's Find function to find it (try saying that three times real fast), but here are four faster ways to find the parent icon of an alias:

- Select the alias icon and choose File⇨Show Original.
- Select the alias icon and press ⌘+R.
- Select the alias icon and use the Action menu's Show Original command.
- Control-click the alias icon and choose Show Original from the contextual menu.

Any of these methods opens the window containing the parent document with its icon preselected for your convenience.

The View(s) from a Window

Views are part of what makes your Mac feel like *your* Mac. Mountain Lion offers four views so you can select the best one for any occasion. Some people like one view so much that they rarely (or never) use others. Other people, like me, memorize the keyboard shortcuts to switch views instantly without reaching for the mouse. Try 'em all, and use the one(s) you prefer.

Moving through folders fast in Column view

Column view is a darn handy way to quickly look through a lot of folders at once, and it's especially useful when those folders are filled with graphics files. The Column view is my favorite way to display windows in the Finder.

 To display a window in Column view, shown in Figure 5-11, click the Column view button on the toolbar (as shown in the margin), choose View➪As Columns from the Finder's menu bar, or press ⌘+3.

Figure 5-11: A Finder window in Column view.

Here's how I clicked around in Column view to see the list of folders and files you see in Figure 5-11:

1. When I click the bobl icon in the Sidebar, its contents appear in the column to the right.

2. When I click the Pictures folder in this column, its contents appear in the second column.

3. When I click the iChat Icons folder in the second column, its contents appear in the third column.

4. When I click the Gems folder in the third column, its contents appear in the fourth column.

5. Finally, when I click the `Emerald Square.gif` icon in the fourth column, the contents of that file appear, along with some information about it: It's a Graphics Interchange Format (GIF) file, 2KB in size, created on 4/12/12, and so on. That's called the Preview column.

TIP

When you're poking around your Mac in Column view, the following tips are good to know:

- **You can have as many columns in a Column view window as your screen can handle.** Just drag any edge or corner of the window to enlarge it so new columns have room to open. Or click the green Zoom (also known as Maximize) gumdrop button to expand the window to "just big enough" to display all columns with content in them.

- **You can use the little grabber handles at the bottom of every column to resize the column widths.**

  They're pretty versatile:

  - If you drag a handle left or right, the column to its left resizes.

  - If you hold down the Option key when you drag, *all* the columns resize at the same time.

  - If you double-click one of these little handles, the column to its left expands to the width of the widest item it contains.

  - If you Option+double-click any handle, all the columns expand at the same time to the width of the widest item each one contains.

- **The preview column displays information about the highlighted item to its left, but only if that item isn't a folder or disk.** (If it is a folder or disk, its contents would be in this column.) For many items, the picture you see in the preview column is an enlarged view of the file's icon. But if the item is a graphic file (even a PDF) saved in a format that QuickTime can interpret (most graphic file formats), a preview picture appears instead, as shown in Figure 5-11. If you don't like having the preview displayed, you can choose View➪Show View Options and turn off Show Preview Column.

Perusing in Icon view

Icon view is a free-form view that allows you to move your icons around within a window to your heart's content. Check out Figure 5-6 to see the icons in my Applications folder in Icon view.

To display a window in Icon view, click the Icon view button in the toolbar (shown in the margin), choose View➪As Icons from the Finder's menu bar, or press ⌘+1.

Icon view: The ol'-stick-in-the-mud view

In all fairness, I must say that many perfectly happy Macintosh users love Icon view and refuse to even consider anything else. Fine. But as the number of files on your hard drive increases (as it does for every Mac user), screen real estate becomes more and more valuable. In my humble opinion, the only real advantages that Icon view has over Column or List view are the ability to arrange the icons anywhere you like within the window and to put a background picture or color behind your icons. Big deal.

I offer this solution as a compromise: If you still want to see your files and folders in Icon view, make them smaller so that more of them fit in the same space on-screen. This is what I do with any icons I have on my Desktop (because the Desktop allows only Icon view).

To change the size of a window's icons, use the little slider in the bottom-right corner of the Finder window when the status bar is showing. If it's not, choose View⇨Status Bar (or press ⌘+/).

Bigger icons make me crazy, but if you like them that way, your Mac can accommodate you. You can also alter the space between icons by dragging the Grid Spacing slider left or right. *Note:* If you like Icon view, consider purchasing a larger monitor; I hear that monitors now come in a 30-inch size.

Learn to love the Icon Size control in the lower-right corner of Icon view windows or in the top-right corner when the Sidebar and Toolbar are hidden.

The Finder's View menu also offers a few commands that might help you glance through your icons more easily:

- **Clean Up:** Choose this command to align icons to an invisible grid; you use it to keep your windows and Desktop neat and tidy. (If you like this invisible grid, don't forget that you can turn it on or off for the Desktop and individual windows by using View Options.) Clean Up is available only in Icon view or when no windows are active. If no windows are active, the command instead cleans up your Desktop. (To deactivate all open windows, just click anywhere on the Desktop or close all open windows.)

If you're like me, you've taken great pains to place icons carefully in specific places on your Desktop. Cleaning up your Desktop destroys all your beautiful work and moves all your perfectly arranged icons. And alas, cleaning up your Desktop is not something you can undo.

If any icons are selected (highlighted) when you pull down the View menu, you see Clean Up Selection rather than Clean Up. If you choose this command, it moves only the icons that are currently selected.

- **Clean Up By:** This new command combines the tidiness of the Clean Up command with the organizational yumminess of the Arrange By command, which I introduce in a moment.

  This command sorts the icons by your choice of criteria, namely:

  - Name (shortcut: ⌘+Option+1)
  - Kind (shortcut: ⌘+Option+2)
  - Date Modified (shortcut: ⌘+Option+5)
  - Date Created (no shortcut)
  - Size (shortcut: ⌘+Option+6)
  - Label (shortcut: ⌘+Option+7)

  It's similar to the Arrange By command, but this one's a one-time affair. After you've used it, you can move icons around and reorganize them any way you like.

- **Arrange By:** This command rearranges the icons in the active window in your choice of nine ways, which happen to be the same nine options (ten if you count "None") in the Arrange pop-up menu (which appears in Figure 5-10).

  Unlike Clean Up By, which is a one-shot command, Arrange By is persistent and will continue to reorganize your icons automatically. In other words, you can't move icons around manually in an arranged window.

  One last thing: The Clean Up and Clean Up By commands are only available for windows viewed as icons; the Arrange By command is available in all four views and remains in effect if you switch to a different view or close the window. To stop the Finder from arranging icons in a window, choose None from either the View➪Arrange By submenu or the Toolbar's Arrange pop-up menu, or use the keyboard shortcut, ⌘+Control+0.

Listless? Try touring folders in List view

Now I come to my second-favorite view, List view (shown in Figure 5-12). The main reason why I like it so much is the little triangles to the left of each folder, known as *disclosure triangles,* which let you see the contents of a folder without actually opening it. This view also allows you to select items from multiple folders at once and move or copy items between folders in a single window. Finally, it's the view used to present Spotlight search results.

Disclosure triangles

Sort indicator   Column resizer

Figure 5-12: A window in List view.

To display a window in List view, click the List view button on the toolbar (shown in the margin), choose View⇨As List from the Finder's menu bar, or press ⌘+2.

When you're in List view, the following tips can help you breeze through your folders to find what you're looking for:

- **To disclose a folder's contents, click the triangle to its left or, if it's selected, press the right-arrow key.** Figure 5-12 shows the result of either clicking the triangle to the left of the iTunes folder or selecting (highlighting) the iTunes folder and pressing the right-arrow key.

    If you press Option+right arrow, all the folder's subfolders also expand. I pressed the Option key before I pressed the right-arrow key in Figure 5-12, so the Album Artwork and iTunes Media folders are expanded. Had any of the sub-folders (Cache, Download, and Automatically Add to iTunes) contained files or folders (they didn't when the screen shot was captured), they would have been expanded as well.

- **Click the column header to sort items in List view.** Notice the little triangle at the right edge of the selected column (the Name column in Figure 5-12). That's the column's sorting indicator. If the triangle points upward, the items in the corresponding column sort in descending order; if you click the header (Name) once, the triangle points downward and the items are listed in the opposite (ascending) order. This behavior is true for all columns in List view windows.

- **You can change the order in which columns appear in a window.** To do so, press and hold a column's name, and then drag it to the left or right until it's where you want it. Release the mouse button, and the column moves.

The exception (isn't there always an exception?) is that the Name column always appears first in List view windows; you can move all other columns about at will. In fact, you can even hide and show columns other than Name if you like using the View Options window.

You can fine-tune all four views and the Desktop by using the View Options window. Just choose View➪Show View Options or press ⌘+J. The options you see apply to the active window or the Desktop. Click the Use as Defaults button to apply these options to all windows in that view (that is, Icon, List, Column, or Cover Flow).

✔ **To widen or shrink a column, hover over the dividing line between that column and drag left or right.** When your cursor is over the dividing line in the header, it changes to a double-headed resizer, as shown in the margin and in Figure 5-12 (where I'm enlarging the Date Modified column by clicking between it and the Date Added column).

You gotta go with the flow

If you're familiar with the Cover Flow feature in iTunes or if you own an iPhone, iPod touch, or iPad (which do a Cover Flow thing when you turn them sideways in their iPod music-player mode), you're already familiar with Cover Flow.

To display a window in Cover Flow view, click the Cover Flow view button on the toolbar (shown in the margin), choose View➪As Cover Flow from the Finder's menu bar, or press ⌘+4. Figure 5-13 shows Cover Flow view.

Figure 5-13: A window in Cover Flow mode.

Cover Flow view has two cool features:

✔ The item that's selected in the list (The Wall Live in Austin (Stills) Part 14.JPG in Figure 5-13) appears in a preview in the top part of the window.

✔ You can flip through the previews by clicking the images to the left or right of the current preview image or by sliding the black scroll bar below the preview to the left or right.

Finder on the Menu

The Finder menu is packed with useful goodies, most of which are available in its menus. In the following sections, I look at those that pertain specifically to using the Finder.

The actual Finder menu

Here are a few of the main items you can find on the Finder menu:

✔ **About Finder:** Choose this command to find out which version of the Finder is running on your Mac. This menu item isn't particularly useful — or at least not for very long. But when a different application is running, the About Finder item becomes About *application name* and usually gives information about the program's version number, the developers, and any other tidbits that those developers decide to throw in. Sometimes these tidbits are useful, sometimes they're interesting, and sometimes they're both.

✔ **Preferences:** Use the choices here to control how the Finder looks and acts. Find out the details in the "Setting Finder preferences" section, later in this chapter.

✔ **Services:** One of the really cool features of OS X applications is the accessibility of Services. If nothing is selected in the Finder, the Services menu is empty, as shown in Figure 5-14 A. When an icon or icons are selected, there are two Services you can choose, as shown in Figure 5-14 B. Finally, if a word or words are selected, you have a myriad of options, as shown in Figure 5-14 C.

Figure 5-14: Services available with nothing selected (A), an icon selected (B), and a word selected (C).

In other words, the items you see in the Services menu are context-sensitive, so what you see in yours will depend on what you have selected. If you look in the Services menu and don't find anything interesting, try selecting something else and looking again; you might be pleasantly surprised.

Choose the last item in the menu, Services Preferences, and you can enable dozens of useful Services that aren't available by default.

✔ **Hide Finder (⌘+H):** Use this command when you have Finder windows open and they're distracting you. Choosing it makes the Finder inactive (another program becomes active) and hides any open Finder windows. To make the Finder visible again, either choose Show All from the Application menu (which bears the name of the active application, such as TextEdit, System Preferences, and so on) or click the Finder icon, shown in the margin here, in the Dock.

The advantage to hiding the Finder — rather than closing or minimizing all your windows to get a clean screen — is that you don't have to open them all again when you're ready to get the windows back. Instead, just choose Show All (to see all windows in all apps) or click the Finder button in the Dock to see all Finder windows.

✔ **Hide Others (Option+⌘+H):** This command hides all windows associated with all running programs except the active program. It appears in most applications' Application menus and is good for hiding distractions so you can focus on one thing: the unhidden application.

Another easy way to hide all open applications and windows while activating the Finder is to hold down the ⌘ and Option keys and click the Finder icon in the Dock. This technique works with whatever application is active, not just the Finder. So if you're surfing the web and decide you want to see only Safari's windows on your screen, ⌘-Option-click the Safari button in the Dock, and it will happen instantly.

✔ **Show All:** Use this command as the antidote to both of the Hide commands. Choose this, and nothing is hidden anymore.

Note that all three of these commands require that at least one application be running in addition to the Finder. Put another way, when the Finder is the only app running these, three commands are grayed out and unavailable.

You can achieve much of the same effect as all this hide-and-show jazz by using Exposé and/or Mission Control, both discussed in Chapter 7.

Finally, if you noticed that the Finder menu's Empty Trash command isn't mentioned here, that's because it's mentioned briefly in Chapter 4 and gets detailed coverage in Chapter 6.

Like a road map: The current folder's pop-up menu

In the center of the window's title bar is the name of the folder that you're viewing in this window: the highlighted folder. You know that already. What you might not know is that it offers a hidden road map to this folder from the top level. The following steps explain how it works:

1. **⌘-click and hold the folder's name (Desktop) in the title bar.**

   A pop-up menu appears, with the current folder (Desktop, in Figure 5-15) at the top.

Figure 5-15: Traverse folders from this convenient pop-up menu.

2. **Select any folder in the menu, and it becomes the highlighted folder in the current window; release the mouse button, and that folder's contents are displayed.**

   As shown in Figure 5-15, the contents of the Desktop folder — a file and a folder — are displayed in the window. If I released the mouse button, the contents of the highlighted folder (bobl) would appear.

3. **After jumping to a new folder, you can click the Back button.**

   Hey, you're right back where you were before you touched that pop-up menu!

Don't forget that you can display the path bar near the bottom of the window (it's showing in Figures 5-12, 5-13, and 5-15) by choosing View⇨Show Path Bar. Then you can double-click any folder displayed in the path bar to open it. Last but not least, this trick also works with the title bar in most document windows, showing you the path to the folder containing the document.

Going places with the Go menu

The Go menu is chock-full of shortcuts. The items on this menu take you to places on your Mac — many of the same places you can go with the Finder window toolbar — and a few other places.

The following list gives you a brief look at the items on the Go menu:

- ✔ **Back (⌘+[ ):** Use this menu option to return to the last Finder window that you had open. It's equivalent to the Back button on the Finder toolbar, in case you have the toolbar hidden.

✔ **Forward (⌘+]):** This command is the opposite of using the Back command, moving you forward through every folder you open. Remember that if you haven't gone back, you can't go forward.

✔ **Enclosing Folder (⌘+↑):** This command tells the Finder window to display the folder where the currently selected item is located.

✔ **All My Files (Shift+⌘+F):** This command shows you all your document files at once.

This is a good time to use the Arrange pop-up menu to sort these files into some semblance of order.

✔ **Documents (Shift+⌘+O):** You'll probably use this command often, because the Documents folder is a great place to save documents you create.

✔ **Desktop (Shift+⌘+D):** Use this command to display the Desktop folder, which contains the same icons as the Desktop you see behind open windows.

✔ **Downloads (Option+⌘+L):** This opens your Downloads folder, which is where files you download in Safari, save as attachments in Mail, or receive via AirDrop (explained shortly) are saved by default.

✔ **Home (Shift+⌘+H):** Use this command to have the Finder window display your Home folder (which is named with your short name).

✔ **Computer (Shift+⌘+C):** This command tells the Finder window to display the Computer level, showing Network and all your disks.

✔ **AirDrop (Shift+⌘+R):** AirDrop lets you share files wirelessly with anyone around you. There's no setup required and no special settings. Just click the AirDrop icon in the Finder sidebar, use this menu item, or use the keyboard shortcut, and your Mac automatically discovers other people nearby who are using AirDrop.

It's great as long as the others are also running OS X Lion or Mountain Lion. Fortunately, that's the case at my house. Before AirDrop, when files needed to be shuffled between family Macs, I would usually take care of it from my Mac in the office because I knew how. AirDrop makes file sharing easy enough that my wife and kids now transfer files at will with no spousal or fatherly intervention required.

✔ **Network (Shift+⌘+K):** This command displays whatever is accessible on your network in the Finder window.

✔ **Applications (Shift+⌘+A):** This command displays your Applications folder, the usual storehouse for all the programs that came with your Mac (and the most likely place to find the programs you install).

✔ **Utilities (Shift+⌘+U):** This command gets you to the Utilities folder inside the Applications folder in one fell swoop. The Utilities folder is the repository of such useful items as Disk Utility (which lets you erase, format, verify, and repair disks) and Disk Copy (which you use to create and mount disk-image files). You find out more about these useful tools in Chapter 18.

✔ **Recent Folders:** Use this submenu to quickly go back to a folder that you recently visited. Every time you open a folder, OS X creates an alias to it and stores it in the Recent Folders folder. You can open any of these aliases from the Recent Folders command on the Go menu.

✔ **Go to Folder (Shift+⌘+G):** This command summons the Go to Folder dialog, shown in Figure 5-16. Look at your Desktop. Maybe it's cluttered with lots of windows, or maybe it's completely empty. Either way, suppose you're several clicks away from a folder that you want to open. If you know the path from your hard drive to that folder, you can type the path to the folder in the Go to the Folder text box (separating folder names with forward slashes [/]) and then click Go to move (relatively) quickly to the folder you need.

Figure 5-16: Go to a folder by typing its path.

The first character you type must also be a forward slash, as shown in Figure 5-16, unless you're going to a subfolder of the current window (bobl in Figure 5-16).

This particular dialog is a tad clairvoyant; it tries to guess which folder you mean by the first letter or two that you type. For example, in Figure 5-16, I typed the letter **A** and paused, and the window guessed that I wanted *Applications.* Then I pressed the right-arrow key to accept the guess and typed **U**, and the window guessed the rest *(tilities)* and filled it in for me.

✔ **Connect to Server (⌘+K):** If your Mac is connected to a network or to the Internet, use this command to reach those remote resources.

One last thing: If you're looking for your Home/Library folder, which appeared in the Go menu prior to OS X 10.7 (Lion), it's now hidden for your protection (as explained in Chapter 6). To reveal it, hold down the Option key and click the Go menu.

Customizing Finder Windows

The Finder is outrageously handy. It not only gives you convenient access to multiple windows, but also offers ways to tweak what you see till you get what works best for you. So whereas earlier sections in this chapter explain what the Finder is and how it works, the following sections ask, "How would you like it to be?"

Adding folders to the Sidebar

Adding whatever folder you like to the Sidebar is easy. All you need to do is select the item you want to add and choose File⇨Add to Sidebar from the menu bar (or press ⌘+T). You can now reach the item by clicking it in any Finder window's Sidebar. And you can move files or folders into that folder by dragging them onto the Sidebar icon for the item.

To remove an item from the Sidebar, right-click or Control-click the item and choose Remove from Sidebar. Or ⌘-click the item and drag it off the sidebar, as shown in Figure 5-17.

Release Drag   Command-click

Figure 5-17: I find the "drag-and-poof" technique much more satisfying than the menu.

Setting Finder preferences

You can find Finder and Desktop preferences by choosing Finder➪Preferences. In the Finder Preferences window that appears, you find four panes: General, Labels, Sidebar, and Advanced, all of which are shown in Figure 5-18.

Figure 5-18: Set Finder preferences here.

General pane

In the General pane, you find the following options:

- ✔ **Show These Items on the Desktop check boxes:** Select or deselect these check boxes to choose whether icons for hard drives; external disks; CDs, DVDs, and iPods; and connected servers appear on the Desktop. OS X Mountain Lion deselects all four options by default (which differs from earlier versions of Mac OS, which enabled all four by default). If you don't want disk icons cluttering your beautiful Desktop, deselect (clear) these check boxes. When they're deselected, you can still work with hard drives, CDs, DVDs, and other types of disks. You just have to open a Finder window and select the disk or disc you want in the Sidebar.

- ✔ **New Finder Windows Open pop-up menu:** Here, you can choose whether opening a new Finder window displays All My Files, your Home folder (which is my preference), the Documents folder, or other disk or folder. (All My Files is the default.)

✔ **Always Open Folders in a New Window check box:** Selecting this box spawns a new window each time you open a folder or disk. (Old-timers may recognize this behavior from Mac OS 9.)

Don't enable it and windows open "in place," which prevents window clutter. If you want a new window, press ⌘ before you double-click. This forces the folder to open in a new window. Between this feature and Column view, I rarely need more than two or three windows on-screen, and I get by most of the time with a single window in Column view.

✔ **Spring-loaded folders and windows:** This one's easier to do than to explain, so do this: Select the check box to enable the feature, and then drag any icon (except a disk icon) onto any folder or disk icon. When the folder or disk icon is highlighted, don't release the mouse button. After a delay (which you set via the Delay slider), the highlighted folder icon "springs" open. If you drag the item onto another folder now, that folder springs open. And so on. This continues until you release the mouse button, at which time the item you're dragging is dropped into whichever folder is open at the time. Notice that each time you drag the item onto a different folder the previous folder springs shut automatically. That's spring-loaded folders for you.

As long as the check box is checked, you can make folders spring open instantly by pressing the spacebar, regardless of the delay you've specified with the Delay slider.

Labels pane

The Labels pane lets you rename the colored labels that appear in the File menu. The default names are the same as their color, but you can change them to anything you like by entering new labels in the text boxes. To demonstrate this, I changed the first item from its default name (Red) to *Urgent (Formerly Red)* in Figure 5-18.

To assign a label to any icon, select the icon, choose File➪Label, and then click one of the colored dots. The selected icon takes on that color. Why would you want to do that? Well, partly because colorized icons are festive, but mostly because you can then use the label as one of the criteria for searches, as described in Chapter 7.

Here's an example: If you apply the red label to every file and folder associated with, say, Project X — all the folders, DOC files, PDF files, JPEG files, and so on — you can later search for items with the red label and see all these items at once, regardless of what folder they're stored in or what application created them. That said, many users find labels useless and go years without ever applying a single label to a file or folder.

Sidebar pane

The Sidebar pane lets you choose which items are displayed in the Sidebar. Select the check box to display the item; deselect the check box to not display it.

Advanced pane

The Advanced pane is just big enough to offer the following check boxes and a pop-up menu:

- The Show All Filename Extensions check box tells the Finder to display the little two-, three-, four-, or more-character filename suffixes (such as .doc in summary.doc) that make your Mac's file lists look more like those of a Linux user. The Finder hides those from you by default, but if you want to be able to see them in the Finder when you open or save files, you need to turn on this option.

- The Show Warning before Changing an Extension check box allows you to turn off the nagging dialog that appears if you attempt to change the two-, three-, four-, or more-character file extension.

- The Show Warning before Emptying the Trash check box (on by default) allows you to turn off the nagging dialog telling you how many items are in the Trash and asking whether you really want to delete them.

- The Empty Trash Securely check box makes Secure Empty Trash the default. The Secure Empty Trash feature overwrites deleted files with meaningless data so neither the files nor their contents can be recovered.

- The When Performing a Search pop-up menu lets you choose the default search location when you initiate a search as described earlier in this chapter. Your choices are Search This Mac, Search the Current Folder, and Use the Previous Search Scope.

Digging for Icon Data in the Info Window

Every icon has an Info window that gives you — big surprise! — information about that icon and enables you to choose which other users (if any) you want to have the privilege of using this icon. (I discuss sharing files and privileges in detail in Chapter 16.) The Info window is also where you lock an icon so that it can't be renamed or dragged to the Trash.

To see an icon's Info window, click the icon and choose File⇨Get Info (or press ⌘+I). The Info window for that icon appears. Figure 5-19 shows the Info window for the QuickTime Player icon.

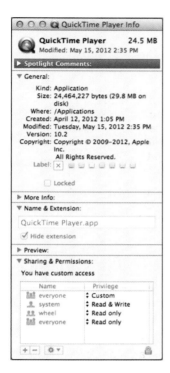

Figure 5-19: A typical Info window for an application (QuickTime Player, in this case).

Documents, folders, and disks each have slightly different Info windows. In this section, I give you highlights on the type of information and options that you can find.

The gray triangles reveal what information for an icon is available in this particular Info window. The sections that you see for most icons include the following:

✔ **Spotlight Comments:** Provides a field in which you can type your own comments about this icon for Spotlight to use in its searches. (I talk about searching a little earlier in this chapter and discuss Spotlight searches in greater detail in Chapter 7.)

✔ **General:** For information of the general kind, such as

- *Kind:* What kind of file this is — an application, document, disk, folder, and so on

- *Size:* How much hard drive space this file uses

- *Where:* The path to the folder that contains this file

- *Created:* The date and time that this file was created

- *Modified:* The date and time that this file was last modified (that is, saved)

- *Version:* Copyright information and the file's version number

- *Label:* Choose or change the color label.

Five other check boxes may or may not appear in the General section of a particular Info window. Here's the scoop on this quintet of optional options:

- *Open in 32-bit mode* (check box): Most late-model Macs can take advantage of Mountain Lion's high-performance 64-bit processing mode. Some applications are designed to take advantage of Mountain Lion's faster 64-bit processing mode, but sometimes programs that should run in 64-bit mode don't run properly. If an application doesn't work properly — it often quits unexpectedly, freezes, or refuses to launch at all — try selecting this check box. It couldn't hurt. Note that this option is only available for applications that are designed to run in both modes; if you don't see this check box, that means the program you're using can only run in one mode.

- *Shared folder* (check box): Designates the folder as Shared, so other users are allowed to see and use its contents. You find out all about sharing in Chapter 16.

- *Stationery Pad* (check box): This one only appears in the Info window of document icons. If you select it, the file becomes a template. When you open a Stationery Pad document, a copy of its contents appear in a new Untitled document that you would typically save with a descriptive name.

- *Locked* (check box): If this box is checked, you receive a warning if you try to put the item in the Trash: "This item is locked. Do you want to move it to the Trash anyway?" Your options are Stop and Continue. If you continue, the item goes into the Trash as usual.

Then, when you try to empty the Trash, you receive another warning: "There are some locked items in the Trash. Do you want to remove all the items, including the locked ones, or just the unlocked ones?" Your choices this time are Cancel, Remove Unlocked Items, and Remove All Items. If you choose to Remove All Items, the locked item(s) are deleted. If you choose Remove Unlocked Items, the locked item(s) remain in the Trash, and you receive the "There are some locked items" warning again the next time you try to empty it.

To remove the locked item from the Trash, click the Trash icon in the Dock and drag the locked item out of the Trash and into a folder or onto the Desktop.

✔ **More Info:** When the file was created, modified, and last opened (documents only).

✔ **Name & Extension:** Tells the full name, including the (possibly hidden) extension.

✔ **Preview:** When you select a document icon, the menu offers a Preview option that you use to see a glimpse of what's in that document. You can also see this preview when you select a document icon in Column view; it magically appears in the rightmost column. If you select a QuickTime movie or sound, you can play your selection right there in the preview pane without launching a separate application. Neat.

✔ **Sharing & Permissions:** Governs which users have access to this icon and how much access they are allowed. (See Chapter 16 for more about access privileges.)

If you press the Option key before you pull down the Finder's File menu, the Get Info command changes to Show Inspector (alternatively, press ⌘+Option+I). The Inspector window looks and acts like a Get Info window for the most part, with two whopping exceptions:

✔ **It displays info for the currently selected icon.** Click a different icon and the inspector displays different info. So you can Get Info on lots of icons by using the arrow keys or pressing Tab or Shift+Tab. Try it — it's cool.

✔ **It displays cumulative info when you select multiple icons.** This is an easy way to determine the total size of several items (files or folders) all at once.

And that's about it for icons, which are among the most fundamental parts of what makes your Mac a Mac (and not a toaster or an Xbox).

Part II

Mountain Lion Taming (Or "Organization for Smart People")

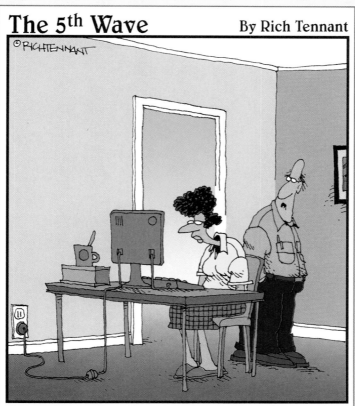

The 5th Wave   By Rich Tennant

"No, that's not the icon for iCal, it's the icon for iCan't, the database of reasons you forgot an appointment."

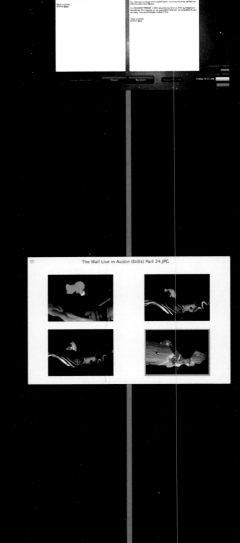

In this part . . .

Peruse the chapters in this part to discover how to organize just about everything on your Mountain Lion. Don't get all worked up — this stuff is easy. In fact, I think of this part as "The Lazy Person's Guide to Getting and Staying Organized."

I start by showing you more about the all-important Finder, and then move on to the two most important skills of all: saving and opening files. You'll then spend a bit of time with Mountain Lion's impressive timesaving tools and discover the joys of dealing with disks (and discs) — a good thing to know indeed! Next is a short discourse on using your calendars to stay organized and other important information, all without tearing your hair out.

It might sound imposing, but I assure you this part is (mostly) painless.

The Care and Feeding of Files and Folders

In This Chapter

▶ Checking out the OS X folder structure

▶ Saving your document before it's too late

▶ Opening icons

▶ Getting (and staying) organized

▶ Copying, pasting, and moving files and folders

---

*T*his could be the most important chapter in this book. If you don't understand how to open and save files by using the Open dialog and Save sheets or how to use the file and folder system, you'll have a heck of a time getting the hang of your Mac. Ask any longtime Mac user; the old lament is pretty common: "Well, I saved the file, but now I don't know where it went." It happens all the time with new users; if they don't master these essential techniques, they often become confused about where files are located on their hard drives. Sure, the sidebar has an item called All My Files that displays all of your files, but if you have thousands or tens of thousands of files, it's more a curse than a blessing.

This chapter is a tonic for finding the file or folder you want. Knowing where your files are is something every Mac user should grok (fully understand). Hang with me and pay attention; everything will soon become crystal clear.

Pad Info

Lion FD cover.pdf

Lion FD cover.pdf

All My Files (in the Sidebar) is a fast and easy way to find a file or folder (although the sheer number of files it displays may overwhelm you, no matter how you sort or arrange them). And Chapter 7 is chock-full of tools and tips for finding files and folders when you misplace them. Furthermore, although you can often find files or folders by using Spotlight, you have to remember enough details about the file or its contents for Spotlight to find it.

At the end of the day, all the aforementioned techniques are useful and good to know, but take it from me: It's often faster and easier if you know exactly where a file or folder is than to hunt for it.

Later in the chapter, I look at using Open dialogs and Save sheets within applications to find files and folders. You see them only *after* you launch a program and use that program's File menu to open or save a file. (For more on launching applications, read the parts of Chapter 5 about icons; for more on creating and opening documents, see the documentation or help file for the program that you're using.)

Spotlight (which you discover in Chapter 7) is OS X's built-in search mechanism. It's available just about everywhere you look in Mountain Lion: The magnifying glass on the menu bar, the Toolbar of Finder windows, and Open dialogs and Save sheets. The point is, if you can't find a file or folder manually as described in the rest of this chapter, try Spotlight.

Understanding the OS X Folder Structure

Start by looking at the folder structure of a typical OS X installation. Open a Finder window, and click the icon for your hard drive (which is typically called Macintosh HD) in the Sidebar. You should now see at least four folders: Applications, Library, System, and Users. Within the User folder, each user with an account on this Mac has his own set of folders containing documents, preferences, and other information that belongs to that user and account.

If you're the sole person who accesses your Mac, you probably have only one user. Regardless, the folder structure that OS X uses is the same whether you have one user or dozens.

Within the Users folder, you find your personal Home folder and a Shared folder, where you can put files you want to share with other users. All these files are stored in a nested folder structure that's a bit tricky to understand at first. This structure makes more sense after you spend a little time with it and figure out some basic concepts.

If you display the path bar at the bottom of your windows by choosing View⟿ Show Path Bar, it'll start to make sense much sooner.

If you take a look at Figure 6-1, you can see how these main folders are related to one another. In the sections that follow, you take a look at each of these folders in more depth and find out more about what's nested inside each one.

Figure 6-1: A bird's-eye view of key folders on your Mac.

Understanding nested folders

Folders within other folders are often called *nested folders*. To get a feel for the way nested folders work in OS X, check out Figure 6-2. You can see the following from the figure:

- The Desktop is the top-level folder in this example; all the other folders and files you see reside within the Desktop folder.

- Folder 1 is inside the Desktop folder, which is one level deep.

- Folder 2 is inside Folder 1, which is one level deeper than Folder 1, or two levels deep.

- Folder 3 is inside Folder 2 and is three levels deep.

- The two files inside Folder 3 are four levels deep.

If the preceding list makes sense to you, you're golden. What's important here is that you're able to visualize the path to Folder 3. That is, to get to files inside Folder 3, you open Folder 1 and then open Folder 2 to be able to open Folder 3. Understanding this concept is important to understanding the relationships between files and folders. Keep reviewing this section, and eventually, the concept will click. You'll slap yourself in the head and say, "Now I get it!"

Folder 1 (on Desktop): One level deep

Folder 2: Two levels deep

Folder 3: Three levels deep

File 1: Four levels deep   File 2: Four levels deep

Path bar

Figure 6-2: Nested folders, going four levels deep.

From the top: The Computer folder

I start with the Computer folder, which is the top level of the folder hierarchy. The Computer folder shows all the storage devices (hard drives, CD- or DVD-ROM, USB flash drive, and so forth) that are currently connected to your Mac. The following steps show how you can start at the Computer folder and drill down through the folder structure:

1. **To find the Computer folder, choose Go⇨Computer or press Shift+⌘+C.**

   In Figure 6-1, the Computer folder is called Bob L's MacBook Pro, and it contains a hard-drive icon (Mountain Lion HD) and a Network icon, with which you can access servers or other computers on your local network. (If that seems mysterious, read Chapter 16 for the whole scoop on sharing files with other Macs and sharing your Mac with other users.)

If you don't see a Computer icon in your Sidebar, choose Finder⇨ Preferences, click the Sidebar icon at the top, and then select the check box for your computer. You can change a Mac's name (Bob L's MacBook Pro in Figure 6-1) in the Sharing System Preferences pane, which you can access by launching the System Preferences application (from the Applications folder, the Dock, or the menu) and then clicking the Sharing icon.

You might have more or fewer icons in your Computer folder than you see in Figure 6-1, depending on how many disks you have mounted.

2. **Double-click the icon that holds your OS X stuff.**

    (Technically, this drive is called your boot drive.) In Figure 6-1, that hard drive is called Mountain Lion HD. I have no idea what yours is called, of course; if you haven't changed it, it's probably called Macintosh HD.

3. **Check out the folders you find there.**

    You should see at least four folders (unless you've added some; if you installed the Xcode programming tools, for example, you have more). In the next few sections, I walk you through what you can find in each one.

Peeking into the Applications folder

The Applications folder, located at the root level of your boot drive (the one with OS X installed on it), is accessible by clicking the Applications icon in the Sidebar, by choosing it in the Go menu, or by pressing Shift+⌘+A. In this folder, you find applications and utilities that Apple includes with OS X. Most users of a given Mac have access to all the items in the Applications folder, with the exception of managed accounts or accounts with Parental Controls, as discussed in Chapter 16.

Finding fonts (and more) in the public Library folder

The Library folder, at the root level of your OS X hard drive, is like a public library; it stores items available to everyone who logs into an account on this Mac.

There are actually three Library folders on your hard drive: the one at the root level of your OS X disk, a second inside the root-level System folder, and a third in your Home folder.

What's that you say? You don't see a Library folder inside your Home folder? Well it's like this: In versions of OS X earlier than OS X Lion (10.7), you would have seen a folder named Library between the Downloads and Movies folders in your Home folder (or mine — bobl — in Figure 6-1). But that was then, and this is now. In OS X Mountain Lion, the Home Library folder is hidden from view to protect you from yourself. You discover the secret to making it visible if you need it in the "Your personal Library card" section of this chapter, which is coming up.

Leave the /System/Library folder alone. Don't move, remove, or rename it, or do anything within it. It's the nerve center of your Mac. In other words, you should never have to touch this third Library folder. You find a bunch of folders inside the Library folder at root level (the "public" Library folder). Most of them contain files that you never need to open, move, or delete.

By and large, the public Library subfolder that gets the most use is the Fonts folder, which houses many of the fonts installed on the Mac. For the most part, fonts can be made available in one of two ways:

- **To everyone who uses the Mac:** If that's the case, they're stored here in the Fonts folder.

- **To a single user:** In this case, you place the fonts in the user's Library folder (the one in the user's Home folder).

I discuss fonts more in Chapter 14. Meanwhile, some other public Library subfolders that you might use or add to are the iMovie, iTunes, iPhoto, and iDVD folders (where you put plug-ins for those programs); the Scripts folder (which houses AppleScripts accessible to all users); and the Desktop Pictures folder (where you can place pictures to be used as Desktop backgrounds).

Don't remove, rename, or move any files or folders in any of your Library folders unless you're sure of what you're doing and why. OS X is very picky about folders in its Libraries being in the proper place and bear the proper name. While I'm on the subject, you probably shouldn't remove, rename, or move applications installed by Mountain Lion in the Applications folder.

Note: Under most circumstances, you won't actually add items to or remove items from folders in this Library yourself. Software installers usually do the heavy lifting for you by placing all their little pieces in the appropriate Library folders. You shouldn't need to touch this Library often, if ever. That said, knowing what these folders are — and who can access their contents — might come in handy down the road a piece.

The locations of the three libraries are illustrated in Figure 6-3.

System Library Folder

"Public" Library Folder

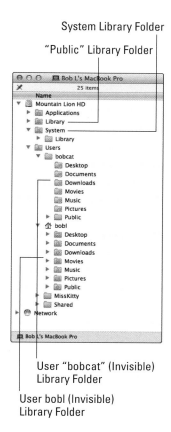

User "bobcat" (Invisible)
Library Folder

User bobl (Invisible)
Library Folder

Figure 6-3: A guide to which
Library is which.

If your Mac is set up for multiple users, only users with administrator
(admin) privileges can put stuff in the public (root-level) Library folder.
(For more information on admin privileges, check out Chapter 16.)

Let it be: The System folder

The System folder contains the files that OS X needs to start up and keep
working.

Leave this folder alone. Don't move, remove, or rename it or anything within
it. It's part of the nerve center of your Mac.

The bottom line is that you should, for the most part, restrict yourself to using the folders within your Home folder. If you're the only user of your Mac, you can pretty much forget about the root level Library. But those with more than one user account on their Mac may someday need to add or remove a file from this folder.

So now you can forget everything outside your Home folder because with few exceptions, that's where all of your "stuff" will reside.

The usability of the Users folder

When you open the Users folder, you see a folder for each person who has a user account on the Mac, as well as the Shared folder.

The Shared folder that you see in the Users folder allows everyone who uses the Mac to use the files stored there. If you want other people who use your Mac to have access to a file or folder, the Shared folder is the proper place to stash it. You can see my Shared folder right below my Home folder (bobl) in Figure 6-1, earlier in this chapter.

I realize that a lot of people don't share their Macs with others, and if you're one of these folks, you may wonder why I keep mentioning sharing and multiple users and the like. Well, OS X is based on the Unix operating system — a multiuser operating system used on high-end servers and workstations that are often shared by several people. OS X has both the benefit of this arrangement and a bit of the confusion caused when a single user (could it be you?) fires up a computer that *could* be set up for several people. That's why OS X folders are organized the way they are — with different hierarchies for each user and for the computer as a whole.

I should also mention that each user account has its own preferences and settings, and that one user can't see another user's files by default.

If your Mac has more than one constant user, consider creating a user account for each person. If you're a parent, separate user accounts mean you can enable Mountain Lion's terrific Parental Controls, which are a very good thing if you ask me. But I'm getting ahead of myself again; Chapter 16 has the scoop on sharing your Mac and Parental Controls.

There's no place like Home

From the Users folder, you can drill down into the Home folder to see what's inside. When the user logs on to this Mac, his Home folder appears whenever he clicks the Home icon in the Sidebar, chooses Go⇨Home, or uses the keyboard shortcut Shift+⌘+H.

Your Home folder is the most important folder to you as a user — or at least the one where you stash most of your files. I strongly recommend that you store all the files you create in subfolders within your Home folder — preferably, in subfolders in your `Home/Documents` folder. The advantage of doing so is that your `Home/Documents` folder is easy to find, and many programs use it as the default folder for opening or saving a file.

When you open your Home folder, you see a Finder window with a little house icon and your short username in the title bar. Seeing your short username in the title bar tells you that you're in *your* Home folder. Every user has a Home folder named after his or her short username (as specified in the Users & Groups System Preferences pane). Figure 6-4 shows that my Home folder is named bobl — the short name I used when I first set up my Mac.

![Figure 6-4: My Home folder.]

Figure 6-4: My Home folder.

If your Mac has more than one user, you can see the other users' Home folders in your Users folder, but OS X prevents you from opening files from or saving files to them.

By default, your Home folder has several folders inside it created by OS X. The following four are the most important:

- **Desktop:** If you put items (files, folders, applications, or aliases) on the Desktop, they're actually stored in the Desktop folder.

- **Documents:** This is the place to put all the documents (letters, spreadsheets, recipes, and novels) that you create.

- **Library:** As I mention earlier in this chapter, this Library folder is invisible in Mountain Lion; I show you how to deal with that shortly. Rest assured that even though it's hidden, it's still one of the most important folders in your Home folder, containing Preferences (files containing the settings you create in System Preferences and other places), fonts available only to you (as described earlier in this chapter) and other stuff that you — and only you — expect to use.

➤ **Public:** If others on your local area network use file sharing to connect with your Mac, they can't see or use the files or folders in your Home folder (unless you've explicitly shared them), but they can share files you've stored in your Home folder's Public folder. (Read more about file sharing and Public folders in Chapter 16.)

You can create more folders, if you like. In fact, every folder that you *ever* create (at least every one you create on this particular hard drive or volume) *should* be within your Home folder. I explain more about creating folders and subfolders and organizing your stuff inside them later in this chapter.

The following are a few more tidbits to keep in mind as you dig around your Home folder:

➤ If you decide that you don't want an item on the Desktop anymore, delete it by dragging its icon from the Desktop folder to the Trash or by dragging its icon from the Desktop itself to the Trash. Both techniques yield the same effect: The file is in the Trash, where it remains until you empty the Trash. Or if you don't want it on the Desktop anymore but don't want to get rid of it either, you can drag it from the Desktop into any other folder you like.

➤ The other five folders that you should see in your Home folder are Downloads, Movies, Music, Pictures, and Sites. All these folders except Sites and Downloads are empty until you (or a program such as iTunes, GarageBand, iPhoto, or iMovie, which create files inside these folders automatically the first time you launch them) put something in these folders. The Sites folder contains a few files that your Mac needs if you enable Web Sharing in the Sharing System Preferences pane, as I describe in Chapter 16. And the Downloads folder might as well be empty, but it contains a document entitled, About Downloads, with a little info on Dock stacks and the Downloads folder and concludes by saying, ". . . when you're done reading this document, feel free to throw it out."

Your personal Library card

The invisible Library subfolder of your Home folder is the repository of everything that OS X needs to customize *your* Mac to *your* tastes. If you want to add something to a Library folder, it's usually best to add it to your Home/ Library folder. You won't spend much time (if any) adding things to the Library folder or moving them around within it, and that's probably why it's now hidden from sight. Still, I think it's a good idea for you to know what's in your Home/Library.

In the "Finding fonts (and more) in the public Library folder" section, earlier in this chapter, I discuss the Library folder that's used to specify preferences for the Mac as a whole. But *this* Library folder is all about you and your stuff.

Be cautious with all Library folders. OS X is very persnickety about how the folders and files within it are organized. As I discuss earlier in the chapter, you can add items to and remove items safely from most Public or Home Library folders, but *leave the folders themselves alone*. If you remove or rename the wrong folder, you could render OS X inoperable. It's like the old joke about the guy who said to the doctor, "It hurts when I do that," and the doctor replies, "Then don't do that."

To find your hidden `Home/Library` folder, do this:

1. **Hold down the Option key on your keyboard.**

2. **Click the Go menu.**

   The (formerly) invisible Library folder appears in the Go menu as long as the Option key is pressed, as shown in Figure 6-5.

3. **Select Library and release the mouse button.**

Figure 6-5: A normal Go menu (left) and a Go menu with the Option key pressed (right).

You should see several folders in the `Home/Library` folder; the exact number depends on the software that you install on your Mac. You probably have folders called Mail, Safari, Logs, and Preferences, for example.

Some of the most important standard folders in the Library folder include the following:

✓ **Application Support:** Some applications store their support files here; others store theirs in the main (root-level) public Library folder.

✓ **Fonts:** This folder is empty until you install your own fonts here. The fonts that come with OS X aren't stored here, but in the Library folder at root level for everyone who uses this Mac. I discuss this topic earlier in this chapter. If you want to install fonts so that only you have access to them, put them in the Fonts folder in *your* Library folder.

The easiest way to install a font is to double-click its icon and let Mountain Lion's Font Book utility handle it for you, as described in Chapter 14. But I'd be remiss if I didn't also mention how to install a font manually:

- *To install a font that only you can use:* Drag the font file's icon to the Fonts folder in your Home/Library. The font is available only to this user account (because other users can't use fonts stored in *your* Home/Library folder).

- *To install a font for all users of this Mac:* Drag the font file's icon into the Fonts folder in the public Library folder — the one at root level that you see when you open your hard drive's icon.

✔ **Preferences:** The files here hold the information about whichever things you customize in OS X or in the applications you run. Whenever you change a system or application preference, that info is saved to a file in the Preferences folder.

Don't mess with the Preferences folder! You should never need to open or use this folder unless something bad happens — if, for example, you suspect that a particular preferences file has become *corrupted* (that is, damaged). My advice is to just forget that you know about this folder and let it do its job. If you don't know why you're doing something to a folder (other than the Fonts folder) in your Home/Library, *don't do it.* There must be some good reasons why Apple decided to hide the Home/Library folder in OS X Mountain Lion, and I'm sure that one of them is to keep you (or me) from accidentally screwing something up.

Saving Your Document before It's Too Late

If you have a feel for the OS X folder structure, you can get down to the important stuff — namely, how to save documents and where to save them. You can create as many documents as you want, using one program or dozens of 'em, but all could be lost if you don't save the files (or versions of the files) to a storage device such as your hard drive or other disk.

When you *save* a file, you're committing a copy to a disk — whether it's a disk connected directly to your Mac, one available over a network, or a removable disk such as a USB flash drive or portable hard disk.

Lion introduced three new features — Resume, Auto Save, and Versions — to make your life easier. In previous versions of OS X, applications generally showed a blank page or nothing at all when you launched them. Mountain Lion's Resume feature automatically reopens all windows that were on-screen when you quit the app. So, when you launch the app again, all the windows are reopened in the same position on-screen as when you quit. Best of all, Resume seems to work with most third-party apps.

Programs have offered Auto Save before, but now it's baked into OS X. Auto Save automatically saves versions of your work as you work, when you pause, and every 5 minutes, whether you need it or not.

For as long as we've had Macs, we've saved unique versions of our files, creating and managing them with the Save As command or by duplicating and renaming them in the Finder. Now Mountain Lion (like Lion before it) takes over version control for you by automatically saving versions as described in the preceding paragraph.

That's the good news, but there's also bad news . . . although Auto Save and versions are baked right into OS X, third-party apps require a software update before they can take advantage of these features. So please don't get too comfortable with Auto Save and Versions until you're sure that your applications take advantage of these features. Most third-party apps still rely on the good old Save and Save As commands, which have been around since time immemorial.

In the following sections, I show you how to save your masterpieces. Prevent unnecessary pain in your life by developing good saving habits. I recommend that you save your work (or save a version in apps that support versions)

- Every few minutes
- Before you switch to another program
- Before you print a document
- Before you stand up

The keyboard shortcut for Save in almost every Mac program is ⌘+S. Memorize it. See it in your dreams. Train your finger muscles to do it unconsciously. Use it (the keyboard shortcut) or lose it (your unsaved work).

If you don't heed this advice — and the program that you're using crashes while switching programs, printing, or sitting idle (the three likeliest times for a crash) — you may lose everything you did since your last save or saved version. The fact that a program crash doesn't bring down the entire system or force a restart is small consolation when you've lost everything you've typed, drawn, copied, pasted, or whatever since the last time you saved or saved a version.

Stepping through a basic Save

This section walks you through the steps you use the first time you save a document. The process is the same whether your app supports Auto Save and Versions or not. It's only after the initial save that Auto Save and Versions come into play.

Does it have Auto Save and Versions or not?

It can be hard to discern at a glance whether or not an app uses the new Auto Save and Versions features. In Mountain Lion, the Save a Version command has gone back to its original (and less confusing) moniker, which is plain ol' Save. Fortunately, there are other ways to determine whether a program supports Auto Save and Versions.

The first is whether the app has a Save As or Duplicate command in its File menu. Programs with a Save As command are old-school and don't support the new Auto Save and Versions features. Programs with a Duplicate command have usually been updated with support for Auto Save and Versions. (Interestingly, the shortcut for Duplicate and Save As is almost always the same, namely ⌘+Shift+S.)

The next is whether the app has Rename and Move To commands in its File menu. If it doesn't, it's old-school; if it does, it's Auto Save and Version-savvy.

The easiest way to tell, however, is to look at the title bar of a document. If it displays a little triangle to the right of the document's name when you hover over it and a pop-up menu when you click the triangle as shown in the following figure, it means that the app supports Auto Save and Versions. (You read more about the options in the pop-up menu later in this chapter.)

In a few sections of this book, I ask you not only to read the instructions while sitting in front of your Mac, but also to perform each step of the instructions as described. This section is one of them. If you read it and follow along, I can pretty much guarantee that it'll make sense. If you read it somewhere other than at your Mac, it could be a mite confusing.

Saving a file works pretty much the same way in any application you use to create documents. For this example, I use OS X's word processing application, TextEdit, but the process would be very similar in Microsoft Word, Adobe Photoshop, Apple Keynote, or any other application.

If you're going to follow along as I recommend, please launch the TextEdit program now (it's in your Applications folder), click the New Document button or choose File⇨New, and type a few words on the Untitled page that appears after you launch it.

Now that we're both on the same page, both literally and figuratively, here's how saving a file works: When you choose to save a file for the first time (by choosing File⇨Save or pressing ⌘+S), a Save sheet appears in front of the document that you're saving, as shown in Figure 6-6. I call this a *basic* Save sheet (as opposed to an *expanded* Save sheet, which I get to in a moment):

1. **In the Save As field, type a name for your file.**

   When a Save sheet appears for the first time, the Save As field is active and displays the name of the document. The document name (usually, Untitled) is selected; when you begin typing, the name disappears and is replaced by the name you type.

2. **If the Where pop-up menu lists the location where you want to save your file, choose that location, and proceed to Step 5; if not, click the disclosure button (the one with the little triangle to the right of the word *Untitled* in Figure 6-6).**

   You can choose from a short list of folders and volumes listed in the basic Save sheet's Where pop-up menu (which are the same devices and favorites you see in the Sidebar of Finder windows). Or, if you click the disclosure button (triangle), the sheet expands so that you can navigate folders just as you would in the Finder: by opening them to see their contents.

Figure 6-6: A basic Save sheet looks a lot like this.

If you clicked the Save button instead of pulling down the Where menu, your file would be saved to iCloud, Apple's free online storage service (which you discover in Chapter 10).

If you switch to expanded view by clicking the disclosure button, the Where pop-up menu shows the path to the folder the file will be saved in (Documents in Figure 6-6 and Figure 6-7).

Figure 6-7: An expanded Save sheet looks similar to this one (shown in List view).

I think that the Where menu should be the same in both basic and expanded Save sheets, as it was before OS X 10.5 Leopard. It seems more confusing to have the contents of this menu change based on whether the Save sheet is expanded or not. I've called it to your attention so it won't confuse you.

Switch between the basic and expanded Save sheets a few times by clicking the disclosure button. Make sure that you see and understand the difference between what you see in the Where menu in a basic Save sheet and what you see in the Where menu in an expanded Save sheet.

3. **To find the folder where you want to save your file, choose among views by clicking the Icon, List, Column, or Cover Flow view button.**

   (The buttons look like their counterparts in Finder windows.) In icon view, you double-click a folder to open it. List and Cover Flow views offer disclosure triangles for folders and disks, so single-click the disclosure triangles of folders to see their contents. In column view, you click an item on the left to see its contents on the right, just as you do in a column-view Finder window.

   You can also use the Forward and Back buttons or the Sidebar, both available only in an expanded Save dialog, to conveniently navigate your disk. Many of these navigation aids work just like the ones in the Finder; flip back to Chapter 5 for more details. You can enlarge the Save sheet to see more the same way you enlarge a Finder window: Drag an edge or corner of the sheet.

If you can't find the folder in which you want to save your document, type the folder's name in the Search box. It works just like the Search box in a Finder window, as described in Chapter 5. You don't even have to press Enter or Return; the Save sheet updates itself to show you only items that match the characters as you've typed them.

4. **Select the folder where you want to save your file in the Where pop-up menu or Sidebar.**

5. **If you want to create a new subfolder of the selected folder to save your file in, click the New Folder button, give the new folder a name, and then save your file in it.**

In Figure 6-8, I've selected an existing folder named Novels. You can tell that it's selected because its name is displayed in the Where menu and highlighted below that in the first column.

The selected folder is where your file will be saved.

Figure 6-8: Saving a file in the Novels folder (which is in the Documents folder).

The keyboard shortcut for New Folder is Shift+⌘+N, regardless of whether you're in a Save sheet or the Finder. If I wanted to create a new folder inside the Novels folder in Figure 6-8, I could have clicked the New Folder button or pressed the shortcut.

6. **In the File Format pop-up menu, make sure the format selected is the one you want.**

7. **If you want to turn off the display of file extensions (such as `.rtf`, `.pdf`, and `.txt`) in Save sheets, select the Hide Extension check box.**

8. **Double-check the Where pop-up menu one last time to make sure that the correct folder is selected; then click the Save button to save the file to the active folder.**

   If you click Save, the file appears in the folder you selected. If you change your mind about saving this file, clicking Cancel dismisses the Save sheet without saving anything anywhere. In other words, the Cancel button returns things to the way they were before you displayed the Save sheet.

After you've saved a file for the first time, choosing File➪Save or pressing ⌘+S won't bring up a Save sheet. Instead, what happens next depends on whether the app supports Mountain Lion's Auto Save and Versions. If the app *doesn't* support AutoSave and Versions, Save and its shortcut, ⌘+S merely resaves your document in the same location and with the same name. If you wanted to save a unique version with a different name you'd choose the Save As command and save the file under a new name. If the app *does* support Auto Save and Versions, however, the upcoming section, "Save As versus Duplicate: Different names for the same result," explains how things work.

When you use apps that don't support Auto Save and Versions, I beg you to get into the habit of pressing ⌘+S often. It can't hurt — and just might save your bacon someday.

One last thing: In Figures 6-6, 6-7, and 6-8, I used the Save sheet for TextEdit as an example. In programs other than TextEdit, the Save sheet might contain additional options, fewer options, or different options and therefore might look slightly different. The File Format menu, for example, is a feature specific to TextEdit; it might not appear in other applications' Save sheets. Don't worry. The Save sheet always *works* the same way, no matter what options it offers.

Save As versus Duplicate: Different names for same result

File➪Duplicate and File➪Save As serve the same purpose and achieve the same result. The difference is that you'll find File➪Duplicate in apps that support Versions and Auto Save, and File➪Save As in apps that don't. They're different names for the achieving the same result: Saving a file that's already been saved with a different name, with the option of saving the renamed file in a different folder.

Before I get into the details, you may be wondering *why* you would want to do save an existing file with a different name? So here's a good (albeit kind of rude) example: Suppose that you have two cousins, Kate and Nancy. You write Kate a long, chatty letter, and save this document with the name Letter to Kate. Later, you decide that you want to send almost the same letter to Nancy, but you want to change a few things. So you change the part about your date last night and replace all references to Kate's husband, Kevin, with references to Nancy's husband, Norman. (Aren't computers grand?)

So you make all these changes in Letter to Kate, but you haven't resaved this document yet, and although the document on your screen is actually a letter to Nancy, its filename is still Letter to Kate. Think of what would happen if you were to save it now without using the Save As feature: Letter to Kate reflects the changes that you just made. (The stuff in the letter meant for Kate is blown away, replaced by the stuff that you just wrote to Nancy.) Thus, the filename Letter to Kate is inaccurate. Even worse, you might no longer have a copy of the original letter you sent to Kate! The solution? Just use Save As or Duplicate to rename this file Letter to Nancy by choosing File⇨Save As or File⇨Duplicate.

If you chose Save As: A Save sheet appears, in which you can type a different filename in the Save As field. You can also navigate to another folder, if you like, and save the newly named version of the file there. Now you have two distinct files: Letter to Kate and Letter to Nancy. Both contain the stuff they should, but both started life from the same file.

If you chose Duplicate: The title bar of the document becomes editable so you can change its name without even seeing a Save sheet. (Refer to the figure in the earlier sidebar, "Does it have Auto Save and Versions or not?") Press Enter or Return and the renamed file will be saved in the same folder as the original. Or, if you want to save the newly renamed file in a different location, choose File⇨Move To or click the little triangle to the right of the document's name, choose Move To in its pop-up menu, and then select a folder to save the file into from the pop-up menu.

Now that you understand what Save As or Duplicate are all about, here's an easier way to get the same result: Before you start, duplicate the document in the Finder (choose File⇨Duplicate or ⌘+D). Rename the copy, and open it. This way, when you're done making changes, you don't have to remember to choose Save As; you can just perform your habitual Save. This approach also protects you from accidentally saving part of the letter to Nancy without changing the file's name first (which you're likely to do if you're following my advice about saving often). So when you decide that you're going to reuse a document, Save As (or duplicate and rename the file) *before* you begin working on it, just to be safe.

Versions give you the benefits of Save As without any action on your part, but only a handful of programs supported Auto Save and Versions at press time.

Some of Apple's apps, as well as most third-party apps, still use the Save As technique, and I expect that to be the status quo for quite some time. But since some of Apple's offerings (most notably TextEdit) use Auto Save and Versions, I'd be remiss if I glossed over the new way of doing things.

One last thing: If the app you're using supports Mountain Lion's Versions, it creates a snapshot called a Version automatically as you work, when you pause, every 5 minutes, and every time you choose File⇨Save (⌘+S). Click the triangle to the right of the title of a document to see various things you can do with Versions, as shown in Figure 6-9.

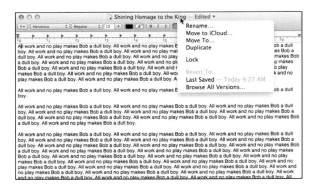

Figure 6-9: Click the triangle to see this menu of options for Versions.

TIP

Choose Browse All Versions to compare different Versions of the document you've saved side-by-side, as shown in Figure 6-10.

Figure 6-10: Browse All Versions lets you compare all versions and revert to an earlier version.

Figure 6-10 is actually Mountain Lion's Time Machine backup utility displaying the various Versions. Read more about Time Machine in Chapter 18.

Tabbing around the Save (or Save As) sheet

In the expanded view, if you press the Tab key while the Save As field is active, it becomes inactive, and the Search box becomes active. Press Tab again, and the Sidebar becomes active. Press the Tab key one more time, and the file list box (more accurately known as the *detail pane* — the part with Icon, List, Column, or Cover Flow view buttons in it) becomes active. That's because the file list box, the Search box, the Sidebar, and the Save As field are mutually exclusive. Only one can be active at any time. You can always tell which item is active by the thin blue or gray border around it.

When you want to switch to a different folder to save a file, click the folder in the Sidebar or click anywhere in the file list box to make the file list active. The following tricks help you get a hold on this whole active/inactive silliness:

🖙 If you type while the file list box is active, the list box selects the folder that most closely matches the letter(s) that you type. It's a little strange because you won't see what you type: You'll be typing blind, so to speak.

🖙 When the file list is active, the letters that you type don't appear in the Save As field. If you want to type a filename, you have to activate the Save As field again (by clicking in it or using the Tab key) before you can type in it.

🖙 If you type while the Sidebar is active, nothing happens. You can, however, use the up- and down-arrow keys to move around in the Sidebar.

🖙 Pressing Shift reverses the order of the sequence. If you press Shift+Tab, the active item moves from the Save As field to the file list box to the Sidebar to the Search box and back to the Save As field again.

Open Sez Me

You can open any icon in the Finder — whether it's a file or a folder — in at least six ways. (Okay, there are at least *seven* ways, but one of them belongs to aliases, which I discuss in great detail back in Chapter 5.) Anyway, here are the ways:

🖙 Click the icon once to select it and choose File➪Open.

🖙 Click the icon twice in rapid succession.

If the icon doesn't open, you double-clicked too slowly. You can test (and adjust) your mouse's sensitivity to double-click speed in the Mouse (or Trackpad) System Preferences pane, which you can access by launching the System Preferences application (from the Applications folder, the Dock, or the menu) and then clicking the Mouse (or Trackpad) icon.

🖙 Select the icon and then press either ⌘+O or ⌘+↓.

🖙 Right-click or Control-click it and then choose Open from the contextual menu.

✔ If the icon is a document, drag it onto the application icon (or the Dock icon of an application) that can open that type of document.

✔ If the icon is a document, right-click or Control-click it and choose an application from the Open With submenu of the contextual menu.

You can also open any document icon from within an application, of course. Here's how that works:

1. **Just launch your favorite program, and choose File➪Open (or press ⌘+O, which works in most Mac programs).**

   An Open dialog appears, like the one shown in Figure 6-11.

Figure 6-11: The Open dialog using column view.

When you use a program's Open dialog, only files that the program knows how to open appear enabled (in black rather than light gray) in the file list. In effect, the program filters out the files it can't open, so you barely see them in the Open dialog. This method of selectively displaying certain items in Open dialogs is a feature of most applications. Therefore, when you're using TextEdit, its Open dialog dims all your spreadsheet files (because TextEdit can open only text, Rich Text Format, Microsoft Word, and some picture files). Pretty neat, eh?

2. **In the dialog, simply navigate to the file you want to open (using the same techniques you use in a Save sheet).**

   Click a favorite folder in the Sidebar or use Spotlight if you can't remember where the file resides.

3. **Select your file, and click the Open button.**

For what it's worth, some applications allow you to select multiple files in their Open dialogs by holding down either Shift (for contiguous selections) or ⌘ (for noncontiguous selections). If you need to open several files, it's worth a try; the worst thing that could happen is that it won't work and you'll have to open the items one at a time.

Some programs, including Microsoft Word and Adobe Photoshop, have a Show or Format menu in their Open dialogs. This menu lets you specify the type(s) of files you want to see in the Open dialog. You can often open a file that appears dimmed by choosing All Documents from the Show or Format menu (in those applications with Open dialogs that offer such a menu).

With drag-and-drop

Macintosh drag-and-drop is usually all about dragging text and graphics from one place to another. But there's another angle to drag-and-drop — one that has to do with files and icons.

You can open a document by dragging its icon onto that of the proper application. You can open a document created with Microsoft Word, for example, by dragging the document icon onto the Microsoft Word application's icon. The Word icon highlights, and the document launches. Usually, of course, it's easier to double-click a document's icon to open it; the proper application opens automatically when you do — or at least, it does most of the time. Which reminds me . . .

With a Quick Look

To use the Quick Look command to peek at the contents of most files in Open dialogs, right-click or Control-click the file and choose Quick Look, or use its easy-to-remember shortcut: Press the spacebar. Whichever way, you'll soon see the contents of that file in a floating window without launching another application.

The Quick Look window, shown in Figure 6-12, shows you the contents of most types of files.

Sometimes Quick Look even works on files the current application can't open. For the most part, if a file can be selected in an Open dialog, you can probably view its contents with Quick Look. Quick Look is so wonderful it's also available for icons in the Finder. But you'll have to wait for Chapter 7 to read about the rest of Quick Look's charms.

Figure 6-12: The Quick Look window showing the contents of the Lion FD cover.pdf file.

When your Mac can't open a file

If you try to open a file, but OS X can't find a program to open that file, OS X prompts you with an alert window. I tried to open a very old (1993) file created on a long-defunct Psion Series 3 handheld PDA — a file so old that most of you have probably never seen the .wrd file extension, shown in Figure 6-13.

Figure 6-13: Oops! OS X helps you find the correct application.

Click Cancel to abort the attempt to open the file, or click the Choose Application or Search App Store button to select another application to open this file.

If you click the Choose Application button, a dialog appears (conveniently opened to your Applications folder and shown in Figure 6-14). Applications that OS X doesn't think can be used to open the file are dimmed. For a wider choice of applications, choose All Applications (instead of Recommended Applications) from the Enable pop-up menu.

Figure 6-14: Choosing an application to open this document.

You can't open every file with every program. If you try to open an MP3 (audio) file with Microsoft Excel (a spreadsheet), for example, it just won't work; you get an error message or a screen full of gibberish. Sometimes, you just have to keep trying until you find the right program; at other times, you don't have a program that can open the file.

When in doubt, Google the file extension. You'll usually find out more than you need to know about what application(s) create files with that extension.

With the application of your choice

I don't know about you, but people send me files all the time that were created by applications I don't use . . . or at least that I don't use for that document type. OS X lets you specify the application in which you want to open a document in the future when you double-click it. More than that, you can specify that you want all documents of that type to open with the specified application. "Where is this magic bullet hidden?" you ask. Right there in the file's Info window.

Assigning a file type to an application

Suppose that you want all .pdf files that usually open in Preview to open instead in Pixelmator, a more capable third-party program. Here's what to do:

1. **Click one of the files in the Finder.**

2. **Choose File⬦Get Info (⌘+I).**

3. **In the Info window, click the gray triangle to disclose the Open With pane.**

4. **From the pop-up menu, choose an application that OS X believes will open this document type.**

In Figure 6-15, I'm choosing Pixelmator. Now Pixelmator opens when I open this file (instead of the default application, Preview).

Figure 6-15: Before (left) and after (right) changing the application that opens this document.

5. **(Optional) If you click the Change All button at the bottom of the Open With pane, as shown on the right side of Figure 6-15, you make Pixelmator the new default application for all `.tif` files that would otherwise be opened in Preview.**

   Notice the handy alert that appears when you click the Change All button and how nicely it explains what will happen if you click Continue.

Opening a file with an application other than the default

Here's one more technique that works great when you want to open a document with a program other than its default. Just drag the file onto the application's icon or alias icon or Dock icon, and presto — the file opens in the application.

If I were to double-click an MP3 file, for example, the file usually would open in iTunes (and, by default, would be copied into my iTunes Library). But I frequently want to audition (listen to) MP3 files with QuickTime Player, so they're not automatically added to my iTunes music library. Dragging the MP3 file onto QuickTime Player's icon in the Applications folder or its Dock icon (if it's in the Dock) solves this conundrum quickly and easily.

If the icon doesn't highlight, and you release the mouse button anyway, the file ends up in the same folder as the application with the icon that didn't highlight. If that happens, just choose Edit⇨Undo (or press ⌘+Z), and the mislaid file magically returns to where it was before you dropped it. Just remember — don't do anything else after you drop the file, or Undo might not work. If Undo doesn't work, you must move the file back to its original location manually.

Only applications that *might* be able to open the file should highlight when you drag the file on them. That doesn't mean the document will be usable — just that the application can *open* it. Suffice it to say that OS X is usually smart enough to figure out which applications on your hard drive can open what documents — and to offer you a choice.

Organizing Your Stuff in Folders

I won't pretend to be able to organize your Mac for you. Organizing your files is as personal as your taste in music; you develop your own style with the Mac. But after you know how to open and save documents when you're using applications, these sections provide food for thought — some ideas about how I organize things — and some suggestions that can make organization easier for you, regardless of how you choose to do it yourself.

The upcoming sections look at the difference between a file and a folder; show you how to set up nested folders; and cover how some special folder features work. After you have a good handle on these things, you'll almost certainly be a savvier — and better organized — OS X user.

Files versus folders

When I speak of a *file,* I'm talking about what's connected to any icon except a folder or disk icon. A file can be a document, an application, an alias of a file or an application, a dictionary, a font, or any other icon that *isn't* a folder or disk. The main distinction is that you can't put something *in* most file icons.

The exceptions are icons that represent OS X packages. A *package* is an icon that acts like a file but isn't. Examples of icons that are really packages include many software installers and applications, as well as "documents" saved by some programs (such as Keynote, GarageBand, or TextEdit files saved in its .rtfd format). When you open an icon that represents a package in the usual way (double-click, choose File⇔Open, press ⌘+O, and so on), the program or document opens. If you want to see the contents of an icon that represents a package, you have to right-click or Control-click the icon first and choose Show Package Contents from the contextual menu. If you see an item by that name, you know that the icon is a package; if you don't see Show Package Contents on the contextual menu, the icon represents a file, not a package.

When I talk about *folders,* I'm talking about things that work like manila folders in the real world. Their icons look like folders, like the one in the margin to the left; they can contain files or other folders, called *subfolders.* You can put any icon — any file or folder — inside a folder.

Here's an exception: If you try to put a disk icon in a folder, all you get is an alias to the disk *unless* you hold down the Option key. Remember that you can't put a disk icon in a folder that exists on the disk itself. In other words, you can copy a disk icon only to a *different disk;* you can never copy a disk icon to a folder that resides on that disk. For more about aliases, flip to Chapter 5; for details on working with disks, see Chapter 8.

File icons can look like practically anything. If the icon doesn't look like a folder, package, or one of the numerous disk icons, you can be pretty sure that it's a file.

Organizing your stuff with subfolders

As I mention earlier in this chapter, you can put folders inside other folders to organize your icons. A folder "nested" inside another folder is called a *subfolder*.

You can create subfolders according to whatever system makes sense to you — but why reinvent the wheel? Here are some organizational topic ideas and naming examples for subfolders:

- **By type of document:** Word-Processing Documents, Spreadsheet Documents, Graphics Documents
- **By date:** Documents May–June, Documents Spring '12
- **By content:** Memos, Outgoing Letters, Expense Reports
- **By project:** Project X, Project Y, Project Z

When you notice your folders swelling and starting to get messy (that is, filling with tons of files), subdivide them again by using a combination of these methods that makes sense to you. Suppose that you start by subdividing your Documents folder into multiple subfolders. Later, when those folders begin to get full, you can subdivide them even further, as shown in Figure 6-16.

My point (yes, I do have one!): Allow your folder structure to be organic, growing as you need it to grow. Let it happen. Don't let any single folder get so full that it's a hassle to deal with. Create new subfolders when things start to get crowded. (I explain how to create folders in the next section.)

If you want to monkey around with some subfolders yourself, a good place to start is the Documents folder, which is inside your Home folder (that is, the Documents folder is a *subfolder* of your Home folder).

Figure 6-16: Before (left) and after (right) organizing the Novels and Finances folders with subfolders.

Creating subfolders . . . or not

How full is too full? When should you begin creating subfolders? That's impossible to say, at least in a one-size-fits-all way, but having too many items in a folder can be a nightmare — as can having too many subfolders with just one or two files in each one. My guideline is this: If you find more than 15 or 20 files in a single folder, begin thinking about ways to subdivide it. On the other hand, some of my biggest subfolders contain things that I don't often access. My Bob's Correspondence 1992 folder, for example, contains more than 200 files. But because I don't use it very often, its overcrowded condition doesn't bother me. (Your mileage may vary.)

Here are some tips to help you decide whether to use subfolders or just leave well enough alone:

✔ **Don't create subfolders until you need them.** That way, you avoid opening an empty folder when you're looking for something else — a complete waste of time.

✔ **Let your work style decide the file structure.** When you first start working with your Mac, you might want to save everything in your Documents folder for a while. When a decent-size group of documents has accumulated in the Documents folder, consider taking a look at them and creating logical subfolders for them.

If you use a particular folder a great deal, put it in your Dock, or make an alias of it and move the alias from the Documents folder to your Home folder or to your Desktop (for more info on aliases, see Chapter 5) to make the folder easier to access. Or drag the folder (or its alias) to the Sidebar, so it's always available, including in Open dialogs and Save sheets. If you write a lot of letters, keep an alias to your Correspondence folder in your Home folder, in the Dock, on your Desktop, or in the Sidebar for quick access. (By the way, there's no reason why you can't have a folder appear in all four places, if you like. That's what aliases are for, right?)

If you create your own subfolders in the Documents folder, you can click that folder in the Dock to reveal them, as shown in Figure 6-17. I show you how to customize the Dock in Chapter 4.

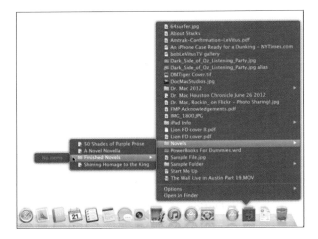

Figure 6-17: It's super-convenient to have your Documents folder in the Dock.

It's even more convenient if you choose to view the Documents folder as a list, as described in Chapter 4 and shown in Figure 6-17!

Creating new folders

So you think that Apple has already given you enough folders? Can't imagine why you'd need more? Think of creating new folders the same way you'd think of labeling a new folder at work for a specific project. New folders help you keep your files organized, enabling you to reorganize them just the way you want. Creating folders is really quite simple.

To create a new folder, just follow these steps:

1. **Decide which window you want the new folder to appear in — and then make sure that window is active.**

   If you want to create a new folder right on the Desktop, make sure that *no* window is active or that you're working within your `Home/Desktop` folder window. You can make a window active by clicking it, and you can make the Desktop active if you have windows on-screen by clicking the Desktop itself.

2. **Choose File⇨New Folder (or press Shift+⌘+N).**

   A new, untitled folder appears in the active window with its name box already highlighted, ready for you to type a new name for it.

3. **Type a name for your folder.**

   If you accidentally click anywhere before you type a name for the folder, the name box is no longer highlighted. To highlight it again, select the icon (single-click it) and press Return (or Enter) once. Now you can type its new name.

Give your folders relevant names. Folders with nebulous titles like `sfdghb` or `Stuff` or `Untitled` won't make it any easier to find something six months from now.

For folders and files that you might share with users of non-Macintosh computers, here's the rule for maximum compatibility: Use no punctuation and no Option-key characters in the folder name. Periods, slashes, backslashes,and colons in particular can be reserved for use by other operating systems. When I say Option-key characters, I'm talking about special-purpose ones such as ™ (Option+2), ® (Option+R), ¢ (Option+4), and even © (Option+G).

Navigating with spring-loaded folders

A *spring-loaded folder* pops open when you drag something onto it without releasing the mouse button. Spring-loaded folders work with all folder or disk icons in all views and in the Sidebar. Because you just got the short course on folders, subfolders, and various ways to organize your stuff, you're ready for your introduction to one of my favorite ways to get around my disks, folders, and subfolders.

Here's how spring-loaded folders work:

1. **Select any icon except a disk icon.**

   The folder highlights to indicate that it's selected.

2. **Drag the selected icon onto any folder or disk icon — but don't release the mouse button.**

    I call this *hovering* because you're doing just that: hovering the cursor over a folder or disk icon without releasing the button.

    In a second or two, the highlighted folder or disk flashes twice and then springs open, right under the cursor. You can press the spacebar to make the folder spring open immediately.

3. **After the folder springs open, perform any of these handy operations:**

    - Continue to traverse your folder structure this way. Subfolders continue to pop open until you release the mouse button.

    - If you release the mouse button, the icon you've been dragging is dropped into the active folder at the time. That window remains open — but all the windows you traversed clean up after themselves by closing automatically, leaving your window clean and uncluttered.

    - If you want to cancel a spring-loaded folder, drag the cursor away from the folder icon or outside the boundaries of the sprung window. The folder pops shut.

After you get used to spring-loaded folders, you'll wonder how you ever got along without them. They work in all four views, and they work with icons in the Sidebar or Dock. Give 'em a try, and you'll be hooked. You can toggle spring-loaded folders on or off in the Finder's Preferences window. There's also a setting for how long the Finder waits before it springs the folders open. See Chapter 5 for more on Finder preferences.

Smart Folders

As Steve Jobs was fond of saying near the end of his annual keynote addresses, "There is one more thing," and when it comes to folders, that one last thing is the Smart Folder.

A Smart Folder lets you save search criteria and have them work in the background to display the results in real time. In other words, a Smart Folder is updated continuously, so it displays all the files on your computer that match the search criteria at the moment.

So, for example, say you create a Smart Folder that contains all the Rich Text Format files on your computer that you've opened in the past two weeks, as shown in Figure 6-18. Or you can create a Smart Folder that displays graphics files, but only the ones bigger (or smaller) than a specified file size. Then all those files appear in one convenient Smart Folder.

Figure 6-18: A Smart Folder that displays only RTF files created in the past six months.

The possibilities are endless. Because Smart Folders use aliaslike technology to display items, the actual files reside in only one location: the folder where you originally put them. True to their name, Smart Folders don't gather the files themselves in a separate place; rather, they gather *aliases* of files, leaving the originals right where you stashed them. Neat!

Also, because Spotlight (discussed in Chapter 7) is built deep into the bowels of the OS X file system and kernel, Smart Folders are updated in real time and so are always current, even after you've added or deleted files on your hard drive since creating the Smart Folder.

Smart Folders are so useful that Apple provides five ways to create one. The following steps show you how:

1. **Start your Smart Folder by using any of the following methods:**

   - Choose File⇨New Smart Folder.
   - Press ⌘+Option+N.
   - Choose File⇨Find.
   - Press ⌘+F.
   - Type at least one character in the Search box of a Finder window.

   If you have All My Files selected in the Sidebar, you can't use the last method, because All My Files is a Smart Folder — one with a weird icon, but a Smart Folder nonetheless.

2. **Refine the criteria for your search by clicking the + button to add a criterion or the – button to delete one.**

3. **When you're satisfied and ready to turn your criteria into a Smart Folder, click the Save button below the Search box.**

   A sheet drops down.

4. **Choose where you want to save your folder.**

   While the Save sheet is displayed, you can add the Smart Folder to the Sidebar, if you like, by clicking the Add to Sidebar check box.

5. **When you're finished editing criteria, click the Save button to save the folder with its criteria.**

After you create your Smart Folder, you can save it anywhere on any hard drive and use it like any other folder. There's also an option to display it in your Sidebar, if you want.

If you want to *change* the criteria for a Smart Folder you created earlier, right-click or Control-click the Smart Folder in the Sidebar and select Show Search Criteria, as shown in Figure 6-19.

Figure 6-19: Right-click or Control-click a Smart Folder in the Sidebar and choose Show Search Criteria.

Alternatively, you can right-click or Control-click the Smart Folder (even one in the Sidebar) and choose Show Search Criteria from the contextual menu.

When you're finished changing the criteria, click the Save button to resave your folder. Don't worry — if you try to close a Smart Folder you've modified without saving your changes, OS X politely asks if you want to save this Smart Folder and warns that if you don't save, the changes you made will be lost. You may be asked whether you want to replace the previous Smart Folder of the same name; usually, you do.

Smart Folders (with the exception of the Sidebar's All My Files, which has its own weird little icon) display a little gear in their center, as shown in Figure 6-19, making them easy to tell apart from regular folders.

Smart Folders can save you a lot of time and effort, so if you haven't played with them much (or at all) yet, be sure to give 'em a try.

Shuffling Around Files and Folders

Sometimes, keeping files and folders organized means moving them from one place to another. At other times, you want to copy them, rename them, or compress them to send to a friend. These sections explain all those things and more.

All the techniques that I discuss in the following sections work at least as well for windows that use list, column, or Cover Flow view as they do for windows that use icon view. I use icon view in the figures in this section only because it's the best view for pictures to show you what's going on. For what it's worth, I find moving and copying files much easier in windows that use list or column view.

Comprehending the Clipboard

Before you start moving your files around, let me introduce you to the Clipboard. The *Clipboard* is a holding area for the last thing that you cut or copied. That copied item can be text, a picture, a portion of a picture, an object in a drawing program, a column of numbers in a spreadsheet, any icon (except a disk), or just about anything else that can be selected. In other words, the Clipboard is the Mac's temporary storage area.

Most of the time, the Clipboard works quietly in the background, but you can ask the Clipboard to reveal itself by choosing Edit⇨Show Clipboard. This command summons the Clipboard window, which lists the type of item (such as text, picture, or sound) on the Clipboard — and a message letting you know whether the item on the Clipboard can be displayed.

As a storage area, the Clipboard's contents are temporary. *Very* temporary. When you cut or copy an item, that item remains on the Clipboard only until you cut or copy something else. When you do cut or copy something else, the new item replaces the Clipboard's contents, and the newcomer remains on the Clipboard until you cut or copy something else. And so it goes.

Whatever is on the Clipboard heads straight for oblivion if you crash, lose power, log out, or shut down your Mac, so don't count on it too heavily or for too long.

The Clipboard commands on the Edit menu are enabled only when they can actually be used. If the selected item can be cut or copied, the Cut and Copy commands in the Edit menu are enabled. If the selected item can't be cut or copied, the commands are unavailable and are dimmed (gray). If the Clipboard is empty or the current document can't accept what's on the Clipboard, the Paste command is dimmed. Finally, when nothing is selected, the Cut, Copy, and Clear commands are dimmed.

Icons can't be cut; they can only be copied or pasted. So when an icon is selected, the Cut command is always gray.

Copying files and folders

One way to copy icons from one place to another is to use the Clipboard. When a file or folder icon is selected, choose Edit⇨Copy (or use its shortcut, ⌘+C) to copy the selected icon to the Clipboard. Note that this doesn't delete the selected item; it just makes a copy of it on the Clipboard. To paste the copied icon in another location, choose Edit⇨Paste (or use its shortcut, ⌘+V).

Other methods of copying icons from one place to another include these:

- ✔ **Drag an icon from one folder icon onto another folder icon while holding down the Option key.** Release the mouse button when the second folder is highlighted. This technique works regardless of whether the second folder's window is open. If you don't hold down the Option key, you move the icon to a new location rather than copy it, as I explain a little later in this section.

  When you copy something by dragging and dropping it with the Option key held down, the cursor changes to include a little plus sign (+) next to the arrow, as shown in the margin. Neat!

- ✔ **Drag an icon into an open window for another folder while holding down the Option key.** Drag the icon for the file or folder that you want to copy into the open window for a second folder (or other hard disk or removable media such as a USB flash drive).

- ✔ **Choose File⇨Duplicate (⌘+D) or right-click or Control-click the file or folder that you want to duplicate, and then choose Duplicate from the contextual menu that appears.** This makes a copy of the selected icon, adds the word *copy* to its name, and then places the copy in the same window as the original icon. You can use the Duplicate command on any icon except a disk icon.

  You can't duplicate an entire disk onto itself. But you can copy an entire disk (call it Disk 1) to any other actual, physical, separate disk (call it Disk 2) as long as Disk 2 has enough space available. Just hold down Option, and drag Disk 1 onto Disk 2's icon. The contents of Disk 1 are copied to Disk 2 and appear on Disk 2 in a folder named Disk 1.

You can cut an icon's name, but you can't cut the icon itself; you may only copy an icon. To achieve the effect of cutting an icon, select the icon, copy it to the Clipboard, paste it in its new location, and then move the original icon to the Trash.

If you're wondering why anyone would ever want to copy a file, trust me: Someday, you will. Suppose that you have a file called Long Letter to Mom in a folder called Old Correspondence. You figure that Mom has forgotten that letter by now, and you want to send it again. But before you do, you want to change the date and delete the reference to Clarence, her pit bull, who passed away last year. So now you need to put a copy of Long Letter to Mom in your Current Correspondence folder. This technique yields the same result as making a copy of a file by using Save As, which I describe earlier in this chapter.

When you copy a file, it's wise to change the name of the copied file. Having more than one file on your hard drive with exactly the same name isn't a good idea, even if the files are in different folders. Trust me that having 12 files called Expense Report or 15 files named Doctor Mac Consulting Invoice can be confusing, no matter how well organized your folder structure is. Add distinguishing words or dates to file and folder names so that they're named something more explicit, such as Expense Report Q3 2010 or Doctor Mac Consulting Invoice 4-4-2011.

You can have lots of files with the same name *on the same disk* (although, as I mention earlier, it's probably not a good idea). But your Mac won't let you have more than one file with the same name and extension (.txt, .jpg, .doc) *in the same folder*.

Pasting from the Clipboard

As I mention earlier in this chapter, to place the icon that's on the Clipboard someplace new, click where you want the item to go and choose Edit⇨Paste or use the keyboard shortcut ⌘+V to paste what you've copied or cut.

Pasting doesn't purge the contents of the Clipboard. In fact, an item stays on the Clipboard until you cut, copy, restart, shut down, log out, or crash. This means that you can paste the same item over and over and over again, which can come in pretty handy at times.

Almost all programs have an Edit menu and use the Macintosh Clipboard, which means you can usually cut or copy something from a document in one program and paste it into a document in another program. Usually.

Moving files and folders

You can move files and folders around within a window to your heart's content, as long as that window is set to icon view. Just click and drag any icon to its new location in the window. Some people spend hours arranging icons in a window until they're just so. But because using icon view wastes so much screen space, I avoid using icons in a window.

You can't move icons around in a window that is displayed in list, column, or Cover Flow view, which makes total sense when you think about it. (Well, you can move them to put them in a different folder in list, column, or Cover Flow view, but that's not moving them around, really.) And you can't move icons around in a window under the spell of the Arrange By command.

As you might expect from Apple by now, you have choices for how you move one file or folder into another folder. You can use these techniques to move any icon (folder, document, alias, or program icon) into folders or onto other disks.

- ✔ **Drag an icon onto a folder icon.** Drag the icon for one folder (or file) onto the icon for another folder (or disk) and then release when the second icon is highlighted (see Figure 6-20). The first folder is inside the second folder. Put another way, the first folder is a subfolder of the second folder. This technique works regardless of whether the second folder's window is open.

- ✔ **Drag an icon into an open folder's window.** Drag the icon for one folder (or file) into the open window for a second folder (or disk), as shown in Figure 6-20.

Figure 6-20: Two ways of putting one folder into another.

If you want to move an item from one *disk* to another disk, you can't use the preceding tricks. Your item is copied, not moved. If you want to *move* a file or folder from one disk to another, you have to hold down the ⌘ key when you drag an icon from one disk to another. The little Copying Files window even changes to read *Moving* Files. Nice touch, eh?

Selecting multiple icons

Sometimes you want to move or copy several items into a single folder. The process is pretty much the same as it is when you copy one file or folder (that is, you just drag the icon to where you want it and drop it there). But you need to select all the items you want before you can drag them en masse to their destination.

If you want to move all the files in a particular folder, simply choose Edit⇪Select All or press ⌘+A. This command selects all icons in the active window, regardless of whether you can see them on-screen. If no window is active, choosing Select All selects every icon on the Desktop.

But what if you want to select only some of the files in the active window or on the Desktop? Here's the most convenient method:

1. **To select more than one icon in a folder, do one of the following:**

    • *Click once within the folder window (don't click any one icon), and drag your mouse (or keypad) while continuing to hold down the mouse button.* You see an outline of a box around the icons while you drag, and all icons within or touching the box become highlighted (see Figure 6-21).

Figure 6-21: Select more than one icon by clicking and dragging with your mouse (or trackpad).

• *Click one icon and hold down the Shift key while you click others.* As long as you hold down the Shift key, each new icon that you click is added to the selection. To deselect an icon, click it a second time while still holding down the Shift key.

• *Click one icon and hold down the ⌘ key while you click others.* The difference between using the Shift and ⌘ keys is that the ⌘ key doesn't select everything between it and the first item selected when your window is in list, cover flow, or column view. In icon view, it really doesn't make much difference.

To deselect an icon, click it while holding down the ⌘ key.

2. **After you select the icons, click one of them (clicking anywhere else deselects the icons) and drag them to the location where you want to move them (or Option-drag to copy them).**

Be careful with multiple selections, especially when you drag icons to the Trash. You can easily — and accidentally — select more than one icon, so watch out that you don't accidentally put the wrong icon in the Trash by not paying close attention. (I detail how the Trash icon works later in this chapter.)

Playing the icon name game: Renaming icons

Icon, icon, bo-bicon, banana-fanna fo-ficon. Betcha can change the name of any old icon! Well, that's not entirely true. . . .

If an icon is locked or busy (the application is currently open), or if you don't have the owner's permission to rename that icon (see Chapter 16 for details about permissions), you can't rename it. Similarly, you should never rename certain reserved icons (such as the Library, System, and Desktop folders).

To rename an icon, you can either click the icon's name directly (don't click the icon itself, because that selects the icon) or click the icon and press Return (or Enter) once.

Either way, the icon's name is selected and surrounded with a box, and you can type a new name, as shown in Figure 6-22. In addition, the cursor changes from a pointer to a text-editing I-beam. An I-beam cursor is the Mac's way of telling you that you can type now. At this point, if you click the I-beam cursor anywhere in the name box, you can edit the icon's original name. If you don't click the I-beam cursor in the name box but just begin typing, the icon's original name is replaced by what you type.

If you've never changed an icon's name, give it a try. And don't forget: If you click the icon itself, the icon is selected, and you won't be able to change its name. If you do accidentally select the icon, just press Return (or Enter) once to edit the name of the icon.

Figure 6-22: Change an icon's name by typing over the old one.

One last thing: If you have two or more icons you want to move to a new folder, select the items and choose File⇨New Folder with Selection, press ⌘+Control+N, or right-click or Control-click one of the selected items and choose New Folder with Selection. All three techniques will create a new folder, move the selected icons into it, and even selects the name of the new folder (which will be New Folder with Items) so you can type a new name immediately.

Compressing files

If you're going to send files as an e-mail enclosure, creating a compressed archive of the files first and sending the archive instead of the originals usually saves you time sending the files and saves the recipient time downloading them. To create this compressed archive, simply select the file or files and then choose File⇨Compress. This creates a compressed `.zip` file out of your selection. The compressed file is smaller than the original — sometimes by quite a bit.

Getting rid of icons

To get rid of an icon — any icon — merely drag it onto the Trash icon on your Dock.

Trashing an alias gets rid of only the alias, not the parent file. But trashing a document, folder, or application icon puts it in the Trash, where it *will* be deleted permanently the next time you empty the Trash. The Finder menu offers a couple of commands that help you manage the Trash:

✓ **Finder⇨Empty Trash:** This command deletes all items in the Trash from your hard drive, period.

I'll probably say this more than once: *Use this command with a modicum of caution.* After a file is dragged into the Trash and the Trash is emptied, the file is gone, gone, gone unless you have a Time Machine or other backup. (Okay, maybe ProSoft Engineering's Data Rescue II or some other third-party utility can bring it back, but I wouldn't bet the farm on it.)

✔ **Finder⟳Secure Empty Trash:** Choosing this command makes the chance of recovery by even the most ardent hacker or expensive disk-recovery tool difficult to virtually impossible. Now the portion of the disk that held the files you're deleting will be overwritten with randomly generated gibberish. You're hosed unless you have a Time Machine or other backup.

If you put something in the Trash by accident, you can almost always return it whence it came: Just invoke the magical Undo command. Choose Edit⟳Undo or press ⌘+Z. The accidentally trashed file returns to its original location. Usually. Unfortunately, Undo doesn't work every time — and it remembers only the very last action that you performed when it does work — so don't rely on it too much.

Four Terrific Timesaving Tools

....

In This Chapter

▶ Taking a quick look inside files with Quick Look

▶ Finding your files and folders, fast

▶ Taking charge with Mission Control

▶ Learning to love Mountain Lion's Launchpad

....

*I*n this chapter, I show you the ins and outs of four terrific timesaving tools: Quick Look, Spotlight, Mission Control, and Launchpad. Each is designed to let you use your Mac better, faster, and more elegantly. Yes, you can use your mouse and click your way to any file or folder on any disk. But these features are built into Mountain Lion for your convenience.

At the risk of repeating myself, Apple frequently provides more than one way to accomplish a task in OS X, so there's duplication and overlap among and between the tools in this chapter and tools you've read about elsewhere in this book. Don't worry. Take what you need, and leave the rest. Most users love Quick Look, but some never use it. Some people love Spotlight; others rarely use it. Mission Control is amazingly helpful, especially on laptops with small screens, but some users don't care for it.

My advice: Try all the tools and techniques in this chapter at least a few times before you decide whether you want or need them.

With a Quick Look

The Quick Look command displays the contents of the selected file in a floating window. The key point is that you can see what's in a file without double-clicking (to open) it and without launching any application. This is quite handy when you want to peek at the contents of a file without having to open it.

To take a Quick Look yourself, select an icon and do any of the following: Choose File➪Quick Look; right-click or Control-click the icon and choose Quick Look from its contextual menu; or use one of its two keyboard shortcuts — ⌘+Y or the easiest shortcut ever, spacebar.

One of my favorite ways to use Quick Look is with a folder full of images, such as the one shown in in Figure 7-1.

Close Quick Look window

Grow (zoom) Quick Look window

Previous

Next   Quick Look window

Index sheet   Open with default app (Preview)

Share menu   Four selected icons

Full screen

Figure 7-1: The Quick Look window (left) displaying an image from one of the selected icons in my *The Wall Live in Austin – Stills* folder.

The cool part is that while the Quick Look window is open, you can select different icons in the Finder window and very quickly peek at their contents in the Quick Look window.

The bad news is that while Quick Look works with many types of files — Microsoft Office, Apple iWork, plain-text, PDF, TIFF, GIF, JPEG, PNG, and most types of audio and video — it doesn't work with *all* files. You'll know it didn't work if Quick Look shows you a big document, folder, or application icon instead of the contents of that file.

If you select multiple items before you invoke Quick Look, as I've done in Figure 7-1, three icons appear at the top of the Quick Look window near the left side — the Next, Previous, and Index Sheet buttons. With these controls you can view all of the selected items at the same time as an *index sheet,* as shown in Figure 7-2, or view them one at a time by clicking the Next or Previous buttons.

Figure 7-2: Four selected files displayed as a Quick Look index sheet.

The blue outline around the image at the bottom on the right indicates that the cursor is hovering over that image; if I were to click, that image (The Wall Live in Austin (Stills) Part 24.JPG) would fill the window, and the icons shown at the top of the Quick Look window in Figure 7-1 would reappear.

Share and share alike with the Share menu

If you use an Apple i-device, you're surely familiar with the rectangular button with an arrow escaping from it, as shown in the margin and in Figure 7-1. It's called the Share menu and it has four options:

- ✔ **E-mail:** Launches the Mail app and attaches the selected file to a blank message, ready for you to address and send.
- ✔ **Message:** Launches the Messages (formerly iChat) app and puts the selected file in an outgoing message, ready for you to address and send.

  You become well acquainted with the Messages app in Chapter 10.
- ✔ **AirDrop:** Sends the selected file to other Mac users on the same network with a single click. Note that only Lion and Mountain Lion support AirDrop; earlier versions of OS X didn't include it. And only recent-vintage Macs (say 2010 or newer) can use it.

 ✔ **Flickr:** Posts the selected file to Flickr, a popular photo-sharing site. (Note that this option only appears if you've selected an image file. So if you don't see it when you click your Share menu, you've probably selected a PDF or other type of file that can't be uploaded to Flickr.)

Slide into Slideshow (full-screen) mode

Quick Look really shines in its Slideshow (full-screen) mode, which you can start with any of these techniques:

 ✔ Hold down Option and choose File⟿Slideshow.

 ✔ Press ⌘+Option+Y.

 ✔ If your file is already open in the Quick Look window, click the double-diagonal-arrow button in the upper-right corner of the window.

When you're in Slideshow mode, a completely different set of controls appears on screen automatically, as shown in Figure 7-3.

Add to iPhoto

Previous   Next   Close Quick Look

Play   Index Sheet   Exit full screen

Figure 7-3: The Slideshow controls appear automatically in the full-screen Slideshow mode.

 TIP

The Slideshow controls disappear after a few seconds of inactivity; if you don't see them when you need them, just move the cursor and they'll magically reappear.

To exit Slideshow (full-screen) mode, press Esc or click the Exit full screen button to return to the Quick Look window or the Exit Quick Look button to both exit Slideshow mode and quit Quick Look.

When you're finished with Quick Look window, click the X button in the top-left corner (refer to Figure 7-1); if you're in full-screen mode, click the X button in the slide show control bar, as shown in Figure 7-3; or press ⌘+Y, which works in either mode.

Spotlight on Finding Files and Folders Faster

Even if you follow every single bit of advice provided in this chapter, a time will come when you won't be able to find a file or folder, although you know for certain that it's right there on your hard drive. Somewhere. Fortunately, Mountain Lion includes a fabulous technology called Spotlight that can help you find almost anything on any mounted disk in seconds. Spotlight can

- Search for files
- Search for folders
- Search for text inside documents
- Search for files and folders by their metadata (creation date, modification date, kind, size, and so on)

Spotlight finds what you're looking for and then organizes its results logically, all in the blink of an eye (on most Macs).

Spotlight is both a technology and a feature. The technology is pervasive throughout Mountain Lion — and is the underlying power behind the search boxes in many Apple applications and utilities such as Mail, Contacts, System Preferences, and Finder. You can also use it right from the Spotlight menu — the little magnifying glass at the right end of the menu bar. Also, you can reuse Spotlight searches in the future by turning them into Smart Folders (which I explain in Chapter 6).

Finding files and folders has never been faster or easier than it is in Mountain Lion. So in the following sections, I look at the two separate but related ways that Spotlight helps you find files, folders, and even text inside document files: the Search box in Finder windows and the Spotlight menu.

Using the Search box in Finder windows

With its power provided by Spotlight, this definitely isn't your father's Search box.

Press ⌘+Option+F to move the cursor to the search box of the active window.

The following steps walk you through all the features:

1. **Type a single character in the Search box.**

   The window starts displaying the results, as shown in Figure 7-4.

Figure 7-4: As soon as you type one character (a) in the Search box the magic begins.

Not only does the window become populated with files that match the letter(s) you typed, at the same time, a menu drops down below your cursor to offer search suggestions, such as Filename, Kinds, and Downloaded From as shown in Figure 7-4, as well as others such as Dates and Sent By (not shown). Typing additional characters narrows the scope, so the more you type, the fewer matches and suggestions you'll see.

If you want to change the criteria for one or more of these items, it's the same as changing criteria for a Smart Folder: Click the item in the Sidebar, and then click the Action-menu button and choose Show Search Criteria. When you're done changing the search criteria, click the Save button to resave your folder.

2. **If the folder or volume you want to search isn't This Mac or your Home folder, open the folder you want to search, and type your query in the Search box in that folder's window.**

   The default is to search files' contents if it can. Mountain Lion's Spotlight can search the contents of files created by most popular applications. To search for a file by its file name, choose Filename Contains (*a* in Figure 7-4) from the drop-down menu.

3. **When you find the file or folder, you can open any item in the window by double-clicking it.**

You can also start a search by choosing File⇨Find (shortcut: ⌘+F).

Keep these points in mind when you perform a search:

- You have a choice of where to search. My Home folder (bob1) is selected in Figure 7-5.

- You can choose additional search criteria — such as the kind of file (PDF in Figure 7-5) and the last date the file was opened (Within Last 60 Days in Figure 7-5) — as well as other attributes, including Modification Date, Creation Date, Keywords, Label, File Contents, and File Size.

Figure 7-5: Search your whole Mac or a specific folder (and its subfolders), and then narrow your search using one or more criterion.

✔ To add another criterion, simply click the + button on the right side of the window.

✔ To save a search for reuse in the future, click the Save button on the right side of the window.

Try choosing different options from the window's Arrange menu — Application, Date Last Opened, and so on — to see the search results presented in different ways.

So there you have it — fast searches made easy in the Finder. But there are many ways to access the power of Spotlight, and the Search box in the toolbar of Finder windows is merely one of them.

Using the Spotlight menu and window

Another way to search for files and folders is to use the Spotlight menu itself — the magnifying-glass icon at the far right end of your menu bar. Click the icon to open the Spotlight Search box, and then type a character, word, or series of words in the Search box to find an item, as shown in Figure 7-6.

Memorize and use the super-convenient and easy-to-remember keyboard shortcut for opening the Spotlight search box, which is ⌘+spacebar by default. If you don't find ⌘+spacebar appealing as a shortcut, you can change it to whatever you like in the Spotlight System Preferences pane.

If you highlight (but don't click) an item in the Spotlight's menu's results list, a preview pops up to its left. I love being able to preview a dictionary definition, like the one in Figure 7-6.

Spotlight is more than just a menu and Search box; it also uses a technology that's pervasive throughout OS X and apps including (but certainly not limited to) Mail, Contacts, and many, many more. The reason why it's so spectacularly speedy is that it "indexes" your files when your Mac is idle. The upshot is that Spotlight knows file locations and contents soon after a file is created or modified.

Figure 7-6: Type in the Search box, and your results appear instantly (bottom).

You can also use the Spotlight window to create and perform more sophisticated searches. You can access this window in two ways:

- Click the Show All in Finder item on the Spotlight menu or press ⌘+Option+spacebar.

  You can change this shortcut to whatever you like in the Spotlight System Preferences pane.
- Use the criteria at the top of the window to narrow your search.

This is exactly the same process you use to create Smart Folders, as discussed in Chapter 6! If you want to make a Smart Folder from a search you perform, just click the Save button.

Regardless of which method you choose to invoke it — the Search box in a Finder window, the Spotlight Search box in the menu bar, or the Spotlight window — Spotlight saves you time and effort.

Finding files by other attributes

After you add a search attribute by clicking the + button, choose a search attribute from its pop-up menu: Kind, Last Opened Date, Last Modified Date, Created Date, Name, or Contents by default. Select an item, and its relevant pop-up menus and/or text entry fields appear, as shown in Figure 7-7.

File Size isn't one of the default search attributes in the pop-up menu; here's how to choose it and many other attributes not on the menu: Choose Other from the pop-up menu and a list of dozens of additional search options (including File Size) appears, as shown in Figure 7-8.

Figure 7-7: Narrowing a search using the Kind, Created Date, Last Opened Date, and File Size search attributes.

Figure 7-8: Just some of the search attributes that appear when you choose Other.

In Figure 7-8, I've selected the File Size search attribute in the list so I can use it for this search. And, because I expect to use this search attribute fairly often, I've also selected its In Menu check box. As a result, the File Size search attribute appears below the Contents attribute in the pop-up menu for easy access, as shown in Figure 7-9.

Figure 7-9: The search attribute pop-up menu before (left) and after (right) adding the File Size attribute.

It took a few steps to use File Size as a search attribute the first time, but the next time I need it, I just choose it from the pop-up menu and search away.

Exposé Yourself to Mission Control's Spaces

Two of my favorite tools in Leopard and Snow Leopard were Exposé and Spaces, a positively peachy pair of utilities that went together like peanut butter and chocolate. They went together so well, in fact, that Apple teamed them up in their very own System Preferences pane: the eponymous Exposé & Spaces System Preferences pane.

You won't find the Exposé & Spaces System Preferences pane in Lion or Mountain Lion, but rest assured that Exposé and Spaces are alive and well in both versions, having survived the name change to Mission Control.

Figure 7-10 shows the Mission Control System Preferences pane (the pane formerly known as Exposé & Spaces) in all its glory.

Figure 7-10: The Mission Control System Preferences pane.

The painless Mission Control pane

The top part of the pane contains four check boxes: Show Dashboard as a Space; Automatically Rearrange Spaces Based on Most Recent Use; When Switching to an Application, Switch to a Space with Open Windows for the Application; and Group Windows By Application. You know what Dashboard is all about (from Chapter 3), but because I haven't introduced you to Spaces yet (but will shortly), these check boxes will make sense to you only after you read the sections that follow. Suffice it to say that they do what you think they'll do. You should experiment with the settings, turning them on and off, to see which way you prefer them.

Moving right along, most of this pane handles keyboard and mouse shortcuts for Mission Control. These eight pop-up menus — four each for keyboard and mouse shortcuts — let you specify the trigger for each of the four features with a keystroke or mouse button. The default keyboard shortcuts appear below, but yours may differ; to change them, click the appropriate pop-up menu and make a new selection.

Hold down the ⌘, Option, Control, and/or Shift keys when you choose an item from the keyboard shortcut menu (the four pop-up menus on the left in Figure 7-10) to add modifier keys to the keyboard shortcuts you create. So, for example, if you held down ⌘+Shift when you selected F11 from a pop-up menu, the keyboard shortcut for that feature would be ⌘+Shift+F11.

Finally, most Apple keyboards made in the past five or six years also include a dedicated Mission Control and Dashboard shortcut keys (F3 and F4 respectively). If you see a tiny picture that looks like the Mission Control icon on your F3 key, or looks like the Dashboard icon on your F4 keys, you can use them in addition to the other shortcuts discussed in this section.

A picture is worth a thousand words, so check out Figures 7-11, 7-12, and 7-13 as you read about each feature.

Figure 7-11: On most days, my screen looks something like this, with a myriad of open windows from numerous apps obscuring one another.

⌐ To see Mission Control, which displays all open windows in all open applications, as shown in Figure 7-12, press Control+↑ (up arrow).

TIP

If you hover over a window on the Mission Control screen (shown in Figure 7-12) and press the spacebar, you see a preview of the window's contents, which is especially helpful when a window is partially obscured by another window.

Figure 7-12: After invoking Mission Control (Control+↑).

- To see all open windows belonging to the current application (TextEdit in Figure 7-13), press Control+↓ (down arrow).

- To hide all open windows and display the Desktop, press F11 or fn+F11.

- To summon forth the Dashboard (which displays your widgets, as I explain in Chapter 3), press F12 (or fn+F12). Or, if your F4 key has a Dashboard icon printed on it, press F4.

Figure 7-13: After invoking Application Windows (Control+↓) when TextEdit was active.

Notice that when you're using Mission Control, windows appear at a reduced size. Identifying information — either the program or window name — appears below it, making it easier to discern what each item contains. When you click any of these small windows, Mission Control deactivates, and the window you clicked becomes the active window.

Check out the way that Mission Control's Application Windows screen (see Figure 7-10) includes a row of document icons near the bottom of the screen. They represent the TextEdit documents I created or modified most recently. Click the stack at the right end of the row to see more documents. You read more about TextEdit in Chapter 14, but trust me that this new feature makes it a cinch to reopen documents you've used recently.

Hot corners!

In the bottom-left corner of the Mission Control System Preferences pane is a Hot Corners button, which lets you designate any or all of the corners of your screen as hot spots to trigger Mission Control, Dashboard, Launchpad, Screen Saver, or Display Sleep. Click the menu for a corner, and select the feature you want associated with that corner. Then, whenever you move your cursor onto that corner and leave it there for a second or two, the feature executes.

Hot corners have been part of Mac OS since time immemorial and are still as useful as ever. I like to set the top-right corner to start my screen saver and the bottom-right corner to disable it, for example.

Mission Control is enabled by default, but you can disable any or all of its features by turning off its trigger: Just choose the minus sign from a pop-up menu instead of a keyboard or mouse-button shortcut. In Figure 7-10, the Dashboard mouse trigger is disabled, and I'm changing the Mission Control mouse trigger to Middle Mouse.

Spaces from 30,000 feet (An overview)

If Mission Control lets you manage your windows in real time, spaces lets you manage windows by organizing them in groups called *spaces* and switch from space to space with a keystroke or gesture.

When you use spaces, only two kinds of windows are shown: windows from applications associated with the active space and windows from applications launched while that space is active.

If you find yourself spending too much time moving and resizing windows on-screen, consider setting up spaces for specific tasks. You might have one space dedicated to a specific project, another for web surfing, and a third for e-mail, each with all its windows arranged just the way you like them.

Think of a space as being a single screen, set up just the way you like it, with its windows arranged just the way you like them. Take, for example, the three spaces shown in Figures 7-14, 7-15, and 7-16. I have one for web surfing (Figure 7-14), one for Mail (Figure 7-15), and one for working in the Finder (Figure 7-16), each one with its windows arranged exactly as I like 'em.

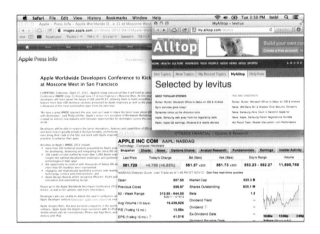

Figure 7-14: My web-surfing space, with three Safari windows (Apple Press Info, my Alltop page, and eTrade) arranged the way I like 'em on my screen.

Figure 7-15: My Mail space, with three Mail windows (Message Viewer, Addresses, and Activity) arranged just so.

Figure 7-16: My Finder space, with two windows in list view (All My Files and Trash), plus a third window in icon view (More Pix).

Moving right along, you manage your spaces with Mission Control, a feature in Mountain Lion that provides an overview of what's running on your Mac, including all your spaces, the Dashboard, and all open windows. In a nutshell, this dynamic duo makes it easier than ever to manage and maintain the mélange of Finder and application windows that conspire to clutter and eventually consume your screen.

To see it in action, press the Mission Control key (Control+↑ by default). If you have a trackpad, you can also swipe upward using three fingers to see Mission Control, which will look something like Figure 7-17 based on the three spaces shown in Figures 7-14 through 7-16.

Note that you won't see the Dashboard in Mission Control if you've cleared the Show Dashboard as a Space check box in the Mission Control System Preferences pane.

In earlier versions of OS X, these desktops were called *spaces*. Mission Control, improbably, uses the words *spaces* and *desktop* interchangeably, so as you see in Figure 7-17, my three spaces are named Desktop 1, Desktop 2, and Desktop 3. I think it's dumb, and I'm going to continue to call a space a space regardless of what Mission Control labels them.

By the way, apps running in full screen mode are considered a space, which bears the name of the app rather than "Desktop X."

Figure 7-17: Mission Control showing off three spaces (Desktops 1, 2, and 3) and the Dashboard.

To add a new space, first enter Mission Control; then move the cursor to the top-right corner of the screen and click the Add (+) button. (My tech editor informs me that if you have your Dock on the right side of the screen, the + will appear in the top-left corner instead of the top-right.)

You don't see a + button? It's hidden and appears only when your cursor is nearby. You can see it in the top-right corner of Figure 7-17; if you don't see a + button there on *your* screen, move the cursor to that general vicinity, and it magically appears.

You can use this technique to add as many spaces as you like. When you're finished using Mission Control, you can

  ✔ Click a space at the top of the screen to switch to it.

   or

  ✔ Press the Mission Control key or swipe with three fingers to return to the space you were using when you entered Mission Control.

These gestures require a Magic Mouse, Magic Trackpad, or laptop with buttonless trackpad.

If you're using a notebook Mac, I implore you to learn to use gestures with Mission Control. Visit the Trackpad System Preferences Pane's More Gestures tab and make sure you've enabled three- or four-finger swipes. I love swiping between Mission Control spaces like the ones in Figures 6-14, 6-15, and 6-16. Swipe and I've got Mail; swipe again and I've got Safari; swipe again and I've got the Finder. Try it — I think you'll like swiping to switch spaces (a.k.a. desktops) as much as I do.

Getting around in space (s)

You just saw one way to move from one space to another — enter Mission Control and click the space you want to use. You can also navigate spaces in the following ways:

- Press the Control key and ← (left-arrow key) or → (right-arrow key) to move to the next or previous space.

- Swipe left or right with three fingers to move to the next or previous space.

- Press the Control key and the number key for the space you want to use. Pressing Control+2, for example, activates Desktop 2.

  You can enable or disable these keyboard shortcuts in the Keyboard Shortcuts tab of the Keyboard System Preferences pane.

There will be times when you want to move a window from one space to another. To do so:

- Drag a window to the left or right edge of the screen, and pause. After a short delay, the window pops into the space on the left or right of the current space.

- Press and hold down the mouse button on the window you want to move while pressing the Control key and the

  - Left-arrow key (←) to move the window to the space on the left of the current space.

  - Right-arrow key (→) to move the window to the space on the right of the current space

  - Number key of the space to move the window to that space

  or

- Start in the space that has the window you want to move. Enter Mission Control, drag the window from the middle part of the screen onto the space you want to move it to, and then release the mouse button.

It's often useful to assign a specific application to a specific space. To do so, first launch the application in question; then press and hold its Dock icon, and choose Options, as shown in Figure 7-18.

Here's the rundown on those options:

- **To have the application open in every space, choose All Desktops.**

  When the application is running, it will appear in every space.

- **To have the application open only in the current space, choose This Desktop.**

The application opens in this space. If you're working in a different space and switch to this application, its assigned space scrolls into view.

✔ **To have the application open in whatever space you're using, choose None.**

Figure 7-18: Press and hold an application's Dock icon to assign the application to a specific space (Desktop).

Finally, should you want to delete one or more spaces, simply enter Mission Control, and move the cursor over the space. A Delete button — an X that should look familiar if you use an iPhone, iPad, or iPod touch, or the Dashboard — appears in the top-left corner, as shown in Figure 7-19. Click it to delete that space.

Figure 7-19: Hover the cursor over a space, and a Delete button (X) appears.

Deleting a space doesn't delete or quit any applications or close any documents. Applications and windows in a deleted space move to the space called Desktop (the one *without* a numeric suffix).

The bottom line is that spaces can be particularly useful for those with a smaller display. This feature is an acquired taste, so even if you have a small screen, you may not care for it.

My advice: Try it for a while, and if you decide that you hate it, turn its triggers off (by selecting the minus sign) and be done with it.

Launchpad: The Place for Applications

Launchpad presents all the applications in your Applications folder in a view that looks like the home screen of any iOS device (that is, iPhone, iPad, or iPod touch). In fact, if you use one of these devices, I suspect that you could skip everything that follows about Launchpad, because it works almost exactly like the home screen on an iPhone or other i-device.

 Click Launchpad's Dock icon (shown in the margin). It fills your screen with big, beautiful application icons, as shown in Figure 7-20.

 I changed my Desktop picture from plain white to a photograph (of a lion) for Figure 7-20. The photo is actually in focus; the nifty blur effect happens only when Launchpad is active. Sure, it's just eye candy, but at least it's *elegant* eye candy.

If your Launchpad has more than one page of apps, you see two or more dots near the bottom of the screen (directly above the arrow cursor). To change pages, press the left-arrow ($\leftarrow$) or right-arrow ($\rightarrow$) key.

Figure 7-20: Launchpad, in all its glory.

To launch an app, just click its icon. In a heartbeat, Launchpad disappears, and the app replaces it on your screen.

Customizing Your Launchpad

Launchpad is configurable, just like home screens on i-devices. As you're about to see, you can rearrange app icons on a page, move them from one page to another, organize them in folders, and delete them. Say it all together now: "Just like on i-devices."

For those who are unfamiliar with iOS or devices that run it, here's how these things work on your Mac:

- **To rearrange app icons:** Click and drag the app to its new location.
- **To move apps to the next or previous page:** Click and drag the app to the left or right edge of the screen. When the next page of apps appears, drag the app to its new location on that page.
- **To add an app to your Dock:** Click and drag the app onto the left side of the Dock.
- **To create a folder for apps:** Drag one app's icon on top of another app's icon to create a folder.
- **To add an app to a folder:** Drag the app onto that folder to add it.
- **To move an app out of a folder:** Click the folder to open it, and drag the app out of the folder.
- **To change a folder's name:** Click to open the folder, click the current name, and then type a new name.
- **To uninstall apps:** Click an app's icon, but don't release the mouse button until all the icons begin to wiggle. Apps that can be uninstalled display a Delete button (X); click to uninstall the app.

  Press Esc to stop the wiggling.

If an icon doesn't have a Delete button, it's installed with OS X Mountain Lion and can't be uninstalled.

8

Dealing with Disks

In This Chapter

▶ Initializing and erasing your disks

▶ Using PC-formatted disks

▶ Creating your own CDs and DVDs

▶ Ejecting disks

*1*n this chapter, I show you disk basics: How to format them for your Mac, how to format them so that your Windows-using brethren (and sisteren) can use them, how to eject them, how to copy or move files between disks, and much more. Onward!

This chapter offers lots of info that applies to every Mac user — including folder management and moving or copying files to and from disks other than your internal hard drive. I also show you how to work with optical media such as CD-R, CD-RW, DVD-R, DVD+R, DVD-RW, DVD+RW, and DVD+R DL (dual-layer) — types of discs that many Mac users deal with regularly. You more than likely have an internal SuperDrive (CD and DVD player/burner). Or you might have added external storage devices such as a USB flash drive; a USB, FireWire, or Thunderbolt hard drive; or an optical disc player/recorder.

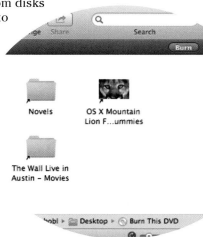

Is that a disk or a disc?

So how do you spell this critter, anyway? Sometimes, you see it spelled d-i-s-k; at other times, you see it spelled d-i-s-c. If you're wondering what's up with that, here's the skinny. In the good old days, the only kind of computer disk was a disk with a k: floppy disk, hard drive, Bernoulli disk, and so on. Then the compact disc (you know, a CD) was invented. The people who invented it spelled it with a c instead of a k, probably because it's round like a discus (think track and field). From that time on, both spellings have been used more or less interchangeably.

Now, some people will tell you that magnetic media (floppy, hard, Zip, Jaz, and so on) are called *disks* (spelled with a k) and that optical media — that is, discs that are read with a laser, such as CD-ROMs, CD-RWs, audio CDs, and DVDs — are called *discs* (spelled with a c).

I'll compromise. When I speak about something that could be either a disk or a disc, I stick with *disk*. If I speak strictly about optical media, I use the term *disc*. I hope that's clear. If not, my editors *made* me do it.

Comprehending Disks

You should think of the disk icons that appear on the Desktop (and/or in the sidebars of Finder windows) as though they were folders. That's because your Mac sees disks as nothing *but* giant folders. When you double-click one, its contents appear in a Finder window; to that extent, it works just like a folder. You can drag stuff in and out of a disk's window, and you can manipulate the disk's window in all the usual ways — again, just like a folder.

If you don't see your hard disk icon(s) on the Desktop or in the Sidebar, open Finder Preferences (choose Finder⇨Preferences or press ⌘+, [comma]) and select the appropriate items in the General and Sidebar tabs, as described in Chapter 5.

Although (for all intents and purposes) disks *are* folders, disks do behave in unique ways sometimes. The following sections explain what you need to know.

Some disks need to be formatted first

Brand-new disks sometimes need to be *formatted* — prepared to receive Macintosh files — before you can use them. When you connect an unformatted hard disk, your Mac usually pops up a dialog that asks what you want to do with the disk. One option is usually to *format* (or *initialize*) the disk — that is, get it ready to record data. If you choose to format the disk, the Disk Utility program launches itself so you can format the disk from the Erase tab.

If you ever need to format or initialize a blank disk and don't see the dialog, all you have to do is open Disk Utility manually (it's in your Applications/ Utilities folder) and use its Erase tab to format the disk.

Moving and copying between disks

Moving a file icon from one on-screen disk to another works the same way as moving an icon from one folder to another, with one notable exception: When you move a file from one disk to another, you automatically make a copy of it, leaving the original untouched and unmoved. If you want to move a file or folder completely from one disk to another, you have to delete that leftover original by dragging it to the Trash or by holding down the ⌘ key when you drag it from one disk to the other.

You can't remove a file from a read-only disc (such as a CD-R or DVD-R) or from a folder to which you don't have write permission. But you should be able to move or delete files and folders from all other kinds of disks that you might encounter.

Copying the entire contents of any disk or volume (CD, DVD, or external hard drive, among others) to a new destination works a little differently:

1. **Click the disk's icon.**

2. **Hold down the Option key, and drag the disk icon onto any folder, any disk icon, or any open Finder window.**

   When the copy is completed, a folder bearing the same name as the copied disk appears in the destination folder or disk. The new folder contains each and every file that was on the disk of the same name.

Copying files in this way is handy when you want to grab all the files from a CD or DVD and put them on your hard drive.

If you don't hold down the Option key when you drag a disk icon to another destination, your Mac creates an *alias* of the disk (that is, a link back to the original) instead of a copy of its contents. As you might expect, the alias will be almost worthless after you eject the disk; if you open it, it will ask you to insert the original disk.

If you like using the Duplicate command, note that you can't use the Duplicate keyboard shortcut (⌘+D) on a disk, although you can use it on a folder. For the full details of moving, copying, and pasting, flip to Chapter 6.

Surprise: Your PC Disks Work, Too!

One of the most excellent features of OS X (if you have friends unfortunate enough not to own Macs, and you want to share files with them) is that it reads and writes CDs and DVDs that can be read by PCs.

Although your Mac can read disks formatted by a PC, the *files* on them might or might not work for you. If the files are documents, such as Microsoft Word .doc or Microsoft Excel .xls files, one of your Mac programs can probably open them. If the files are Windows programs (these often sport the `.exe` extension, which stands for *executable*), your Mac can't do anything with 'em without additional software designed to run Windows programs.

So if you want to run Windows on your Mac, you need to use either Mountain Lion's built-in utility called Boot Camp or a third-party program such as Parallels Desktop from Parallels (`www.parallels.com`), Fusion from VMware (`www.vmware.com`), or the free VirtualBox (`www.virtualbox.org`). Boot Camp requires you to reboot your computer each time you want to use Windows; the third-party programs emulate PC hardware so that you can run genuine Microsoft Windows operating systems in Mountain Lion *without* rebooting your Mac.

So with a commercial app such as Parallels Desktop or VMware Fusion (both around $60), the free VirtualBox from Oracle, or Mountain Lion's included Boot Camp utility, your Mac *can* run those `.exe` files (which is to say most Windows programs).

None of these comes with a copy of Windows (required).

Parallels Desktop and VMware Fusion are almost as fast as a PC when running most Windows applications. Depending on which Intel-based Mac you have, they might even be speedy enough to play first-person shooters. Boot Camp is even faster but has the disadvantage of requiring you to leave Mountain Lion and restart your Mac before you can use it. For most other stuff (including the Windows-bundled Solitaire), all three are capable of running Windows a heck of a lot faster than many PCs are.

Burning CDs and DVDs

With OS X, you can play, create, and publish audio and video on optical media. Depending on which type of optical drive your Mac is equipped with, you can burn some or all of the following types of discs: CD-R, CD-RW, DVD-R, DVD+R, DVD-RW, DVD+RW, and DVD+R DL (dual layer).

In the sections that follow, I show you two ways to burn files on a CD or DVD. For the first way, you insert a disc and select the files you want to burn. The second method, creating a burn folder, enables you to save the list of files you've burned.

Burning a music CD is a different process that's performed using iTunes. Don't worry — you find out all about that process in Chapter 12.

What kind of discs can my Mac burn?

Great question. If you don't know what types of discs your Mac can burn, here's an easy way to find out:

1. **In your Applications folder, open the Utilities folder, and then open the System Information application.**

2. **In the Contents pane on the left, click the disclosure triangle to expand the Hardware category if necessary, and then click Disc Burning, as shown in the following figure.**

   The right side of the window now reveals lots of information about the disc-burning capabilities of this Macintosh. The CD-Write and DVD-Write items tell you the types of discs your Mac is capable of burning.

   The disc burner in the following figure can burn CD-R and -RW, and DVD-R, -R DL (dual

layer), -RW, +R, +R DL (dual layer), and +RW optical discs. When you purchase blank discs, make sure that they're one of the types your burner supports.

Burning on the fly

One way to burn files to a CD or DVD is to simply insert a blank disc and select the files you want to burn on the fly. Just follow these steps:

1. **Insert a blank CD or DVD disc.**

   You see an alert (as shown in Figure 8-1) that asks you what you want to do with the disc.

   In this case, the blank disc happened to be a DVD-R, but the same thing happens if you insert any supported recordable blank CD or DVD disc.

Figure 8-1: Insert a blank DVD into your optical media drive, and get ready to feel the burn.

2. **Choose Open Finder from the Action pop-up menu.**

   Open Finder is the default choice unless you've changed that default in the CDs & DVDs System Preferences pane or as explained in the following tip.

   Your choices in the CDs & DVDs System Preferences pane for the default action when you insert a blank CD or DVD are

   - *Open Finder:* Mounts the blank disk in the Finder (as shown in the instructions that follow this tip)

   - *Open iTunes:* Opens iTunes automatically when you insert a blank CD

   - *Open Disk Utility:* Opens the Disk Utility application automatically

   - *Open iDVD* (for DVDs only, not CDs): Opens iDVD automatically

   - *Open Other Application:* Lets you choose the application to use when you insert a blank CD or DVD disc

   - *Run Script:* Runs a specified AppleScript when you insert a blank disc.

   - *Ignore:* Leaves the disk in your drive but does nothing (that is, none of the above).

   If you want to make any of these actions the default in the alert shown in Figure 8-1 and thus avoid a trip to the CDs & DVDs System Preferences pane, select the Make This Action the Default check box.

   For the purposes of these steps, go with Open Finder for now.

3. **Click OK.**

   Your blank DVD *mounts* (appears as an icon) on the Desktop just like any other removable disc, but its distinctive icon tells you that it's a recordable DVD (or CD), as shown in Figure 8-2.

Figure 8-2: Recordable optical discs get a distinctive labeled icon.

4. **Drag files or folders onto the disc icon on your Desktop (or in the Sidebar) until the disc contains all the files you want on it.**

5. **(Optional) If you like, you can change the disc's name from Untitled DVD (or CD) the same way that you change the name of any file or folder.**

   I've changed the name of the CD in Figure 8-3 to *Burn This DVD*.

6. **When you're ready to finish (burn) your DVD (or CD), open its disc icon and click the Burn button in the top-right corner of the disc's window, or click the Burn icon (which looks like the warning symbol for radioactivity) to the right of the disc in the Sidebar, both shown in Figure 8-3.**

Burn icon in sidebar   Burn button

Figure 8-3: Click the Burn button in the window or the burn icon next to the disc's icon in the Sidebar to burn your disc.

Notice that the amount of free space remaining on the disc (638.8MB in Figure 8-3) is displayed in the status bar at the bottom of the window. If you don't see the status bar, choose View⇨Status Bar.

Alternatively, you could

- Control-click or right-click the disc's icon and choose Burn *Your Disc's Name Here* from the contextual menu (that is, Burn "Burn This DVD" in Figure 8-4).

- Select the icon, and choose File⇨Burn *Disc Name* (left side of Figure 8-4). If you choose Eject, from either the contextual menu or the File menu, you're asked whether you want to burn the disc first.

- If you drag the disc icon to the Trash/Eject Disk icon in your Dock, the Trash/Eject Disk icon turns into the Burn Disc icon (which still looks like the warning symbol for radioactivity). Drop the disc icon on the radioactivity icon in the Dock, and the burning begins.

After you've chosen to burn a disc, you see the dialog shown in Figure 8-5.

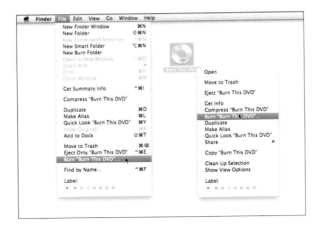

Figure 8-4: Two more ways to burn a disc.

7. Choose a speed from the Burn Speed pop-up menu, click the Burn button, and you're done.

I usually use a slower but more reliable burn speed (8x in Figure 8-5) unless I'm in a huge hurry. I've had many discs fail when burned at the default highest speed possible. You can call those discs drink coasters unless they were rewritable (RW) discs. If that's the case, you can erase them with Disk Utility and try again.

Figure 8-5: The last step before the burning begins.

I feel obliged to mention that CD-RW and DVD-RW discs rarely (if ever) work in devices other than your Mac, including CD (audio) players and DVD (video) players. When you burn a music CD or a video DVD and plan to watch it on a device other than your Mac, you shouldn't burn it on rewritable (RW) media.

Select the Save Burn Folder To check box if you think that you may want to burn another copy of this disc someday. (You find out more about burn folders in the next section of this chapter.)

Creating a burn folder

A burn folder lets you burn selected files to a CD or DVD many times. Perhaps the most useful thing you can do with a burn folder is to create one that contains your most important files and then regularly burn the current versions of those files to a CD or DVD as a backup.

Whenever you drag an item to a burn folder, the Finder creates an alias of that item in the burn folder. So when you burn a disc using a burn folder, the parent (original) files are burned to the disc, not the aliases.

Here's how to create and use a burn folder:

1. **Choose File⇨New Burn Folder.**

   A folder titled Burn Folder appears on the Desktop.

2. **Name the burn folder.**

3. **Drag some icons into the burn folder.**

4. **When you're ready to burn the folder's contents to a disc, double-click it, and click Burn.**

5. **Insert a disc and follow the on-screen instructions.**

If the Finder can't find the parent file for an alias, it asks whether you want to cancel the burn or to continue without that item. If you cancel, the disc remains empty.

Here are a couple of other ways to burn the contents of a burn folder:

- If a burn folder is in the Sidebar of a Finder window, you can burn its contents to a disc quickly by clicking the burn icon to its right, as shown in Figure 8-3.

- Right-click or Control-click the burn folder and then choose Burn *Disc Name* (in Figure 8-4 it says, *"Burn This DVD"*) from the contextual menu.

Getting Disks out of Your Mac

The preceding sections tell you almost everything there is to know about disks except one important thing: How to eject a disk. Piece of cake, actually. Here are several ways, all simple to remember:

- Click the disk's icon to select it and choose File⇨Eject (or use the keyboard shortcut ⌘+E).

- Drag the disk's icon to the Trash. When you drag a disk's icon, the Trash icon in the Dock changes into an Eject icon, like the one shown in the left margin.

The preceding method of ejecting a disk is something that used to drive me (and many others) crazy before OS X. In the olden days, the Trash icon didn't change into an Eject icon. This confused many new users, who then asked me the same question (over and over and over): "But doesn't dragging something to the Trash erase it from your disk?"

As I mention earlier in the chapter, this technique does something completely different if you've dragged any files onto the disc. In that case, the Trash icon turns into the radioactive symbol, and your Mac offers to burn the disc, as shown in Figure 8-5. Put another way, this ejection technique works only if the disc is blank, has already been burned, or is a store-bought prerecorded (read-only) CD or DVD.

- Click the little Eject icon to the right of the disc's name in the Sidebar.

- Press the Eject key on your keyboard if it has one. (If it has one, it probably has the Eject icon on it.)

If your keyboard doesn't have an Eject key, press the F12 key, and continue to hold it down for a second or two. On many keyboards that don't have an Eject key, this keyboard shortcut ejects a disc.

- Right-click or Control-click the disk icon and choose Eject from the contextual menu.

There's one more way, if you like little menus on the right side of your menu bar. To install your own Eject menu on the menu bar, navigate to `System/Library/CoreServices/MenuExtras`, and then open (double-click) the Eject.menu icon. Your Eject menu appears on the right side of your menu bar, as shown in Figure 8-6 (left). If you get tired of the icon on your menu bar, just press ⌘ and drag it off, and it disappears with a satisfying poof, as shown in Figure 8-6 (right).

Figure 8-6: Using the Eject menu to eject a disc (left) and removing the Eject menu from the menu bar by ⌘-dragging it (right).

Organizing Your Life

* *

In This Chapter

▶ Introducing Calendar

▶ Creating and using Calendar calendars

▶ Creating and organizing Calendar events

▶ Make forgetting a thing of the past with Reminders and Notification Center

▶ Taking notes with Notes

* *

*W*hen you buy OS X Mountain Lion, the folks at Apple generously include applications that can help simplify and organize your everyday affairs — namely, Calendar, Reminders, and Notes (to name three you discover in this chapter).

In fact, OS X comes with a whole folder full of applications — software you can use to do everything from surfing the Internet to capturing an image of your Mac's screen to playing QuickTime movies to checking the time. Technically, most of these applications aren't even part of OS X. Rather, the vast majority of them are what are known as *bundled* apps — programs that come with the operating system but are unrelated to its function. Readers (bless them) tend to complain when I skip bundled applications, so I mention almost all of them in this book.

But in this chapter, you get a look at only the applications that help you organize your everyday life: your appointments, to-do items, notes to yourself, and all the various gadgets you may attach to and detach from your Mac.

The applications discussed in this chapter are stored in (where else?) the Applications folder, which you can get to in four ways:

- Click the Applications folder in the Sidebar of any Finder window.
- Choose Go⇨Applications.
- Press ⌘+Shift+A.
- Click the Launchpad icon in the Dock to see all the applications installed on this Mac (as you see in Chapter 7).

Other bundled apps you might be especially interested in include Safari (Chapter 10), Contacts and Mail (Chapter 11), iTunes (Chapter 12), a whole handful of multimedia applications that enable you to play video and more on your Mac (Chapter 13), and TextEdit (Chapter 14). For even more information on the OS X bundled applications, check out *Macs For Dummies,* 10th Edition, by *USA Today* columnist Edward C. Baig or Mark Chambers' *OS X Mountain Lion All-in-One For Dummies,* both published by Wiley.

Keeping Track with Calendar

Calendar is a wonderful program that provides multiple appointment calendars with alerts. More precisely, you can have multiple color-coded calendars, several types of visual, audible, and e-mailed alerts, repeating events, and more. You can publish your calendar(s) on the web for others to view (which requires an iCloud account or other WebDav server), and you can subscribe to calendars published by other Calendar users.

I love Calendar and keep it open at all times on my Macs. In the sections that follow, I share a handful of the features I find most useful.

Navigating Calendar views

Calendar lets you display the main Calendar window just the way you like it:

- **You can view your calendar by the day, week, month, or year.** Figure 9-1 shows a weekly view. To select a view, click the Day, Week, Month, or Year button at the top.

- **To move back or forward,** click the arrow buttons on either side of the Today button. You see the previous or next week in week view, yesterday or tomorrow in day view, and so on.

- **To go to today's date,** click the Go to Today button.

- **To add a new calendar,** click the New Calendar (+) button.

Show/Hide calendars   Next day, week, month, or year   Full screen

Create Quick Event   Views   Go to Today

Calendars   Events   Event Info

Previous day, week, month, or year

Search

Figure 9-1: The Calendar main window displaying the view I prefer: week view.

You can find all these items, most of which have shortcuts, in the Calendar View menu, as shown in Figure 9-2. This menu offers almost total control of what you see and how you navigate.

If you want to master Calendar, it would behoove you to spend some time experimenting with these views and with their navigation commands and options.

Creating calendars

If you refer to Figure 9-1, you see a list of my calendars in the top-left corner: Bob's Teaching Schedule, Bob's Appointments, Bob's Deadlines, Bob's Travel, and so on. The check boxes turn the visibility of a calendar on (checked) and off (unchecked).

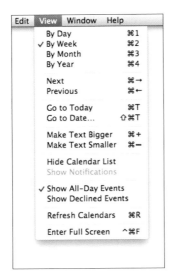

Figure 9-2: The Calendar View menu.

The calendars appear in three sections — On My Mac, iCloud, and Subscriptions — because there are all three types of calendars on my Mac. You can read much more about iCloud in Chapter 10, but for now, if you are not an iCloud user, your calendars will appear in the On My Mac section instead of the iCloud section. Because I don't actually have any calendars stored on my Mac (all of my calendars are stored in and synced by iCloud), the Sample On My Mac calendar you see in Figure 9-1 exists solely for this demonstration.

To create a new calendar in Calendar, follow these steps:

1. **Choose File⇨New Calendar⇨iCloud or On My Mac.**

   A new calendar named Untitled is created and added to the appropriate calendar list.

2. **To give your calendar a name, select Untitled and type a new name.**

3. **(Optional) To color-code the entries for this calendar, first select the calendar (by clicking it); choose Edit⇨Get Info or press ⌘+I; and then select a color by clicking and holding the color swatch, as shown in Figure 9-3.**

   In my humble opinion, Other is the handy choice because it lets you select thousands of colors in addition to the seven colors available in the menu.

Color swatch

Figure 9-3: Choose Other for even more colors.

Now any item you create while this calendar is selected (in the list that pops up from the Calendars button) appears on the selected calendar in the color you selected. While you're in the Info sheet, you can also add a description of your calendar.

Grouping calendars

You can also organize calendars in groups that contain more than one calendar. To create a new calendar group in Calendar, follow these steps:

1. **Choose File⇨New Calendar Group, or press ⌘+Shift+N.**

   A new calendar group named Group is created and added to the On My Mac section of the calendar list.

2. **Give the new group a name by selecting Group and typing a new name.**

3. **To add calendars to the group, create a new calendar while the group is selected, or drag existing calendars below the group name in the list, as shown in Figure 9-4.**

   When you release the mouse button, the Personal calendar moves below the Family + Personal group. Note that the Personal calendar is indented and the Family + Personal group has a disclosure triangle to its left.

   Now you can show or hide all calendars in the group by selecting or deselecting a single check box. You can still show or hide individual calendars by selecting or deselecting their check boxes, of course.

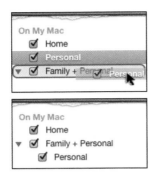

Figure 9-4: Adding the Personal calendar to the Family + Personal group.

Here's how you might deploy this feature. You could create individual calendars for each member of your family and put all the individual family calendars in a group called Family. Then you could make all the family-member calendars visible or invisible with a single click of the group calendar's check box.

If you have an iCloud account (as discussed in Chapter 10), you can publish your calendars and invite others to subscribe to them by choosing Calendar⇨ Publish. The others receive an e-mail inviting them to subscribe to your calendar. This is what my family does. Each of us maintains and publishes his or her own calendar and subscribes to everyone else's. That way, we can all see at a glance who's doing what and when they're doing it. This is by far the slickest solution we've found.

Deleting a calendar or group

To delete a calendar or calendar group, select it in the list and choose Edit⇨Delete or press ⌘+Delete. If the calendar has events on it or the group has calendars in it, you see an alert box asking if you're sure you want to delete that calendar or group; if not, the calendar or group will be deleted as soon as you choose Edit⇨Delete or press ⌘+Delete.

When you delete a calendar or group, all the events and reminder items in that calendar or group are also deleted. Although you *can* Undo a deleted calendar or group (choose Edit⇨Undo or press ⌘+Z), you must do so before you quit Calendar. If you quit Calendar without undoing a calendar or calendar-group deletion, everything on that calendar (or calendars) will be gone forever (unless, of course, you have Time Machine or another backup, as explained in Chapter 18).

Creating and managing events

The heart of Calendar is the event. To create a new one, follow these steps:

1. **Choose File⇨New Event, press ⌘+N, double-click, or drag up or down anywhere on the calendar.**

   If you double-click or click and drag on the day of the event, you can skip Step 2, and you don't need to specify the date in Step 3.

   Alternatively, try the Create Quick Event (+) button. It's smart enough to interpret commands like "Family Movie at 7PM on Thursday" and create a new event, as shown in Figure 9-5.

Figure 9-5: Creating a Quick Event (upper left) and the resulting event bubble (lower right) for this one-hour event on my Appointment calendar.

2. **If the event doesn't appear in the proper place, just click it and drag it wherever you like.**

3. **To edit an event, select it and choose Edit⇨Edit Event, press ⌘+E, or double-click it to open its event bubble, as shown in Figure 9-5.**

   All the items with little arrows on their right sides — *Repeat, Show As, Calendar*, and *Alerts* — are pop-up menus. An *Alert* menu is popped up in Figure 9-5.

4. **When you're satisfied with all of the event's items, click the Done button.**

If you prefer working in a little window rather than the event bubble, check out the Edit➪Show Inspector command (⌘+Option+I), which displays the selected event in a window. Click a different event, and its info instantly fills the Inspector window. Try it; you might like it.

The difference is that the Inspector window changes contextually and displays information about the currently selected event. Get Info windows, on the other hand, display info for a specific event. Put another way, a Get Info window displays the info for a specific event, and you can have as many Get Info windows on the screen as you like. There's only one Inspector window; it displays info for whichever event is currently selected.

Inviting others to attend an event

To invite other people to your event, you can open Contacts or the Calendar Address Panel (Window➪Address Panel or ⌘+Option+A) and drag the contacts onto the event in Calendar. Alternatively, you can type the first few letters of the name in the Invitees field, and names that match magically appear. In Figure 9-6, I typed the letters *st,* and Calendar offered me a choice of my two contacts with names that start with *st* — namely, Stan LeVitus and Stan Lee. Sweet! (If you're unfamiliar with Contacts, flip to Chapter 11 for details.)

Figure 9-6: Type the first few letters of a contact's name.

After you've added one or more invitees, click the Send button to invite them to the event. If the invitees have Calendar (or its predecessor iCal), they can open the enclosure (which is included with your invitation e-mail), which adds the event to Calendar with Accept, Decline, and Maybe buttons. All they have to do is click the appropriate button, and you receive an e-mail informing you of their decision along with an enclosure that adds their response to the event in Calendar. Nice, eh?

If the invitee doesn't have Calendar (or doesn't open the enclosure that was included with the e-mail invitation), he or she has to respond the old-fashioned way: by replying to your e-mail or calling you on the telephone.

Setting an alert

What's the point of putting an event on your calendar if you forget it? If you set an alert, Calendar won't let you forget. To set an alert, click the word *None* with the double-headed arrow (just to the right of the word *alert*) in the Event info window. A menu appears. Choose the type of alert you want from the menu and change its values to suit your needs. I find the Message with Sound and Email alerts so useful that I use both for almost every event I create.

You can have as many alerts as you like for each event. When you add an alert, a new alert item appears below it. Just click the word *None* with the double-headed arrow just to the right of the word *alert* to create a second (or third or fifteenth) alert. To remove an alert, click the word *alert* and choose *None* from the pop-up menu.

You can choose separate default alerts for Events, All Day Events, and Birthdays in Calendar Preferences. Choose Calendar➪Preferences or press ⌘+, (comma), and then click the Alerts tab at the top of the window.

All the features mentioned so far are wonderful, but my very favorite Calendar feature has to be alerts. I rarely miss an important event anymore; Calendar reminds me of them with time to spare. Better still, I sync events and alerts among my Mac and iPhone and iPad. I can create an event or alert, and within a few minutes — through the magic of iCloud — it appears on the other devices.

You don't have to have iCloud to sync calendars on your Mac and iPhone, but without it, you can synchronize only when you connect your iPhone to your Mac with its included USB cable or perform a wireless sync.

Are you available?

A relatively new feature is the Availability panel (choose Window➪ Availability Panel or press Shift+⌘+A). To take advantage of it because it requires at least one calendar administered through a CalDAV server or Microsoft Exchange Server 2007 or later. If you don't know what CalDAV or Exchange servers are, you can safely skip to the next section. If your calendar is hosted on a CalDAV server, you may designate events as Free or Busy; if your calendar is hosted on an Exchange server, you may designate events as Free, Busy, Tentative, or Out of Office. The result is that workgroup members with access to this calendar can schedule events that don't conflict with other members' events.

Unfortunately, this feature currently doesn't work if your calendars are hosted on Apple's iCloud online service.

Reminders: Protection Against Forgetting

Reminders is a brand-new Mac app that will be familiar to anyone with an iDevice because it bears more than a passing resemblance to the iOS Reminders app.

Reminders help you stay organized. Unlike an event, a Reminder item isn't necessarily associated with a particular day or time (though it can be). Furthermore, Reminders can be location-based, which is handier on an iDevice than a Mac, but a great feature if you have such a device. Finally, Reminders can have a priority level of Low, Medium, High, or None.

If you have an iDevice and use iCloud, your Reminders will appear on all your Apple devices — other Macs, iPhones, iPads, and iPod touches — simultaneously, which means you should never miss a Reminder. Just set a Reminder on your Mac or any iDevice, and you'll never forget anything.

Getting started with Reminders

Before you create or manage your own Reminders, there are a couple of things you should know, starting with the concept of Lists. Reminders includes a List called *Reminders* by default. You can delete or rename it if you like, and you can create additional Lists if you care to by choosing File⇨New List, pressing ⌘+L, or clicking the plus button at the bottom of the window.

I like to have two to-do Lists and call them Bob's To Dos and Bob's Shopping List. I also have a third List called Completed, which Reminders creates the first time you click the check box to indicate a task is "done," such as the *Advanced iPhone book proposal* Reminder shown in Figure 9-7.

In other words, when you check the box for an item, the item is moved from whichever List it's on to the Completed List.

Here are more helpful techniques for working with Lists:

- **To rename a List:** Right-click or Control-click the List, choose Rename from the contextual menu, type the new name, and press Return or Enter when you're done. Or, select the list, press Return or Enter, type the new name, and then press Return or Enter again when you're done.

- **To display a List in a separate window:** Double-click the List's name; right-click or Control-click the List and choose Open List in New Window from the contextual menu; choose Window⇨Open in New Window; or press ⌘+Return or Enter.

- **To show or hide the little calendar:** Choose View⇨Show/Hide Calendar; press ⌘+Option+K; or click the little calendar button below the little calendar.

✔ **To show or hide the List sidebar:** Choose View⇨Show/Hide Sidebar; press ⌘+Option+S; or click the little triangle in a button on the left beneath the little calendar.

Figure 9-7: Three Lists (upper left) and some of the Reminders on Bob's To Dos (right).

You don't have to have more than one List. You don't even have to change the default List's name from *Reminders* if you don't want to. That being said, I like having Reminders organized into separate To Do and Shopping Lists. The point is that you can make a bunch of Lists or dump everything into a single List; just use Lists to organize your Reminders so they make sense to you.

To do or not to do: Setting reminders

The preceding sections tell you pretty much everything about Reminders except how to create one, so it's time to find out how to create Reminders. It couldn't be easier: Just choose File⇨New Reminder; press ⌘+N; click the Plus button in the top-right corner of the Reminders window; or click the first blank line in any List and begin typing.

Ah, but there's much more to a Reminder. Reminders can:

✔ Remind you at a specific time on a specific date.

✔ Repeatedly remind you at a specified interval.

✔ Remind you at a specific location (great for iPhone and 3G/4G iPad owners).

And Reminders can also have a priority and notes. To access these features, you need to Show Info for the Reminder by choosing View➪Show Info; pressing ⌘+I; clicking the little "i" that appears on the right side of the Reminder (hover your cursor over the right side of the reminder if you don't see it); or double-click a blank spot on the Reminder. Show Info for the Pizza and Wings Reminders is shown in Figure 9-8.

Figure 9-8: A Reminder to get Pizza and a Reminder to get Wings when I'm near the store.

The first time you try to use At a Location, your Mac will present a dialog asking if you want to Enable Location Services to Allow "Reminders" to Use Your Current Location. If you agree, click the Open Privacy Preferences button, select the check box to enable Location Services in Reminders, and then close the System Preferences app. If you don't want to enable Location Services for the Reminder app, just click the Cancel button.

If you have an iPhone, Location-based Reminders are awesome. Give them a try, and I'm sure you'll be as hooked as I am.

Finally, to reorder Reminders in a List, click a blank spot on any Reminder, drag it up or down, and drop it into its new position.

Everything you need to know about the Notification Center

The item on the right in Figure 9-9 should look familiar to those of you who use an iPhone, iPad, or iPod touch. It's the Mac Notification Center, and while it's new in Mountain Lion, it's been part of the iOS for years (well, at least a year or more).

Figure 9-9: This is what the Pizza Reminder looks like on my Mac (top left and right) and on my iPhone (bottom left).

Notification Center displays communications from apps that support it. You can make it appear regardless of what application is currently active by clicking its menu bar icon (shown in the margin) or swiping from the left edge to the right on your trackpad.

You manage notifications in the Notifications System Preference pane. Choose ■⬧System Preferences, click System Preferences' Dock icon, or click the little gear near the bottom of Notification Center, which is a shortcut that opens the Notifications System Preference pane. On the left are all the apps on your hard disk that support the Notification Center protocol. To specify settings for an app, click it in the list. When you've selected an app, here's what you can do:

✔ **To have an app's notifications not appear in Notification Center:** Either deselect the Show in Notification Center check box or drag the app down to the Not in Notification Center section of the list.

✔ **To change how apps are sorted in Notification Center:** Choose Manually or By Time from the Sort Notification Center pop-up menu. Choose Manually if you prefer to arrange the order the apps appear in Notification Center by dragging them up or down; choose By Time to sort them with the most recent ones at the top.

✔ **To specify the alert style for the app:** Your choices are Banners, Alerts, or None. Alerts stay onscreen until you dismiss them; Banners appear in the upper-right corner of the screen below the Notification Center icon and fade away a few seconds after they appear.

✔ **To see the number of new notifications for the app on its Dock icon:** Select the Badge App Icon check box.

✔ **To hear a sound when receiving notifications:** Select the Play Sound when Receiving Notifications check box.

✔ **To specify the number of recent items the Notification Center displays for the app:** Click the Show in Notification Center pop-up menu and choose 1, 5, 10, or 20 recent items.

Here's a look at the Notification Center itself:

✔ **To temporarily turn off all alerts and banners:** Open Notification Center, scroll to the top, and then click the Show Alerts and Banners switch so it's ON.

✔ **To respond to a notification:** Open Notification Center and click the notification to launch its app, or click its banner before it disappears.

✔ **To repeat a notification in 9 minutes:** Click the Snooze button.

✔ **To close all notifications for an app:** Hover over the right side of the app's name (Reminders in Figure 9-9) and click the little x when it appears.

Use Notes for Making Notes

Notes is an electronic notepad for your Mac. A note is a convenient place to jot quick notes, recipes, phone numbers, or whatever. Some Notes are shown in Figure 9-10.

To create a new Note, choose File⯈New Note; press ⌘+N; or click the little Plus button below the list of Notes.

Notes is supremely flexible; here are just a few things you can do:

✔ Double-click a Note to open it in its own window so you can drag it around on-screen by its title bar.

✔ Change text to any font, color, size, and style by selecting it and using the myriad of tools in the Format menu.

✔ Search for a word or phrase in any Note by typing your query in the Search box.

✔ Create bulleted, numbered, or dashed lists (the baked potato recipe in Figure 9-10 is a bulleted list) by selecting the text and choosing Format⇨Lists.

"Tasty Bacon" note
in a window

"42-min. Perfect
Baked Potatoes"
Folders List   Search box   Note (contents)

Show Folders   Hide Folders   Share note
List button   List button
                                    Trash (Delete) Note

Figure 9-10: Notes is for making notes on your Mac.

✔ Create folders to organize your Notes by choosing File⇨New Folder or pressing ⌘+Shift+N.

The Notes window must be selected to create a new folder. If a note in a window is active, the New Folder command will be unavailable. So click the main Notes window if the New Folder command is grayed out.

Folders in the Notes application are exclusive to Notes. In other words, the folders described in the following bullets aren't folders in the Finder. You won't find them on your hard disk; they live only in the Notes app. And also remember that folders are strictly optional. If you don't have a ton of notes, keeping them all in a single folder and using the Search box to filter them may work for you.

- Show or hide the Folders List by choosing View⇨Show/Hide Folders List or clicking the Hide folders button.

- Show only Notes in a folder by clicking the folder's name in the Folders List.

- Automatically sync notes with your iDevice by using iCloud as your Default Account (choose Notes⇨Default Account⇨iCloud).

- Send the contents of a Note via the Mail or Messages apps by choosing File⇨Share or clicking the Share icon.

- Print a Note by choosing File⇨Print or pressing ⌘+P.

Anything that you type on a Note is saved automatically as you type. So you never have to Save or Save a Version. Other Notes goodies include a spell checker, spoken notes, text substitutions (such as Smart Quotes and Smart Dashes), and transformations (such as Make Upper or Lowercase). You can find all of these options in the Edit menu.

Part III
Do Unto Mountain Lion: Getting Things Done

The 5th Wave — By Rich Tennant

"Wow, I didn't know OSX could redirect an email message like that."

In this part . . .

Moving right along, Part III comprises how to do stuff with your Mac. In this section, it's off to the Internet first — how to get it working and what to do with it after that. Next, you discover three of Apple's most imaginatively named programs: the excellent e-mail application called Mail; the wonderful contact manager named Contacts; and the instant message and chatting app called Messages. That's followed by a pair of chapters devoted to working with media — music, movies, DVDs, and digital photos. Finally, you discover the basics of processing words and using fonts.

This is an excellent section, chock-full of useful information (if I do say so myself), and it's one you definitely don't want to miss.

Internet-Working

In This Chapter

▶ Getting an overview of the Internet

▶ Pre-surfing with the Network System Preferences pane

▶ Surfing the web with Safari

▶ Searching with Google

▶ Going face to face with FaceTime

These days, networking online is easier than finding a log to fall off: You simply use the Internet to connect your Mac to a wealth of information residing on computers around the world. Luckily for you, OS X has the best and most comprehensive Internet tools ever shipped with a Mac operating system.

OS X offers built-in Internet connectivity right out of the box. OS X Mountain Lion comes with

✔ Apple's Safari web browser, which you use to navigate the web, download remote files, and more

✔ The FaceTime app for video chats with other Mac or iDevice users

✔ Messages, Apple's instant message and live online chatting client that works with other Messages users; people using AOL Instant Messaging (AIM) clients; and people using Jabber (an open-source chatting protocol), Google Talk, and Bonjour (which discovers other users on your local area network)

✔ The Mail application (for e-mail)

In this chapter and the next, I cover the top things most people use the Internet for: the *World Wide Web* (that's the www. you see so often in Internet addresses) and *video and audio chatting.* You discover Safari and FaceTime in this chapter, and find out about Mail and Messages in Chapter 11.

But before I can talk about browsers, chatting, e-mail software, or messaging, I have to help you configure your Internet connection. When you're finished, you can play with your browsers, mail, and chat applications to your heart's content.

Getting Connected to the Internet

Before you can surf the Internet, you need to connect to it. If you're a typical home user, you need three things to surf the Internet:

- ✏ **A connection to the Internet,** such as a Digital Subscriber Line (DSL), a cable modem, or a satellite Internet service.

  If you use technology other than DSL or cable modem to connect your computer to the Internet, your network administrator (the person you run to at work when something goes wrong with your computer) or ISP might have to help you set up your Mac because setting up those other configurations is (sigh) beyond the scope of this book.

- ✏ **An account with an ISP** (an Internet service provider such as AT&T, Comcast, or RoadRunner).

  The technical reviewer for this book reminds me that these days, that's not necessarily true. All you really need is free Wi-Fi, which is available everywhere — in stores, restaurants, parks, libraries, and other places — and a free e-mail account from Apple's iCloud, Microsoft's Windows Live Hotmail, Google's G-Mail, or Yahoo! Mail.

- ✏ **A Mac** (preferably one running OS X 10.8 Mountain Lion).

  You might need to tweak a few settings, as I explain in the upcoming section "Plugging in your Internet-connection settings."

After you set up each of these components, you can launch and use Safari, Mail, Messages, and any other Internet application you care to use.

Setting up your modem

If you have a cable modem, DSL, or other high-speed Internet connection — or are thinking about getting any of these — you can use them with your Mac. In most cases, you merely connect your Mac to the Internet via a cable plugged into the Ethernet port of your Mac and into an external box — which is connected to a coaxial or optical TV cable or plugged into a telephone outlet, depending on what kind of access you have to the Internet.

For a wireless connection, the setup is the same, but rather than plug the cable into the Ethernet port on your Mac, you plug it into a wireless router or AirPort or Time Capsule base station. After this device is connected to the box supplied by your ISP, any Wi-Fi–equipped Mac (or PC) within range can connect to the Internet wirelessly on your network.

Your cable or DSL installer should have set everything up for you before leaving your home or office. If you still cannot connect to the Internet, you should call that service provider and give them heck. Troubleshooting a high-speed connection is pretty abstruse (which puts it beyond the purview of this book).

Your Internet service provider and you

After you make sure that you have a working modem, you have to select a company to provide you access to the Internet. These companies are called *Internet service providers* (ISPs). The prices and services that ISPs offer vary, often from minute to minute. Keep the following in mind when choosing an ISP:

- **If your connection comes from a cable or telephone company, your ISP is probably that company.** In effect, the choice of ISP is pretty much made for you when you decide on cable or DSL service.

- **The going rate for unlimited broadband access to the Internet starts at around $25 or $30 per month.** If your service provider asks for considerably more than that, find out why. Higher-throughput packages for cable and DSL connections might run you twice that. For example, at this writing, the highest-speed DSL package from AT&T is around $60 per month.

Because most Mac users like things to be easy, OS X includes a cool feature in its Setup Assistant to help you find and configure an account with an ISP. When you installed OS X 10.8 (assuming that you did and that it didn't come preinstalled on your Mac), the Setup Assistant might have asked you a bunch of questions about your Internet connection and set up everything for you. (Installing OS X is detailed in this book's Appendix.) If you didn't have an Internet connection (an ISP) at that time, you need to configure the Network System Preferences pane yourself. Although I cover the Network System Preferences pane in depth in the next section, how to configure it so that your Mac works with your ISP is something you have to work out with that ISP. If you have questions or problems not answered by this book, your ISP should be able to assist you. And if your ISP can't help, it's probably time to try a different ISP.

Plugging in your Internet-connection settings

If you didn't set up your Internet connection when you installed OS X, you need to open System Preferences (from the Applications folder, the Dock, or the menu) and click the Network icon. The Network pane offers options for connecting your Mac to the Internet or to a network. Setting up your Internet connection manually in the Network System Preferences pane is beyond the purview of this book. The easiest way to use it is to click the Assist Me button at the bottom and let your Mac do the heavy lifting.

If you're part of a large office network, check with your system administrator before you change anything in this pane. If you ignore this advice, you run the risk of losing your network connection completely.

If your Mac asks you a question you can't answer during set up, ask your ISP or network administrator for the answer. I can't possibly tell you how in this book because there are just too many possible configurations, and each depends on your particular ISP and service.

That said, here's a brief rundown on the most common things you might need to know to set up a network connection:

- **TCP/IP:** TCP/IP is the language of the Internet. You might be asked to specify things such as your IP address, domain name servers, and search domains.

- **PPP or PPPoE:** These acronyms stand for *Point-to-Point Protocol* and *Point-to-Point Protocol over Ethernet.* Which one you see depends on what service you're using to connect. All analog modems use PPP; some cable and DSL modems use PPPoE.

- **Proxies:** If you're on a large network or your Mac is behind a firewall, you might need to specify one or more proxy servers. If so, your network administrator or ISP can help you with configuration. (Most home users will never need to touch this tab.) Some ISPs require you to specify proxy servers; if you need to do this, ask your ISP what to do.

If you use your Mac in more than one place, you can set up a separate configuration for each location and choose it from the Location menu. A *location,* in this context, consists of all settings in all items in the Network System Preferences pane. After you have this entire pane configured the way that you like, follow these steps to create separate locations:

1. **Pull down the Location menu and choose Edit Locations.**

2. **Click the + button at the bottom of the Locations list.**

   A new, untitled Location appears in the list.

3. **Type a descriptive name for the new location, such as** AirPort at Starbucks **or** Ethernet at Joe's Office**.**

4. **Click Done, and then click Apply.**

   From now on, you can change all your network settings at the same time by choosing the appropriate location from the Location pop-up menu.

If, on the other hand, your Mac has a single network or Internet connection (as most home users have), just leave the Location menu set to Automatic and be done with it.

 Using the Network Setup Assistant (click the Assist Me button at the bottom of the Network System Preferences pane, and then click the Assistant button) to create a network connection usually makes it unnecessary for you to have to deal with most of these items. Still, I thought you should at least know the basics.

Browsing the Web with Safari

With your Internet connection set up, you're ready to browse the web. In the following sections, I concentrate on browsing the web with Safari because it's the web browser installed with OS X Mountain Lion.

 If you don't care for Safari, check out OmniWeb, Firefox, or Chrome, which are all free and have features you won't find in Safari.

To begin, just open your web browser. No problem. As usual, there's more than one way. You can launch Safari by any of these methods:

- ✐ Clicking the Safari icon in the Dock or LaunchPad (look for the big blue compass that looks like a stopwatch, as shown in the margin)
- ✐ Double-clicking the Safari icon in your Applications folder
- ✐ Single-clicking a URL link in an e-mail or other document
- ✐ Double-clicking a URL link document (a `.webloc` file) in the Finder

When you first launch Safari, it automatically connects you to the Internet and displays the default Apple start page (see Figure 10-1). In the sections that follow, I cover the highlights of using Safari, starting at the top of the screen.

Navigating with the toolbar buttons

The buttons along the top of the window do pretty much what their names imply. From left to right, these buttons are

- ✐ **Back/Forward:** When you open a page and move to a second page (or third or fourth), the Back button takes you to a previously visited page. Remember that you need to go back before the Forward button will work.

- ✐ **iCloud:** iCloud automatically displays all the open web pages on your other devices. So click this button to see pages you've opened on other Macs or your iDevice.

✔ **Share:** When you find a page of interest or a page you know you'll want to remember, click this button (which is actually a drop-down menu) to tell Safari to remember it for you in Mountain Lion's cool Reading List or as a Bookmark — two topics I explore further a little later in this chapter. Or send a link to it via Mail or Messages, both covered in Chapter 11.

Figure 10-1: Safari displaying the Apple start page.

To the right of the Share button is the Address field. This is where you type web addresses, or *URLs* (Uniform Resource Locators), that you want to visit. Just type one and press Return to surf to that site.

Then, on the right of the Address field, are two more buttons

✔ **Reader:** Reader lets you view stories and other articles in a window optimized for easy reading by stitching together articles that are continued over multiple web pages and broken up by ads, menu bars, and other items. Reader is only available for certain pages. When it's available, the icon turns blue, as shown in the margin; otherwise it appears grayed out and can't be clicked.

✔ **Downloads:** Click this button to see a list of files you've downloaded in the past and ones currently being downloaded.

But wait — there's more. To add other useful buttons to your toolbar, choose View⟶Customize Toolbar (or right-click anywhere in the toolbar and choose Customize Toolbar from the contextual menu). The Customize Toolbar sheet drops down, and you can drag items into or out of the toolbar to create your own custom set of buttons. In Figure 10-2, for example, I added (left to right) Home, AutoFill, Zoom In/Out, New Tab, and Email (a link to this page) to my toolbar.

Figure 10-2: The Customize Toolbar sheet (bottom) and my customized toolbar (top, highlighted).

Web addresses almost always begin with `http://www`. But Safari has a cool trick: If you just type a name, you usually get to the appropriate website that way without typing `http`, `://`, or `www`. If you type **apple** in the Address field and press Return, for example, you go to `www.apple.com`. Or if you type **boblevitus**, you're taken to `www.boblevitus.com`. Try it — it's pretty slick.

Below the Address field is the Bookmark Bar, already populated with some buttons of web pages Apple thinks you might enjoy, including Apple, Yahoo!, Google Maps, YouTube, and Wikipedia.

The News and Popular buttons are actually *drop-down menus*. You can tell by the little black triangles after their names, as shown in Figure 10-3.

Figure 10-3: The News (and Popular) buttons are actually drop-down menus.

You can delete these bookmarks and/or add your own bookmarks to the Bookmark Bar, as described in the next section.

Bookmarking your favorite pages

When you find a web page you want to remember and return to, you bookmark it. Here's how it works:

1. **Choose Bookmarks⇨Add Bookmark, press ⌘+D, or click the Share button and choose Add Bookmark.**

2. **Choose where to store the bookmark from the pop-up menu, as shown in Figure 10-4.**

Figure 10-4: This page will appear in the Bookmarks Bar as "Consulting by Dr. Mac."

3. **Rename the bookmark or use the name provided by Safari.**

4. **Click the Add button to save the bookmark.**

 To return to a bookmarked page, click it in the Bookmarks Bar, select it in the Bookmarks Menu, choose Bookmarks⇨Show All Bookmarks, press ⌘+Option+B, or click the Show All Bookmarks button (shown in margin) to see all your bookmarks in the Bookmarks window, as shown in Figure 10-5.

Figure 10-5: The Bookmarks window in all its glory.

Open bookmarked pages in the Bookmarks window by double-clicking them.

You can view the contents of any collection (that is, a folder full of bookmarks) by clicking its name in the Collections pane on the left side of the window. Figure 10-5 shows, in particular, the contents of the Bookmarks Bar folder with the contents of the News subfolder expanded.

To organize your Bookmarks window or place bookmarks on the toolbar or Bookmarks menu, move bookmarks by dragging them. You can place bookmarks and folders of bookmarks on the Safari Bookmarks Bar or Bookmarks menu by dragging them to the appropriate folder. If you drag a folder of bookmarks to the Bookmarks Bar folder (or directly onto the Bookmarks Bar itself), the result is a drop-down menu, as shown in Figure 10-3, earlier in this chapter.

To delete a bookmark, select it in the Bookmarks window and press Delete key.

If you enable Auto-Click for a folder of bookmarks, you don't get a drop-down menu when you click its button. Instead, all the pages in that folder open at once, each in its own separate tab. You can still use the drop-down menu, but you have to click and hold the button rather than just click. Conversely, if you want to open all the bookmarks in a folder that doesn't have Auto-Click enabled, you can ⌘-click it to open the pages in separate tabs.

Bookmarks are favorites, and favorites are bookmarks. Both words refer to exactly the same thing: shortcuts to websites. In this chapter, I use *bookmarks* because that's what Safari calls them. Some other browsers call them *favorites.*

What's on your reading list?

The Reading List serves as a repository for pages or links you want to read but don't want to read right now. It's a lot like a bookmark, but easier to create on the fly, which makes the Reading List perfect for sites or links you don't need to keep forever (that's what bookmarks are for).

In the previous section, you saw one of the ways you can add a page by clicking the Share button in the Toolbar and choosing Add to Reading List.

Another way to add a page to your Reading List is to open the page and click the Reading List icon (the eyeglasses, as shown in the margin). The Reading List sidebar appears on the left side of the window, as shown in Figure 10-6. Click the Add Page button in the Reading List sidebar.

To add a link to your Reading List without visiting the page, press the Shift key when you click. It's fast and works even when the Reading List sidebar is closed. Or right-click the link and choose Add to Reading List from the contextual menu.

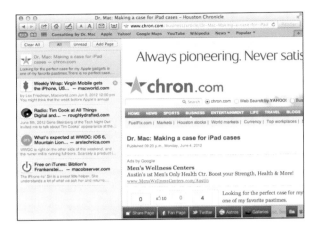

Figure 10-6: Use the Reading List for pages you want to visit soon.

Finally, to delete an item from your Reading List, click the X in its top-right corner, as shown in Figure 10-6. To delete them all at once, click the Clear All button.

If you don't see an X, move the cursor over the item you want to delete, and it magically appears.

Using the terrific Top Sites page

The Top Sites page has quickly become one of my favorite Safari features. It displays a selection of sites you visit frequently, as shown in Figure 10-7.

Figure 10-7: Top Sites displays your favorite sites.

To see it, choose History⊏⇨Show Top Sites, press ⌘+Option+1, or click the Top Sites button (shown in the margin), which you'll find to the right of the Show All Bookmarks button.

As you surf the web, Safari learns your favorite sites and replaces the sites on the Top Sites page with the ones you visit most.

The little stars you see in the top-right corner of some sites in Figure 10-7 indicate that the page has changed since the last time you visited it (a very nice touch).

Click the Edit button in the bottom-left corner, and you can

- **Delete a site you don't want on your Top Sites page.** Click the little X in its top-left corner.

- **"Pin" a site to your Top Sites page to make it remain one of your Top Sites, even if you don't visit that page for a while.** Click the pushpin in its top-left corner. All the items in the top row of Figure 10-8 are marked as permanent Top Sites.

- **Change the number and size of the sites shown.** Choose Small (24 sites), Medium (12 sites, as shown in Figure 10-7), or Large (6, as shown in Figure 10-8).

Figure 10-8 shows all these actions.

Figure 10-8: This is what editing the Top Sites page looks like.

Searching with Google

Looking for something on the Internet? Check out Google, the fantastic search engine that's totally integrated with Safari to help you hunt down just about anything on the Internet in no time.

In this section, you discover how to use Google to search the Internet and find almost anything, as well as how to get help with Google when all else fails.

To search the Internet with Google, follow these steps:

1. **Type the beginning of a word or phrase in the Address field.**

   As you type, Safari offers a list of suggestions and recent searches, as shown in Figure 10-9. Note that I had only typed *vizsla p* when Safari offered this list.

2. **Click one of the list items, finish typing the word or phrase, or use the arrow keys to select a list item, and then press Return or Enter to start the search.**

   Google almost immediately offers your search results, as shown in Figure 10-9.

Figure 10-9: A Google search for pictures of Vizsla dogs.

3. **Click one of the result links.**

   Links appear in blue and are underlined. You're taken instantly to that particular page.

4. **If a particular result isn't just what you're looking for, click the Back button, and try another result link.**

5. **If Google offers too many results that aren't just right, click the gear button near the top of the results page and choose Advanced Search.**

Advanced searches refine your search with a multitude of options, some of which are shown in Figure 10-10.

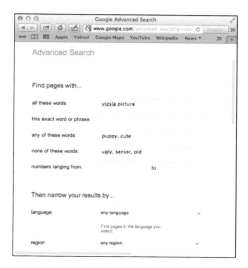

Figure 10-10: A Google advanced search for pictures of Vizsla dogs that are cute or puppies and not ugly, senior, or old.

6. **Click the Advanced Search button.**

   A refined results page quickly appears. As before, click a result link to visit that page. If it's not just what you're looking for, click the Back button, and try a different result link.

If you prefer to use Yahoo! or Bing rather than Google for your searches, choose Safari➪Preferences, click the General tab at the top of the window, and choose your preferred search engine from the Default Search Engine pop-up menu.

One last thing: The little angle bracket icons on the right side of the toolbar and Bookmarks Bar in Figure 10-10 (and shown in the margin) indicate that the window is too narrow to display all the tools or bookmarks. Click it, and a menu shows you the previously hidden choices, as shown in Figure 10-11.

That's pretty much all you need to know to have a great time searching the web with Google.

Figure 10-11: The Toolbar overflow menu (top) shows the four hidden toolbar icons; the Bookmarks Bar overflow menu (bottom) shows the two hidden bookmark folders.

Checking out Help Center

Safari has a lot more features, and I could write an entire chapter about using Safari, but one of the rules we *For Dummies* authors must follow is that our books can't run 1,000 pages long.

So I'm going to give you the next best thing: Open the Help Center (by choosing Help⇨Safari Help). A special Safari Help window appears; you can search for any Safari-related topic or solution to any Safari-related problem right there.

Video Calls with FaceTime

In the beginning, FaceTime brought video calling to the iPhone 4. It was iPhone 4-to-iPhone 4 only and required Wi-Fi (not 3G). Still, it was pretty cool and worked quite well. Not surprisingly, it soon spread to the second and third generation iPads, the iPod touch, and in OS X Lion, the Mac as well.

I haven't told you about Messages yet (I will in Chapter 11), but one of its features is video chat. Alas, Messages can only video chat with folks on Macs or PCs; FaceTime lets you do it with other Mac users as well as users of iPhone 4s, iPads, and iPod touches.

In addition to its aforementioned video-with-iDevices prowess, FaceTime works very nicely for Mac-to-Mac video calls. And because it's a single-purpose application, many users find it easier and less intimidating to set up and use than Messages or Skype.

By the way, there's no Windows version of FaceTime at the moment, so you'll have to use Messages (or third-party software like Skype) to have cross-platform video chats.

To get started, just launch FaceTime from either your Applications folder, your LaunchPad, or your Dock, and the main (only) FaceTime window appears, as shown in Figure 10-12.

Figure 10-12: The FaceTime window, ready to make a call.

The left side of the window shows what your Mac's camera is seeing (which happens to be me in Figure 10-12).

I clicked the iPhone entry to initiate a call from my Mac to my wife's iPhone. She was at the football game with my son Jacob, and I was soon talking to both of them, as shown in Figure 10-13.

Figure 10-13: What I saw on my Mac screen (left) and what they saw on their iPhone screen (right).

FaceTime uses Mountain Lion's Contacts (covered in Chapter 11), so if you have friends or family who have an iPhone 4, iPad 2 or later, iPod touch, or a Mac, just click their phone number or e-mail address to initiate a video call.

Communications Made Easy

In This Chapter

▷ Managing contacts with Contacts

▷ Mastering e-mail with Mail

▷ Conquering chats and iMessages with Messages

*I*n this chapter, you look at a trio of terrific programs that work together and make managing your contacts, e-mail, and messages (chats) a breeze. You're about to find out how these eponymous programs — Contacts, Mail, and Messages — work, and how to use them individually and as a team.

I cover a lot of material in not a lot of space in this chapter, so if there's something you want to find out about Contacts, Mail, or Messages that I don't cover, don't forget about the wonderful assistance you can find in Help⇨Mail Help, Help⇨Contacts Help, and Help⇨Messages Help.

Collecting Your Contacts

Contacts stores and manages information about your family, friends, and anyone else you want to keep in touch with. It works seamlessly with the Mail and Messages applications, enabling you to quickly look up e-mail addresses when you're ready to send an e-mail, text, or start a chat.

stationery is

In fact, Contacts works with several applications, both on and beyond your Mac, including the following:

✔ Use it with FaceTime (covered in Chapter 17) to video chat with friends and family.

✔ Use it with Calendar (covered in Chapter 9) by choosing Window⇨ Address Panel or pressing ⌘+Option+A. You can then drag any person in your Contacts from the Address Panel to any date and time on the calendar, and a special Meeting event is created automatically by Calendar. The event even has a Send Invitation button; if you click it, it launches Mail and sends the person an invitation to this meeting. Very cool stuff.

✓ The Contacts application can also work with any other application whose programmers choose to make the connection or with any device that is compatible with Contacts. For example, FileMaker's Bento application ($49.99 in the Mac App Store) exchanges data with Contacts seamlessly, so changes made in Contacts appear in Bento (and vice versa) almost immediately.

✓ It's also available in most programs that have a Share button or menu so you can share with your contacts via whichever method is appropriate, usually their e-mail or .Mac address (for iMessages).

✓ If you use iCloud, you can sync contacts with devices that include (but are not limited to): other Macs, iPhones, iPads, and iPod touches.

In the following sections, you find out the best ways to fill Contacts with contacts and keep those contacts organized.

Adding contacts

Follow these steps to create a new entry in the Contacts:

1. **Launch the Contacts application by double-clicking its icon in the Applications folder, clicking its Dock icon, or clicking its Launchpad icon.**

   The Contacts window appears. The first time that you open Contacts, you see two cards: Apple Computer and the one with the personal identification information you supplied when you created your account.

2. **To create a new entry, click the + button at the bottom of the Contacts window's Name column.**

   An untitled address card appears. The First name text field is initially selected. (It's highlighted in Figure 11-1.)

3. **Type the person's first name in the First text field.**

   Here, I type **Bob.**

4. **Press Tab.**

   Your cursor should now be in the Last text field.

   You can always move from one field to the next by pressing Tab — in fact, this shortcut works in almost all Mac programs with fields. (Move to the previous field by pressing Shift+Tab.)

Figure 11-1: A new address card in Contacts.

5. Type the last name for the person you're adding to your Contacts.

Here, I type **LeVitus**. Continue this process, filling in the rest of the fields shown in Figure 11-2.

Figure 11-2: The address card displayed in the Contacts window.

6. When you're done entering information, click the Done button to exit the editing mode.

The contact I created with this step appears in Figure 11-2.

The little triangles (actually up and down arrows) between the labels and their contents fields in Figure 11-1 are pop-up menus that offer alternative labels for the field. For example, if you were to click the arrows next to the word *Mobile,* you could choose Home, Work, Main, Home Fax, Work Fax, Pager, Other, or Custom to replace the label Mobile.

To add more info about any Contacts entry, select the name in the Name column (Bob "Dr. Mac" LeVitus in Figure 11-2). You can tell when a name is selected because it is highlighted, as mine is in Figure 11-2. Then click the Edit button at the bottom of the Contacts window, and make your changes.

Repeat these steps for everyone you want to keep in touch with.

Importing contacts from other programs

If you already have contacts you created in another program, you might be able to import them into Contacts. Contacts can import contacts in vCard, LDIF, or Text file format.

The first thing you need to do is export the data from the other program in one of these formats. Then choose File➪Import➪vCard (or LDIF or Text file, as the case may be), choose the exported data file in the Open File dialog, and then click the Open button.

Creating a basic group

Now let me explain how to organize your contacts into groups. Why would you want to organize your contacts into groups? The main reason, at least for me, is practical: I can send e-mail to everyone in a group that I've defined with a single click. So when it's time to send out a press release, I can simply send it to my Press group, shooting the e-mail off to all 50 people I have in that group. And when I want to send an e-mail to all the parents of kids on my son's indoor football team, I merely address it to my Flag Football Parents group, and all 12 families in that group receive it.

Here's how to create a group and add contacts to it:

1. **Launch the Contacts application by double-clicking its icon in the Applications folder or clicking its Dock icon.**

2. **To create a new group, choose File➪New Group or press ⌘+Shift+N.**

   An untitled Group appears in the Group column with "untitled group" highlighted.

3. **Type a descriptive name for this group and then press Enter or Return.**

   I named mine Family.

4. **Click All Contacts on the left side of the window to show all your contacts on the right side.**

5. **Click the contacts you want in the group on the right side.**

Hold down the ⌘ key as you select contacts if you want to select more than one contact.

You can use the Search field (magnifying-glass icon) at the top of the window to find a contact or contacts, and then drag them onto the group to add them.

6. **Drag the selected contact names onto the group, as shown in Figure 11-3.**

Figure 11-3: Adding six contacts to the Family group.

Contacts considerately displays the number of contacts you're dragging, which happens to be six in this instance.

Another way to create a group is to select contacts by clicking, ⌘-clicking, and/or Shift-clicking and choosing File➪New Group from Selection.

Setting up a Smart Group (based on contact criteria)

A second type of group — called a Smart Group — might be even more useful to you. A Smart Group gathers contacts in your Contacts based on criteria you specify. So, for example, you could create a group that automatically selects Apple staff members.

The big advantage of a Smart Group over a regular group is that when I add a new Apple contact, that contact automatically becomes a member of the Apple Smart Group with no further action on my part. And if you delete a card or modify it so the contact no longer matches the Smart Group criteria, the contact is removed from the group automatically.

To create a Smart Group, follow these steps:

1. **Choose File➪New Smart Group or press ⌘+Option+N.**

A Smart Group sheet appears in front of the Contacts window, as shown in Figure 11-4.

Figure 11-4: Creating a new Smart Group.

2. **Give the Smart Group a name.**

   I named mine Apple.

3. **Select the appropriate items from the menus: Any, Company, Contains, Email, and so on.**

   In Figure 11-4, I've created a Smart Group that includes any contact that contains *Apple* in the Company field or *@apple.com* in any e-mail field.

4. **When you're happy with the criteria specified, click OK.**

To delete a group or Smart Group from your Contacts, click to select it and choose Edit⇨Delete Group.

The Views are lovely

 Notice the three similar-looking icons under the Contacts list and shown in the margin. These are shortcut buttons for three views, which can also be selected using the View menu or keyboard shortcuts.

The three views, shown in Figure 11-5, are:

- **Groups view:** Click the Groups (left) icon, choose View⇨Groups, or press ⌘+1 to view Contacts in three panes: a list of Groups on the left, a list of Contacts in the middle, and details for the selected contact on the right.

- **List and Card view:** Click the List and Card (middle) icon, choose View⇨List and Card or press ⌘+2) to hide the list of Groups and display only the list of Contacts on the left and the details for the selected contact on the right.

- **Card Only view:** Click the Card Only (right) icon, choose View⇨ Card Only or press ⌘+3), to hide the Groups and Contacts lists and display only the details for the selected Contact.

Groups (Command + 1)

List and Card (Command + 2)   Card Only (Command + 3)

Figure 11-5: Groups view (top), Card Only view (right), and List and Card view (bottom).

iCloud + Contacts = Your contacts everywhere

If you're not an iCloud user (see Chapter 10), your contacts will be stored locally on your hard disk. iCloud users, on the other hand, can choose to store their contacts either locally or in iCloud. The difference is if you store them on iCloud, you can sync all your devices so they all display the same information. In other words, if you add a contact to your iPhone, you'll see it on your Mac in the Contacts app within a few minutes. Conversely, if you add a contact on your Mac, within a few minutes, it magically appears in the Contacts app on your iDevice.

To enable iCloud for Contacts, choose Contacts⟹Preferences (shortcut: ⌘+,), click the Accounts icon at the top of the window, and then select the Enable This Account check box.

If you use iCloud, there's no reason to store contacts locally (that is, On My Mac). And, in fact, if you use iCloud, you shouldn't even see an On My Mac section in the Groups list. My advice is that if you do see both sections (On My Mac and iCloud) in the Groups list, as in the Groups View shown in Figure 11-5, copy the contacts stored On Your Mac to iCloud by clicking All on My Mac in the Groups list and selecting all its contacts (Edit⟹Select All or ⌘+A) and dragging them onto the iCloud group. Now click the iCloud group and confirm that the contacts you just dragged are visible, and then delete the On My Mac group (select it and choose Edit⟹Delete Group). Finally, look for duplicate contacts by choosing Card⇨Look for Duplicates. If any duplicates are found, you're invited to either delete one (if they're the same) or merge them (if one is different).

Sending e-mail to a contact or group

You don't even have to open Contacts to send an e-mail to a contact or group contained in your Contacts. In the following sections, you see how Mail finds contacts or groups for you without launching Contacts. But if you already have Contacts open, this technique for sending e-mail to a contact or group is probably most convenient.

To create a blank e-mail message to a contact, click and hold the label next to the e-mail address, and choose Send Email from the pop-up menu that appears, as shown in Figure 11-6.

Figure 11-6: Sending e-mail to a contact is as easy as clicking.

The Mail program becomes active, and a blank e-mail message addressed to the selected contact appears on your screen. Just type your e-mail as you normally would.

As you can see in Figure 11-6, in addition to sending an e-mail, the pop-up menu next to e-mail addresses lets you:

- Start a FaceTime video chat (see Chapter 10).
- Send an iMessage (see the "Communicating with Messages" section, later in this chapter).
- Search for this e-mail address in documents on your Mac using Spotlight (see Chapter 7).
- Send your vCard (see the following Tip) to this e-mail address.

The information for each contact can be sent to others in an industry-standard file format known as a *vCard* (virtual business card). Choosing Send My Card works the same as Send Email, but instead of starting with a totally blank e-mail message, the message starts with your vCard enclosed. When the recipient opens the vCard file, all your contact information will be added to his or her Contacts (or other contact manager in Windows).

Sending and Receiving E-Mail with Mail

Mail is a program for sending, receiving, and organizing your e-mail. Mail is fast and easy to use, too. Click the Mail icon in the Dock or Launchpad or double-click the Mail icon in the Applications folder to launch Mail. The Mail icon looks like a canceled postage stamp, as shown in the margin.

You can use other applications to read e-mail. Mozilla (Thunderbird) and AOL, for example, have their own mail readers, as does Microsoft Office (Entourage or Outlook). But for Macs, the easiest and best mail reader around (meaning the best one on your hard drive by default) is almost certainly Mail. And of course, you can't beat the price; it's free!

The following sections, in some cases, offer you starting points. Even so, you should find everything perfectly straightforward. If you run into a question that the following sections don't answer, remember that you can always call upon the assistance of Help (Help➪Mail Help).

Setting up Mail

If this is your first time launching Mail, you need to set up your e-mail account(s) before you can proceed. A set of New Account screens appears automatically. Just fill in the blanks on each screen and click the Continue button until you're finished.

If you don't know what to type in one or more of these fields, contact your ISP (Internet service provider) or mail provider for assistance.

After you've set up one or more e-mail accounts, you see a Welcome message asking whether you'd like to see what's new in Mail. If you click Yes, Help Viewer launches and shows you the What's New in Mail page (while Mail's main window, which looks like Figure 11-7, appears in the background). Or if you click No, Mail's main window appears as the active window immediately.

Mail's main window is actually called a *viewer window* or *message viewer window*. You can have more than one of them on your screen, if you like; just choose File➪New Viewer Window or press ⌘+Option+N.

Show/Hide Mailbox pane button

Mailbox pane   Toolbar   Favorites bar

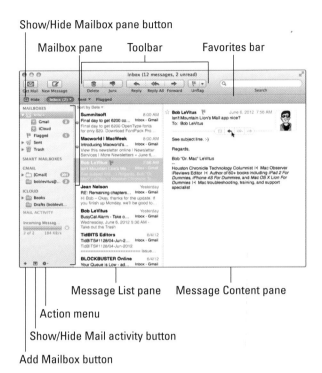

Message List pane   Message Content pane

Action menu

Show/Hide Mail activity button

Add Mailbox button

Figure 11-7: Mail's main window.

Composing a new message

Here's how to create a new e-mail message:

1. **Choose File⇨New Message, click the New button on the toolbar, or press ⌘+N.**

   A new window appears. This is where you compose your e-mail message, as shown in Figure 11-8.

2. **Place your cursor in the To field, and type someone's e-mail address.**

   Use my address (`MountainLion4Dummies@boblevitus.com`) if you don't know anyone else to send mail to.

   If the recipient is in your Contacts (as Barack Obama and Barry the Electrician are in mine), just type a few letters, and Mail's intelligent autocomplete function matches it up with Contacts. So, for example, I typed the letters *b-a-r,* and a list of people in my Contacts with *bar* in their names — namely, Barack Obama and Barry the Electrician in

Figure 11-8 — appeared. I can select a name by clicking it, typing an additional letter or letters to narrow the search (typing an **r** would leave only Barry the Electrician; typing an **a** would leave only Barack Obama), or using the arrow keys and pressing Return or Enter.

Figure 11-8: Composing an e-mail message.

3. Press the Tab key twice to move your cursor to the Subject text field and type a subject for this message.

I typed **Isn't Autocomplete neat?** in Figure 11-8.

4. Click in the main message portion of the window, and type your message there.

I typed **Your message here...** in Figure 11-8.

5. When you're finished writing your message, click the Send button to send the e-mail immediately, or close it to save it in the Drafts mailbox so you can work on it later.

If you save your message to the Drafts mailbox (so you can write more later, perhaps), you can send it when you're ready by opening the Drafts mailbox, double-clicking the message, and then clicking the Send button.

Just for the record, here's what the buttons in the toolbar in Figure 11-8 are all about:

🖙 **Send:** D'oh. Sends the message.

🖙 **Attach:** Opens a standard Open File sheet so you can pick a file or files to enclose with this message. To enclose multiple files, hold down the ⌘ key as you click each file you want to enclose.

If the recipients of this message use Windows, you probably want to select the Send Windows-Friendly Attachments check box at the bottom of the Open File sheet.

✓ **Format:** Shows or hides the Formatting toolbar, which is showing (between the toolbar and the To field) in Figure 11-8.

✓ **Photo Browser:** Opens the Photo Browser panel, which displays the photos in your iPhoto library and lets you drag and drop them into a mail message.

✓ **Show Stationery:** Opens a sheet with a selection of stationery you can use for your e-mail message. (You find out more about this feature in the upcoming section, "Working with stationery.")

✓ **The little arrow thingie to the left of the From pop-up menu (shown in the margin):** This little doohickey is actually a pop-down menu that lets you add fields to your message header. What fields? Glad you asked. . . . You can choose CC Address Field, BCC Address Field, Reply-To Address Field, or Priority Field. Or if you choose Customize, you see all the available fields with check boxes next to them so you can turn them on or off at will.

Changes you make using this menu become defaults. In other words, if you add a BCC field to this message, *all* subsequent messages also have a BCC field.

If you don't see text labels for the items in your toolbar, as you do in Figures 11-7 and 11-8, choose View⇨Customize Toolbar. The Customize Toolbar sheet appears in front of the active window; choose Icon and Text from the Show menu in its lower-left corner.

A quick overview of the toolbar

Before you go any further, look at the nine handy buttons and a search field in the viewer window's toolbar by default:

✓ **Get Mail:** Checks for new e-mail.

✓ **New Message:** Creates a new, blank e-mail message.

✓ **Delete:** Deletes selected message or messages ("Hi" in Figure 11-7, shown earlier).

To select more than one message in the list, hold down the ⌘ key when you click the second and subsequent messages.

✓ **Junk:** Marks the selected message or messages as junk mail. Mail has built-in junk-mail filtering that can be enabled or disabled in Mail Preferences. (Choose Mail⇨Preferences and click the Junk Mail icon on the toolbar.) If you receive a piece of *spam* (junk mail), select it and click this button to help train Mail's junk-mail filter. If a selected message has been marked as junk mail, the button changes to read Not Junk.

For more info on junk-mail filtering, click the question-mark button in the Junk Mail pane of the Mail Preferences window.

- ✔ **Reply:** Creates a reply to the sender only.

- ✔ **Reply All:** Creates a reply to the sender and everyone who was sent the original message.

- ✔ **Forward:** Creates a copy of this message you can send to someone other than the sender or other recipients.

- ✔ **Flag/Unflag:** This drop-down menu lets you mark or unmark one or more messages with any of seven colored flags. The selected message in Figure 11-7, for example, is flagged in green.

Finally, on the toolbar is a Search field that finds a word or phrase in any item stored in Mail. When you begin typing, a drop-down menu appears, as shown in Figure 11-9, so you can narrow the search to people or subjects matching your search phrase. You can also click the buttons in the Favorites bar to limit your search to specific mailboxes or to search only specific parts of messages — All, Inbox (2), Sent, Flagged, and Drafts (1) in Figure 11-9.

Figure 11-9: Searching for items with "bob" reveals 57 items.

The little numbers next to the mailbox buttons in the Favorites bar indicate the number of unread messages in that mailbox. A message is considered "read" after you click it.

Searching in Mail should be familiar to you; it works the same way as searching in the Finder. So, for example, if you want to save a search as a Smart Mailbox (Mail's version of a Smart Folder in the Finder), you click the Save button, which is behind the drop-down menu in Figure 11-9.

I've mentioned the Favorites bar, a new feature in Mountain Lion, a couple of times now. Mail populates it with mailboxes you use often: Inbox, Sent, Drafts, and Flagged in Figure 11-9. Add your own mailboxes by dragging them from the Mailbox pane to the Favorites bar.

Working with stationery

I personally find stationery for e-mail dorky. But since you might think it's the greatest thing since sliced kittens, here are some tips for working with it. First, to use it, click the Show Stationery button in a New Message window.

I'm a Luddite when it comes to e-mail. When I started using e-mail a long, long time ago, it was considered bad form to add anything but text to an e-mail message. It was generally agreed that e-mail messages should include only what was necessary to convey the information and nothing more. That's why all these froufrou flowers and borders irritate me and why I find them a waste of bandwidth. So please do me a favor: If you decide to send me an e-mail message, please don't use goofy stationery.

Here are some tips to help you have more fun with stationery:

- **Adding favorites:** If you find you're using a particular stationery a lot, you can add it to the Favorites category to make it easier to use. To do so, merely click the appropriate category in the list on the left (Birthday, Announcements, Photos, Stationery, and Sentiments in Figure 11-10); then click the stationery you want to make a favorite and drag it onto the word *Favorites* in the list on the left. When *Favorites* highlights, drop the stationery, and presto — that piece of stationery will appear in the Favorites category evermore.

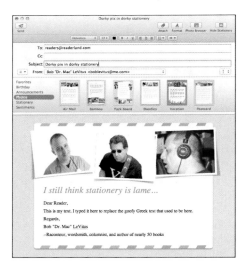

Figure 11-10: Drag and drop your own pictures in a stationery.

✔ **Greeking out:** You can change the Greek/pseudo-Latin text that appears in all the stationery by selecting it, deleting it, and typing whatever text you want to appear. You have to do it only once; the text you type in any stationery appears in all other stationeries.

✔ **Replacing pictures:** You can replace any picture in any stationery with a picture of your own. Just drag a picture — from the Photo Browser (Window➪Photo Browser) or the Finder — onto any picture in any piece of stationery. I've replaced the boilerplate text and all three of the dorky pictures in the Air Mail stationery, as shown in Figure 11-10.

✔ **Removing stationery:** If you decide you don't want to use stationery with a message after you've applied it, click the Stationery category and choose the Original stationery, which changes your message back to a clean, blank page.

Checking your mail

How do you check and open your mail? Easy. Just click the Get Mail button at the top of the main Mail window (refer to Figure 11-9) or press ⌘+Shift+N.

✔ **To read a new message,** select it. Its contents appear in the Message Content pane.

✔ **To delete a selected message,** click the Delete button on the toolbar.

✔ **To retrieve a message you accidentally deleted,** click Trash on the left and drag the message into the Inbox or other mailbox.

✔ **To configure Mail to send and check for your mail every *X* minutes,** choose Mail➪Preferences and click the General icon at the top of the window. Click the Check for New Mail pop-up menu and make a selection — every 1, 5, 15, 30, or 60 minutes — or choose Manually if you don't want Mail to check for mail automatically at all. (The default setting is to check for mail every 5 minutes.)

✔ **To add a sender to Contacts,** when someone who isn't already in your Contacts sends you an e-mail message, simply choose Message➪Add Sender to Contacts (shortcut: ⌘+Y).

Adding a sender to your Contacts has an additional benefit: It guards messages from that person against being mistaken for junk mail. In other words, your Contacts is a *white list* for the spam filter; if specific senders appear in your Contacts, their messages will never be mistakenly marked as junk mail.

Dealing with spam

Speaking of junk mail, although e-mail is a wonderful thing, some people out there try to spoil it. They're called *spammers,* and they're lowlifes who share their lists among themselves — and before you know it, your e-mail box is flooded with get-rich-quick schemes, advertisements for pornographic websites and chat rooms, and all the more traditional buy-me junk mail.

Fortunately, Mail comes with a pretty darn good Junk Mail filter that analyzes incoming message subjects, senders, and contents to determine which ones are likely to contain bulk or junk mail. When you open Mail for the first time, it's running in its training mode, which is how Mail learns to differentiate between what it considers junk mail and what you consider junk mail; all it needs is your input. Mail identifies messages it thinks are junk, but if you disagree with its decisions, here's what you do:

- Click the Not Junk button in the brown bar for any message that *isn't* junk mail.

- Conversely, if a piece of junk mail slips past Mail's filters and ends up in the Inbox, select the message and click the Junk button in the Mail window's toolbar.

After a few days (or weeks, depending upon your mail volume), Mail should be getting it right almost all the time. When you reach that point, choose Move it to the Junk Mailbox on the Junk Mail tab of Mail's preferences window. Now Mail starts moving junk mail automatically out of your Inbox and into a Junk mailbox, where you can scan the items quickly and trash them when you're ready.

If (for some reason that escapes me) you prefer to receive and manually process your junk mail, you can turn off junk-mail processing by disabling it on the Junk Mail tab of Mail's preferences pane.

Changing your preferences

Actually, Mail's preferences (Mail⇨Preferences or ⌘+,) are more than you might expect from the name. This is the control center for Mail, where you can

- Create and delete e-mail accounts.

- Determine which fonts and colors are used for your messages.

- Decide whether to download and save attachments (such as pictures).

- Decide whether to send formatted mail or plain text.

- Decide whether to turn on the spell checker.

    The default is to check spelling as you type, which many people (myself included) find annoying.

- Decide whether to have an automatic signature appended to your messages.

- Establish rules to process mail that you receive.

Mail rules rule

If you really want to tap the power of Mail, you need to set *rules*. With some cool rules, you can automatically tag messages with a color; file them in a specific mailbox; reply to/forward/redirect the messages automatically (handy when you're going to be away for a while); automatically reply to messages; and *kill-file* messages (just delete them without even bothering to look at them — what better fate for mail from people you hate?).

There's no way I can do rules justice in a page or so, but here's a quick look at how to create one:

1. **Choose Mail↩Preferences.**

2. **Click the Rules icon on the toolbar of the Preferences window.**

3. **Click the Add Rule button.**

   The first condition should say From in its first pop-up menu and Contains in its second pop-up menu. Look at your options in these menus but return them to their original state — From and Contains — when you're done looking.

4. **In the field to the right of the Contains pop-up menu, type a word you want to filter for (I typed** LeVitus**).**

   Below the condition you just created, you should see an action under the words Perform the Following Actions. It should say Move Message in its first pop-up menu and No Mailbox Selected in its second pop-up menu.

5. **Look at the options on these menus, but this time, change the first one from Move Message to Play Sound and the second one from No Mailbox Selected to Blow.**

6. **Type a description of the rule, such as** Message from LeVitus**, in the Description field.**

   Your rule should look identical to Figure 11-11 now.

Figure 11-11: When you get a message from me, Mail plays the Blow sound.

7. **Click OK.**

   Mail asks whether you want to apply your rule(s) to the selected mailboxes.

8. **Choose Apply if you want Mail to run this rule on the selected mailboxes, or choose Don't Apply if you don't.**

   And that's how you build a rule. From this point forward, every time you get a message from me, you hear the Blow sound.

Notice the little + (plus) and – (minus) buttons to the right of each condition and action. Use the + button to add more conditions or actions and the – button to delete a condition or action. If you have multiple conditions, you can choose Any or All from the pop-up menu above them, which executes this rule when either any of the conditions or all of the conditions are met. Either way, all the actions you create are always executed when this rule is triggered.

Mailboxes smart and plain

The following sections take a closer look at both types of mailboxes — plain and smart.

Plain old mailboxes

Plain mailboxes are just like folders in the Finder; you create them and name them, and they're empty until you put something in them. They even look like folders in Mail's mailbox pane. You use mailboxes to organize any messages you want to save.

Here are several ways to create a plain mailbox:

- ✔ Choose Mailbox⇨New Mailbox.
- ✔ Click the little + sign at the bottom of the mailbox pane on the left side of the viewer window.
- ✔ Click the Action menu at the bottom of the mailbox pane (the one that looks like a gear), and choose New Mailbox.
- ✔ Right-click or Control-click in the mailbox pane and choose New Mailbox from the contextual menu.

Whichever way you choose, the next thing that happens is that a sheet drops down with a Location pop-up menu and a field for you to type the name you want to give this mailbox. Choose On My Mac from the Location menu, and name the mailbox anything you like. Click OK, and the mailbox is created in the mailbox pane.

You can create *submailboxes* (mailboxes inside other mailboxes) to further subdivide your messages. To do so, click a mailbox to select it before you create a new mailbox.

In Figure 11-12, I've divided my Books mailbox into three submailboxes: iPhone For Dummies, Lion For Dummies, and Mountain Lion For Dummies.

Figure 11-12: My Books mailbox is divided into three submailboxes.

You can also drag and drop a mailbox from the top level of the list (such as Drafts, Junk, and Other Dumb Mail in Figure 11-12) onto another mailbox (such as Books or any of its three submailboxes) to make them submailboxes. If you drag a mailbox into a submailbox, it becomes a sub-submailbox. And so on.

To delete a mailbox, click it to select it and then

- ✔ Choose Mailbox⇨Delete Mailbox.

- ✔ Right-click or Control-click the mailbox, and choose Delete Mailbox.

- ✔ Click the Action menu at the bottom of the mailbox pane (the one that looks like a gear), and choose Delete Mailbox.

Intelligent smart mailboxes

A *smart mailbox* is Mail's version of the Finder's Smart Folder. In a nutshell, smart mailboxes are mailboxes that display the results of a search. The messages you see in a smart mailbox are *virtual;* they aren't really in the smart mailbox itself. Instead, the smart mailbox displays a list of messages stored in other mailboxes that match whatever criteria you've defined for that smart folder. As with Smart Folders in the Finder, smart mailboxes update automatically when new messages that meet the criteria are received.

Here are two ways to create a smart mailbox:

- Choose Mailbox⬏New Smart Mailbox.
- Click the + button at the bottom of the mailbox pane, and choose Smart Mailbox from the pop-up menu.

Whichever way you choose, the next thing that happens is that a sheet drops down with a field for the smart mailbox's name, plus some pop-up menus, buttons, and check boxes, as shown in Figure 11-13.

Figure 11-13: This smart mailbox gathers messages with the words *Mountain Lion* in the body or subject.

Name your smart mailbox; determine its criteria (by using the pop-up menus, plus and minus buttons, and check boxes), and then click OK. The smart folder appears in the mailbox pane with a little gear on it to denote that it's smart. You can see the Smart Mountain Lion smart mailbox in Figure 11-13, though only the first part of its name — Smart Mountain — is visible. Notice that it has a gear, and plain mailboxes don't.

Sign here, please

If you're like me, you'd rather not type your whole signature every time you send an e-mail message, and you don't have to with Mail. If you create canned signatures, you can use them in outgoing messages without typing a single character.

Here's how it works:

1. **Choose Mail⬏Preferences or press ⌘+, (that's ⌘+comma).**
2. **Click the Signatures icon in the Preferences window's toolbar.**
3. **Click the name of the mail account you want to create this signature for in the left column (iCloud in Figure 11-14).**

Figure 11-14: My newly created BL Long signature.

4. **Click the little + sign at the bottom of the middle column to create a new, blank signature.**

5. **Type a descriptive name for this signature to replace the default name Signature #1 (BL Long in Figure 11-14).**

6. **Type the signature exactly as you want it to appear in outgoing messages in the right column** (Regards, Bob "Dr. Mac" LeVitus – * Houston Chronicle, **and so on in Figure 11-14).**

7. **Drag the name you've assigned this signature (BL Long in Figure 11-14) onto the mail account you're using it with (iCloud in Figure 11-14).**

If you have more than one signature, you can choose the one you want to use as the default: Choose the account in the column on the left; then choose the signature from the Choose Signature pop-up menu.

If you have more than one signature, another cool thing happens: A Signature menu appears in new messages, as shown in Figure 11-15, so you can choose a signature other than the one you chose from the pop-up menu as the default (it's BL Short in Figure 11-15).

Take a (Quick) look and (Slide) show me some photos

One last cool feature, and you're finished with Mail. That cool feature is QuickLook, which includes a slick Slideshow option. Notice that there's a QuickLook button in the header of messages you receive that contain one or more pictures, as shown on the left in Figure 11-16. If you click the QuickLook button, a new window appears, displaying one of the enclosed pictures as shown on the right in Figure 11-16.

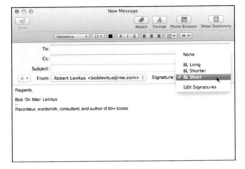

Figure 11-15: Choosing my BL Short signature from the Signature menu.

If you don't see a QuickLook button, click the blue Details button in the top-right corner (which says *Hide* in Figure 11-16 because the details are showing).

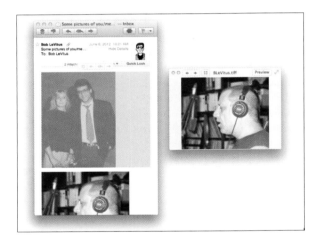

Figure 11-16: Click the QuickLook button (left), and it displays a picture in its own window (right).

Above my smiling face in the QuickLook window on the right in Figure 11-16 is a set of buttons. Here's the lowdown on what they do (from left to right):

- ✓ **Previous:** Click this button to see the previous picture.
- ✓ **Next:** Click this button to see the next picture.
- ✓ **Index Sheet:** Displays all the enclosed pictures at the same time, shrinking them to a smaller size if necessary to fit them all on the screen. Click a picture once to see its name; click a second time to display it full screen.

   ✏ **Open with Preview:** Opens the picture in the Preview application.

   ✏ **Full screen:** Adjusts the picture so it fills the screen, as shown in
     Figure 11-17.

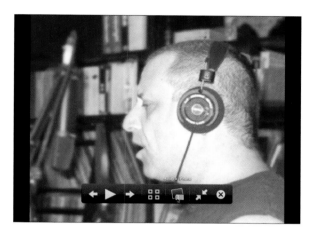

Figure 11-17: QuickLook's full screen mode.

To close the QuickLook window, either click the little X in its top-left corner
or click the QuickLook button in the message header again. Notice that when
you're in full-screen mode, there are a couple of new buttons in addition to
the ones I just mentioned in Figure 11-16. These new buttons are

   ✏ **Play/Pause:** Click this button to start or pause the slide show. It displays
     each of the enclosed pictures for around 5 seconds with a smooth dissolve
     transition between them.

   ✏ **Add to iPhoto:** Copies the picture into your iPhoto library.

To escape from full-screen mode, click the big X, shown in the bottom-right
corner of Figure 11-17, or press the Esc key.

Communicating with Messages

Instant messaging and chat rooms provide for interactive communication
among users all over the world. If you're into instant messaging, Messages
gives you immediate access to all the other users of AIM, Jabber, Google Talk,
and iCloud. All you need are their screen names, and you're set to go. You
can even join any AOL chat room just by choosing File➪Go to Chat Room.
To get started, just launch Messages from either your Applications folder,
Launchpad, or Dock.

By the way, if you're a fan of the iChat application in previous OS X releases and wonder where it went in Mountain Lion, Messages is the answer. The program you knew and loved as iChat is now called Messages. Same great iChat tastiness and now with support for iMessages!

What the heck is an iMessage?

iMessage is Apple's inter-device messaging protocol. That means you can send unlimited iMessages to anyone with an iPhone, iPad, or iPod touch running iOS 5 (or later) or Mac running Mountain Lion (OS X 10.8).

Think of it as MMS messaging, similar to what you find on smartphones, but you can send and receive them from your Mac. Better still, an iMessage can include photos, videos, locations, and contacts in addition, of course, to text. And if you have more than one iOS device, iMessage keeps all your conversations going across all of them. You can also get delivery receipts letting you know your messages went through. You'll know it's been read, too, if your friend has enabled read receipts.

Chit-chatting with Messages

Your chats can be one to one, or they can be group bull sessions. Messages is integrated with Contacts, so you don't have to enter your buddies' information twice. It also communicates directly with the Mail application. Here's all the essential info you need to get started:

- ✔ **To start a text chat,** open Messages, select a buddy in your buddy list, and choose Buddies⇨Invite to Chat. If you don't see your Buddies List, choose Window⇨Buddies or press ⌘+1.

  Each participant's picture (or icon) appears next to anything she says, which is displayed in a cartoonlike thought bubble, as shown in Figure 11-18. If you find the thought bubbles a little too childish, you can turn them off by choosing View⇨Messages and an option other than Show as Balloons.

- ✔ **To start a group text chat,** hold down the ⌘ key, click each person in your buddy list that you want to include, and then click the A button at the bottom of the buddy list. In a group text chat, everyone sees every message from every participant.

- ✔ **To attach a picture to a person in your Contacts** (as I have for myself on both Macs), copy a picture of the person to the Clipboard in your favorite graphics application (Preview, for example). Now open Contacts, and display the card for the person you want to add a picture to. Click the empty picture box at the top of the card, and paste the picture on the Clipboard. You should now see that picture on the Contacts card and also when you chat in Messages with the person. Neat!

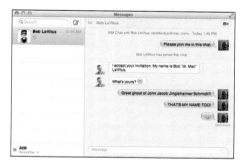

Figure 11-18: A chat with myself. (I have two Macs on the same network.)

If you've already attached a picture to a contact in Contacts, that picture will appear automatically when you chat.

✔ **To transfer files,** just drag the document's icon to the message box, as demonstrated in Figure 11-19, and press Return or Enter. The file zips across the ether. This is a very convenient way to share photos or documents without resorting to file sharing or e-mail.

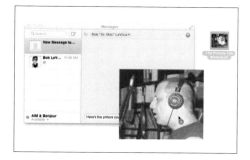

Figure 11-19: Transferring a file with Messages.

When you drag an image file (The Picture You Wanted, in Figure 11-19) onto the Messages window's message box, you see an oversize semitransparent preview, so you're sure you're sending them the right image and not something totally embarrassing. Way to go, OS X Mountain Lion.

✔ **To send an e-mail from Messages,** just select a buddy in Messages's buddy list and choose Buddies⇨Send Email (or press ⌘+Option+E). Mail launches (if it's not already open) and addresses a new message to the selected buddy, ready for you to begin typing.

Chatting with audio and video

The greatest Messages feature is audio/video chatting, which is why it was once known as *iChat AV*. Apple dropped the *AV* part and changed its name to Messages, but whatever you call it, the program still has fantastic audio and video features that are lots of fun — and ever-so-easy to set up and use.

With Messages, you can conference a video chat with up to three other people at the same time and audio chat with up to nine other folks at the same time.

To conduct a video or audio chat, follow these steps:

1. **Connect a FireWire camera and/or a supported microphone to your Mac.**

   Although many FireWire and USB camcorders and webcams will work fairly well for video chatting, Apple's iSight and FaceTime HD camera/ microphone combinations are designed just for this purpose (and works even better in most cases). The latter is built into all Mac notebooks, iMacs, and Apple displays these days; the former was built into previous generations of Macs. In other words, you probably have a camera and mic, so you won't have to buy a thing to video (and audio) chat.

   When you have appropriate hardware connected to your Mac, your buddies' names in the buddy lists display little green telephone or camera icons if they have the right hardware and an adequate Internet connection on their end.

2. **To start an audio- or videoconference, click the appropriate green icon(s).**

   Your buddies receive an invitation to begin an audio or video chat.

3. **If they accept the invitation, a Video Chat window appears, as shown in Figure 11-20.**

Figure 11-20: I'm Messagesting with my buddy Dave Hamilton.

Sending files and messages with Bonjour and Messages

OS X offers built-in support for Bonjour (Apple used to call it Rendezvous), which makes chatting even better. With Bonjour, OS X can automatically recognize others on a local network who are available to chat. So you can send a message or files from one computer to another quickly and with minimum hassle. Just choose Window↪Bonjour, and select the person with whom you want to chat from the Bonjour window. From there, you can send a message or file.

For Bonjour to connect to another computer, both users need to have Bonjour enabled and must either be connected to the same network or have AirPort for wireless networking built in. Beyond that, the connection is configuration-free; you don't have to do anything to be part of a Bonjour network because your Mac configures itself and joins up automatically.

If you're in the same Wi-Fi network and are both running Mountain Lion or Lion, however, Mountain Lion's AirDrop (described in Chapter 16) is an even faster, easier way to transfer files between two Macs.

If your Mac has a built-in iSight camera or you have a compatible camcorder or webcam handy, why not give it a try? My chat handle is `boblevitus@mac.com`; feel free to invite me to video chat if you see me online.

Remote Screen Sharing: Remarkable and superbly satisfying

I'd like to call your attention to one last Messages feature. It's called Remote Screen Sharing, was introduced in OS X 10.5 Leopard, and is possibly the most useful Messages feature of all time. It lets you control another Mac anywhere in the world, or another Mac user can control your Mac.

So now when my lovely wife Lisa calls out to me and says something like, "I'm trying to get my mail, but the thing I click to get mail disappeared," I don't have to try to decipher her description and explain how to replace the Mail icon in the Dock. Instead, I calmly say, "Honey, just open up your Messages app and let me show you how to fix that."

Here's how that works:

1. She launches Messages on her Mac. I launch Messages on mine.

2. She clicks *my* name in *her* buddy list and chooses Buddies↪Share My Screen with Bob LeVitus; or, I click *her* name in *my* Buddies list and choose Buddies↪Ask To Share Lisa LeVitus's Screen.

3. A window pops up on Lisa's screen, where she grants me permission to control her screen; when permission is granted, I can see her screen on *my* Mac and control her Mac with my mouse and keyboard.

   More specifically, I see a *proxy image* of her screen that says *Switch to Lisa LeVitus's Computer,* as shown in Figure 11-21.

Figure 11-21: If I click *Switch to Lisa LeVitus's Computer*, my screen will be taken over by my wife's computer's screen.

4. When I click in the little Computer window *(Switch To Lisa LeVitus's Computer)*, my screen changes — and instead of my stuff I see my wife's Desktop, as shown in Figure 11-22.

Figure 11-22: This is my computer displaying my wife's computer screen.

Now I can open her Applications folder, find her Mail application icon, and drag it to the Dock. Like magic, her issue is resolved. And I didn't have to leave my desk to fix it. Best of all, you can remotely control remote buddies via the Internet just as easily. For example, when mom calls from Boca with a Mac problem, I click her name in my Buddies list and in seconds I'm controlling her Mac from my office in Austin.

My consulting business has been using similar software to help Mac users for years. It's fantastic to be able to talk to someone on the phone while I'm controlling their Mac. I can fix things in a fraction of the time it would take to explain over the phone.

5. To go back to my Mac screen, I click the Switch to My Computer window at bottom left in Figure 11-22, and the remote computer screen disappears and mine comes back.

Before you get excited about having all that control, note these provisos:

- ✔ You and the other user must both be running OS X Leopard (OS X 10.5) or higher.
- ✔ You and the other user must both have iMessage accounts (or iCloud, AIM, Jabber, or Google Talk accounts).
- ✔ You and the other user both need high-speed Internet access.

When you share your screen, the person you share it with has the same degree of access to your files that you have. Only share your screen only with people you deeply trust. Furthermore, if you have files on your Mac that you would prefer the other person didn't see, I suggest you hide them deep in a subfolder somewhere or delete them before you begin your screen-sharing session. And, of course, don't forget that you can end the screen sharing session by ending the chat or quitting the Messages application.

Shine On You Crazy Diamond (Parts I–V)
Pink Floyd — Wish You Were Here
3:27   -10:

Shine On You Crazy Di
Pink Floyd — Wish
3:27

12

The Musical Mac

In This Chapter

▶ Using iTunes

▶ Working with media

▶ Playing with playlists

A long time ago, before the iPod and the iTunes Store were born, iTunes was a program you used to store and manage your MP3 music files. Over the ensuing years, it has grown into much more. Today, iTunes not only manages your music collection, but manages your video collection as well. And if you use devices such as an iPod, Apple TV, iPad, or iPhone, you manage the music or video on *them* by using iTunes, too.

So the anachronistically named iTunes is the program you use to manage audio and video files on your hard drive and to manage syncing files with your iPod, Apple TV, iPhone, and iPad devices.

Although entire books have been dedicated to iTunes alone, I share the most important stuff — the handful of things you really need to know — in this chapter.

Introducing iTunes

iTunes is the Swiss Army knife of multimedia software. After all, what other program lets you play audio CDs; create (burn) your own audio or MP3 CDs; listen to MP3, AIFF, AAC, WAV, Audible.com, and several other types of files; view album cover art; enjoy pretty visual displays in time to the music; view and manage TV shows, movies, and other video files; manage iPods (or other MP3 players), Apple TVs, iPads, and/or iPhones; listen to Internet radio stations; and more? On top of all that, it's your interface to the iTunes Store, the world's leading (legitimate) source of downloadable music and video content. (Whew!)

To open iTunes, click its icon in the Dock or double-click its icon in the Applications folder. The iTunes window opens (see Figure 12-1).

Source list

Rewind/Previous item

Play/Pause

Fast Forward/Next item

Info

Volume

Grid view

Album List view

Cover Flow view

Song List view

Column Browser

Search field

Show/Hide album artwork or video viewer

Info   Main List

Repeat

Choose Speakers

Start Genius

Shuffle

Add playlist

Show/Hide iTunes sidebar

Album artwork/ video viewer

Figure 12-1: Dissecting the iTunes interface.

In a nutshell, whatever you select in the Source List on the left is reflected in the main list on the right. In Figure 12-1, the Music library is selected. At the bottom of the window, you can see that there are 12,521 songs in my Music library, which would take 36.1 days to listen to from start to finish and uses 114.10GB of space on my hard drive.

Rather than try to explain what every item shown in Figure 12-1 does, I encourage you to click anything and everything you see in the main iTunes window. Experiment with the views, show and hide the iTunes browser and album art, click different items in the Source List, and see what happens.

I'd like you to take note of a few other items:

✔ The iTunes main window shrinks to a much more manageable size when you click its green gumdrop button, as shown in the top part of Figure 12-2. Click the green gumdrop again to expand it back to its normal size.

To switch between the small (top left) and ultra-small (top right) windows, click the bottom-right corner of the little window and drag left to shrink it or drag right to expand it.

The most recent versions of iTunes include two new ways to switch to the Mini Player: Choose Window⇨Switch to Mini Player or press ⌘+Shift+M. To switch back to the normal-sized iTunes window, choose Window⇨Switch *from* Mini Player, press ⌘+Shift+M again, or click the green gumdrop (again).

✔ iTunes offers a ten-band graphic equalizer that can make your music (or video) sound significantly better. Just choose Window⇨Equalizer to invoke it on-screen. You can see the equalizer in the lower part of Figure 12-2.

Figure 12-2: The iTunes equalizer (bottom) and minimized main window (top).

✔ Don't miss the iTunes Visualizer, which offers a groovy light show that dances in time to the music, as shown in Figure 12-3. You turn it on by choosing View⇨Show Visualizer or pressing ⌘+T. If you like the default Visualizer, check out some of iTunes' other built-in Visualizers such as Lathe, Jelly, or Stix, which are available in the Visualizer submenu. Search the web for *"iTunes Visualizer"* to find even more.

TIP

When you get sick of the Visualizer (as you surely will), just choose View⇨Hide Visualizer or press ⌘+T again to make it disappear.

Try this: Choose View⇨Full Screen or press ⌘+F while the Visualizer is running, and the Visualizer takes over your entire screen. Click anywhere on the screen to bring the iTunes window back.

Figure 12-3: The iTunes psychedelic light show is known as the iTunes Visualizer.

Working with Media

iTunes is, first and foremost, a media manager and player, so the next thing I examine is how to get your favorite media *into* iTunes. Of course, you can acquire media a number of ways, depending upon the type of media and where the files reside. For example, you can add song or video files you've downloaded from websites or received as enclosures in e-mail messages. Or you can add songs by ripping audio CDs. You can buy music, movies, TV shows, audiobooks, and apps for your iPhone/iPod/iPad at the iTunes Store (and, to be fair, from many other online vendors, including www.amazon.com and www.audible.com). You can subscribe to free podcasts at the iTunes Store as well. And you can listen to all sorts of music on the Internet radio stations included with iTunes.

REMEMBER

The iTunes Store and Internet radio require that you be connected to the Internet before you can use them.

In the following sections, you discover the various ways to add media — songs, movies, videos, and podcasts — to your iTunes library, followed by a quick course in listening to iTunes Internet radio stations.

Adding songs

You can add songs from pretty much any source, and the way you add a song to iTunes depends on where that song comes from. Here are the most common ways people add their songs:

✔ **Add a song file such as an MP3 or AAC file from your hard drive.** Either drag the document into the iTunes window, as shown in Figure 12-4, or choose File➪Add to Library (shortcut: ⌘+O) and choose the file in the Open File dialog. In either case, the file is added to your iTunes Music library.

Drag

Figure 12-4: Drag and drop songs to the iTunes window to add them to your Music library.

✔ **Add songs from a store-bought or homemade audio CD.** Launch iTunes and insert the CD. A dialog appears, asking whether you would like to import the CD into your iTunes library. Click the Yes button, and the songs on that CD are added to your iTunes Music library. If you don't see a dialog when you insert an audio CD, you can import the songs on that CD anyway. Just select the CD in the Source List on the left, and click the Import button near the bottom-right corner of the iTunes window.

If your computer is connected to the Internet, iTunes magically looks up the song title, artist name, album name, song length, and genre for every song on the CD. Note that this works only for store-bought CDs containing somewhat popular music — and that iTunes might not be able to find information about a very obscure CD by an even more obscure band, even if the disc is store-bought. And in most cases, it can't look up information for homemade (home-burned) audio CDs. Finally, it sometimes gets things wrong.

✔ **Buy your songs from the iTunes Store.** Click the iTunes Store option in the Source List on the left. From the iTunes Store's home screen, you can either click a link or type a song title, album title, artist name, or keyword or phrase in the Search field, and then press Return or Enter to start the search. When you've found an item that interests you, you can double-click any song to listen to a 30-second preview of it or click the Buy Song or Buy Album button to purchase the song or album, as shown in Figure 12-5.

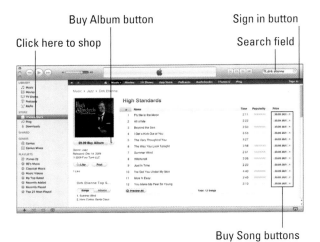

Figure 12-5: At the iTunes Store, buying music is as easy as clicking the Buy Song or Buy Album button.

✔ **Buy your songs from other online vendors such as Amazon.** Amazon (www.amazon.com) has a huge downloadable music store on the web. Its MP3 Downloads section has more than a million songs, with more being added every day. The prices at Amazon are often lower than the prices for the same music at the iTunes Store.

The first time you make a purchase from the iTunes Store, you have to create an Apple account, if you don't already have one. To do so, just click the Sign In button, and then click the Create New Account button in the Sign In dialog. After your account is established, future purchases require just one or two clicks.

Adding movies and videos

To add a video file such as an MOV or MPEG from your hard drive, either drag the file to the iTunes window, as shown in Figure 12-4, earlier in this chapter, or choose File⇨Add to Library (shortcut: ⌘+O) and choose the file in the Open File dialog. In either case, the file is added to your iTunes Movie library.

You can also buy movies, TV shows, and other video content from the iTunes Store. Shopping for video is almost the same as shopping for music. Here are the steps:

1. **Click the iTunes Store in the Source List on the left.**

2. **Either click a link or type a movie title, music-video name, actor or director name, or other keyword or phrase in the Search field, and press Return or Enter to start the search.**

3. **When you find a video item that interests you, double-click it to see a preview, or click the Buy Episode or Buy Video button to purchase the episode or video.**

Adding podcasts

Podcasts are like radio or television shows, except that when you subscribe to them, you can listen to or watch them (using iTunes or your iPod, iPad, or iPhone) at any time you like. Thousands of podcasts are available, and many (or most) are free. To find podcasts, follow these steps:

1. **Click the iTunes Store in the Source List on the left.**

2. **Click the Podcasts link on the store's home screen.**

3. **Click a link on the Podcasts screen, or type a keyword or phrase in the Search field.**

4. **When you find a podcast that appeals to you, double-click it to listen to a preview, click the Get Episode button to download the current episode of that podcast, or click the Subscribe button to receive all future episodes of that podcast automatically.**

   Figure 12-6 shows all these things for the Mac Geek Gab audio podcast from The Mac Observer.

Subscribe button

Get Episode button

Get Info button

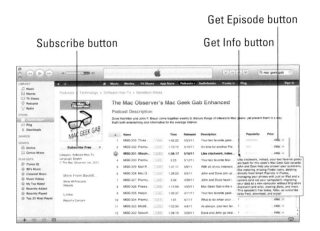

Figure 12-6: The Mac Geek Gab podcast from The Mac Observer.

For more information on most podcasts, just point at the little *i* button on the right side of the description field, as shown in Figure 12-6. You don't even have to click (though you can if you want to).

Subscribing to a podcast is a cool deal. You can configure how often iTunes checks for new episodes (hourly, daily, weekly, or manually) and what to do when new episodes become available (download the most recent one, download all episodes, or do nothing) and how many episodes to keep in your iTunes Library (all, all unplayed, or a specific number between 2 and 10). To specify these settings, choose Podcasts in the Source List, click the name of the podcast you want to configure, and then click the Settings button near the bottom of the window.

Learning from iTunes U

Want to learn something for free? Click the iTunes U tab in the iTunes Store and you can choose from tens of thousands of free audio and video courses, including a good number produced by colleges and universities that include Harvard, Oxford, Stanford, and hundreds more.

You download or subscribe to a course the same way you download or subscribe to a podcast. Check it out the next time you're in the iTunes Store. It's a great way to learn something new for free.

Listening to Internet radio

Streaming audio is delivered over the Internet in real time. Think of streaming audio as being "just like radio" but using the Internet rather than the airwaves as its delivery medium.

iTunes offers two ways to listen to streaming Internet radio stations: the easy way and the less-easy way. The easy way is to listen to one of the hundreds of Internet radio stations included with iTunes. They're even organized into convenient categories such as Alt/Modern Rock, Blues, Country, Jazz, Public, Top 40/Pop, Urban, and many more.

To listen to one of iTunes' included Internet radio stations, click the Radio item in the Source List on the left, and then click a disclosure triangle to the left of each category name to reveal the stations in that category, as shown in Figure 12-7.

Figure 12-7: Listening to All Classic Hits (181.FM), one of 248 streams in the Classic Rock category.

The less-easy way is to find an Internet radio station on your own by surfing or searching the web using Safari (or another web browser). When you find an Internet radio station you'd like to listen to using iTunes, here's how to get it into iTunes:

1. **Copy its address (its URL) by highlighting it and choosing Edit⇨Copy (shortcut: ⌘+C).**

2. **Switch to (or launch) iTunes.**

3. **Choose Advanced⟲Open Stream (shortcut: ⌘+U).**

4. **Choose Edit⟲Paste (shortcut: ⌘+V).**

5. **Click OK.**

The station appears in your iTunes library.

Strangely, there's no way to make an Internet radio station you've added yourself appear in iTunes' Radio category. Apparently, only Apple is allowed to decide what is and is not "radio." Harrumph.

All about Playlists

Playlists are a big deal in iTunes. Playlists let you manage otherwise-unmanageable amounts of media, such as the 12,000+ songs I have in my iTunes library. Playlists let you create subsets of a large collection, so it's easier to enjoy exactly the kind of music you want in iTunes or on your iPod. Two types of playlists exist:

- ✓ **Regular playlists** contain the songs (or videos, podcasts, or radio stations) that you specify by dragging them to the playlist.

- ✓ **Smart playlists,** on the other hand, select songs from your library based on criteria you specify. Furthermore, smart playlists are updated automatically if you add new items to your library that meet the criteria.

All playlists appear in the Source List on the left side of the iTunes window.

Creating a regular playlist

To create a regular playlist, follow these steps:

1. **Either click the + button in the bottom-left corner of the iTunes window or choose File⟲New Playlist (shortcut: ⌘+N).**

A new playlist named "untitled playlist" appears in the Source List.

2. **(Optional) As long as the playlist's name, "untitled playlist," is selected and ready to be edited, you probably want to rename it something meaningful by typing a new name for it.**

If you decide not to name it now, you can double-click it and type a new name anytime.

3. **To add a song to a playlist, click the song in your library and drag it to the playlist's name, and when the playlist's name becomes high-lighted, release the mouse button.**

The song is added to that playlist. Note that adding a song to a playlist doesn't remove it from the library. Conversely, if you delete a song from a playlist, the song isn't deleted from your library. And if you delete a playlist from the Source List, the songs it contains aren't deleted from your library. In other words, think of songs in playlists as being aliases of songs in your library.

4. **Select the playlist in your Source List, and click Play to listen to the songs it contains.**

If you don't want to drag songs to your playlist one by one, there's an easier way. To create a regular playlist that includes songs you've selected from your library, ⌘-click the songs you want to include in the playlist and choose File➪New Playlist from Selection (shortcut: ⌘+Shift+N), as shown in Figure 12-8.

Figure 12-8: How to create a playlist from songs you've selected in your Music library.

You can also use that ⌘-click multiple songs technique to add a batch of songs to an existing playlist.

Working with smart playlists

To create a smart playlist that builds a list based on criteria and updates itself automatically, follow these steps:

1. **Either Option-click the + button in the bottom-left corner of the iTunes window or choose File➪New Smart Playlist (shortcut: ⌘+Option+N).**

The Smart Playlist window appears, as shown in Figure 12-9.

2. **Use the pop-up menus to select the criteria that will build your smart playlist, and click the + button to add more criteria.**

Figure 12-9: The Smart Playlist window lets you specify the criteria for your smart playlist.

3. **Click OK when you're done.**

The playlist appears alongside your other playlists in the Source List. You can tell it's a smart playlist by the gear on its icon. To modify the criteria of a smart playlist after it's been created, hold down the Option key, and double-click the smart playlist to reopen the Smart Playlist window and change the smart playlist's criteria.

Burning a playlist to CD

Another use for playlists is for burning audio CDs you can listen to on almost any audio CD player. The only trick is to make sure the total playing time of the songs in the playlist is less than the capacity of the blank CD you're using, which is usually 74 to 80 minutes. Don't forget to account for the gap between tracks, which is two seconds by default. When you have all the songs you want on your CD on the playlist, choose File⇨Burn Playlist to Disc. The Burn Settings dialog appears.

Note that although the default type of disc iTunes burns is an audio CD, it can also burn two other types — MP3 CDs or data CDs (and DVDs):

- MP3 CD is a special format that can be played in many CD audio players and set-top DVD players. The cool thing about an MP3 CD is that rather than holding a mere 74 to 80 minutes of music, it can hold more than 100 songs! The uncool thing about MP3 CDs is that many older audio CD players won't play them.

- A data CD or DVD is nothing more than a disc formatted to be read and mounted by any computer, Mac or Windows.

If you click the Burn button now, you'll get an audio CD. To burn an MP3 CD or Data CD or DVD, click the appropriate radio button in the Burn Settings dialog.

When you're satisfied, click the Burn button. In a few minutes, you have an audio CD that contains all the songs on the playlist — and plays the songs in the order in which they appeared on the playlist (unless, of course, you elected to burn a data CD or DVD.)

Looking at two specific playlists

There are a couple more relatively new playlists I'd like to draw your attention to: The Genius and the iTunes DJ (that's the feature once known as *Party Shuffle*).

Who is the Genius?

The Genius is actually more of a "what": an iTunes feature that lets you find new music — in your iTunes library or the iTunes Store — that's related to a song of your choosing. Or, as the Genius splash screen you see when you turn the Genius on puts it, "Genius makes playlists and mixes from songs in your library that go great together. And the Genius sidebar recommends music from the iTunes Store that you don't already have." To get started, choose Store⟳Turn On Genius, if you haven't done so already. When you've finished reading, the Genius splash screen appears; click the Turn On Genius button in the bottom-right corner.

Turning Genius on sends information about your iTunes library to Apple. There's a Learn More button on the What Is Genius screen if you want to (d'oh!) learn more about it.

To use Genius, you must (for some unknown reason) have an iTunes Store account, even though the information the Genius sends to Apple about your iTunes library is stored anonymously. And even though no purchase is required, I think it's a dumb requirement — but that's the way it works, take it or leave it.

Assuming you take it, sign into your iTunes Store account if you have one or create one if you don't. After agreeing to the Genius Terms of Service, the Genius gathers info about your iTunes library, sends the info to Apple, and then (finally) delivers your results. When all this is done, you can create Genius playlists and use the Genius sidebar.

How? Glad you asked! Click a song in your Library, and then click the Start Genius button in the bottom-right corner of iTunes main window (that's it in the margin). After a bit of cogitation, iTunes presents you with its Genius selections based on the song you clicked. As shown in Figure 12-10, the song was *Wild Horses* by The Rolling Stones, and the Genius suggested *What Is and What Shall Never Be* by Led Zeppelin, *Keep Talking* by Pink Floyd, and 22 other songs.

Figure 12-10: The Genius suggests songs in the playlist that go nicely with the song the suggestions are based on.

If you're not a fan of British Invasion rock music, let me assure you that most of the songs in the Genius playlist pretty much do "go great together." If you don't have issues with all the legal mumbo jumbo, the iTunes Store account, or sending information about your iTunes library to Apple, give the Genius a try.

What do you say to iTunes DJ?

iTunes DJ is the new and improved version of the iTunes feature once known as Party Shuffle.

The big news here is that iTunes DJ is now actually *fun* at parties. Any guest who has the free Remote application lurking on an iPhone, iPad, or iPod touch can request any song in your iTunes library — and cast votes for songs in the current list. Figure 12-11 shows the iTunes DJ Settings window and the iTunes DJ voting screen on my iPhone.

To start the festivities, first click the iTunes DJ icon in the Playlists section of the Source List. iTunes selects some songs to get you started. Click the Settings button at the bottom right of the window to configure iTunes DJ, as shown in Figure 12-11. Click the Refresh button next to the Settings button to have the iTunes DJ select a fresh batch of songs.

Songs that have votes or songs that have been requested are not replaced when you click the Refresh button, so vote for all the songs you want to keep *before* you click the Refresh button.

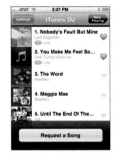

Figure 12-11: The iTunes DJ Settings window in iTunes on your Mac (left) and the iTunes DJ screen on my iPhone (right).

One last thing: If you're new to iTunes, may I suggest exploring the excellent iTunes Tutorials, which you'll find in the Window menu, as shown in Figure 12-12.

Figure 12-12: You can discover a lot about iTunes from its most excellent tutorials.

13

The Multimedia Mac

In This Chapter

▷ Watching DVD movies on your Mac with DVD Player

▷ Watching movies with QuickTime Player

▷ Taking pictures and movies with Photo Booth

▷ Opening, viewing, printing, and converting file formats with Preview

▷ Importing media — photos and videos — to your Mac

"*M*edia content" is more than just music (the topic of Chapter 12), and your Mac is ready, willing, and able to handle almost any type of media (with any type of content) you can throw at it. Which is why, in addition to the aforementioned iTunes, OS X Mountain Lion includes applications for viewing and working with media such as DVD movie discs, QuickTime movie files, as well as graphics in a variety of file formats such as PDF, TIFF, and JPEG.

In this chapter, you look at some bundled applications you can use to work with such media — namely, DVD Player, QuickTime Player, Preview, Photo Booth, and Image Capture — followed by a brief section about importing your own media (photos and videos) into your Mac.

Watching Movies with DVD Player

The DVD Player application includes snazzy little on-screen controllers, as shown in Figure 13-1. They enable you to watch your movies on your Mac in pretty much the same way you'd watch them on your TV with your DVD player.

Figure 13-1: DVD Player's on-screen controller gadgets.

If you've changed your preferences, DVD Player might not start automatically. See the upcoming sidebar for details.

Follow these steps to watch a DVD:

1. **Insert a video DVD into your Mac.**

   This step automatically launches the DVD Player application; if it doesn't, you can double-click the DVD Player icon in the Applications folder or single-click it in Launchpad to start it.

   If you don't see the little controller gadgets, you can choose Window⬄Show Controller (shortcut: ⌘+Option+C) to display the gray remote control–like gadget shown at the top of Figure 13-1, or you can move your cursor to the very bottom of the screen to see the transparent overlay controls shown at the bottom of Figure 13-1.

   The transparent overlay works only in Full Screen mode.

2. **Use the controls to play, stop, or pause your DVD and more.**

   The controls themselves should be self-explanatory to anyone who has ever used a set-top DVD player. If they're not familiar to you, hover the cursor over any control to reveal a tooltip. This works for buttons on either type of controller.

3. **Use the Controller drawer if you like to give DVD Player less commonly used, but still useful, commands.**

   To open (top right, Figure 13-1) or close (top left, Figure 13-1) the little Controller drawer, choose Controls⬄Open/Close Control Drawer, press ⌘+], or click the little pull tab (where you see the arrow cursors in Figure 13-1) and drag.

   The controller might disappear after a few seconds. To make it reappear, jiggle the mouse or choose Window⬄Show Controller (shortcut ⌘+Option+C).

If you're in Full Screen mode, the menu bar won't appear unless you move the cursor to the *top* of the screen. Doing so also makes the chapters/bookmarks/video clips overlay — which you use to choose a chapter, bookmark, or clip — appear just below the menu bar.

And the transparent controller shown at the bottom of Figure 13-1 won't appear unless you move the cursor to the *bottom* of the screen.

So move the cursor to the top of the screen to see the menu bar and chapters/bookmarks/video clips overlay, and move it to the bottom of the screen to see the transparent controller.

4. **Sit back and enjoy the inserted DVD movie on your Mac screen.**

There really isn't much more to it than that, but here are a few other useful tips and hints for using DVD Player:

  ✓ The View menu lets you choose viewing sizes for your movie, including Full Screen, which usually looks best.

  ✓ The Go menu lets you navigate to the DVD menu, beginning of the disc, previous or next chapter, or forward or back 5 seconds, with convenient keyboard shortcuts for each of these commands. It also includes several convenient submenus including Title, Chapter, and (my personal favorite) Bookmarks.

  ✓ To create a bookmark so you can jump directly to this exact moment in the movie, use the on-screen controls to find the point you want to bookmark. Pause at that point and choose Go⇨Bookmarks. The Bookmarks window opens. Click the little plus button at the bottom and then type a name for this bookmark (or accept the name DVD Player offers — Bookmark 1, Bookmark 2, and so). Click the Add button and you're done. Now you can skip right to this frame of the movie from the Bookmarks submenu (in the Go menu) by double-clicking it in the Bookmarks window, or by selecting it in the bookmarks panel of the chapters/bookmarks/video clips overlay.

Move your cursor to the top of the screen in Full Screen mode to see the movie's chapters and bookmarks.

  ✓ Many user-configurable options are available in the Preferences window: DVD Player⇨Preferences (keyboard shortcut: ⌘+,).

  ✓ For more information about almost any DVD Player feature, choose Help⇨DVD Player Help.

Troubleshooting DVD Player settings

DVD Player is a pretty-easy-to-use application. However, you might find it's not working as expected for a couple of reasons:

✔ **You've changed the default setting:** The default setting, Open DVD Player when You Insert a Video DVD — is in the CDs & DVDs System Preferences pane, which you find in the System Preferences application.

✔ **Certain external DVD drives won't be recognized by DVD Player:** If that's the case, you need to use either the viewing software that came with the drive or a program such as VLC (VideoLAN Client).

✔ **Your Mac might not have a DVD player (although unless you have a MacBook Air or a Mac mini, it's unlikely):** If you choose ⬛⏵About This Mac in the Finder, the About This Mac window has a More Info button. Click it to launch an application called System Information. Or you can launch System Information (which you find in the Utilities folder) the old-fashioned way — by double-clicking its icon. Either way, it can tell you whether you have a DVD drive in your Mac. Just click the Disc Burning item in the contents column on the left; the details appear on the right.

Playing Movies and Music in QuickTime Player

QuickTime is Apple's technology for digital media creation, delivery, and playback. It's used in a myriad of ways by programs such as Apple's iMovie, by websites such as YouTube (www.youtube.com), and in training videos delivered on CD or DVD.

QuickTime Player is the OS X application that lets you view QuickTime movies as well as streaming audio and video, QuickTime VR (Virtual Reality), and many types of audio files as well. The quickest way to launch it is by clicking its icon in the Dock. It also opens automatically when you open some QuickTime movie document files.

I say "some" QuickTime movies because some will open QuickTime Player and others will open iTunes. To change the app that opens for a particular movie, right-click or Control-click its icon in the Finder and choose the application you prefer from the Open With submenu. This opens the file with that program this one time only. To make the change permanent, press Option, and the Open With command becomes the Always Open With command.

To play a QuickTime movie, merely double-click its icon — and QuickTime Player (or iTunes) launches itself.

Using QuickTime Player couldn't be easier. All its important controls are available right in the player window, as shown in Figure 13-2.

Figure 13-2: QuickTime Player is simple to use.

Here are a few more QuickTime Player features you might find useful:

- ✔ **The Movie Inspector window** (Window➪Show/Hide Movie Inspector or ⌘+I) provides a lot of useful information about the current movie, such as its location on your hard drive, file format, frames per second, file size, and duration.

- ✔ **The Trim control** (Edit➪Trim or ⌘+T) lets you delete frames from the beginning and/or end of a movie.

- ✔ **The Share Menu** lets you send your movies to others via the Mail or Messages apps; publish them to iTunes so you can watch them on your iPods, iPhones, and AppleTVs; send them to iMovie for additional editing and post-production work; or upload them to YouTube, Vimeo, Flickr, or Facebook, and other similar sites.

See Chapter 17 details about Mountain Lion's cool new AirPlay Mirroring option, which lets you "mirror" what's on your Mac screen and view it on an HDTV wirelessly. The only thing you need is an Apple TV ($99) connected to your HDTV.

You're the Star with Photo Booth

The Photo Booth application provides all the fun of an old-time (or new-time) photo booth like the ones you sometimes see in malls or stores. It lets you shoot one photo, a burst of four photos in a row, or shoot a movie using your Mac's built-in camera. If yours is one of the rare Macs with no built-in camera (such as the Mac Mini), or you own a better USB or FireWire webcam than the built-in model, you'll be pleased to hear that most USB and FireWire webcams work with Photo Booth right out of the box with no drivers or other software necessary. Just launch Photo Booth and look in the Camera menu, where any compatible cameras appear.

If you only have one camera available — mine's called FaceTime HD Camera (Built-in) — it's selected automatically so you shouldn't have to even bother with the Camera menu.

Photo Booth couldn't be easier to use. Start by clicking one of the three buttons in the lower-left corner of the Photo Booth window: Burst (of four photos), Single Photo, or Movie, and then click the big red camera button to take a picture, as shown in Figure 13-3.

Figure 13-3: Photo Booth about to take a picture of yours truly.

Before you shoot, you might want to explore the five pages of special effects — Sepia Tone, Color Pencil, Pop Art, and dozens more — by clicking the Effects button (lower right), and then clicking the particular effect you want to try. If you like it, click the big red camera button and shoot a picture, pictures, or video; if you don't, click the Effects button again and click another effect. Or, click the Normal effect in the center of all the Effects pages, if you prefer to shoot with no effects.

Photo Booth includes a feature called Screen Flash, which uses your computer display as a camera flash by turning the screen all-white as it shoots the photo. If *your* screen isn't flashing when you shoot, look in the Camera menu for the Enable Screen Flash command. If there's not a check mark before its name, select it and there will be. Finally, Screen Flash is (understandably) disabled when shooting movies.

After you shoot, your pictures or movies drop into the tray at the bottom of the window (there are two in Figure 13-3). You can then select one or more photos in the tray and then do any of the following:

✔ Delete them by pressing the Delete or Backspace key.

✔ Share them by clicking the Share button (shown in the margin), which replaces the Effects button when one or more photos are selected in the tray.

✔ Export them as JPEG files by choosing File➪Export.

✔ Print them by choosing File➪Print or pressing ⌘+P.

✔ Drag them from the tray to the Desktop, a folder, an e-mail, or iMessage, where they appear as JPEG files, or drag them onto the icon (Dock or Applications Folder) of an image editor such as iPhoto.

So that's the scoop on Photo Booth. It's fun and easy, and if you've got a camera (as most of you do), you should definitely launch Photo Booth and give it a try.

If you have kids that are old enough to trust with a Mac, Photo Booth and its effects will entertain them for hours (or, more likely, for a few minutes). It's guaranteed to entertain and delight kids of all ages the first time they play with it.

Viewing and Converting Images and PDFs in Preview

You use Preview to open, view, and print PDFs as well as most graphics files (TIFF, JPEG, PICT, and so on). *PDF files* are formatted documents that can include text and images. User manuals, books, and the like are often distributed as PDF files. You can't edit the existing text in a PDF file with Preview, but you can leaf through its pages, annotate and mark it up, and print it. You can often select text and graphics in a PDF file, copy them to the Clipboard (⌘+C), and paste (⌘+V) them into documents in other applications. It's also the application that pops open when you click the Preview button in the Print dialog, as described in Chapter 15.

Actually, that's not entirely true. You can edit one certain type of PDF file: a form that has blank fields. Preview allows you to fill in the blanks and then resave the document. And although it's technically not editing, you can annotate a PDF document by using the Annotate tools on the toolbar.

One of the most useful things Preview can do is change a graphic file in one file format into one with a different file format. For example, say you're signing up for a website and want to add a picture to your profile. The website requires pictures in the JPEG file format, but the picture file on your hard drive that you'd like to use is in the TIFF file format. Preview can handle the conversion for you:

1. **Open the TIFF file with Preview by double-clicking the file.**

   If another program (such as Adobe Photoshop) opens instead of Preview, drag the TIFF document onto the Preview icon or launch Preview and choose File⇨Open (shortcut: ⌘+O) to open the TIFF file.

2. **Choose File⇨Export.**

3. **Choose the appropriate file format — such as JPEG — from the Format pop-up menu, as shown in Figure 13-4.**

Figure 13-4: Preview makes it easy to convert a TIFF graphic file into a JPEG graphic file.

4. **If you want to make sure you don't confuse your original image with the one in the new format, change the name of your file in the Export As field, too.**

5. **Click Save.**

As you can see in Figure 13-4, Preview lets you convert any file it can open to any of the following file formats: JPEG, JPEG-2000, OpenEXR, PDF, PNG, and TIFF.

Chances are good that you'll never need to convert a file to most of these formats, but it's nice to know that you could if you needed to.

Almost every OS X program with a Print command lets you save your document as a PDF file. Just click and hold the PDF button (found in all Print dialogs) and choose Save As PDF. Then, should you ever need to convert that PDF file to a different file format, you can do so by using the preceding steps.

Importing Media

Chances are good that you'll want to import pictures or video from your digital camera or DV camcorder someday. It's a piece of cake. So in the following sections, I show you how easy it is to get your digital photos into your Mac and help you get started with digital video (which is a bit more complex).

In the sections that follow, I focus on applications that are a part of OS X. Technically, that doesn't include the iLife applications. What I mean is that if you bought an OS X Mountain Lion upgrade in a box at a store, it doesn't include iLife applications, such as iMovie and iPhoto. Your Mac almost certainly came with the iLife suite preinstalled, but depending upon how old your Mac is, you might not have the current versions, and the various versions all work slightly differently. See the nearby sidebar "Living the iLife" for more details about iLife.

Downloading photos from a camera

This is the Mac I'm talking about, so of course, getting pictures from your digital camera onto your hard drive is a pretty simple task. Here's how to do it step by step using Image Capture:

1. **Turn on the camera, and set it to review or playback mode.**

   This step might not be necessary for some cameras. It was for my old Olympus, but isn't for my Nikon Coolpix P1.

2. **Connect the camera to your Mac with its USB cable.**

   At this point, Image Capture may launch automatically, or, if you have iPhoto, it may launch instead.

   If you have both programs on your hard drive and the wrong one opens when you connect your camera, you can change that behavior in Image Capture's Device Settings pane. Launch Image Capture (it's in your Applications folder) if it didn't launch when you connected your camera. Now choose the application you prefer for photo management (Image Capture in Figure 13-5; other options could include iPhoto, Aperture, Photoshop, Photoshop Elements, Adobe Bridge, or whatever photo-management app you happen to have installed on your hard disk) from the Connecting This Camera Opens pop-up menu.

3. **From the Image Capture window, you can either click Import All to download all the photos in your camera or click Import to import only the select photos, as shown in Figure 13-5.**

- *To choose contiguous photos,* click the first photo you want to download, press Shift, and then click the last photo you want to download.

- *To choose noncontiguous photos,* press ⌘ and click each photo you want to download. Either way, an orange highlight shows you which photos are going to be downloaded when you click the Download button (such as the first, third, fourth, and sixth photos in Figure 13-5).

Eject Button   Save to Folder

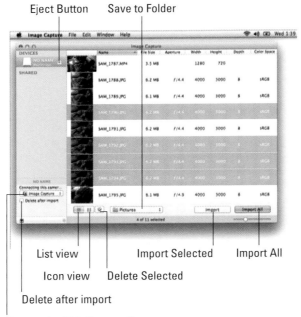

List view   Import Selected   Import All

Icon view   Delete Selected

Delete after import

Connecting This Camera Opens:

Figure 13-5: I've told my Mac to open Image Capture when I connect this camera.

In Figure 13-5, the Download To pop-up menu is set to the Pictures folder, which is the default setting. If you were to click the Download or Download All button now, Image Capture would download the photos in your camera to the Pictures folder inside your Home folder.

If you want to delete the photos from your camera after they're downloaded to your hard drive, select the photos you want to delete, and click the Delete button. To delete all photos after you've imported them, check the Delete after Import check box.

If a disk icon, often named No Name (see Figure 13-5), appears in the Devices section of the Sidebar when you plugged in your camera, you have to eject that disk by clicking the Eject Disk icon next to its name in the Image Capture window (or by ejecting it in the Finder in the usual way) before you disconnect your camera, or you could lose or damage files in your camera. So try to remember. If you don't, Image Capture scolds you with the scary warning dialog shown in Figure 13-6.

Figure 13-6: This warning means you forgot to eject your camera's disk.

Downloading DV video from a camcorder

Getting video from a DV camcorder to your hard drive is almost as easy as importing photos from your digital camera. Although it's beyond the scope of this book to explain how you download video, the following tips can help you get started.

iMovie works well for downloading video from miniDV and HD camcorders that include output via FireWire or USB 2.

If you do plan to use iMovie, don't forget about the built-in Help system (⌘+Shift+?). Here, you find extensive assistance, as shown in Figure 13-7 which is the main Help page for iMovie.

Never insert a mini-DVD into a slot-loading optical drive like the ones in all Macs (except the Mac Pro). If your camcorder records on mini-DVDs, you'll need to spring for a tray-loading optical drive.

Living the iLife

In previous editions of this book, I called iLife "one of the fantastic bargains in software" and said, "if you had to buy all these programs from other vendors (or for a Windows PC), you'd pay a whole lot more." And that was when the only way to get iLife was on a DVD for $79.

You can still get iLife '11 (latest version as of this writing) on DVD for $79, or iMovie, iPhoto, and GarageBand are available a la carte in the Mac App Store for $14.99 each. At present, you can't buy iWeb or iDVD a la carte, but both are included if you buy the suite on disc.

Figure 13-7: Don't forget that help is just a click (or a keystroke) away.

So if you don't have the latest version of iLife on your hard drive, take a look at the features and programs it includes (www.apple.com/ilife) and consider whether you'd benefit from all the new goodies you don't currently have.

Words and Letters

In This Chapter

▶ Processing words with TextEdit

▶ Finding out all about Mountain Lion's fonts

▶ Managing fonts with Font Book

*A*s I discuss in previous chapters, your Mac is well equipped for creating and managing media — music, movies, DVDs, and photos. But your Mac is also ready to handle more common tasks, such as typing a letter or writing an essay.

I think it's fair to say that Mountain Lion's TextEdit application is all that many users will ever need for writing letters or essays.

If you need more control over your pages, try Pages from Apple (available in the Mac App Store for $19.99).

Furthermore, your Mountain Lion comes with a wide variety of fonts (sometimes called *typefaces*), plus a handy little app called Font Book for managing those fonts. Fonts allow you to change the way text looks on the screen and the printed page.

In this chapter, you look at the OS X Mountain Lion text-composition and editing program, called TextEdit, and then explore fonts and how to manage them.

ng and Composing a Document.rtf

ar,

e first sentence in a document called, "Creating and Composing
nt.rtf." This is the second sentence in a document called, "Creati
ling a Document.rtf." **This is the third sentence and it is now B**

This is the first sentence in the second paragraph
of a document called, "Creating and Composing a
Document.rtf." This is the second sentence in the
second paragraph of a document called, "Creating
nd Composing a Document.rtf."

sentence in the third paragraph. And so on...

Processing Words with TextEdit

TextEdit is a word processor/text editor that you can use to write letters, scribble notes, or open Read Me files. It's not as sophisticated as Microsoft Word (or Apple's Pages, Quark Xpress, or Adobe InDesign, for that matter), but you can definitely use it for light word processing and text editing. TextEdit is capable of performing a respectable amount of text formatting, and it can even check your spelling and read text to you in a natural-sounding (if somewhat creepy) voice.

TextEdit supports images, too. Just copy an image from another program and paste it into a TextEdit document. Or you can drag-and-drop an image into a TextEdit document from many applications.

TextEdit can even open Microsoft Word documents (.doc and .docx files). This is fabulous if you don't happen to have a copy of Microsoft Word on your hard drive.

If you like Microsoft Word, you may enjoy my *Office 2011 For Mac For Dummies*, also from Wiley.

Like all apps included with Mountain Lion, you find TextEdit in the Applications folder at root level on your hard disk.

The Dock doesn't have a TextEdit icon but if you like it, use it regularly, or would just like to have it in your Dock, either drag its icon from the Applications folder to the left side of the Dock or launch it, right-click (or Control-click) its Dock icon, and then choose Keep in Dock.

Creating and composing a document

In every version of TextEdit I can ever remember, when you launched TextEdit, the next thing you saw was a blank, untitled document. Mountain Lion's rendition of TextEdit, however, presents you with an Open dialog (which you may recall from Chapter 6). If you want to open an existing document, select it and click the Open button near the bottom-right corner of the dialog. Or, if you want a new, blank document, click the New Document button near the lower-left corner of the dialog; choose File➪New; or press ⌘+N.

You should now have a blank document called Untitled on your screen. Let its name — Untitled — be a message to you that before you begin working on this document you should probably give it a name and save it to your hard drive. To do so now, choose File➪Save or press ⌘+S. (If you're new to Mac OS Mountain Lion Save sheets, flip to Chapter 6 for details.)

As you work with the document, it's a good idea to save it every few minutes, just in case. After you've named a file, all you need to do to save its current state is choose File➪Save a Version or press ⌘+S.

TextEdit uses Mountain Lion's version support and autosave features, so your work is saved on the fly. Don't be lulled into a false sense of security; most third-party apps don't support this feature. At least not yet. (Chapter 6 has the lowdown on versions and saving.)

RANT & RAVE

So why would I need Microsoft Word?

The free word processor included with OS X Mountain Lion can not only open Microsoft Word files — even ones in the latest file format, `.docx` — but it can modify and save them again, too.

Why does this make me rave and marvel? Because now, even if you don't own a copy of Microsoft Word, you can open documents created by others using Word, edit, and resave them — all *without* having to buy your own copy of Word.

Don't get me wrong: If you need Microsoft Word, you need Microsoft Word. I use it as much as any other program, and there's nothing else like it. Yes, it's a bit bloated and may be overkill for some, but since TextEdit doesn't support many of Word's features — including

but not limited to comprehensive style sheets, revision tracking, and embedded graphics editing and effects — TextEdit really is no replacement for Word.

For example, here is a Word document in TextEdit (left) and Microsoft Word (right).

Note the Reviewing Toolbar in the Word version and all the red and pink that denotes changed text; TextEdit offers no revision tracking or tools at all. To TextEdit's credit, the two versions look remarkably alike otherwise.

So TextEdit lets you open, edit, and save Word documents, which may be all you need. If you think you can get by without a full-featured, professional-quality writing tool like Word, this freebie (TextEdit) may very well be the perfect word processor for you.

Now begin typing your text. When you type text in a word processor, you should know a few handy things:

- ✏ **Press the Return (or Enter) key only when you reach the end of a paragraph.** You don't need to press Return at the end of a line of text; the program automatically wraps your text to the next line, keeping things neat and tidy.

- ✏ **Type a single space after the punctuation mark at the end of a sentence, regardless of what your typing teacher might have told you.** Word processors and typewriters aren't the same. With a typewriter, you want two spaces at the end of a sentence; with a word processor, you don't. (Typewriters use *fixed-width* fonts; computers mostly use fonts with variable widths. If you put two spaces at the end of a sentence in a computer-generated document, the gap looks too wide.) Trust me on this one.

- ✏ **Limit most documents to a maximum of two different fonts.** OS X offers you a wide selection of fonts — but that doesn't mean you have to use them all in one document.

To put certain characters in your TextEdit document, choose Edit⟹Special Characters (shortcut: ⌘+Option+T). This command opens the Character Palette, where you can choose special characters such as mathematical symbols, arrows, ornaments, stars, accented Latin characters, and so on. To insert a character into your document at the insertion point, simply click it and click the Insert button.

Working with text

TextEdit operates on the "select, then operate" principle, as do most Macintosh programs, including the Finder. Before you can affect text in your document — change its font face, style, size, margins, and so on — you need to select the text you want to operate on.

You can use several methods to select text in a document:

- ✏ If you double-click a word, the word is selected.

- ✏ If you triple-click a word, the entire paragraph that contains the word is selected.

- ✏ You can click anywhere in the document, hold down the Shift key, and then click again somewhere else in the document, and everything between the two clicks will be selected.

- ✏ You can click anywhere in the document, hold down the Shift key, and use the keyboard arrow keys to extend the selection. Figure 14-1 shows some text that is selected.

Give all these methods of selecting text a try, decide which ones feel most comfortable, and then memorize them for future use.

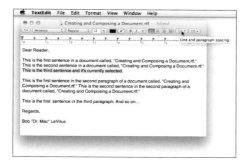

Figure 14-1: A highlighted sentence means it's currently selected.

Rather than bore you with a rundown of what the buttons on TextEdit's toolbar do, just hover the cursor over any item to display its tooltip, as I've done for the Line and Paragraph Spacing drop-down menu in Figure 14-1.

When text is selected, you can operate on it. For example, you can use the Format menu's Font submenu to make text Bold, Italic, Outlined or Underlined, as shown in Figure 14-2.

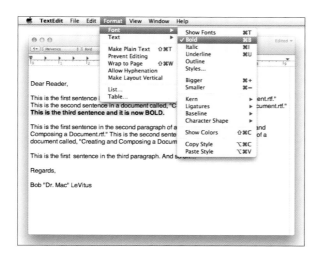

Figure 14-2: Only the selected sentence is affected by these formatting commands.

Another way I could have applied the Bold style to the text in Figure 14-2 is by clicking the B (for Bold) button on the toolbar. Note that the toolbar is only visible when working on a Rich Text document; if you were to choose Format⇨Make Plain Text (⌘+Shift+T), the toolbar would disappear.

The same idea applies to tabs and margins. In Figure 14-3, I've dragged the left-margin markers from 0 inches to the one inch mark. Notice that the selected text is now indented by one inch.

Left margin marker   Right margin marker

Figure 14-3: The selected paragraph is now indented.

Select some text in your document, and try all the items in the Format menu's Font and Text submenus. As you see, you have a great deal of control over the way your words appear on the screen. And because TextEdit, like most Macintosh software, is WYSIWYG (What You See Is What You Get), when you print the document (by choosing File⇪Print), the printed version should look exactly like the version you see on the screen. For help with printing, see Chapter 15.

Before you print your masterpiece, however, you might want to check your spelling and grammar — something that TextEdit makes extremely simple. Merely choose Edit⇪Spelling and Grammar⇪Check Document Now or press ⌘+; (semicolon). TextEdit highlights and underlines what it perceives to be mistakes in your document. Right-click (or Control-click) to correct the error, as shown in Figure 14-4.

Don't put too much faith in Mountain Lion's spelling and grammar checker. It's good, but not perfect, and no substitute for a good proofreading.

Adding graphics to documents

Last but not least, you have a couple of ways to add pictures to a TextEdit document. The first works as follows:

 1. **Copy a picture in another program — Preview, Safari, or whatever.**

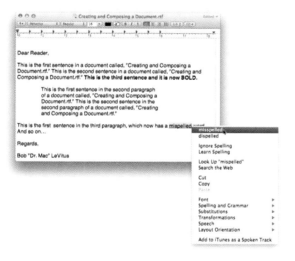

Figure 14-4: Right-click (or Control-click) to correct a spelling or grammar error.

2. **Put the cursor where you want the picture to appear in your TextEdit document.**

3. **Choose Edit⇨Paste.**

   The picture magically appears on the page.

Or you can drag a picture from the Finder or some application (such as Safari or Mail) to a TextEdit document, as I did in Figure 14-5.

Drag file from here
(the Desktop or a folder)

Drag file to here
(the TextEdit document)

Figure 14-5: Dragging a picture into a TextEdit document.

Font Mania

You can jazz up your documents — or make them a little more serious — with different fonts. To a computer user, *font* means *typeface* — what the text characters look like. Although professional typographers will scream at my generalization, I'll go with that definition for now.

Tens of thousands of different fonts are available for the Macintosh. You don't want to use the same font for both a garage-sale flyer and a résumé, right? Luckily for you, OS X comes with hundreds of fonts. Some are pretty predictable, such as Times New Roman (the font of this paragraph), but OS X gives you some artsy ones, too, such as Brush Script. If you *really* get into fonts, you can buy single fonts and font collections anywhere you can buy software. Plenty of shareware and public-domain fonts are also available from online services and user groups. Some people have thousands of fonts. (Maybe they need to get out more.)

The preinstalled fonts live in two different folders, both called Fonts. One is in the Library folder at root level on your hard drive; the other is in the Library subfolder within the System folder.

OS X actually has four Font folders. A third one, also called Fonts, is in the (hidden) Library folder in your home directory. The upcoming section explains the subtle distinctions among those three locations. The fourth one is in the Network/Library folder, and you see it only when you're connected to a NetBoot network server.

Types of fonts

You can find many font formats with names like OpenType, Mac TrueType, Windows TrueType, PostScript Type 1, bitmap, and dfont. No problem — OS X supports them all. In fact, the only font format I know that Mountain Lion *doesn't* support is PostScript Type 3.

That said, the three most common formats for Macs are TrueType, PostScript Type 1, and OpenType.

- **TrueType fonts:** These standard-issue Apple fonts come with OS X. They're in common use on Macs as well as on Windows machines. That's partly because these fonts are *scalable:* They use only a single outline per font, and your Mac can make their characters bigger or smaller when you choose a font size in a program.

- **Type 1 fonts:** These fonts are often referred to as *PostScript Type 1* fonts, and they're the standard for desktop publishing on the Mac (as well as Windows and Unix). Tens of thousands of Type 1 fonts are available. (Not nearly as many high-quality TrueType fonts exist.)

Type 1 fonts come in two pieces:

- A *suitcase* file to hold the bitmap that tells the computer how to draw the font on your screen.

- A *printer font* that tells the printer how to print the font on a page.

Some Type 1 fonts come with two, three, or four printer fonts, which usually have related names. Just keep all the parts together, and they should just work.

✔ **OpenType fonts:** OpenType fonts are really TrueType fonts in which PostScript information is embedded. This gives you the greater typographic control that high-end typesetters require while keeping the one-file convenience of TrueType. OpenType is one of the most popular file formats and the one favored by most major type vendors including Adobe and Linotype.

Managing your fonts with Font Book

Font Book lets you view your installed fonts, install new fonts, group your fonts into collections, and enable and disable installed fonts. As usual, you find the Font Book application in the Applications folder at root level on your hard disk.

The easiest way to install a new font is to double-click it in the Finder. Font Book opens and displays the font. Click the Install Font button to install the font.

Other ways you can install new fonts are to choose File⇨Add Fonts or press ⌘+O. A standard Open dialog allows you to select a font or fonts to be installed.

Note that, by default, new fonts are installed in your Home folder's Fonts folder, which is inside your invisible Library folder (`Users/Home/Library/Fonts`). You can change the default installation location in the Font Book preferences pane (Font Book⇨Preferences or ⌘+,).

To view a font or font family, click its name in the Font list. Click the disclosure triangle before the name of a font to see all the variants that are installed.

To change the size of the viewed font, click the triangle next to the font size (18 in Figure 14-6) in the top-right corner of the Font Book window and choose a new size from the drop-down list that appears, or type a different number where the number 18 appears in Figure 14-6, or move the size slider — the white dot and gray line that run along the right edge of the window — up or down.

To *disable* a font so it no longer appears on any applications' Font menus, choose Edit⇨Disable or click the Disable button (the check mark in a square button) at the bottom of the window.

Figure 14-6: Click a font in the Font list to display its characters in the right pane.

To enable a previously disabled font, choose Edit⇨Enable or click the Enable button (same as the Disable button).

Mountain Lion's Font Book looks out for your best interests; it won't allow you to disable or delete any fonts required by Mountain Lion — including (but not limited to) Lucida Grande, Helvetica, and Helvetica Neue.

Installing fonts manually

To install any new font manually, drag its icon into one of the two Fonts folders that you have access to. Why might you want to install them manually? If you install a font via the double-click-and-use-Font Book method, the font will be installed in your `Home/Library/Fonts` folder, and available only to you.

If you want other users to be able to access the new font, drag the font's icon to the Fonts subfolder inside the Library folder, which is at the root level of your hard drive. This Fonts folder has universal access. Or, if you usually want to install fonts for everyone, change the Default Install Location in Font Book Preferences (Font Book⇨Preferences or ⌘+,).

The Fonts folder in the Library inside the System folder is reserved for OS X and can't be modified easily. If you try to remove a font from it — or add one, for that matter — you first have to authenticate yourself as an administrator. Do yourself a favor, and *never* remove fonts from `/System/Library/Fonts`. You can really screw up your Mountain Lion operating system if you remove the wrong font. So don't go messing with the fonts in folders unless you know what you're doing. Otherwise, just use Font Book, which prevents you from doing anything bad to fonts.

Part IV
Making This Mountain Lion Your Very Own

In this part . . .

1 start this part by helping you decipher the myriad Print options so you can become a modern-day Gutenberg. Then you get a look at all the different ways you can share data with others and access data other users have shared. Finally, you look at a bunch of other cool technologies included with OS X Mountain Lion to help you make your big cat look, feel, and act just the way you want her to.

There is something in this part for everyone, so don't touch that dial.

15

Publish or Perish: The Fail-Safe Guide to Printing

In This Chapter

▶ Connecting a printer

▶ Using Page Setup to prepare your document for printing

▶ Printing to most printers

▶ Mastering the printing process

*W*hen you want to get what's on your screen onto paper, printing under OS X should be as simple as pressing the keyboard shortcut ⌘+P and pressing Return or Enter. Happily, that's usually just how easy printing something is; when it isn't, printing can turn into a raging nightmare. If you configure your printer and printing software properly, however, printing is pretty darn simple.

In this chapter, I scare away the bogeymen to help you avoid any printing nightmares. I walk you through the entire process as though you just unpacked a new printer and plugged it in.

Before Diving In . . .

Before I even start talking about hooking up printers, you should know a few essential things. So here's a little list that tells you just what those things are:

> ✔ **Read the documentation that came with your printer.** Hundreds of different printer makes and models are available for the Mac, so if I contradict something in your printer manual, follow your manual's instructions first. If that effort doesn't work, try the techniques in this chapter.

✔ **The Print and Page Setup sheets differ slightly (or even greatly) from program to program and from printer to printer.** Although the examples I show you in this chapter are representative of what you'll probably encounter, you might come across sheets that look a bit different. For example, the Print and Page Setup sheets for Microsoft Word include choices that I don't cover in this chapter (such as Even or Odd Pages Only, Print Hidden Text, and Print Selection Only). If you see commands in your Print or Page Setup sheet that I don't explain here, they're specific to that application; look within its documentation for an explanation. Similarly, many graphics apps — such as Apple's iPhoto, Adobe Illustrator, and Photoshop — have added numerous gadgets, list boxes, radio buttons, and so forth to their Print dialogs, to the point where you might not even recognize them as Print dialogs.

✔ **Don't forget about the Help.** Of course it's built into Mountain Lion and better than ever, but many third-party programs support this excellent Apple technology, which can be the fastest way to figure out a feature that has you stumped. So don't forget to check out the Help menu before you panic. (I cover the Help menu in Chapter 1.)

Ready: Connecting and Adding Your Printer

Before you can even think about printing something, you have to connect a printer to your Mac and tell OS X that the printer exists.

If you have a printer and are able to print documents already, you can skip ahead to the "Set: Setting Up Your Document with Page Setup" section. The info between here and there pertains only to setting up a *brand-new* printer — one that still has its manual.

Connecting your printer

Once again, I must remind you that you *could* connect your Mac to thousands of printer models, and each one is a little different from the next. In other words, if what you're about to read doesn't work with the printer you're trying to connect, RTFM *(Read the Fine Manual)*. It should tell you how to load your ink or toner cartridges.

That said, here are some very general steps to connect a printer to your Mac:

1. **Connect the printer to your Mac with the cable snugly attached at both ends (printer and Mac).**

   For your printer to work, you have to somehow connect it to a data source. (Think of your phone — you can't receive calls without some sort of connector between callers.)

What about wireless printing?

For those who wish to print wirelessly over Wi-Fi (assuming your printer supports it), I'm afraid you're on your own. Here's why: The procedure for setting up a Wi-Fi printer is different for each manufacturer; hence, I can't provide such instructions in the allotted number of pages. Here's some good news, though: I have set up a number of Epson, Canon, HP, and Kodak Wi-Fi printers and have never had a problem. Each was easy to set up for wireless printing by following the instructions that came with the printer. If you don't have the instructions or can't find them, visit the manufacturer's website and search for your printer model's manual.

2. **Plug the printer's AC power cord into a power outlet.**

   Yup, I mean the regular kind of outlet in the wall; on a power strip; or, best of all, on a UPS (Uninterruptible Power Supply). Some printers require you to plug one end of the AC power cord into the printer; others have the AC power cord attached permanently. The point is that your printer won't work if it's not connected to a power source.

3. **Turn on your printer.**

   Look in the manual if you can't find the power switch.

4. **If your printer came with software, install it on your Mac, following the instructions that came with the printer.**

5. **(Optional) Restart your Mac.**

   You need to do this only if you had to install software and the Installer told you to restart.

Any port on a Mac

Mac technology has changed dramatically since the previous editions of this book, when I used to say, "Begin by connecting the printer to the Printer port (with both the Mac and the printer turned off — but you knew that)." Ah, nostalgia. Now I tell you, "You need to plug the printer cable into the appropriate port. . . ." You see, these days, printers might connect via a USB, Ethernet, or (rarely) FireWire port. Or it might connect wirelessly via Wi-Fi or Bluetooth.

Typically, your printer connects to your machine via USB. If your printer didn't come with a cable that fits into one of the ports on your Mac, contact your printer manufacturer and ask for one; it's cheesy not to provide the proper cable with a printer.

Setting up a printer for the first time

After you connect your computer and printer, provide a power source for your printer, and install the software for your printer, you're ready . . . to configure your Mac. You have to do that so your Mac and your printer can talk to each other.

Many, if not all, of the steps involving the Print & Scan System Preferences pane require that your printer be turned on and warmed up (that is, already run through its diagnostics and startup cycle) beforehand. So before doing anything else, make sure your printer is turned on, warmed up, and connected to your Mac.

The first time you connect your printer, you may see an alert asking whether you want to download and install software for your printer. My printer is an Epson Workforce 630, as shown in Figure 15-1.

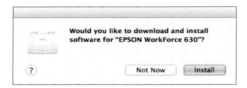

Would you like to download and install software for "EPSON WorkForce 630"?

Not Now   Install

Figure 15-1: Connecting a printer to your Mac.

You do, so click the Install button. At this point, you may see a License Agreement window. If so, click the Agree button to proceed. (You may click Disagree if you wish, but that halts the installation process.)

After clicking the Install and Agree buttons, a Software Update window may appear and tell you it's finding software. If it does, just leave it alone; it disappears after a minute or two. Don't click the Stop button unless you want to abort the installation.

If you've connected a new printer and *didn't* see an alert like the one shown in Figure 15-1, it's not an issue; just follow the upcoming instructions.

Here are the steps to set up a printer for the first time:

1. **Launch System Preferences, click the Print & Scan icon, and then click your printer's name in the Printers list on the left side of the window.**

   You can open System Preferences from the menu, or launch it from the Applications folder, Dock, or Launchpad.

Mountain Lion is a pretty smart cat; it should have already recognized your printer at this point. If so, your printer's name appears in the Printers list of the Print & Scan System Preferences pane, as shown in Figure 15-2. My printer's name, as you can see in Figure 15-2, is Epson WorkForce 630.

Figure 15-2: Printers Mountain Lion recognizes; click the plus sign (+) button to add other printers.

If your printer *isn't* in the list at this point, click the + button at the bottom of the Printers list and either select it from the list of nearby printers or choose Add Other Printer or Scanner.

If you still can't "see" your printer, you probably need to install (or reinstall) its driver software manually, either from the CD or DVD that came with the printer or by downloading the latest driver software from your printer manufacturer's website. See the nearby sidebar "Go for a driver" for more on drivers.

2. **Select the printer you want selected by default when you print documents from the Default Printer pop-up menu (Last Used is selected in Figure 15-2).**

3. **Select the default paper size you want to use with this printer from the Default Paper Size menu (usually US Letter if you live in the United States).**

That's all there is to it. Close System Preferences, and you're ready to print your first document! Before you do, however, make sure you have the document set up to look just the way you want it to look printed. Read through "Set: Setting Up Your Document with Page Setup" for more info.

Go for a driver

Many printer manufacturers periodically introduce new drivers with enhanced functionality. So the driver software on the CD in the box with your printer could be out of date when you buy that printer. Check whether the CD contains the latest version of the printer driver on the manufacturer's website, and download a more recent version of the driver if necessary.

Apple includes a library of printer drivers with Mountain Lion, which cover most popular printer brands and models. These drivers are installed by default. Mountain Lion also checks to see whether a newer driver is available — for every driver in its library — and if it finds one, offers to download and install the new driver (refer to Figure 15-1).

If you chose *not* to install some or all of them when you installed OS X Mountain Lion, you almost certainly need to manually install the appropriate printer drivers before your printer appears in the Print & Scan System Preferences pane's Printers list.

One last thing: Printer sharing

To share a printer with others on your local area wired or wireless network, select it in the Printers list on the left side of the Print & Scan System Preferences pane, and then click the Share This Printer on the Network check box.

If the lock in the bottom-left corner of the Print & Scan pane is locked, you may have to click it and provide your administrator password before you can select the check box.

If Printer Sharing is not enabled, an alert that says Printer Sharing Is Turned Off appears below the check box, as shown in Figure 15-2. Click the Sharing Preferences button on the right and the Sharing System Preferences pane (which I discuss in much detail in Chapter 16) replaces the Print & Scan pane. Just select the check box next to Printer Sharing to turn it on.

Set: Setting Up Your Document with Page Setup

After you set up your printer, the hard part is over. You should be able to print a document quickly and easily — right? Not so fast, bucko. Read here how the features in the Page Setup sheet can help you solve most basic printing problems.

Many programs have a Page Setup command on their File menu. Note that some programs use the name *Page Setup,* and others use *Print Setup.* (Print Setup is the quaint, old term, more popular in the System 6 era and in

Windows than on today's Macs.) Either way, this is the sheet where you can choose your target printer, paper size, page orientation, and scale (as shown in Figure 15-3).

Become familiar with Page Setup. You might not need to use it right this second, but it's a good friend to know. Even though some apps offer some of these Page Setup settings in their Print sheets, Page Setup is the only place you find these options in many programs.

Figure 15-3: The Page Setup sheet in the TextEdit application.

Users of network printers or PostScript printers might see slightly different versions of the Print and Page Setup sheets. The differences should be minor enough not to matter.

Click the little question mark in the bottom-left corner of the Page Setup sheet at any time for additional help. If you do, Page Setup help opens immediately in the Help Center. (Okay, maybe not *immediately,* but Help Center in Mountain Lion is much, much faster than the Help Viewer in previous OS X incarnations.)

The options within the Page Setup sheet are as follows:

- **Settings:** When you have everything else in the Page Setup sheet configured just the way you want it for most documents, choose Save As Default to save this configuration as the default Page Setup for this application.

- **Format For:** In this pop-up menu, you find the name of the active printer. If you have several printers configured, you can choose any of them from this menu.

This menu usually defaults to Any Printer, the least effective setting. Unless the printer you want to use appears here, you might not get the full functionality the printer offers.

✔ **Paper Size:** Use this pop-up menu to choose the type of paper currently in the paper tray of your printer or to choose the size of the paper that you want to feed manually. The dimensions of the paper that you can choose appear below its name.

Page Setup sheet settings (including Paper Size) remain in effect until you change them. For example, when you print an envelope, don't forget to change back to Letter before trying to print on letter-size paper again.

✔ **Orientation:** Choose among options here to tell your printer whether the page you want to print should be *portrait-oriented* (like a letter, longer than it is wide) or *landscape-oriented* (sideways, wider than it is long).

Some programs offer additional Page Setup choices. If your program offers them, they usually appear in the Settings pop-up menu in the Page Setup sheet. (Adobe Photoshop and Microsoft Word have them; TextEdit doesn't.)

✔ **Scale:** To print your page at a larger or smaller size, change this option to a larger or smaller percentage.

Print: Printing with the Print Sheet

After you connect and configure your printer and set up how you want your document to print, you come to the final steps before that joyous moment when your printed page pops out of the printer. Navigating the Print sheet is the last thing standing between you and your output.

Although most Print sheets that you see look like the figures I show here, others might differ slightly. The features in the Print sheet are a function of the program with which you're printing. Many programs choose to use the standard-issue Apple sheet, but not all do. If I don't explain a certain feature in this chapter, chances are good that the feature is specific to the application or printer you're using (in which case, the documentation for that program or printer should offer an explanation).

Printing a document

If everything has gone well so far, the actual act of printing a document is pretty simple. Just follow the steps here, and in a few minutes, pages should start popping out of your printer like magic. (In the sections that follow, I talk about some print options that you'll probably need someday.)

1. **Open a document that you want to print.**

2. **Choose File⇨Print (or press ⌘+P).**

   You see the basic Print sheet, as shown in Figure 15-4.

Figure 15-4: Your basic Print sheet.

3. **Click Print.**

   Wait a few minutes for the network to tell the printer what to do, and then walk over to your printer to get your document.

Choosing File⇨Print (⌘+P) *won't* work for you if any one of the following is true for the software you're using:

- ✔ The Print command is on a different menu.

- ✔ There *is* no Print command. (Hey, it could happen.)

- ✔ The Print keyboard shortcut is anything but ⌘+P.

If any of the preceding is true for a program you're using, you just have to wing it. Look in all the menus and check out the product's documentation to try to get a handle on the Print command for that pesky program.

Choosing among different printers

Just as you can in the Page Setup sheet, you can choose which printer you want to use from the Printer pop-up menu of the Print sheet.

You can choose only among the printers you've added via the Print & Scan System Preferences pane, as I describe earlier in this chapter in the section I lovingly call "Setting up a printer for the first time." This includes printers connected to wireless base stations and routers, as well as Wi-Fi–enabled printers. After they're set up, Macs (and PCs) within wireless range can print to these printers wirelessly.

Choosing custom settings

If you've created a custom group of settings previously, you can choose them from the Presets pop-up menu of the Print sheet. I touch more on this feature in the "Saving custom settings" section, later in this chapter.

By default, the Print sheet is displayed with its details hidden. As such, just three menus are available: Printer, Pages, and PDF. To reveal the rest of the Print options, click the Show Details button near the bottom of the Print sheet. An expanded Print sheet with all the details you're likely to need, as shown in Figure 15-5, replaces the more streamlined version shown in Figure 15-4.

Figure 15-5: Your expanded Print sheet.

Click in any of the fields and press the Tab key. Your cursor jumps to the next text field; likewise, press Shift+Tab to jump to the previous field. By the way, this shortcut works in almost any program, window, dialog, or web page that has text fields.

The expanded Print sheet has the following options:

- ✔ **Copies:** In this text field, set how many copies you want to print. The Print sheet defaults to one copy (1) in most applications, so you probably see the numeral 1 in the Copies field when the Print sheet appears. Assuming that's the case, don't do anything if you want to print only one copy. If you want to print more than one copy of your document, highlight the 1 that appears in the Copies field and replace it, typing the number of copies you want.

- ✔ **Pages:** Here, you find two radio buttons: All and From. The default behavior is to print your entire document, so the All option is preselected. But if you want to print only a specific page or range of pages, select the From radio button and type the desired page numbers in the From and To text fields.

  Suppose that you print a 10-page document — and then notice a typo on Page 2. After you correct your error, you don't have to reprint the whole document — only the page with the correction. Reprint only Page 2 by typing **2** in both the From and To fields. You can type any valid range of pages (um, you can't print page 20 if your document is only 15 pages long) in the From and To fields.

- ✔ **Paper Size:** Use options in this pop-up menu to choose the type of paper currently in your printer's paper tray — or to choose the size of the paper that you want to feed manually. The dimensions of the paper appear below its name.

  You've already seen this setting in Page Setup. The difference is that the settings here (in the Print sheet) apply only to this document, whereas the settings in Page Setup are the default for all documents and remain in effect until you change them in Page Setup. This can be very handy when, for example, you print an envelope. If you change the paper-size setting for the envelope document, you don't have to remember to change it back to Letter in Page Setup.

- ✔ **Orientation:** Once again, you've seen this setting in Page Setup. And once again, the choice you make in Page Setup is the default for all pages you print. Keep in mind that the setting you choose here (in the Print sheet) applies only to this document. Choose among options here to tell your printer whether the page you want to print should be portrait or landscape oriented.

The following list describes the features you can find in the unlabeled menu found in the expanded Print sheet (the one that says *TextEdit* in Figure 15-5). In addition to the TextEdit, Layout, and other options I cover in a moment, your pop-up menu might offer options such as Quality & Media, Color

Options, Special Effects, Borderless Printing, and so on. (Whether you have these options depends on your printer model and its driver.) Check out these options if you have 'em; they usually offer useful features:

- **TextEdit:** The only TextEdit–specific options, as shown in Figure 15-5, are two check boxes. One governs whether to print a header and footer for this document; the other lets you choose to rewrap the contents of the document to fit the page.

  You can see the results of clicking these check boxes in the proxy image of your document on the left half of the sheet.

- **Layout:** Choose Layout to set the number of pages per printed sheet, the layout direction, and whether you prefer a border. Here are your options for Layout:

  - *Pages per Sheet:* Choose preset numbers from this pop-up menu to set the number of pages that you want to print on each sheet.

    Pages appear on-screen smaller than full size if you use this option.

  - *Layout Direction:* Choose one of the four buttons that govern the way pages are laid out on the printed page.

  - *Border:* Your choices from this pop-up menu are None, Single Hairline, Single Thin Line, Double Hairline, and Double Thin Line.

  - *Two-Sided:* If your printer supports two-sided (known as *duplex*) printing, the three radio buttons allow you to specify whether you're going to use two-sided printing and, if so, whether you'll be binding (or stapling) along the long or short edge of the paper.

  Two check boxes — Reverse Page Orientation and Flip Horizontally — do just what they say if you enable them.

- **Color Matching:** Choose Color Matching to choose a color-conversion method (usually, either Apple's ColorSync or Vendor Matching). The idea here is to get the printed page to look as much like what's on your screen as possible.

- **Paper Handling:** Choose Paper Handling if you want to reverse the order in which your pages print or to print only the odd- or even-numbered pages. You can also specify whether the document's paper size is to be used (in which case, you might have lines that break across pages) or whether the output should be scaled to fit the chosen paper size.

- **Cover Page:** Choose Cover Page to add a cover page.

- **Print Settings:** Choose Print Settings to choose paper type and print quality.

Saving custom settings

After you finalize printer settings, you can save them for future use. Just click the Presets pop-up menu and choose Save Current Settings as Preset, and provide a name for this preset. From then on, the preset name appears as an option in the Presets pop-up menu. Just choose your saved set before you print any document, and all the individual settings associated with that preset are restored.

To manage your custom settings, known in Mountain Lion-speak as *presets,* choose Show Presets from the Print sheet's Presets pop-up menu. This nifty feature displays a list of your presets and their settings and allows you to delete, duplicate, or rename (by double-clicking their current name) your presets.

Preview and PDF Options

To see a preview of what your printed page will look like, choose Open PDF in Preview from the PDF pop-up menu in the bottom-left corner of the expanded Print sheet. When you do so, you see the page or pages that you're about to print displayed by the Preview application, as shown in Figure 15-6.

Figure 15-6: A preview of a TextEdit document.

If you have any doubt about the way a document will look when you print it, check out Preview first. When you're happy with the document preview, just choose File➪Print, press ⌘+P, or click the Print button at the bottom of the Preview window. Or click the Cancel button to return to your application and make changes to the document.

Preview works with the Preview application. With the Preview feature, you can do cool things like these:

- ✔ See all the pages in your document the way they will be printed, one by one.

- ✔ Zoom in or out to get a different perspective on what you're about to send to the printer (pretty cool!).

- ✔ Rotate the picture 90 degrees to the left or right.

- ✔ Spot errors before you print something. A little up-front inspection can save you paper, ink/toner, and frustration.

Check out the Preview program's View menu, where you'll find (among other things), four useful views: Content Only, Thumbnails (shown in Figure 15-6), Table of Contents, and Contact Sheet, as well as the zoom commands and more.

While you're checking out menus, you won't want to miss the Tools menu, which lets you rotate pages, move forward or backward (through multipage documents); and unleash the awesomeness of the Magnifier, shown in Figure 15-7.

Figure 15-7: Preview app includes this useful Magnifier tool.

The Magnifier tool is so very darn cool that it has a rare single-key keyboard shortcut. That key is the ` (the grave accent, which shares a key with the tilde); press it to show or hide the Magnifier. One last thing: Many of the tools and commands mentioned in this section are also available in the toolbar.

Add or delete buttons from the toolbar by choosing View⇨Customize Toolbar.

Just the Fax . . .

OS X includes the capability to fax a document right from the Print sheet. But before you can take advantage of it, you have to connect and add a fax modem. Fortunately, doing so is as easy as connecting and adding a printer (as described in the "Ready: Connecting and Adding Your Printer" section, earlier in this chapter): Just follow the same steps, replacing the word *printer* with the words *fax modem,* and you're good to go. Note that many printers today are actually multifunction devices combining a printer with a scanner, a fax machine, or all three.

After your device is connected and you see it in the Printer list in the Print & Scan System Preference Pane, you're ready to fax. To fax a document, choose the Fax device from the Printer pop-up menu at the top of every Print sheet. When you do, the sheet becomes a Fax sheet, as shown in Figure 15-8.

Figure 15-8: With Mountain Lion, faxing is just as easy as printing.

To fax a document, follow these steps:

1. **Choose Fax PDF from the menu that appears when you press and hold the PDF pop-up menu on the Print sheet.**

2. **Type the fax phone number of the recipient in the To field.**

   If you click the button with the silhouette on the right of the To field, you can select a recipient from the OS X Address Book.

3. **Add a dialing prefix if your phone requires one (such as 1, which most U.S. phones require to dial a 10-digit, long-distance phone number).**

4. **Click the Use Cover page check box if you want a cover page, and if you do, you can type a subject in the Subject field and a brief message in the Message field.**

5. **Select your fax modem from the Printer pop-up menu, if it isn't already selected (FaxModem in Figure 15-8).**

   Everything else in the Fax sheet is just the same as in the Print sheet, which you can read all about in the previous sections.

6. **Click the Fax button to send your fax.**

Before you try to fax something, make sure you have a functioning fax modem — and that it's configured, set up properly, connected to a phone line, and turned on. If you don't get all those ducks in a row, this whole faxing process will (of course) fail. Note that no Mac that can run Mountain Lion includes an analog modem, so those machines don't have built-in hardware that supports faxing; you would need to purchase a modem or other hardware to use this feature (for example, a multifunction printer with fax capability).

Mountain Lion supports a new Bluetooth feature known as Dial-Up Networking (DUN) Profile, which allows a Bluetooth-enabled mobile phone to act as a modem and connect to an Internet service provider (ISP) and the Internet. Unfortunately, after repeated experimentation, I was unable to get any of my mobile phones to act as a fax modem. I mention it only because it's entirely possible that it *will* work with *your* mobile phone. (If it does, please drop me a note at `MountainLion4Dummies@boblevitus.com`, and let me know how you did it, what kind of phone you have, and what wireless carrier [for example, AT&T] you use. Thanks!)

16

Sharing Your Mac and Liking It

In This Chapter

▶ Comprehending networks and file sharing

▶ Setting up file sharing

▶ Finding out about users

▶ Understanding access and permissions

▶ Sharing files, folders, and disks with other users

▶ Sharing remotely

*H*ave you ever wanted to grab a file from your Mac while you were halfway around the world or even around the corner? If so, I have good news for you: It's not difficult with OS X (believe it or not), even though computer networking in general has a well-deserved reputation for being complicated and nerve-wracking. The truth is that you won't encounter anything scary or complicated about sharing files, folders, and disks (and printers, for that matter) among computers as long as the computers are Macintoshes. And if some of the computers are running Windows, OS X Mountain Lion even makes that (almost) painless. Your Macintosh includes everything that you need to share files and printers — except the printers and the cables (and maybe a hub). So here's the deal: You supply the hardware, and this chapter supplies the rest. And when you're done hooking it all up, you can take a rest.

The first sections of this chapter provide an overview and tell you everything that you need to know to set up new user accounts and share files successfully. I don't show you how to actually share a file, folder, or disk until the "Connecting to a Shared Disk or Folder on a Remote Mac" section, later in this chapter. Trust me, there's a method to my madness. If you try to share files without doing all the required prep work, the whole mess becomes confusing and complicated pretty fast — kind of like networking PCs.

One last thing: If you're the only one who uses your Mac, you don't intend to share it or its files with anyone else, and you never intend to access your Mac from another computer in a different location, you can safely skip this whole chapter if you like.

Introducing Networks and File Sharing

Macintosh file sharing enables you to use files, folders, and disks from other Macs on a network — including the Internet — as easily as though they were on your own local hard drive. If you have more than one computer, file sharing is a blessing.

Before diving in and actually sharing, allow me to introduce a few necessary terms:

- **Network:** For the purposes of this chapter, a *network* is two or more Macs connected by Ethernet cables, wireless networking (Apple refers to this as AirPort or Wi-Fi), or FireWire cables (which are by far the least common type of network connection).

- **Ethernet:** A network protocol and cabling scheme that lets you connect two or more computers so they can share files, disks, printers, or whatever.

  - **Ethernet ports:** Where you plug an Ethernet cable into your Mac. Be careful to match the cable to its specific jack. On your Mac and printer, the Ethernet ports look a lot like phone jacks, and the connectors on each end of an Ethernet cable look a lot like phone cable connectors. But they aren't the same. Ethernet cables are typically thicker, and the connectors (RJ-45 connectors) are a bit larger than the RJ-11 connectors that you use with telephones. (See examples of both types of ports in the margin.) Standard phone cables fit (very loosely) into Ethernet ports, but you shouldn't try that, either; they'll probably fall out with the slightest vibration. It's unlikely that such a mistake will cause damage, but it won't work and will be frustrating.

- **Local devices:** Devices connected directly to your computers, such as hard or optical drives. Your internal hard drive, for example, is a local device.

- **Remote devices:** Devices you access (share) over the network. The hard drive of a computer in the next room, for example, is a remote device.

- **Protocols:** Kinds of languages that networks speak. When you read or hear about networks, you're likely to hear the words *AppleTalk, EtherTalk* (or *Ethernet*), *SMB,* and *TCP/IP* bandied about with great regularity. These are all protocols. Macs can speak several different protocols, but every device (Mac or printer) on a network needs to speak the same protocol at the same time to communicate.

Support for the TCP/IP protocol is built into every Mac. Your Mac includes all the software you need to set up a TCP/IP network; the hardware you provide consists of Ethernet cables and a hub (if you have more than two computers) or an AirPort or other Wi-Fi base station. Here, I'm using *hub* generically; its more powerful networking cousins, switches and routers, also work for this purpose.

By the way, in addition to providing wireless networking, the AirPort Extreme wireless Base Stations — as well as the Time Capsule device — are all members of the router class of devices. The Time Capsule is a pretty cool deal; it combines a wireless Base Station, three-port Ethernet router, and a big hard disk that can be shared by all computers on the network and also used as a Time Machine backup disk.

Portrait of home-office networking

A typical Mac home-office network consists of two Macintoshes, an AirPort Extreme wireless Base Station (or other type of Ethernet hub or router), and a network printer. Check out Figure 16-1 to see the configuration of a simple network. In the figure, the black lines between the devices are Ethernet cables; the rectangular device with those cables going into it is an Ethernet hub, router, AirPort Extreme Base Station, or Time Capsule. (I tell you more about cables and such devices in the section "Three ways to build a network," later in this chapter.) You need enough Ethernet cable to run among all your devices.

Figure 16-1: Two Macs and a printer make up a simple Mac network.

File sharing made easy with AirDrop

Perhaps all you want to do is share an occasional file (not necessarily a printer or a home Internet connection or a folder of music files or pictures). In that case, check out AirDrop (for Lion and Mountain Lion only on Macs built in the last couple of years), which uses Apple's proprietary zero-configuration network protocol, known as *Bonjour* (formerly *Rendezvous*). It's a big part of the secret sauce that makes Mac networking so simple.

Here's how it works: If two devices (and this includes all Macs running OS X Jaguar or later) speak Bonjour, you don't have to do *any* configuration other than, possibly, turning on the sharing capability, as I explain in "Setting Up File Sharing," later in this chapter. Bonjour queries the other available networked devices to see what services they support, and then configures the connections for you automatically. Sweet!

It gets even better if you're using Lion or Mountain Lion, 'cause you can use the nifty sharing feature called *AirDrop*. It appears in your Finder window Sidebar and locates all other AirDrop-capable Macs on your local wireless network. The only caveat is that it's Wi-Fi only.

For AirDrop to work you don't need to turn on File Sharing or do anything else. Just click AirDrop in the Finder Sidebar, and you see AirDrop in the Finder window, as shown in the following figure.

While AirDrop is front and center in a Finder window and incredibly simple to use, its limitations are that it is Lion- and Mountain Lion-only and requires Wi-Fi; Messages, on the other hand, works with both Bonjour and your Buddy List to exchange files with anyone with whom you can chat, including PC users. On the third hand, using Messages involves a few more steps (and isn't as pretty, if aesthetics matter to you).

The key here is that both Macs must be on the same Wi-Fi network and have an open Finder window with AirDrop selected. To send a file (or multiple files and/or folders) to the other Mac, just drag it onto the other Mac's icon. AirDrop displays a dialog on the other Mac asking whether the user wants to accept delivery; if so, the items are transferred immediately to the Downloads folder.

When you close the AirDrop window, you are no longer visible to other AirDrop users. Thus, if you want to transfer files to other Bonjour Macs, use Messages as described in Chapter 11, selecting the other Bonjour Mac, establishing a chat, and dragging the item(s) into the message box.

TIP

With the setup shown in Figure 16-1, either Mac can use the other Mac's files, and both Macs can print to the same printer. If you have a broadband Internet connection, you can also connect the cable or DSL modem to the hub/switch/router so all Mac users on the network can share the Internet connection.

A network can — and often does — have dozens or hundreds of users. Whether your network has 2 nodes (machines) or 2,000, the principles and techniques in this chapter apply.

Three ways to build a network

In this chapter, I assume you're working on a small network, the kind typically found in a home or small business. If you're part of a megamonstrous corporate network, and you have questions about your particular network, talk to the PIC (*person in charge,* also known as your *network administrator).* In other words, if you're trying to build a meganetwork, you're going to need a book a lot thicker and harder to understand than this one.

The following list gives you three common ways to build a modern small home or office network:

- ✔ **AirPort:** If all your Macs are equipped with AirPort wireless cards, and you have an (AirPort or) AirPort Extreme Base Station or Time Capsule, you don't need cables at all. Just plug in the Base Station, and Macs with AirPort cards can communicate with one another. If you use an Ethernet printer (connected to your Mac by Ethernet cable), you have to connect it to the Base Station before you can print from your wireless Macs. Both the Base Station and printer have Ethernet ports, so you can use a crossover cable (more about that in a minute) to make the connection.

    Recent vintage AirPort Extreme and Time Capsule devices from Apple include a USB port so you can connect any printer via USB and share it wirelessly (rather than having to use a more expensive Ethernet-equipped "networkable" printer).

    Although this setup is more expensive than connecting everything with Ethernet cables and a cheap hub or router, it's also more flexible because you can move your devices anywhere. (Well, almost anywhere; you're limited to a maximum of 150–200 feet from each Base Station, and that's assuming that there's absolutely nothing in the way to block your signal. Your mileage may vary.)

- ✔ **Traditional Ethernet:** All modern Macs have an Ethernet port, with the exception of the MacBook Air. To connect your Mac to a network, you need Ethernet cables for each Mac and a little device called a *hub, switch,* or *router.* This device is like the center of a wheel; the wires coming out of it are the "spokes."

    A typical Ethernet hub includes two to eight Ethernet ports. You plug the hub into an electrical outlet and then connect Ethernet cables from each of your Macs and printers (from their Ethernet ports) to the hub. Voilà — instant network. These gadgets are pretty cheap, starting at around $10; cables start at a few bucks, increasing in price with the length and quality.

> ✓ **Small Ethernet:** If you have only two devices to network (two Macs or a Mac and an Ethernet printer, in most cases), you can use an Ethernet cable to connect them directly to each other via the Ethernet ports. You can purchase an Ethernet cable at your local electronics store. Plug one end of the Ethernet cable into one device and the other end into the other device.

For each of these setups, if you have a cable modem or Digital Subscriber Line (DSL) as your Internet connection, you might need a router or switch instead of a (cheaper) hub. Routers and switches are similar to hubs but cost a tiny bit more and have additional features that you might or might not need. Your ISP can tell you whether you're going to need one. For what it's worth, I have a cable modem, but it works fine with a cheap hub.

If you use an Apple AirPort Extreme Base Station or Time Capsule, you may not need a hub or router at all because all these devices incorporate small routers (each with three Ethernet ports). So they're all you need for up to three Ethernet devices. If, on the other hand, you have more than three Ethernet devices, you'll need to add a hub, switch, or router with some additional Ethernet ports to accommodate them all.

Setting Up File Sharing

Before you get into the nitty-gritty of sharing files, you must complete a few housekeeping tasks, such as enabling the appropriate type of file sharing. Follow these steps to do so:

1. **Choose ⇨System Preferences, and then click the Sharing icon.**

   The Sharing System Preferences pane appears. The first word of the long username of the first Admin account created on this computer appears in the Computer Name field by default, followed by the type of Mac (for example, Bob L's MacBook Pro).

2. **If you want to change the name of your computer from whatever Mountain Lion decided to call it to something more personal, do that now in the Computer Name text field at the top of the Sharing pane.**

   In Figure 16-2, you can see that I named mine Bob L's MacBook Pro. You can name yours anything you like.

3. **Select the File Sharing check box, as shown in Figure 16-2.**

   Now other users on your network can access files and folders on your computer, as you see later in this chapter.

Figure 16-2: Turning file sharing on and off.

By default, only one folder in your Home folder is shared, and that folder is your Public Folder. If you want to access files or folders on this computer while you're using another computer on the network, you can so long as you first provide your username and password. Everyone else on the network can see only your Public folder.

These are the safest settings. Unless you have good reason to tinker with them, you should probably not change anything here. That said, if you feel you must change these settings, you find out how to do so in the next section of this chapter.

4. **(Optional) If you want remote users to upload and download files to and from this computer, click the Options button, and then select either or both of the Share Files and Folders Using AFP or SMB check boxes.**

   • Doing so gives users on the Internet but not on your local area network some alternatives to file sharing: an Apple File Protocol (AFP) or a client program that uses Server Message Block (Samba or SMB).

   • If you want to enable Windows or Linux users — or users of other operating systems — to share files with you, the SMB check box must be selected.

   • Select the On check box (in the leftmost column) for each account you want to enable to use these protocols to access your Mac, providing the password when prompted.

5. **Click the Done button when you're done, and then proceed to the following section to continue setting up your network.**

Access and Permissions: Who Can Do What

After you set up file sharing (as I explain in the preceding section), your next step on the path to sharing files on a network is telling your Mac who is allowed to see and access specific folders. Luckily for you, this just happens to be what I cover in the following sections.

Users and groups and guests

Macintosh file sharing (and indeed, OS X as well) is based on the concept of users. You can share items — such as drives or folders — with no users, one user, or many users, depending on your needs.

- **Users:** People who share folders and drives (or your Mac) are *users*. A user's access to items on your local hard drive is entirely at your discretion. You can configure your Mac so only you can access its folders and drives, or so only one other person or group — or everyone — can share its folders and drives.

  When you first set up your Mac, you created your first user. This user automatically has administrative powers, such as adding more users, changing preferences, and having the clearance to see all folders on the hard drive.

  For the purposes of this book, I assume that some users for whom you create identities won't be folks who actually sit at your Mac, but those who connect to it only from remote locations when they need to give or get files. But you could allow such a user to use the same name and password to log in while sitting at your desk.

  For most intents and purposes, a remote user and a local user are the same. Here's why: After you create an account for a user, that user can log in to your Mac while sitting in your chair in your office; from anywhere on your local area network via Ethernet; or anywhere in the world via the Internet if you give him or her an Administrator, Standard, or Managed account.

- **Administrative users:** Although a complete discussion of the special permissions that a user with administrator permissions has on a Mac running OS X is far beyond the scope of this book, note two important things:

  - The first user created (usually when you install OS X for the first time) is automatically granted administrator (Admin) powers.

  - Only an administrator account can create new users, delete some (but not all) files from folders that aren't in his or her Home folder, lock and unlock System Preferences panes, and a bunch of other stuff. If you try something and it doesn't work, make sure you're logged in as an Administrator or can provide an Administrator username and password when prompted.

You can give any user administrator permissions by selecting that user's account in the Users & Groups System Preferences pane and selecting the Allow User to Administer This Computer check box. You can select this check box when you're creating the user account or subsequently, if that works for you.

✔ **Groups:** *Groups* are Unix-level designations for privilege consolidation. For example, there are groups named staff and wheel (as well as a bunch of others). A user can be a member of multiple groups. For example, your main account is in the wheel and Admin groups (and others, too). Don't worry — you find out more about groups shortly.

✔ **Guests:** Two kinds of guests exist. The first kind lets your friends log into your Mac while sitting at your desk without user accounts or passwords. When they log out, all information and files in the guest account's Home folder are deleted automatically.

If you want this kind of guest account, you need to enable the Guest Account in the Users & Groups System Preferences pane. To do so, click the Guest Account in the list of accounts on the left and select the Allow Guests to Log In to This Computer check box.

The second kind of guest is people who access Public folders on your Mac via file sharing over your local area network or the Internet. They don't need usernames or passwords. If they're on your local network, they can see and use your Public folder(s), unless you or the Public folder's owner has altered the permissions. If they're on the Internet and know your IP address, they can see and use your Public folder(s) if you don't have a firewall blocking such access. Public folders are all that guests can access, luckily. You don't have to do anything to enable this type of guest account.

Creating users

Before users can share folders and drives (or have their own accounts on your computer, for that matter), they must have an account on your Mac. You can create two different kinds of accounts for them — a User Account or a Sharing Account.

✔ **When you create a User Account** for a person (I call that person and account *User 1*), the account has its own Home folder (called — what else? — User 1), which is filled with User 1's files. Nobody but User 1 can access files in this Home folder unless, of course, User 1 has provided someone the account name and password.

✔ **When you create a Sharing Account** for a person (I call that person and account *Sharing 1*), the person using that account doesn't have a Home folder and can't access other users' Home folders. Sharing 1 can access only the Public folders inside all the Home folders on that Mac.

You can create a new *User* Account only in the Users & Groups System Preferences pane. You can create a new *Sharing* Account in either the Users & Groups or Sharing System Preferences panes.

When you click the + button under the Users list in the Sharing System Preferences pane and choose a contact in your Contacts (as opposed to choosing an existing user account), you create a Sharing Account for that person.

Anyone can remotely access files or folders in your Public folder(s) over a LAN (local area network) or the Internet. But if you want them to be able to access folders or files other than those in the Public folder(s) on your Mac, they need either a User Account or a Sharing Account.

When you add (create) a user, you need to tell your Mac who this person is. This is also the time to set passwords and administrative powers for this new user. Here's the drill:

1. **Choose ⌘⇨System Preferences (or click the System Preferences icon in the Dock), click the Users & Groups icon, and then make sure that the Password tab is selected.**

   The Users & Groups System Preferences pane appears. In this pane (shown in Figure 16-3), you can see the name of the first user (Bob LeVitus) and the administrative control that this user is allowed. (Note that the Allow User to Administer This Computer check box is selected.)

Figure 16-3: The Users & Groups System Preferences pane is where you manage user accounts on this Mac.

The first user created (usually at the same time you installed OS X) always has administrator permissions.

2. **Click the + button beneath the list of users.**

A sheet appears in which you enter the new user's information.

If the + button is dimmed, here's how you get it functioning: First click the lock (at bottom left), supply an administrator name and password in the resulting dialog, and then click OK.

3. **Choose Standard from the New Account menu.**

4. **In the Name text box, type the full name of a user you want to add.**

In the Account Name text box, your Mac inserts a suggested abbreviated name (formerly known as the *short name*). Check out Figure 16-4 to see both.

Figure 16-4: Name the new user and your Mac suggests a short name and password.

In Figure 16-4, I added Steve Wozniak as a user, typing his full name in the Full Name field. You don't really need to type the user's full name, but I do so in this example to show you the difference between a Full Name and an Account Name.

5. **Press the Tab key to move to the next field.**

OS X suggests an abbreviated version of the name in the Account Name field (as shown in Figure 16-4).

Because he's the only Steve who matters around here, I change the suggested Account Name from SteveWozniak to just plain Steve, which is shorter than the short name recommended by OS X. (In other words, I type **Steve** in the Account Name field, replacing the suggested SteveWozniak.) The name of each user's folder (in the Users folder) is taken from the short name that you enter when you create a user.

Users can connect to your Mac (or log in from their own Macs, for that matter) by using the short name, rather than having to type their full names. The short name is also used in environments in which usernames can't have spaces and are limited to eight or fewer characters. Although OS X Mountain Lion allows longer usernames (but no spaces), you might be better off keeping your short name shorter than eight characters, just in case.

6. **Tab to the Password field, and enter an initial password for this user.**

The small, square button with the key to the right of the Password field, when clicked, displays the Password Assistant. You can use the Password Assistant, as shown on the right in Figure 16-4, to help generate a password that should be fairly easy for the user to remember (choose Memorable from the Password Assistant's Type pop-up menu) but hard for a cracking program to guess (or meet other requirements).

To make your password even harder to guess or crack, choose Random or FIPS-181-compliant from the Password Assistant's Type pop-up menu. It will also make it harder for you to remember, so make sure you either memorize it or store it in a safe place.

7. **Press the Tab key to move your cursor to the Verify text field.**

8. **In the Verify text box, type the password again to verify it.**

9. **(Optional) To help remember a password, type something in the Password Hint text box to jog the user's memory.**

If a user forgets her password and asks for a hint, the text that you type in the Password Hint field pops up, ideally causing the user to exclaim, "Oh, yeah . . . *now* I remember!" A password hint should be something simple enough to jog the user's memory, but not so simple that an unauthorized person can guess. Perhaps something like "Your first teddy bear's name backward" would be a good hint.

10. **Click the Create Account button to create the account.**

The sheet disappears, and the new user now appears in the Users & Groups System Preferences pane's Users list.

11. **(Optional) Click the account picture above the Full Name field, and choose a different one.**

TIP

OS X suggests a picture from its default collection for each account, but you can select a different one from the pop-up mini-window shown in Figure 16-5, drag one in from the Finder (or iPhoto), or take a photo with an attached or built-in camera (such as an iSight) by clicking the Edit button (shown in the margin).

Figure 16-5: Choosing a different picture for the user (here, it's Steve Wozniak).

12. **(Optional) Click the Set button next to Apple ID to enter (or create) the user's Apple ID.**

Changing a user

Circumstances might dictate that you need to change a user's identity, password, or accessibility, or perhaps delete a user. Follow these steps to change a user's name, password, or account type:

REMEMBER

1. **Choose ⌘⇨System Preferences (or click the System Preferences icon in the Dock or Launchpad).**

   The System Preferences window appears.

2. **In the System Preferences window, click the Users & Groups icon.**

   The Users & Groups System Preferences pane appears.

   If the lock icon at the bottom of the window is locked, you have to click it and provide an administrator password before you can proceed.

3. **Select the user's name in the accounts list.**

   The information for that person appears.

4. **Make your changes by selecting the existing username and replacing the old with new text or a different setting.**

   - If you want to change the password, click the Reset Password button and make your changes in the sheet that appears.

   - To change the picture or other capabilities, click the Picture, Login Options, Allow User to Administer This Computer (to enable or disable administrator privileges), or Enable Parental Control check box (more on this in a moment) and make the appropriate changes.

   To change a user, you must be logged in using an account that has administrator powers.

5. **Quit the System Preferences application or choose a different System Preferences pane.**

   Your changes are saved when you leave the Users & Groups pane.

Removing a user

To delete a user — in effect, to deny that user access to your Mac — select the user you want to delete in the list of accounts and click the – button. A sheet appears, offering three choices:

- **Save the Home folder in a disk image** saves a disk image of the user's Home folder in a folder named Deleted Users (which it creates inside the Users folder).

- **Don't change the Home folder** removes the user from the Users & Groups System Preferences pane and login screen but leaves that user's Home folder in the Users folder. *(Deleted)* is appended to the folder's name, so if I had selected this option in the previous example, Steve Wozniak's Home folder would be renamed *steve (Deleted)*.

- **Delete the Home folder** does what it says. You have the option of a secure erase (the contents get overwritten multiple times) if you select this option.

To remove a user from your Mac, you must be logged in using an account that has administrator permissions. And you can't remove the first user ever created on this Mac.

Limiting a user's capabilities

Sometimes — especially with younger children, computerphobic family members, or employees in a small business — you want to limit what users can access. For example, you might want to make certain programs off-limits. You do this by clicking the Parental Controls button in the Users & Groups System Preferences pane.

1. **Choose ➪System Preferences (or click the System Preferences icon in the Dock).**

   The System Preferences window appears.

2. **In the System Preferences window, click the Users & Groups icon.**

   The Users & Groups System Preferences pane appears.

3. **Click the user's name to select it, click the Enable Parental Controls check box, and then click the Open Parental Controls button.**

   Note that clicking the Open Parental Controls button without first selecting the Enable Parental Controls check box puts you in the Parental Controls preference pane with a button front and center for you to click to turn Parental Controls on. So either select the check box as instructed or click the Enable Parental Controls button here.

   To change any of these items, you must be logged in using an account that has administrator powers, and the account you're modifying *can't* have administrator powers.

   The Parental Controls System Preferences pane for that person appears with five tabs: Apps (shown in Figure 16-6), Web, People, Time Limits, and Other.

Figure 16-6: You can control an account's access in five categories.

   4. **Set the controls in each of the five tabs.**

     • *Apps:* Determine which applications the user may access. Set whether she can modify the Dock. Also determine whether she's restricted to a very limited and simplified Finder interface.

     • *Web:* Control access to websites.

     • *People:* Determine whether Mail or Messages (or both) communicants will be limited to a specified list. This option also lets you notify someone (usually yourself) when the user tries to exchange e-mail with a contact not in the approved list. You can also maintain a log of all Messages text conversations.

     • *Time Limits:* Set time limits for weekdays and weekends, and prevent access to this computer during specified hours on school nights and weekends. *School night* doesn't take vacations or holidays into consideration.

     • *Other:* Determine whether profanity is hidden during Dictionary access, control whether the user can add or remove printers or modify printer settings, prevent (or allow) burning CDs and DVDs in the Finder, and control whether the user is allowed to change his password.

   5. **Quit the System Preferences application or choose a different System Preferences pane.**

     Your changes are saved when you leave the Parental Controls pane.

A quicker way to set or change Parental Controls for an already-existing account is to click the Parental Controls icon in the System Preferences application (instead of Users & Groups).

Last but not least, you can apply Parental Controls to the Guest Account, but you can't apply them to any account that has administrator permissions.

To turn off Parental Controls for a Managed account, navigate to the Parental Controls System Preferences pane, select the account in the list on the left, click the Action menu at the bottom of the list (the one that looks like a gear), and choose Turn off Parental Controls for *<username>*.

If you want to apply the same Parental Controls settings to more than one user, set them as described above for the first user, and then select that account in the Accounts list in Parental Controls, click the Action menu, and choose Copy Settings. Then select the user you wish to have the same settings, click the Action menu, and choose Paste Settings.

OS X knows best: Folders shared by default

When you add users in the Users & Groups System Preferences pane as I describe earlier, OS X automatically does two things behind the scenes to facilitate file sharing: It creates a set of folders, and it makes some of them available for sharing.

Each time you add a Managed, Standard, or Administrator user, OS X creates a Home folder hierarchy for that user on the Mac. The user can create more folders (if necessary) and also add, remove, or move anything inside these folders. Even if you create a user account solely to allow him or her to exchange files with you, your Mac automatically creates a Home folder for that user. Unless you, as the owner of your Mac, give permission, the user can't see inside or use folders outside the Home folder (which has the user's name), with only three exceptions: the Shared folder in the Users folder, the top level of other user account folders, and the Public folders in every other user's folder, as well as the Shared folder within the Users folder. A description of the latter follows:

✔ **Public:** A Public folder is located inside each user's folder. That folder is set up to be accessible (shared) by any user who can log in to the Mac. Furthermore, any user can log in (as a guest) and copy things out of this folder as long as she knows your Mac's IP address, even if she doesn't have an account on this Mac at all. Files put into the Public folder can be opened or copied freely.

   It's not hard for someone to obtain your IP address. For example, when you visit most web pages, your IP address is saved to that site's log file. So be careful what you put in your Public folder. This is also an excellent reason to employ a firewall. Mountain Lion has an excellent software implementation available via the Firewall tab in Security & Privacy System Preferences (see Chapter 18), and most routers (for example, AirPort Extreme) include a hardware firewall.

   Inside each user's Public folder is a Drop Box folder. As the name implies, this folder is where others can drop a file or folder for you. Only the owner can open the Drop Box to see what's inside — or to move or copy the files that are in it. Imagine a street-corner mailbox; after you drop your letter in, it's gone, and you can't get it back out.

✔ **Shared:** In addition to a Public folder for each user, OS X creates one Shared folder on every Mac for all users of this Mac. The Shared folder *isn't* available to guests, but it's available to all users who have an account on this machine. You find the Shared folder within the Users folder (the same folder where you find folders for each user). The Shared folder is the right place to put stuff that everyone with an account on this Mac might want to use. (Check out my introduction to the Mac OS Mountain Lion folder structure in Chapter 6.)

Sharing a folder or disk by setting permissions

As you might expect, permissions control who can use a given folder or any disk (or partition) other than the startup disk.

Why can't you share the startup disk? Because OS X won't let you. Why not? Because the startup disk contains the operating system and other stuff that nobody else should have access to.

Throughout the rest of this chapter, whenever I talk about *sharing a folder,* I also mean *sharing disks and disk partitions other than your startup disk* (which, when you think of it, are nothing more than big folders anyway). Why am I telling you this? Because it's awkward to keep typing *a folder or any disk (or partition) other than your startup disk.* So anything that I say about sharing a folder also applies to sharing any disk (or partition) other than your startup disk. Got it?

You can set permissions for

- The folder's owner
- A subset of all the people who have accounts on the Mac (a group)
- Everyone who has the Mac's address, whether they have an account or not (guests)

To help you get a better handle on these relationships, a closer look at permissions, owners, and groups is coming right up.

Contemplating permissions

When you consider who can use which folders, three distinct kinds of users exist on the network. I describe each of them in this section. Then, in the "Useful settings for permissions" section, later in this chapter, I show you how to share folders with each type of user. Here's a quick introduction to the different user types:

- **Owner:** The *owner* of a folder or disk can change the permissions to that folder or disk at any time. The name you enter when you log in to your Mac — or the name of your Home folder — is the default owner of Shared folders and drives on that machine. Ownership can be given away (more on that in the "Useful settings for permissions" section, later in this chapter). Even if you own the Mac, you can't change permissions for a folder on it that belongs to another user (unless you get Unix-y and do so as root). The owner must be logged in to change permissions on his folders.

    OS X is the owner of many folders outside the Users folder. If OS X owns it, you can see that system is its owner if you select the folder and choose File➪Get Info (or press ⌘+I).

    Folders that aren't in the User directories generally belong to system; it's almost always a bad idea to change the permissions on any folder owned by system.

If you *must* change permissions on a file or folder, select its icon and choose File➪Get Info (shortcut: ⌘+I), and then change the settings in the Sharing & Permissions section at the bottom of the resulting Get Info window. I urge you not to change permission settings if you're not absolutely sure of what you're doing and why.

✔ **Group:** In Unix systems, all users belong to one or more *groups.* The group that includes everyone who has an account with administrator permissions on your Mac is called Admin. Everyone in the Admin group has access to Shared and Public folders over the network, as well as to any folder that the Admin group has been granted access to by the folder's owner.

For the purpose of assigning permissions, you can create your own groups the same way you create a user account: Open the Users & Groups System Preferences pane, click the little plus sign, choose Group from the New Account pop-up menu, type the name of the group, and then click the Create Group button.

The group appears in the list of users on the left, and eligible accounts appear with check boxes on the right, as shown in Figure 16-7.

Figure 16-7: This group, Outsiders, contains my Bobcat and Miss Kitty accounts.

✔ **Everyone:** This category is an easy way to set permissions for everyone with an account on your Mac at the same time. Unlike the Admin group, which includes only users with administrative permissions, this one includes, well, everyone (everyone with an account on this Mac, that is).

If you want people without an account on this Mac to have access to a file or folder, that file or folder needs to go in your Public folder, where the people you want to see it can log in as guests.

Sharing a folder

Suppose you have a folder you want to share, but it has slightly different rules than those set up for the Public folder, for the Drop Box folder within the Public folder, or for your personal folders. These rules are *permissions,* and they tell you how much access someone has to your stuff.

Actually, the rules governing Shared and Public folders are permissions, too, but they're set up for you when OS X is installed.

I suggest that you share only folders located in your Home folder (or a folder within it). Because of the way Unix works, the Unix permissions of the enclosing folder can prevent access to a folder for which you *do* have permissions. Trust me, if you share only the folders in your Home folder, you'll never go wrong. If you don't take this advice, you could wind up having folders that other users can't access, even though you gave them the appropriate permissions.

By the way, you can set permissions for folders within your Public folder (like the Drop Box folder) that are different from those for the rest of the folder.

I said this before, but it bears repeating: Whenever I talk about *sharing a folder,* I also mean sharing disks — and disk partitions other than your startup disk (which you just can't share, period). So don't forget that anything I say about sharing a folder also applies to sharing any disk (or partition) other than your startup disk. Though you can't explicitly share your startup disk, anyone with administrator access can mount it for sharing from across the network (or Internet).

To share a folder with another user, follow these steps:

1. **Choose System Preferences (or click the System Preferences icon in the Dock).**

   The System Preferences window appears.

2. **In the System Preferences window, click the Sharing icon.**

   The Sharing System Preferences pane appears.

3. **Click File Sharing in the list of services on the left.**

   The lists of shared folders and their users appear on the right, as shown in Figure 16-8.

   If an entry in, for example, the Shared Folders list is too long for you to make out the folder name, hover your pointer over it, and a tooltip will appear, giving you the full name.

Figure 16-8: Changing the privileges of the Recipes folder for the group Everyone.

4. **Click the + (plus) button under the Shared Folders column to add the folder you wish to share (Recipes in Figure 16-8).**

   If you select the Shared Folder check box in a folder's Get Info window, that folder already appears in the list of Shared Folders, so you won't have to bother with Step 4.

   Alas, while checking the Shared Folder check box in a folder's Get Info window causes it to appear in the Sharing System Preferences pane's Shared Folders list, you still have to complete the steps that follow to assign that folder's users and privileges.

5. **Click the + (plus) button under the Users column to add a user or group if the user or group you desire isn't already showing in the Users column.**

6. **Click the double-headed arrow to the right of a user or group name and change its privileges.**

   I'm changing the permission for Everyone to Read & Write in Figure 16-8. You can choose among three types of access (in addition to no access) for each user or group, as shown in Table 16-1. If you're the folder's owner (or have administrator access), you can click the padlock icon and change the owner and/or group for the file or folder.

Table 16-1	Privileges
Permission	**What It Allows**
Read & Write	A user with Read & Write access can see, add, delete, move, and edit files just as though they were stored on her own computer.
Read Only	A Read Only user can see and use files that are stored in a Shared folder but can't add, delete, move, or edit them.
Write Only (Drop Box)	Users can add files to this folder but can't see what's in it. The user must have read access to the folder containing a Write Only folder.
No Access	With no permissions, a user can neither see nor use your Shared folders or drives.

Useful settings for permissions

The following sections show you just some of the most common ways that you can combine permissions for a folder. You'll probably find one option that fits the way you work and the people you want to share with.

Owner permissions — in this case, single silhouette; Bob LeVitus (Me) in Figure 16-9 — must be at least as expansive as Group permissions (double silhouette; Staff in Figure 16-9) and Group permissions must be at least as expansive as Everyone's permissions (triple silhouette; Everyone in Figure 16-9). So to set the Everyone privilege to Read & Write, the Group and Owner privileges must also be set to Read & Write.

In the following examples, I show how to set permissions in the Sharing System Preferences pane. Another way to set permissions is by selecting an icon in the Finder and choosing File⇨Get Info (shortcut: ⌘+I), and then changing the settings in the Sharing & Permissions section at the bottom of the resulting Get Info window. The two methods are pretty much interchangeable, so you can use whichever is more convenient.

Figure 16-9: Allow everyone access, if you want.

✔ **Allow everyone access:** In Figure 16-9, I configure settings that allow everyone on a network to access the Bob's Downloads folder. Everyone can open, read, and change the contents of this Shared folder. Do this by choosing Read & Write for Others from the pop-up menu to the right of the user's name in the Sharing System Preferences pane or the folder's Get Info window.

✔ **Allow nobody but yourself access:** The settings shown in Figure 16-10 reflect appropriate settings that allow owner-only access to the Bob's Downloads folder. No one but me can see or use the contents of this folder. Members of the Staff group can drop files and folders into this folder (see the later bullet "Allow others to deposit files and folders without giving them access: A drop box"). Use the pop-up menus to choose Write Only (Drop Box) as the Staff privilege and No Access as the Everyone privilege.

Figure 16-10: Allow access for no one but the folder's owner.

✔ **Allow all administrative users of this Mac access:** Check out Figure 16-11 to see settings that allow the group Staff (in addition to the owner, Bob LeVitus) access to see, use, or change the contents of the Bob's Downloads folder. Use the pop-up menu to choose Read & Write for the Staff privilege.

Figure 16-11: Allow access for the Staff group and the folder's owner.

✔ **Allow others to deposit files and folders without giving them access: A drop box:** The settings in Figure 16-12 enable everyone to drop their own files or folders in the Bob's Downloads folder without being able to see or use the contents of the Shared folder. After a file or folder is deposited in a drop folder, the dropper can't retrieve it because she doesn't have permission to see the items in the drop folder.

Figure 16-12: Everyone can drop files and folders into this folder.

- ✔ **Read-only bulletin boards:** If you want everyone to be able to open and read the files and folders in this Shared folder — but not to modify them — choose Read Only from the pop-up menus for Group and Others. If you do this, however, only the owner can make changes to files in this folder.

- ✔ **One more privilege:** The Apply to Enclosed Items button, at the bottom of the Sharing and Permissions section of Get Info windows in the Finder, does exactly what its name implies. This feature (which is only available in Get Info windows and doesn't appear in the Sharing System Preferences pane) is a fast way to assign the same permissions to many subfolders at the same time. After you set permissions for the enclosing folder the way you like them, click this button to give these same permissions to all folders inside it.

What is true of Get Info windows is also true of their Inspector window variant. Show Inspector replaces Get Info on the File menu when the Option key is pressed (also Option+⌘+I).

Be careful — there is no Undo for this action.

Unsharing a folder

To unshare a folder that you own, change the permissions for every other user and/or group to No Access. When you do, nobody but you has access to that folder. If you're not sure how to do this, see the "Sharing a folder" and "Useful settings for permissions" sections, earlier in this chapter.

Connecting to a Shared Disk or Folder on a Remote Mac

After you set up sharing and assign permissions, you can access folders remotely from another computer. (Just make sure first that you have the correct administrative permissions to it.)

 File sharing must be activated on the Mac where the shared files/folders reside; it doesn't have to be activated on the Mac that's accessing the files/folders. When file sharing is turned off, you can still use that Mac to access a remote Shared folder on another machine as long as its owner has granted you enough permissions and has file sharing enabled. If file sharing is turned off on your Mac, others won't be able to access your folders, even if you've assigned permissions to them previously.

 If you're going to share files, and you leave your Mac on and unattended for a long time, logging out before you leave it is a very good idea. This prevents anyone who just walks up to your Mac from seeing your files, e-mail, applications, or anything else that's yours — unless you've given that person a user account that has permissions for your files. If you don't want to log out, at least consider requiring that your password be entered when waking from sleep or dismissing the screen saver (General tab of Security & Privacy System Preferences).

On to how to access your Home folder from a remote Mac — a supercool feature that's only bound to get more popular as the Internet continues to mature.

 The following steps assume that you have an account on the remote Mac, which means you have your own Home folder on that Mac.

To connect to a Shared folder on a Mac other than the one you're currently on, follow these steps:

1. **Make sure that you're already set up as a user on the computer that you want to log in to (Lisa & Jacob's Eye Mac, in this example).**

   If you need to know how to create a new user, see the "Creating users" section, earlier in the chapter.

2. **On the computer that you're logging in from (my MacBook Pro in this example), click the Show button to show the Shared section in the Sidebar if it's not already showing.**

(The button says Hide in Figure 16-13 because the shared section is showing.)

All available servers appear. (There are eight in Figure 16-13.)

3. Click the name of the remote Mac (Lisa & Jacob's Eye Mac) you want to access in the Sidebar.

At this point, you're connected to the remote Mac as a guest, as shown in Figure 16-13.

Figure 16-13: Connected to Lisa & Jacob's Eye Mac as a guest.

4. Click the Connect As button.

The Connect dialog appears. The name of the person logged in on Bob L's MacBook Pro automatically appears in the Name field (my account name, bobl, in Figure 16-14).

If that's not your user name on the Mac you're trying to access, type that username in the Name field.

If you select the Remember This Password in My Keychain check box in the Connect dialog, OS X remembers your password for you the next time you connect to this server. Sweet!

5. Select the Guest radio button if you don't have an account on the remote computer, and then click Connect; if you're logging in as a user, skip to Step 6.

Pressing ⌘+G is the same as selecting the Guest radio button, and pressing ⌘+R is the same as selecting the Registered User radio button.

As a guest user, you see Public Folders for users who have accounts on Lisa & Jacob's Eye Mac (Lisa LeVitus, Bob LeVitus, and Jacob in Figure 16-13) but nothing else.

Figure 16-14: The Connect dialog needs my password.

6. **Type your password and click the Connect button.**

After I've connected as a registered user, I see my Home folder (bobl in Figure 16-15), everyone else's Public folders, and hard disks connected to that Mac (BiggestBoy in Figure 16-15).

Figure 16-15: Connecting to Lisa & Jacob's Eye Mac as Bob LeVitus (bobl).

File sharing must be active on Lisa & Jacob's Eye Mac (the Mac I'm accessing remotely in the example). If file sharing weren't active on Lisa & Jacob's Eye Mac, its name wouldn't appear in the Shared section of the Sidebar, and I wouldn't be able to connect to it. But file sharing doesn't have to be active on the computer *you're* using (Bob L's MacBook Pro in this example) to give you access to the remote computer and make this trick work.

When you access your Home folder on a remote Mac as I've done in this example, you see an icon with the short name of your Home folder on that Mac (bobl in Figure 16-16) on the Desktop of the Mac you're using (unless you've deselected Connected Servers in Finder's General Preferences pane, under Show These Items on the Desktop).

Figure 16-16: Accessing my Home folder on Lisa & Jacob's Eye Mac remotely.

7. **When you finish using the remote Mac, disconnect by using one of these methods:**

   - Drag the shared-volume icon (bobl in Figure 16-16) to the Eject icon in the Dock.

     When a disk or volume is selected (highlighted), the Trash icon turns into a little arrow, which represents *eject*. Nice touch, eh?

   - Right-click or Control-click the shared volume icon and choose Eject from the contextual menu that appears.

   - Select the shared-volume icon and choose File⇨Eject.

   - Select the shared-volume icon and press ⌘+E.

   - In a Finder window Sidebar, click the little Eject symbol to the right of the remote computer's name (Lisa & Jacob's Eye Mac in Figure 16-16).

   - If you've finished working for the day, and you don't leave your Mac on 24/7 (as most folks do), choose ⌘⇨Shut Down or Log Out. Shutting down or logging out automatically disconnects you from shared disks or folders. (Shut Down also turns off your Mac.)

Changing Your Password

You can change your password at any time. Changing your password is a good idea if you're concerned about security — for example, if there's a chance your password has been discovered by someone else.

You can change the password for your account on your own Mac, or you can change the password you use to connect to your account on a remote Mac. I show you how to do both in the following sections.

Changing your account password on your Mac

To change the password on your own Mac, just follow these steps:

1. **Choose System Preferences, or double-click its icon in your Applications folder and click the Users & Groups icon.**

   The Users & Groups System Preferences pane appears.

2. **Select your account in the list on the left.**

   Your account information appears in the area on the right.

3. **Click the Change Password button.**

   A sheet drops down.

4. **Type your current password in the Old Password field.**

   This demonstrates that you are who you're supposed to be, not someone who just walked up to your unattended Mac.

5. **Type your new password in the New Password field.**

6. **Retype your new password in the Verify field.**

7. **(Optional but recommended) Type a hint in the Password hint field.**

8. **Click the Change Password button.**

   Assuming that you entered your old password correctly, the sheet disappears.

9. **Close the System Preferences window.**

Changing the password of any account but your own on your Mac

To change a password on your own Mac, just follow these steps:

1. **Choose ⌘⇨System Preferences, or double-click its icon in your Applications folder and click the Users & Groups icon.**

   The Users & Groups System Preferences pane appears.

   You may have to click the lock (at bottom left), supply an administrator name and password in the resulting dialog, and then click OK before you can proceed.

2. **Select the account you want to change the password for in the list on the left.**

   The account information appears in the area on the right.

3. **Click the Reset Password button.**

   A sheet drops down.

4. **Type the new password in the New Password field.**

5. **Retype the new password in the Verify field.**

6. **(Optional but recommended) Type a hint in the Password Hint field.**

7. **Click the Reset Password button.**

8. **Close the System Preferences window.**

Changing the password for your account on someone else's Mac

When you log in to a remote Mac, you can change your own password if you like. Follow these steps to do so:

1. **Log in to the remote computer on which you want to change your password.**

   See the "Connecting to a Shared Disk or Folder on a Remote Mac" section, earlier in this chapter, if you don't know how to log in to a remote computer.

   The Connect dialog appears.

2. **Type your username in the Connect dialog, if it's not already there.**

3. **Click the Change Password button in the bottom-left corner of the dialog.**

   A sheet for changing your password appears.

4. **Type your current password in the Old Password field.**

5. **Type your new password in the New Password and Verify fields.**

   You can use the Password Assistant (the little key to the right of the New Password text box) to help you generate a secure password.

6. **Click the Change Password button.**

   Your password is changed, and you return to the Connect dialog.

7. **(Optional) Type your new password and click Connect to log in to the other Mac.**

   You can skip this step by clicking the Cancel button in the Connect dialog if you don't need to use anything on the remote Mac at this time. Your password is still changed, and you need to use the new password the next time you log in to this Mac.

Select the Add Password to Keychain check box in the Connect dialog to store your passwords in a single place on the Mac; this way you don't have to retype them each time you access a Mac or other remote resource. (Read more about the Keychain in Chapter 19.)

More Types of Sharing

Several more types of sharing exist, and I'd like to at least mention a few in passing. All are found in (where else?) the Sharing System Preferences pane, which you can find by launching the System Preferences application (from the Applications folder, menu, or Dock) and clicking the Sharing icon.

Screen Sharing

Here's the sharing that I consider the coolest. Screen Sharing lets you control another Mac on your network from your Mac. In essence, you see the other Mac's screen on *your* Mac — and control it using *your* mouse and keyboard.

To set up Screen Sharing on the Mac you want to control remotely, follow these steps:

1. **Open the Sharing System Preferences pane by launching the System Preferences application (from the Applications folder, , Launchpad, or Dock) and clicking the Sharing icon.**

2. **Select the check box for Screen Sharing in the list of services on the left.**

3. **Click either the All Users or Only These Users radio button.**

   If you clicked Only These Users, click the + button and add the user or users you want to allow to control this Mac remotely. Notice that the Staff group is included by default.

To take control of your Mac from another Mac, follow these steps:

1. **Click the now-you-see-it-now-you-don't Show tag to the right of Shared to open the Shared section in the Sidebar, if it's not already open.**

All available servers appear.

2. **Click the name of the remote Mac you want to control.**

3. **Click the Share Screen button.**

   Depending on whether you clicked the All Users or Only These Users radio button, you may have to enter your name and password, and then click the Connect button.

   A window with the name of the remote Mac in its title bar appears. In it, you see the screen of the Mac you're looking to control remotely.

4. **Go ahead and click something.**

   Pull down a menu or open a folder. Isn't that cool? You're controlling a Mac across the room or in another room with your mouse and keyboard!

Web Sharing

Web Sharing enables others to share documents on your computer through the web. You can set up a website just by adding Hypertext Markup Language (HTML) pages and images to the Sites folder in your Home folder, and then activating Web Sharing in the Sharing pane of System Preferences.

In a perfect world, that would be all it took. To get it to work, however, you may need to modify settings for your network, router, firewall, DNS server, and other web publishing-related minutiae.

Web Sharing works only while your Mac is connected to the Internet or an internal network, and it requires the speed of a direct connection. If you use a modem and connect to the Internet by dialing up, this capability won't be a lot of use to you.

Furthermore, even if you keep your Mac connected to the Internet 24 hours a day with a Digital Subscriber Line (DSL) or cable-modem connection, using this feature could violate your agreement with your Internet service provider (ISP), because some ISPs prohibit you from hosting a website. Also, most cable and DSL connections use dynamic IP address assignment through Dynamic Host Configuration Protocol (DHCP), which means your IP address will change from time to time.

On the other hand, some ISPs don't care whether you run a website. Check with yours if you're concerned. I do turn on this feature occasionally, but (because I don't use it 24/7) I never bothered to check with my ISP. Do me a favor, and don't rat me out.

Internet Sharing

If your Mac has an Internet connection and another Mac nearby doesn't, you can enable Internet Sharing, and the other Mac can share your Internet connection. The following steps show you how:

1. **Open the Sharing System Preferences pane by launching the System Preferences application (from the Applications folder, ⌘ menu, Launchpad, or Dock) and clicking the Sharing icon.**

2. **Select the Internet Sharing check box in the list of services on the left.**

3. **Choose the connection you want to share — AirPort, FireWire, or Ethernet — from the Share Your Connection From pop-up menu.**

4. **Select the check boxes next to connections other computers will use — Wi-Fi, Ethernet, or Built-In FireWire.**

   Figure 16-17 shows Internet Sharing configured to share my Ethernet Internet connection with another Mac by using Wi-Fi.

Figure 16-17: Sharing my Ethernet Internet connection with another Mac using Wi-Fi.

5. **(Optional) Click the Wi-Fi Options button to name, select a wireless channel for, enable encryption for, and/or set a password for your shared network.**

   That's all there is to it.

And yet more ways to share

A few more cool ways to share your Mac include

- ✓ **DVD or CD Sharing:** When you select this one, remote users can access CDs and DVDs in your Mac's optical drive(s). You can select to have Mountain Lion notify you and request permission when a remote user makes such a request. This feature is especially handy if you have a MacBook Air or Mac mini, which don't ship with optical drives.

- ✓ **Printer Sharing:** If you turn on Printer Sharing in the Sharing System Preferences pane, other people on your local network can use any printer connected to your computer.

- ✓ **Scanner Sharing:** Analogous to Printer Sharing, Scanner Sharing allows others on your local network to use scanners connected to your Mac.

- ✓ **Bluetooth Sharing:** If you have a Bluetooth mobile phone or PDA, and your Mac has Bluetooth, you can configure many of the default behaviors for transferring files to and from your Mac. A picture is worth a thousand words, so Figure 16-18 shows all the things Bluetooth Sharing lets you configure.

Figure 16-18: Configure items for Bluetooth file transfers between your phone and Mac.

Features for the Way You Work

In This Chapter

▶ Talking to your Mac

▶ Listening to your Mac

▶ Enhancing productivity by using automation

▶ Trying out more useful technologies and techniques

▶ Running Microsoft Windows on your Mac (really!)

▶ Mirroring your Mac screen to your HDTV screen wirelessly

*T*his chapter delves into some OS X Mountain Lion features that might very well improve the ways you interact with your computer. Unlike the more mainstream applications and utilities I discuss in Part I — Desktop, Finder, Screen Saver, Appearance, Keyboard, Trackpad, Mouse, and such — the items in this chapter are a little more esoteric. In other words, you don't *have* to use any of the technologies I'm about to show you. That said, many of these items can make you more productive and can make using your Mac even better. So I'd like to believe that at least some of you will *want* to use the cool features I'm about to introduce.

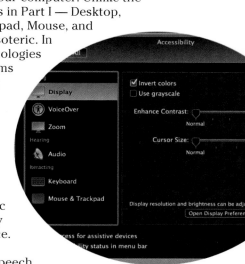

Talking and Listening to Your Mac

Your primary methods for interacting with your Mac are typing and reading text. But there's another way you can commune with your faithful computer: voice.

Whether you know it or not, your Mac has a lot of speech savvy up its sleeve (er . . . up its processors?) and can talk to you as well as listen, type the words you speak, and obey your spoken commands. In the following sections, you discover how to make your Mac do all of the above and more.

Dictation: You talk and your Mac types

Mountain Lion is the first version of OS X to include Dictation, so you can now talk instead of type. It's almost identical to the dictation feature found on the iPhone 4S and third-generation iPad.

First, make sure Dictation is enabled in the Dictation & Speech System Preference pane's Dictation tab; if it's set to Off, click the On button.

After it's enabled, Dictation couldn't be easier to use. First, click where you want your words to appear, and then choose Edit⇨Start Dictation, or press the Fn key twice in rapid succession.

If your keyboard doesn't have an Fn key, click the Shortcut pop-up menu in the Dictation & Speech System Preference pane to change the shortcut one that works with your keyboard.

When you start dictation, a little microphone icon appears. The purple filling indicates the level (relative loudness) of your voice. Try to keep the purple near the middle; not too high and not too low, as shown in Figure 17-1

Figure 17-1: Volume levels for dictation
(left to right): Too soft, just right, and too loud.

When you see the microphone icon, start speaking. After you've dictated a few sentences, click Done and let your Mac catch up. When the words appear you can start dictation again. Repeat as necessary.

It might not be a bad idea to save your document after you speak a few sentences or paragraphs; if you don't, the words you dictated since your last Save will be lost if the app or your Mac crashes.

You can insert punctuation by speaking its name, such as "period" or "comma." You can also perform simple formatting by saying "new line" or "new paragraph" to add space between lines.

Here are a few more tips to help you get the best results when you dictate:

- **Speak in a normal voice at a moderate volume level.** Try to keep the purple in the microphone icon about half-full (or half-empty if you're a pessimist).

- **Avoid background noise.** If you expect to use dictation in a noisy environment or a room with a lot of ambient echo, you should consider using a headset microphone.

  The headset that comes with iPhones and iPod touches is compatible with many Mac models.

- **Be sure the microphone is not obstructed.** Check your Mac's User Guide for the location of your built-in microphone (if you have one).

- **Be sure the input volume of an external microphone is sufficient.** If you're using an external microphone and the purple meter doesn't respond to your voice, select the microphone in the Input pane of the Sound System Preference pane and adjust its input level (volume).

One last thing — Dictation requires an Internet connection. When you dictate text, what you say is sent to Apple's servers to convert it to text.

Other information, such as your contacts, may also be sent to help your Mac understand what you're saying. If that makes you uncomfortable, you probably shouldn't use the Dictation feature.

Commanding your Mac by voice

Speech Recognition enables your Mac to recognize and respond to human speech. The only thing you need to use it is a microphone, and all laptops and iMacs have a built-in mic these days, as does the Apple LED Cinema Display that you can (optionally) purchase for use with any (Mountain Lion-capable) Mac.

Speech Recognition lets you issue verbal commands such as "Get my mail!" to your Mac and have it actually get your e-mail. You can also create AppleScripts and trigger them by voice.

An *AppleScript* is a series of commands, using the AppleScript language, that tells the computer (and some applications) what to do. You find out more about AppleScript later in this chapter.

Setting up for Speech Recognition

To start using Speech Recognition, launch System Preferences and follow these steps:

1. **Open the Accessibility System Preferences pane.**

2. **Click Speakable Items in list on the left and then click the Settings tab.**

3. **Click the On button for Speakable Items, as shown in Figure 17-2.**

Figure 17-2: Turn Speech Recognition on and off.

4. **Choose the microphone you want to use from the Microphone pop-up menu.**

   If you have a laptop or an iMac, you may get better results from just about any third-party microphone. The one that's built into your Mac works, but it isn't the greatest microphone on the planet.

5. **To test that microphone, click the Calibrate button, and follow the on-screen instructions.**

   There are two ways — called *listening methods* — you can use with Speech Recognition. The first listening method is to press a listening key — Esc by default — when you want to talk to your Mac. The second listening method is to have your Mac listen continuously for you to say a special keyword — "Computer" by default — when you want to talk to your Mac.

6. **(Optional) To change the listening key from Esc to a different key, click the Change Key button and press the key you want to use as your listening key.**

7. **(Optional) To change the listening method from Listening Key to Listening Continuously with Keyword, click the appropriate radio button.**

If you select Listening Continuously, you have two more options:

a. To change the way your Mac listens for the keyword — Optional before commands, Required before each command, or Required 15 or 30 seconds after last command — make your selection from the Keyword Is pop-up menu.

b. To change the keyword from Computer to something else, type the word you want to use in the Keyword field.

I call mine OK MacBook Pro, so when people are watching, I can casually say things like "OK, MacBook Pro, log me out," and watch their jaws drop when they realize that I'm talking to my laptop and it's actually doing what I ask.

8. **(Optional) You can have your commands acknowledged by your Mac, if you like, by selecting the Speak Command Acknowledgement check box.**

9. **(Optional) You can choose a sound other than Whit from the Play This Sound pop-up menu.**

10. **Click the Commands subtab on the Speech System Preferences pane's Speech Recognition tab, and then select the check box for each command set you want to enable.**

I can't see any reason not to enable them all unless you don't use Apple's Contacts, in which case you don't need to enable it.

11. **Click the Helpful Tips button and read the tips.**

12. **Click each command-set name, and if the Configure button is enabled, click it and follow the on-screen instructions.**

13. **If you create an AppleScript you want to be speakable, click the Open Speakable Items Folder.**

The Speakable Items folder is opened for you.

14. **Place the script in the folder.**

When you speak its name, the script is executed.

If the Speech System Preferences pane isn't open, and you want to open the Speakable Items folder, you can find it in your `Home/Library/Speech` folder.

15. **Close the Speech System Preferences pane when you're done.**

Using Speech Recognition

Here's how Speech Recognition works. For the sake of this discussion, I use the "Press Esc" listening method.

When Speech Recognition is turned on, a round feedback window appears on-screen, as shown in Figure 17-3.

Figure 17-3: The round Speech Recognition feedback window.

I'm not pressing the Esc key in Figure 17-2, so the word *Esc* appears in the middle of the window to remind me which key to press before I speak a command.

Now, here's how to actually use Speech Recognition:

1. **To see what commands are available, click the little triangle at the bottom of the feedback window, and select Open Speech Commands Window, as shown in Figure 17-3.**

   As you might expect, selecting Speech Preferences from this menu opens the Speech System Preferences pane for you.

   The Speech Commands window appears on-screen, as shown in Figure 17-4.

2. **Peruse the Speech Commands window to find a command you'd like to execute by speaking its name.**

3. **Speak that command exactly as written.**

   In this example, I press the Esc key and say to my Mac, "Tell me a joke." At this point, several things happen:

   - In the feedback window, Esc disappears, and the microphone lights up to subtly indicate that my Mac is waiting for speech input.
   - The command and my Mac's response appear in little boxes above and below the Feedback window.
   - The Speech Commands window changes to reflect the command I've spoken.

   My Mac then says, "Knock, knock," and the bottom part of the Speech Commands window displays the commands I can speak in response.

   You can see all this in Figure 17-5. And that's pretty much it for Speech Recognition.

Figure 17-4: The Speech Commands window.

Figure 17-5: Here's what happened when I pressed Esc and said, "Tell me a joke."

This technology is clever and kind of fun, but it can also be somewhat frustrating when it doesn't recognize what you say. And it requires a decent microphone — although the mic built into most Macs sometimes works okay. The bottom line is that I've never been able to get Speech Recognition to work well enough to continue using it beyond a few hours at best. Still, it's kind of cool (and it's a freebie), and I've heard more than one user profess love for it. Which is why it's included here.

Listening to your Mac read for you

The camera pans back — a voice tells you what you've just seen, and suddenly it all makes sense. Return with me now to those thrilling days of the off-camera narrator. . . . Wouldn't it be nice if your Mac had a narrator to provide a blow-by-blow account of what's happening on your screen?

Or . . . Your eyes are tired from a long day staring at the monitor, but you still have a lengthy document to read. Wouldn't it be sweet if you could sit back, close your eyes, and let your Mac read the document to you in a (somewhat) natural voice? The good news is that both are possible with OS X Mountain Lion — the former with VoiceOver and the latter with Text to Speech.

VoiceOver

Mountain Lion's VoiceOver technology is designed primarily for the visually impaired, but you might find it useful even if your vision is 20/20. VoiceOver not only reads what's on the screen to you, but also integrates with your keyboard so you can navigate around the screen until you *hear* the item you're looking for. When you're there, you can use Keyboard Access to select list items, select check boxes and radio buttons, move scroll bars and sliders, resize windows, and so on — with a simple key press or two.

To check it out, launch the System Preferences application (from Launchpad, the Applications folder, menu, or Dock), click the Accessibility icon, and then click VoiceOver or press ⌘+F5 (⌘+Fn+F5 on notebook/laptop models and most Apple keyboards).

After VoiceOver is enabled, you can turn it on and off in the Accessibility System Preferences pane or by pressing ⌘+F5 or (⌘+Fn+F5 on notebook/laptop models and most Apple keyboards).

While it's on, your Mac talks to you about what is on your screen. For example, if you clicked the Desktop, your Mac might say something along the lines of "Application, Finder; Column View; selected folder, Desktop, contains 8 items." It's quite slick. Here's another example: When you click a menu or item on a menu, you hear its name spoken at once, and when you close a menu, you hear the words "Closing menu." You even hear the spoken feedback in the Print, Open, and Save (and other) dialogs.

VoiceOver is kind of cool (talking alerts are fun), but having dialogs actually produce spoken text becomes annoying really fast for most folks. Still, I urge you to check it out. You might like it and find times when you want your Mac to narrate for you.

The VoiceOver Utility

The VoiceOver Utility lets you specify almost every possible option the VoiceOver technology uses. You can adjust its verbosity; specify how it deals with your mouse and keyboard; change its voice, rate, pitch, and/or volume; and more.

You can open the VoiceOver Utility by clicking the Open VoiceOver Utility button in the Accessibility System Preferences pane or the usual way: by double-clicking its icon (which you find in your Applications/Utilities folder).

Of course, you might get the machines-are-taking-over willies when your Mac starts to talk to you or make sounds — but if you give it a try, it could change your mind.

I wish I had the space to explain further, but I don't. That's the bad news. The good news is that VoiceOver Help is extensive and clear, and it helps you harness all the power of VoiceOver and the VoiceOver Utility.

Text to Speech

The second way your Mac can speak to you is using Text to Speech, which converts on-screen text to spoken words. If you've used Text to Speech in earlier versions of OS X, you'll find that it's pretty much unchanged.

Why might you need Text to Speech? Because sometimes hearing is better than reading. For example, I sometimes use Text to Speech to read a column or page to me before I submit it. If something doesn't sound quite right, I give it another polish before sending it off to my editor.

You can configure this feature in the Speech System Preferences pane:

1. **Open the System Preferences (from Launchpad, the Applications folder, Dock, or menu), click the Speech icon, and then click the Text to Speech tab.**

2. **Choose one of the voices in the System Voice pop-up menu to set the voice your Mac uses when it reads to you.**

3. **Click the Play button to hear a sample of the voice you selected.**

4. **Use the Speaking Rate slider to speed up or slow down the voice.**

5. **Click the Play button to hear the voice at its new speed.**

   I really like Alex, who says, "Most people recognize me by my voice." My second favorite is Fred, who says, "I sure like being inside this fancy computer."

6. **Select the Announce When Alerts Are Displayed check box if you want to make your Mac speak the text in alert boxes and dialogs.**

   You might hear such alerts as "The application Microsoft Word has quit unexpectedly" or "Paper out or not loaded correctly."

7. **Click the Set Alert Options button to choose a different voice to announce your alerts — the phrase your Mac speaks ("Alert," "Attention," "Yo, dude," and the like) when alerting you.**

   You can also set the delay between the time the alert appears and when it's spoken to you.

8. **(Optional) If you like, select either of these two check boxes: Announce When an Application Requires Your Attention or Speak Selected Text When the Key Is Pressed.**

   They both do what they say they'll do. In the case of the latter, you assign the key you want to press by clicking the Set Key button.

9. **(Optional) If you want to have the clock announce the time, click the Open Date & Time Preferences button, and you're whisked to that System Preferences pane; then click the Clock tab and select the Announce the Time check box.**

Now, to use Text to Speech to read text to you, copy the text to the Clipboard, launch TextEdit, paste the text into the empty untitled document, click where you want your Mac to begin reading to you, and then choose Edit⇨Speech⇨Start Speaking. To make it stop, choose Edit⇨Speech⇨Stop Speaking.

Another great place Text to Speech is available is in the Safari web browser. It works the same as TextEdit but you don't have to paste — just select the text you want to hear and choose Edit⇨Speech⇨Start Speaking.

Automatic Automation

OS X Mountain Lion offers a pair of technologies — AppleScript and Automator — that make it easy to automate repetitive actions on your Mac.

AppleScript is "programming for the rest of us." It can record and play back things that you do (if the application was written to allow the recording — Finder, for example, was), such as opening an application or clicking a button.

You can use it to record a script for tasks that you often perform, and then have your Mac perform those tasks for you later. You can write your own AppleScripts, use those that come with your Mac, or download still others from the web.

Automator is "programming without writing code." With Automator, you string together prefabricated activities (known as *actions*) to automate repetitive or scheduled tasks. How cool is that?

Automation isn't for everyone. Some users can't live without it; others could go their whole lives without ever automating anything. So the following sections are designed to help you figure out how much — or how little — you care about AppleScript and Automator.

AppleScript

Describing AppleScript to a Mac beginner is a bit like three blind men describing an elephant. One man might describe it as the Macintosh's built-in automation tool. Another might describe it as an interesting but often-overlooked piece of enabling technology. The third might liken it to a cassette recorder, recording and playing back your actions at the keyboard. A fourth (if there were a fourth in the story) would assure you that it looked like computer code written in a high-level language.

They would all be correct. AppleScript, a built-in Mac automation tool, is a little-known (at least until recently) enabling technology that works like a cassette recorder for programs that support AppleScript recording. And scripts do look like computer programs. (Could that be because they *are* computer programs? Hmm . . .)

If you're the kind of person who likes to automate as many things as possible, you might just love AppleScript because it's a simple programming language you can use to create programs that give instructions to your Mac and the applications running on your Mac. For example, you can create an AppleScript that launches Mail, checks for new messages, and then quits Mail. The script could even transfer your mail to a folder of your choice. Of course, OS X 10.4 Tiger also introduced Automator, which includes a whole lot of preprogrammed actions that makes a task like the one just described even easier.

I call AppleScript a time-and-effort enhancer. If you just spend the time and effort it takes to understand it, using AppleScript can save you oodles of time and effort down the road. Therein lies the rub. This stuff is far from simple; entire books have been written on the subject. So it's far beyond the purview of *OS X Mountain Lion For Dummies.* Still, it's worth finding out about if you'd like to script repetitive actions for future use. To get you started, here are a few quick tips:

- ✔ **You can put frequently used AppleScripts in the Dock or on your Desktop for easy access.**

- ✔ **Apple provides a script menu extra that you can install on your menu bar in AppleScript Utility's Preferences window** — along with a number of free scripts to automate common tasks, many of which are in the Example Scripts folder. (An alias to that folder is present in the AppleScript folder.) Furthermore, you can always download additional scripts from www.apple.com/applescript.

- ✔ **Many AppleScripts are designed for use in the toolbar of Finder windows,** where you can drag and drop items onto them quickly and easily.

- ✔ **Other scripts can enhance your use of iTunes, iPhoto, and iDVD.**

- ✔ **AppleScript Editor (in the Utilities folder inside the Applications folder) is the application you use to view and edit AppleScripts.** Although more information on AppleScript Editor is beyond the scope of this book, it's a lot of fun. And the cool thing is that you can create many AppleScripts without knowing a thing about programming. Just record a series of actions you want to repeat and use AppleScript Editor to save them as a script. If you save your script as an application (by choosing Format⇨Application in the Save sheet), you can run that script by just double-clicking its icon.

- ✔ **If the concept of scripting intrigues you, I suggest that you open the Scripts (in the root-level Library) folder.** Rummage through this folder to check out the scripts available at www.macosxautomation.com/applescript. Furthermore, you can always download additional scripts from www.apple.com/applescript. When you find a script that looks interesting, double-click it to launch the AppleScript Editor program, where you can examine it more closely.

Automator

Automator does just what you'd expect: It enables you to automate many common tasks on your Mac. If it sounds a little like AppleScript to you (which I discuss in the preceding section), you're not mistaken; the two have a common goal. But this tool (introduced in OS X Tiger) is a lot simpler to use, albeit somewhat less flexible, than AppleScript.

For example, in AppleScript, you can have *conditionals* ("if *this* is true, do *that*; otherwise do something else"), but Automator is purely *sequential* ("take *this*, do *that,* then do the next thing, and then . . .").

The big difference is that conditionals allow AppleScripts to take actions involving *decision-making* and *iteration* ("while *this* is true, do *these* things"); Automator workflows can't make decisions or iterate.

The upsides to Automator are that you don't have to know anything about programming, and you don't have to type any archaic code. Instead, if you understand the process you want to automate, you can just drag and drop Automator's prefab Actions into place and build a *workflow* (Automator's name for a series of Actions).

You do need to know one thing about programming (or computers), though: Computers are stupid! You heard me right — even my top-of-the-line MacBook Pro is dumb as a post. Computers do only what you tell them to do, although they can do it faster and more precisely than you can. But all computers run on the GIGO principle — garbage in/garbage out — so if your instructions are flawed, you're almost certain to get flawed results.

Another similarity between Automator and AppleScript is that it's up to the developers of the applications you want to automate to provide you the Actions or scripting support. Not all developers do so. For example, in Apple's wonderful iLife suite of multimedia applications, iTunes, iPhoto, and iDVD are all AppleScript-able — and they've supplied Actions for Automator users. iMovie and versions of GarageBand prior to GarageBand '09 don't support AppleScript. Furthermore, iMovie, GarageBand, and iWeb don't include any Automator actions at this time.

When you launch the Automator application, you see the window and sheet shown in Figure 17-6. Choose one of the starting points if you want Automator to assist you in constructing a new workflow, or choose Workflow to start building a workflow from scratch.

Figure 17-6: Choose Workflow to start a workflow from scratch.

I choose Service for the sake of this demonstration (you see why in a second). When I do, I see the window shown in Figure 17-7.

Figure 17-7: Convert text I select to an audio file.

The Library window on the left contains all the applications Automator knows about that have actions defined for them. Select an application in the top part of the Library window, and its related actions appear below it. When you select an action, the pane at the bottom of the Library window (Text to Audio File in Figure 17-6) explains what that Action does, what input it expects, and what result it produces. Just drag Actions from the Action list into the window on the right to build your workflow.

This particular Service, which took me less than 5 minutes of trial and error to perfect, is quite useful. First, I select text from any source — a web page, Microsoft Word document, e-mail message, or whatever. Then I right-click or Control-click and select my newly created Text-to-Audio Service from the Services menu. OS X then converts the selected text into an audio file, which I can have read to me in iTunes at home, or on my iPhone or iPad in the car, on a plane, or just about anywhere. Sweet!

Automator is a very useful addition to OS X; it's deep, powerful, and expandable, yet relatively easy to use and master. Do yourself a favor, and spend some time experimenting with ways Automator can save you time and keystrokes. You won't regret it.

A Few More Useful Goodies

Even more neat and useful technologies are built into Mountain Lion, but I'm running out of space. So here are, at least in my humble opinion, the best of the rest.

App Store

The App Store app is the OS X software version of the iTunes Store for media and iOS apps. Here, you'll find applications of all types — Business, Entertainment, Graphics, Productivity, Social Networking, and more — at prices that start at zero (free).

Just about everything I tell you in Chapter 12 about the iTunes Store could be said for the App Store. It looks and works the same, and it uses the same credit card you have on file at the iTunes Store.

TIP

If you see a little number on the App Store icon in your Dock, it means that number of your apps have updates available. Launch the App Store app and click the Updates tab to see the apps with updates awaiting them. Even if you don't see a little number in the App Store's Dock icon, it wouldn't hurt to launch the App Store every once in a while to check for updates manually, as the little number sometimes fails to appear in the App Store Dock icon.

Accessibility

Accessibility is mostly designed for users with disabilities or who have diffi-culty handling the keyboard, mouse, or trackpad. The Accessibility System Preferences pane has three sections — Seeing, Hearing, and Interacting — each of which has one or more subsections, as shown in Figure 17-7.

The Seeing section

Seeing has three subsections. The Display subsection lets you display the screen with inverted colors, as shown in Figure 17-8. Check the Use Grayscale box to desaturate your screen into a *grayscale display* (so it looks kind of like a black-and-white TV).

Figure 17-8: The Invert Colors option reverses what you see on-screen.

Select the Show Accessibility Status in Menu Bar check box to see the status of all of the Accessibility Preferences in your menu bar, as shown in Figure 17-7.

The Zoom subsection is where you can turn on a terrific feature called *hardware zoom,* which lets you make things on your screen bigger by zooming in on them. To control it by keyboard, select the Use Keyboard Shortcuts to Zoom check box. Then you can toggle it on and off with the shortcut ⌘+Option+8 and zoom in and out using the shortcuts ⌘+Option+= (the equals key) and ⌘+Option+– (the minus key), respectively. Try this feature even if you're not disabled or challenged in any way; it's actually a great feature for everyone.

Finally, the More Options button lets you specify minimum and maximum zoom levels, display a preview rectangle when zoomed out, and toggle image smoothing on or off.

The Hearing section

The Hearing section has a single subsection called Audio, which lets you choose to flash the screen whenever an alert sound occurs.

This feature, created for those with impaired hearing, is quite useful if you have a MacBook Pro or MacBook and want to use it where ambient noise levels are high or if you don't want your Mac to disturb those around you.

There's also a Play Stereo Audio as Mono check box. Not sure why you'd need it, and I couldn't hear any difference when I tried it with a variety of stereo audio sources. The only thing I can think of is that it might be helpful for those who listen to audio using a monaural (that is, one ear only) Bluetooth headset or those with hearing impairment in only one ear.

The Interacting section

The Keyboard subsection offers two types of assistance:

- The **Sticky Keys** application treats a *sequence* of modifier keys as a key combination. In other words, you don't have to simultaneously hold down ⌘ while pressing another key. For example, with Sticky Keys enabled, you can do a standard keyboard shortcut by pressing ⌘, releasing it, and then pressing the other key. You can select check boxes to tell you (with a beep and/or an on-screen display) what modifier keys have been pressed.

  As useful as Sticky Keys can be, they're really awkward in applications like Adobe Photoshop, Adobe Illustrator, and other applications that toggle a tool's state when you press a modifier key. So if you're a big Photoshop user, you probably don't want Sticky Keys enabled.

- **Slow Keys** lets you adjust the delay between when a key is pressed and when that key press is accepted.

The Mouse & Trackpad subsection offers options for those who have difficulties using a mouse or trackpad by using keys on the keyboard to navigate rather than a mouse or trackpad.

You can also increase the cursor size from the normal setting (16x16) to about 64x64.

Energy Saver

All Macs are Energy Star–compliant (and have been for years), allowing you to preset your machine to turn itself off at a specific time or after a specified idle period. To manage your Mac's energy-saving features, open the Energy Saver System Preferences pane by choosing ❖⇨System Preferences and clicking the Energy Saver icon.

If you have a notebook computer, you have two mostly identical tabs — Battery and Power Adapter — in your Energy Saver System Preferences pane. The battery tab controls your MacBook, MacBook Air, or MacBook Pro's behavior when it's running on battery power (not plugged in); the Power Adapter tab controls its behavior when it *is* plugged in.

If you have a desktop Mac, you won't have tabs, but you do have most of the same controls, including a pair of sliders that control sleep times for your computer and display. To enable Computer or Display sleep, move the appropriate slider to the desired amount of time. You can choose any number between 1 minute and 3 hours, or turn off either type of sleep entirely by moving its slider all the way to the right, to Never.

Setting the display to sleep is handy if you want your Mac to keep doing what it's doing, but you don't need to use the monitor. And if you're a notebook user, display sleep will save you battery power.

To wake up your Mac from its sleep, merely move your mouse or press any key.

Below the Sleep sliders are some check boxes for other useful energy settings, such as

- ✔ **Put the Hard Disk(s) to Sleep When Possible:** Enabling this option forces your hard drive to sleep after a few minutes of inactivity. It's not a particularly useful feature on a desktop Mac, but if you have a laptop, letting your hard drive sleep when it's idle will save you some battery power.

- ✔ **Wake for Network Access:** Enable this option if you want your Mac to wake up automatically for Ethernet network access (handy in a corporate setting where an IT person maintains system configurations).

- ✔ **Restart Automatically if the Computer Freezes:** Enabling this option tells your Mac you want it to restart automatically if it becomes totally hosed.

- ✓ **Allow Power Button to Put the Computer to Sleep:** Does just what it says: Enable it, and tapping your Mac's power (on/off) button puts your computer to sleep immediately.

  To turn your Mac off, use the menu's Shut Down command or its keyboard shortcut (Control+power key).

- ✓ **Automatically Reduce Brightness Before Display Goes to Sleep:** Another one that does what it says.

If you have a laptop, you'll have some additional options, including

- ✓ **Slightly Dim the Display When Using This Power Source (Battery tab only):** The display dims slightly and uses less power when running on the battery.

- ✓ **Show Battery Status in the Menu Bar:** This option adds a little battery-status indicator icon and menu.

Finally, to start up, shut down, or put your Mac to sleep at a predetermined time, click the Schedule button, and then select the appropriate check box and choose the appropriate options from the pop-up menus.

Bluetooth

Bluetooth is wireless networking for low-bandwidth peripherals, including mice, keyboards, and mobile phones. If your Mac has Bluetooth built in or is equipped with a USB Bluetooth adapter, you can synchronize wirelessly with phones and Palm devices, print wirelessly to Bluetooth printers, and use Bluetooth mice and keyboards.

To manage your Mac's Bluetooth features, open the Bluetooth System Preference pane by choosing ⌘⇨System Preferences and clicking the Bluetooth icon.

Ink

Ink is the OS X built-in handwriting-recognition engine. If you have a stylus and tablet connected to your Mac, just turn it on in this pane, and you can hand-write anywhere your Mac accepts typing with the keyboard.

To manage your Mac's Ink features, open the Ink System Preferences pane by choosing ⌘⇨System Preferences and clicking the Ink icon.

The Ink pane is one you see only if you have one of the pen-input tablets that Ink supports connected to your Mac. Most of the supported tablets come from Wacom (www.wacom.com), with prices starting under $100 for a small wireless stylus and tablet.

Automatic Login (Users & Groups System Preferences pane)

Some users don't care for the fact that OS X Mountain Lion is a multiuser operating system — and dislike having to log in when they start up their Mac. For those users, here's a way to disable the login screen:

1. **Open the Users & Groups System Preferences pane, select yourself in the list of users, and click the Login Options button below the list.**

2. **Choose the account you want to be logged in automatically from the Automatic Login pop-up menu.**

   To disable the logging-in requirement, you have to be an administrator, and you might need to unlock the Users & Groups System Preferences.

When you disable logging in, you also affect all the preferences set by anyone else who uses your Mac unless they log out of your account and log into theirs. (Yikes.) So if your Desktop pattern, keyboard settings, and so forth are different from those of someone else who uses your machine, those preferences won't be properly reflected unless each of you has a separate, individual login account. Even if you're not worried about security, consider keeping logging in enabled if any other users have accounts on your machine, or if you don't want just anyone to be able to turn on your Mac and see your personal stuff.

Note that only one account is allowed to use autologin. If another user wants to use this Mac, you need to choose ⌘⇧Log Out, press ⌘+Shift+Q, or have Fast User Switching enabled. And if you've disabled automatic login in the Security System Preferences pane, you can't enable it here.

Boot Camp

Boot Camp is Mountain Lion's built-in technology that allows you to run Microsoft Windows Vista, or Windows 7 on any Intel-based Mac. If your Mac meets the following requirements, you can run Windows on your Mac (if you so desire):

- An Intel-based Mac (of course)
- At least 10GB of free hard drive space (though you'll almost certainly need more)
- A hard drive that isn't partitioned
- A blank recordable CD
- A printer (for printing the instructions)
- A full install copy of Microsoft Windows Vista, or Windows 7 Home Premium, Professional, or Ultimate

You really do need a *full retail* copy of Windows, one that was purchased in a retail box. If your copy of Windows came with your Dell or HP, you probably can't install it under Boot Camp.

To install Windows on your Mac, here are the basic steps:

1. **Launch the Boot Camp Assistant application, which is in your `Applications/Utilities` folder.**

   This step creates a partition on your hard drive for Windows and then burns a special CD with all the drivers you'll need to use Windows on your Mac.

2. **Install Windows on the new partition.**

3. **Install the drivers from the CD you just burned.**

   From now on, you can hold down Option during startup and choose to start up from either the OS X Mountain Lion disk partition or the Windows partition.

If running Windows on your Mac appeals to you, you might want to check out Parallels Desktop or VMWare Fusion (around $80 each) or VirtualBox (free). All three programs not only allow you to run Windows on your Mac, but also let you do so without partitioning your hard drive or restarting every time you want to use Windows. In fact, you can run Mac and Windows programs simultaneously with all three of these products. For more information, read the section on PC disks in Chapter 8.

AirPlay Mirroring

There is one last feature I'd be remiss by not mentioning, even though most of you won't be able to use it without buying an Apple TV. (See the "What's an Apple TV" sidebar for my take on this marvelous little device.)

The feature is called AirPlay Mirroring, and with it, you can stream whatever is on your Mac (or iOS device) screen wirelessly to your HDTV with a connected Apple TV.

It couldn't be easier to use. If an Apple TV is on the same Wi-Fi network as your Mac, an option for AirPlay Mirroring will appear in the Displays System Preference pane. Just enable AirPlay Mirroring, and what is on your Mac screen will appear on your HDTV screen almost instantaneously.

Enable Show Mirroring Options in the Menu Bar When Available in the Displays System Preference pane, and a handy menu lets you switch AirPlay Mirroring on and off without the bother of first opening the Displays System Preference pane.

What's an Apple TV?

Simply put, Apple TV is a shiny little black cube (3.9 x 3.9 x 0.9-inches; 0.6 pounds) that costs $99. It connects to your HDTV via an HDMI cable and lets you rent or buy movies and TV shows from the iTunes Store, as well as stream movies, TV shows, photos, and other media from computers and other devices to your HDTV.

Unlike so many audio/video devices, Apple TV is the model of simplicity. Just plug it in to AC power and connect it to your HDTV using an HDMI cable (not included). For those with a Wi-Fi network, that's all there is to it. You can also connect it via Ethernet cable (also not included), but that's much less convenient. I had both Wi-Fi and an HDMI cable, so I had it up and running in less than 10 minutes.

The on-screen interface — what you see on the HDTV — is clean and uncluttered, making it easy to navigate using either the included aluminum Apple Remote or the free Apple Remote app for iPhone, iPad, and iPod touch. It's a pleasure to sit on the couch and rent or buy movies and TV shows in standard or high definition from the iTunes Store. It's also great to watch streaming video on Netflix. But the best part, at least for me, is that I have complete access to almost all my audio, video, and pictures, all without leaving the comfort of the sofa. More precisely, my family can enjoy TV shows, movies, music, podcasts, audiobooks, and photos, regardless of whether they're actually stored on my Mac Pro, my wife's iMac, or my son's MacBook.

If that were all it did I'd still recommend it, but there's more! Through the magic of Apple's AirPlay technology, you can also stream media to an Apple TV from your iPhone, iPod touch, or iPad. How can you not love that? Here's how that might work: Say you come over and want to show me some pictures. You whip out your iPhone, tap the AirPlay icon in the Photos app, and select my Apple TV. Presto! Your pictures are beamed wirelessly to my Apple TV and appear on my 46-inch HDTV. Beats the heck out of viewing them on a 3.5-inch iPhone screen, don't you think?

There's even more, including MLB and NBA game subscriptions, as well as videos from YouTube and Vimeo. If it offered video from Amazon and Hulu, like my Roku XS box, it would be darn near perfect.

Part V
The Care and Feeding of Your Mountain Lion

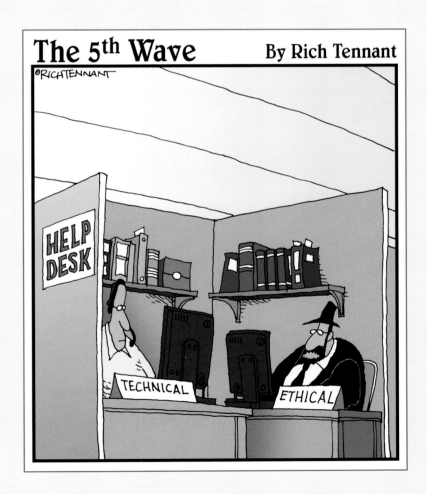

The 5th Wave By Rich Tennant

HELP DESK

TECHNICAL ETHICAL

In this part . . .

ere, I get into the nitty-gritty underbelly of handling trouble in OS X. In this part, I cover topics such as protecting your valuable data by backing it up, and I discuss everything you need to know about Macintosh security (which, thankfully, isn't all that much). Next, you look at some utilities that might or might not be useful but that you should know about anyway. Finally, you find out what to do when things go wonky (which also, thankfully, doesn't happen very much) and experience a quick run-through of Dr. Mac's (okay, Dr. Bob's) top troubleshooting tips for those infrequent times when a good Mountain Lion goes bad.

This material is a little geekier than the first four parts, but it could very well be the most important information in the book. Don't miss out!

18

Safety First: Backups and Other Security Issues

In This Chapter

▶ Backing up . . . it's easy

▶ Discovering why you should back up

▶ Finding out what happens to you if you don't back up

▶ Keeping your Mac safe from rogue viruses and malicious attacks

▶ Protecting your data from prying eyes

*A*lthough Macs are generally reliable beasts (especially Macs running OS X), someday your hard drive (or SSD) will die. I promise. They *all* do. And if you don't back up your drive (or at least back up any files that you can't afford to lose) before that day comes, chances are good that you'll never see those files again. And if you do see them again, my friend, it will be only after paying someone like my buddy Scott Gaidano, the founder of DriveSavers Data Recovery Service. And even if you pay, there's no guarantee of success.

DriveSavers is the premier recoverer of lost data on hard drives. The people there understand Mac hard drives quite well, do excellent work, and can often recover stuff that nobody else could. (Ask the producers of *The Simpsons* about the almost-lost episodes.) Understandably, DriveSavers charges accordingly. Here are some phone numbers for DriveSavers: 800-440-1904 toll free and 415-382-2000.

In other words, you absolutely, positively, without question *must back up* your files if you don't want to risk losing them. Just as you adopt the Shut Down command and make it a habit before turning off your machine, you must remember to back up important files on your hard drive to another disk or device — and back them up often.

How often is often? That depends on you. How much work can you afford to lose? If your answer is that losing everything you did yesterday would put you out of business, you need to back up hourly or perhaps even continuously. If you would lose only a few unimportant documents, you can back up less frequently.

Following the comprehensive coverage of backup options, I look at the possible threat to your data from viruses and other icky things, as well as how you can protect against them.

Finally, I look at what you can do to keep other people from looking at your stuff.

Backing Up Is (Not) Hard to Do

You can back up your hard drive in basically three ways: the super-painless way with Mountain Lion's excellent Time Machine, the ugly way using the brute-force method, or the comprehensive way with specialized third-party backup and disk-cloning software. Read on and find out more about all three. . . .

Backing up with Mountain Lion's excellent Time Machine

Time Machine is a most excellent backup system that was introduced with OS X Leopard — and it's only gotten better. I say it's a system because it consists of two parts: the Time Machine System Preferences pane, shown in Figure 18-1, and the Time Machine application, shown in Figure 18-2.

Figure 18-1: The Time Machine System Preferences pane and menu.

Figure 18-2: The Time Machine application is ready to restore a file in the Finder.

To use Time Machine to back up your data automatically, the first thing you need is another hard drive that's the same size as or larger than your startup disk. It can be a FireWire hard drive, a USB 2 hard drive, a Thunderbolt hard drive, an SSD (if you can afford to use a Solid State Drive for backups), or even another internal hard drive, if your Mac is a Mac Pro like one of mine.

Another option is an Apple Time Capsule, a device that combines an AirPort Extreme wireless base station with a large hard drive so you can automatically back up one or more Macs over a wired or wireless network.

The first time a new disk suitable for use with Time Machine is connected to your Mac, a dialog asks if you want to use that disk to back up with Time Machine. If you say yes, the Time Machine System Preferences pane opens automatically, showing the new disk already chosen as the backup disk.

If that doesn't happen, or you want to use an already-connected hard drive with Time Machine, open the Time Machine System Preferences pane, and click the big On/Off switch to On. Now click the Select Disk button, and select the hard drive you want to use for your backups. Mine is called Bob's Time Machine 500GB (because that's what I named my backup disk) in Figure 18-1.

The only other consideration is this: If you have other hard disks connected to your Mac, you should click the Options button to reveal the Do Not Back Up list, which tells Time Machine which volumes (disks) *not* to back up. To add a volume to this list, click the little + button; to remove a volume from the list, select the volume and then click the – button.

The Options sheet also has a check box for warning you when old backups are deleted; check it if you want to be warned. And if your Mac is a laptop, a second check box governs whether Time Machine backs up your Mac when it's on battery power.

For the record, Time Machine stores your backups for the following lengths of time:

- Hourly backups for the past 24 hours
- Daily backups for the past month
- Weekly backups until your backup disk is full

When your backup disk gets full, the oldest backups on it are deleted and replaced by the newest.

When does it run? Glad you asked — it runs approximately once per hour.

If you enable and set up Time Machine as I've just described, you'll never forget to back up your stuff, so just do it.

What does Time Machine back up?

Time Machine backs up your whole hard disk the first time it runs, and then backs up files and folders that have been modified since your last backup. That's what backup systems do. But Time Machine does more — it also backs up things like contacts in your Contacts, pictures in your iPhoto Library, and events in your Calendar calendars, not to mention its support of versions and locking. Those features — sweet ones indeed — make Time Machine unlike any other backup system.

How do I restore a file (or a contact, a photo, an event, and so on)?

To restore a file or any other information, follow these steps:

1. **Launch the appropriate program — the one that contains the information you want to restore.**

   If what you want to restore happens to be a file, that program is the Finder, which, as you know, is always running. So to restore an individual file, you don't actually need to launch anything. But to restore a contact, a photo, an e-mail message, or an event, for example, you need to launch Contacts, iPhoto, Mail, or Calendar, respectively.

2. **With the appropriate application running (or the appropriate Finder window open), launch the Time Machine application, as shown in Figure 18-2.**

   If you selected the Show Time Machine in Menu Bar check box in the Time Machine System Preference Pane, you can choose Enter Time Machine in the Time Machine menu, as shown in Figure 18-1.

It will be easier to restore a file in the Finder if the folder the file is in (or was in) is the *active* folder (that is, open and frontmost) when you launch the Time Machine application. If not, you have to navigate to the appropriate folder before you can perform Step 3.

3. **Click one of the bars on the right side of the screen *or* click the big "forward" and "back" arrows next to them to choose the backup you want to restore from (Tuesday, May 22, 2012 at 3:29PM in Figure 18-2).**

While the current backup is Tuesday, May 22, 2012 at 3:29PM, note that my cursor is hovering over the bar for Monday, May 21, 2012. If I were to click that bar, I'd see the contents of the Documents folder as they were on May 21.

4. **Select the file, folder, Contacts contact, iPhoto photo, e-mail message, or Calendar event you wish to restore.**

5. **Click the big Restore button below the big forward and back arrows.**

If the file, folder, Contacts contact, iPhoto photo, e-mail message, or Calendar event exists in the same location today, Time Machine politely inquires as to your wishes, as shown in Figure 18-3.

Figure 18-3: Time Machine asks what to do with the file you're restoring.

Backing up by using the manual, brute-force method

If you're too cheap to buy a second hard drive, the most rudimentary way to back up is to do it manually. You would accomplish this by dragging said files a few at a time to another volume — a CD-R, CD-RW, DVD-R, or DVD-RW. (If you use an optical disc, don't forget to actually *burn the disc;* merely dragging those files onto the optical-disc icon won't do the trick.)

By doing this, you're making a copy of each file that you want to protect. (See Chapter 8 for more info on removable storage.)

Yuck! If doing a manual backup sounds pretty awful, trust me — it is. This method can take a long, long time; you can't really tell whether you've copied every file that needs to be backed up; and you can't really copy only the files that have been modified since your last backup. Almost nobody in his right mind sticks with this method for long.

Of course, if you're careful to save files only in your Documents folder, as I suggest several times in this book, you can probably get away with backing up only that. Or if you save files in other folders within your Home folder or have any files in your Movies, Music, Pictures, or Sites folders (which often contain files you didn't specifically save in those folders, such as your iPhoto photos and iTunes songs), you should probably consider backing up your entire Home folder.

As you read in the following section, backing up your Home folder is even easier if you use special backup software.

Backing up by using commercial backup software

Another way to back up your files is with a third-party backup program. Backup software automates the task of backing up, remembering what's on each backup disc (if your backup uses more than one disc), and backing up only files that have been modified since your last backup.

Furthermore, you can instruct your backup software to back up only a certain folder (Home or Documents) and to ignore the hundreds of megabytes of stuff that make up OS X, all of which you can easily reinstall from the OS X Install DVD.

Your first backup with commercial software might take anywhere from a few minutes to several hours and use one or more optical discs — CD-R, CD-RW, DVD-R, DVD-RW, magneto-optical disc — or nonoptical media, such as another hard drive or any kind of tape backup. Subsequent backups, called *incremental backups* in backup-software parlance, should take only a few minutes.

If you do incremental backups, be sure to label all the discs you use during that operation; if you use multiple discs, number them. Your backup software may prompt you with a message such as `Please insert backup disk 7`. If you haven't labeled your media clearly, you could have a problem figuring out which disc *is* disc 7 or which disc 7 belongs to that particular backup set.

One of the best things about good backup software is that you can set it up to automate your backups and perform them even if you forget. And although Time Machine is a step in the right direction and might be sufficient for your needs, it's not good enough for me. I use a total of nine hard drives for backups.

Why You Need Two Sets of Backups

You're a good soldier. You back up regularly. You think you're immune to file loss or damage.

My backup recommendations

I am continually testing new backup solutions, so the software I use can change from month to month. I've tried most of the popular backup solutions and many of the more obscure ones, but before I say anything about my current setup, here is what I'm trying to accomplish (at a minimum): I want at least three (reasonably) current backup "sets" with copies of all my files. I want to update two of them every day and keep the third somewhere offsite (in my safe deposit box at the bank). Every week or two, I swap whichever backup is at the bank for a fresh one — one of the two I update daily.

This scheme ensures that no matter what happens — even if my office burns; floods; is destroyed by tornado, hurricane, or an earthquake; or robbed — I won't lose more than a week or two of work. I can live with that.

Note that once I set them up, all four programs run automatically in the background with no further action on my part, a feature I think of as "set and forget."

My first line of defense, of course, is Mountain Lion's excellent Time Machine. There's no excuse not to use it. But although Time Machine maintains multiple copies of files, they're all stored on the same disk. And I always say, if something's worth backing up to one place, it's worth backing up to three.

And so, in addition to Time Machine, I use the excellent CrashPlan (www.crashplan.com; from $1.50/month), which backs up my Documents folder four times a day to two different hard drives. It also backs up my Home folder continuously to yet another hard drive, so every time I make a change to a document, the backup copy is updated in real time. Finally, it backs up my Home folder over the Internet to the CrashPlan cloud-based servers.

Every night at midnight, SuperDuper! (www.shirtpocket.com; $27.95) clones (duplicates) my startup disk to another hard drive, which provides me a bootable backup I can use with almost any other Mac.

Finally, I use the excellent and free Dropbox (www.dropbox.com) service to synchronize my current project folders among several Macs and my iPhone and iPad, giving me even more backup copies of my most important files.

There is one last thing: I test the integrity of each backup regularly, and so should you. For one thing, it confirms that the files I think are there are actually there, and it reassures me that the files in that backup set aren't corrupted or damaged and are capable of being restored successfully.

Now picture yourself in the following scenario:

You leave the office one day for lunch. When you return, you discover that your office has been burglarized, struck by lightning, flooded, burned to the ground, or buried in earthquake rubble — take your pick.

Alas, while you did have a backup, the backup disk was in the same room as your Mac, which means it was either stolen or destroyed along with your Mac.

This scenario is totally unlikely — but it *could* happen, and it does demonstrate why you need multiple backups. If you have several sets of backup disks, and don't keep them all in the same room as your Mac, chances are pretty good that one of the sets will work even if the others are lost, stolen, or destroyed.

Non-Backup Security Concerns

As you've probably surmised by now, backing up your files is critical unless you won't mind losing all your data someday. And although backing up is by far your most important security concern, several other things could imperil your data — things like viruses or other types of malware, including worms, spyware, and intruder attacks. That's the bad news. The good news is that all those things are far more likely to affect Windows users than Mac users. In fact, I'd venture to say that viruses, worms, malware, spyware, and intruder attacks are rarer than hens' teeth for Mac users.

That said, here are a few precautions Mac users should consider, just in case.

About viruses and other malware

A computer *virus,* in case you missed it in *Time* magazine, is a nasty little piece of computer code that replicates and spreads from disk to disk. A virus could cause your Mac to misbehave; some viruses can destroy files or erase disks with no warning.

Malware (short for *malicious software*) is software that's hostile, intrusive, annoying, or disruptive. Malware is often designed to gain unauthorized access to your computer and/or collect personal data (including passwords) without your knowledge.

The difference between a virus and other types of malware is that malware doesn't spread by itself. It relies upon trickery, mimicry, and social engineering to induce unsuspecting users to open a malicious file or install a malicious program. So a virus is a type of malware, but not all malware is viral.

You don't hear much about viruses on the Mac because there have been few (if any) since the dawn of the modern OS X era (so many big cats ago). Almost all viruses are specific to an operating system — Mac viruses won't affect Windows users, Windows viruses won't affect Mac users, and so forth, and the vast majority of known viruses affect only (you guessed it) Windows.

The one real exception here is a "gift" from the wonderful world of Microsoft Office (Word and Excel, for example) users: the dreaded *macro viruses* that are spread with Word and Excel documents containing macros written in Microsoft's VBA (Visual Basic for Applications) language. But you're safe even from those if you practice safe computing as I describe (although you can unknowingly pass them along to Windows users).

As it happens, so far, much of the viral activity affecting OS X involved various Windows macro viruses. Sadly, a very real threat known as Flashback appeared in early 2012. It exploited a security flaw in Java and stealthily installed itself on Macs. Soon after its discovery, Apple issued software updates for OS X that removed the malware and corrected the security flaw.

By default, your Mac automatically checks for software updates every week, but you can change that setting in the Software Update System Preference Pane. Click the Check Now button to run Software Update manually and check for the latest updates. The moral of the story is that it's usually a good idea to install Apple updates sooner rather than later.

So while there was at least one piece of truly malicious software spotted in the wild, others are spread mostly via social engineering. So here's how to protect yourself:

- Disable Open Safe Files after Downloading in Safari Preferences.

- If a suspicious alert or window appears on your screen, Force Quit your web browser (⌘⇨Force Quit or ⌘+Option+Esc) immediately.

- If the OS X Installer launches for no apparent reason, *do not click Continue!* Don't install the software, and for heaven's sake, don't type your administrator password.

- Don't run *any* installer — the one built into OS X or a third-party kind — unless you're absolutely certain that it came from a trusted source.

- Don't use credit or debit cards with unfamiliar vendors and/or insecure websites.

If you use disks that have been inserted into other computers, you need some form of virus-detection software. If you download and use files from web and File Transfer Protocol (FTP) sites on the Internet, you need some form of virus detection as well.

You don't have too much to worry about if

- You download files only from commercial online services, such as AOL, CNET, or MacUpdate, which are all very conscientious about malware.

- You use only commercial software and never download files from websites with strange names.

You should definitely worry about malicious infection if

- An unsavory friend told you about a website called `Dan'sDenOf PiratedIllegalStolenBootlegSoftware.com`, and you actually visited it.

- You swap disks or USB thumb drives with friends regularly.

- You shuttle disks or USB thumb drives back and forth to other Macs.

- You use your disks or USB thumb drives at public computers or printing shops.

- You download files from various and sundry places on the Internet, even ones that don't sound as slimy as `Dan'sDenOfPiratedIllegal StolenBootlegSoftware.com`.

- You receive e-mail with attachments (and open them).

If you're at risk, do yourself a favor, and buy a commercial antivirus program. I'm not quite ready to install antivirus software myself; I find that it's obtrusive and slows my Mac. If you think you need protection, consider VirusBarrier X6 ($49.95; `www.intego.com`), MacScan ($29.99; `www. macscan.securemac.com`), or ClamXAV (free; `www.clamxav.com`).

If you decide to do as I do and not as I just suggested, I urge you to visit some or all of the websites in Chapter 23 regularly. If nothing else, you'll get advance warning the next time a particularly heinous piece of Mac malware is on the loose. I don't know about you, but I'll wait until then to reassess my position on this antivirus conundrum.

Firewall: Yea or nay?

According to the OS X built-in Oxford American Dictionary, a firewall is

Part of a computer system or network that is designed to block unauthorized access while permitting outward communication.

Using a firewall protects your computer from malicious users on other networks or the Internet and keeps them from gaining access to your Mac.

Unlike older versions of Windows, OS X is quite difficult to crack. There have been few (if any) reports of outsiders gaining access to Macintosh computers running OS X. One reason might be that OS X has a built-in firewall. That's the good news. The bad news is that said firewall is disabled by default. You'll need to activate it if you want to be protected against unauthorized access to your computer.

If you use a router with its own firewall (and the router's firewall is enabled), do not activate the Mountain Lion firewall. Running multiple firewalls can cause issues.

To activate your firewall, follow these steps:

1. **Open the System Preferences application (from the Applications folder, 🍎 menu, Launchpad, or Dock).**

2. **Click the Security & Privacy icon and click the Firewall tab.**

   The default setting is Allow All Incoming Connections, which is the least secure option.

3. **Click the Turn On Firewall button to turn the firewall on, if it's not already running.**

   (Optional) If the lock in the bottom-left corner of the Security & Privacy pane is locked, click it, and provide your administrator password.

4. **Click the Firewall Options button to configure your firewall's settings.**

5. **For the highest level of protection, select the Block All Incoming Connections check box.**

6. **Click OK.**

Alas, you probably won't want to keep this setting for long, because you won't be able to use awesome OS X features such as Messages and file, screen, printer, and music sharing, to name a few. If (or when) it becomes desirable to allow certain incoming connections from outside computers, enable them in the Sharing System Preference pane.

The only other issue you're likely to face is when a particular application needs you to allow outside connections to it in order to function. How would you know? Check the user manual, Read Me file, or application Help. Or you might see an error message that the program can't connect to the Internet. Don't worry — if a program requires you to open your firewall, you can almost certainly find some information in one (or more) of these places.

The solution is to click the little + button on the left near the bottom of the Firewall Options window. A standard Open File sheet drops down over the window; select the appropriate program and click the Add button. Your firewall will then allow incoming connections to that particular application evermore.

Install recommended software updates

I mentioned this before in a short tip but it bears repeating: By default, your Mac checks with the mothership (Apple) once a week to see if there's any new or updated software for your Mac. If there is, your Mac informs you that a new Software Update is available and asks whether you'd like to install it. In almost all cases, you do. Apple issues Software Updates to fix newly discovered security concerns, to fix serious bugs in OS X, or to fix bugs in or add functionality to Apple applications.

You can perform this check manually by clicking the Software Update icon in the System Preferences window, and then clicking the Check Now button. You also use the Software Update System Preferences pane to change the frequency of these checks, disable automatic checking completely, and/or instruct your Mac to automatically download any updates it finds.

Every so often, one of these Software Updates has an unintended side effect; while fixing one problem, it introduces a different problem. Apple is generally pretty careful, and this doesn't happen very often, but if you want to be safe, don't install a Software Update until you've visited MacFixIt (www. macfixit.com), Macworld (www.macworld.com), or MacInTouch (www. macintouch.com) and looked at their reports on the update you have in mind. If there are widespread issues with a particular Software Update, these sites will have the most comprehensive coverage (and possible workarounds).

Apps need updates too. So make a habit of launching the Mac App Store application now and then, clicking the Updates tab, and then updating any apps that require it.

Many third-party programs, including Microsoft Office and Adobe Creative Suite, use their own update-checking mechanism. Check and make sure you've got yours enabled. Many third-party apps offer a Check for Updates option in the Help (or other) menu or as a preference in their Preferences window.

One last thing: If you see a little number on the App Store's icon in the Dock, you have that many updates waiting. Launch the Mac App Store, and click the Updates tab.

Protecting Your Data from Prying Eyes

The last kind of security I look at in this chapter is protecting your files from other users on your local area network and users with physical access to your Mac. If you don't want anyone messing with your files, check out the security measures I describe in the following sections.

Blocking or limiting connections

The first thing you might want to do is open the Sharing System Preferences pane by launching the System Preferences application (from the Applications folder, ⌘ menu, or Dock) and clicking the Sharing icon. Nobody can access your Mac over the network if all the services in the Sharing pane are disabled and your firewall is set to Block All Incoming Connections. See the section "Firewall: Yea or nay?" earlier in this chapter for details on these settings.

Locking down files with FileVault

If you absolutely, positively don't ever want anyone to be able to access the files in your Home folder, FileVault allows you to encrypt your entire disk and protect it with the latest government-approved encryption standard: Advanced Encryption Standard with 128-bit keys (AES-128).

When you turn on FileVault, you're asked to set a *master password* for the computer. After you do, you or any other administrator can use that master password if you forget your regular account login password.

If you turn on FileVault and forget both your login password and your master password, you can't log in to your account — and your data is lost forever. Really. Not even DriveSavers has a hope of recovering it. So don't forget both passwords, okay?

FileVault is useful primarily if you store sensitive information on your Mac. If you're logged out of your user account and someone gets access to your Mac, there is no way they can access your data. Period.

Because FileVault encrypts your Home folder, some tasks that normally access your Home folder might be prevented. For one thing, some backup programs choke if FileVault is enabled. Also, if you're not logged in to your user account, other users can't access your Shared folder(s).

And because FileVault is always encrypting and decrypting files, it often slows your Mac when you add or save new files, and it takes extra time before it lets you log out, restart, or shut down.

To turn on FileVault, follow these steps:

1. **Open the Security & Privacy System Preferences pane.**

2. **Click the FileVault tab.**

3. **Click the Turn on FileVault button to enable FileVault.**

To turn off FileVault, click the Turn off FileVault button. At least that's how it's supposed to work, *but.* . . .

Setting other options for security

The General tab of the Security & Privacy System Preferences pane offers several more options that can help keep your data safe. They are

- ✓ **Change Password:** Click this button to change the password for your user account.

- ✓ **Require Password after Sleep or Screen Saver Begins:** Enable this option if you want your Mac to lock itself up and require a password after the screen saver kicks in or it goes to sleep. It can become a pain in the butt, having to type your password all the time. But if you have nosy co-workers, family members, or other individuals you'd like to keep from rooting around in your stuff, you should probably enable this option.

  When enabled, this option offers a pop-up menu that lets you specify how long after sleep or screen saver this password protection should kick in. The options range from immediately to four hours.

- ✓ **Show a Message When the Screen Is Locked:** Type the message you want on your screen when it's locked in this text entry box.

- ✓ **Disable Automatic Login:** One of the login options in the Users & Groups System Preferences pane is automatic login. With automatic login enabled, you don't have to choose an account or type a password when you start up this Mac. Instead, it bypasses all that login stuff and goes directly to the Desktop of the designated account. If you want to disable this feature for all accounts — so that every user of this Mac sees the login screen and is required to choose an account and type a password — you should enable this option.

- ✓ **Allow Applications Downloaded from Mac App Store, Mac App Store and Identified Developers, or Anywhere:**

  Last, but certainly not least (at least with regard to the General tab), is a new feature called Gatekeeper, which helps protect you from downloading and running malicious software by limiting the applications your Mac can run.

  These three options are mutually exclusive; click the radio button next to the level of protection you desire. Here's what you get with each:

  - *Mac App Store:* This option only allows you to run apps you download from the Mac App Store. It's the safest and most restrictive setting.

- *Mac App Store and Identified Developers:* Apple offers a Developer ID program to certified members of the Mac Developers Program. Apple gives them a unique Developer ID, which allows Gatekeeper to verify that their app is not known malware and that it hasn't been tampered with. If an app doesn't have a Developer ID associated with it, Gatekeeper can let you know before you install it.

  This is probably the best choice for most users. It allows third-party apps from Apple-vetted vendors, such as Microsoft, Adobe, and thousands more. It's a lot less restrictive than the Mac App Store option, and a lot safer than choosing Anywhere.

- *Anywhere:* What its name suggests; this option lets you run any app, no matter where it came from.

Finally, two items in the Privacy tab of the Security & Privacy System Preferences pane are

 ✓ **Enable Location Services:** Select this option for each app you wish to allow use of your computer's current location to provide information, services, and features appropriate to where you are.

 ✓ **Send Diagnostic & Usage Data to Apple:** Anonymously sends details of system crashes, apps that quit unexpectedly, freezes, or kernel panics to the mothership in Cupertino, Apple's world HQ. Engineers then pore over the data and issue software updates to eliminate the bugs. At least that's the theory. . . .

And that's all you really need to know about security and privacy (or at least enough to make you dangerous).

Utility Chest

In This Chapter

▶ Crunching numbers with the Calculator
▶ Setting up lots of stuff, including AirPort Base Stations and Bluetooth devices
▶ Plumbing your Mountain Lion's innards
▶ And much, much more . . .

O S X Mountain Lion comes with a plethora of useful utilities that make using your computer more pleasant and/or make you more productive when you use your computer. In this chapter, I give you a glimpse of the ones that aren't covered elsewhere in this book.

The first item, Calculator, is in your Applications folder; all the other items in this chapter are in your Utilities folder, *inside* your Applications folder (or you can use the Utilities folder's keyboard shortcut, ⌘+Shift+U).

Calculator

Need to do some quick math? The Calculator application gives you a simple calculator with all the basic number-crunching functions that your pocket calculator has. To use it, you can either click the keys with the mouse or type numbers and operators (math symbols such as +, –, and =) using the number keys on your keyboard (or numeric keypad, if you have one). Calculator also offers a paper tape (Window➪Show Paper Tape) to track your computations — and, if you want, provide a printed record. It can even speak numbers aloud (Speech➪Speak Button Pressed and Speech➪Speak).

Check out the Calculator in Figure 19-1.

Figure 19-1: The Calculator (left), Convert menu (middle), and Paper Tape (right).

In my humble opinion, the most useful feature in the Calculator (after the paper tape) is the Convert menu — more specifically, the currency-conversion feature. It actually checks the Internet for the exchange rate before calculating the conversion for you. That's very cool.

Beyond that, Calculator has three modes: Basic, Scientific, and Programmer. Basic is the default, and you access the other two modes as follows:

✓ Pressing ⌘+2 (View➪Scientific) turns the formerly anemic calculator into a powerful scientific calculator.

✓ Choosing View➪Programmer (⌘+3) turns it into the programmer's friend, letting you display your data in binary, octal, hexadecimal, ASCII, and Unicode. It also performs programming operations such as shifts and byte swaps. (If you're a programmer, you know what all that means; if you aren't, it really doesn't matter.)

Activity Monitor

In Unix, the underlying operating system that powers OS X, applications and other things going on behind the scenes are called *processes.* Each application and the operating system itself can run a number of processes at the same time.

In Figure 19-2, you see 78 different processes running, most of them behind the scenes. Note that when this picture was taken, I had half a dozen or more programs running, including the Finder, FaceTime, the Mac App Store, and Activity Monitor itself.

Figure 19-2: The Activity Monitor window (left) and the three little CPU Monitor windows (right).

To display the three CPU Monitor windows on the right side of the Activity Monitor window as shown in Figure 19-2, choose Window⇨CPU Usage (keyboard shortcut ⌘+2), CPU History (keyboard shortcut ⌘+3), and/or Floating CPU Window (no keyboard shortcut).

You also select what appears in the Activity Monitor's Dock icon — CPU Usage, CPU History, Network Usage, Disk Activity, Memory Usage, or the Activity Monitor icon — by choosing View⇨Dock Icon. All but the Activity Monitor icon appear *live*, meaning that they update every few seconds to reflect the current state of affairs.

To choose how often these updates occur, choose View⇨Update Frequency.

But be careful — setting Activity Monitor to update more frequently causes it to use more CPU cycles, which can decrease overall performance slightly.

Finally, the bottom portion of the Activity Monitor window can display one of five monitors. Just click the appropriate tab — CPU, System Memory, Disk Activity, Disk Usage, or Network — to see that particular monitor.

Because all Macs that can run Mountain Lion have at least a dual-core processor, you'll see at least two, and possibly four or more, CPUs displayed in Activity Monitor, one for each core.

Geeks and troubleshooters (and even you) can use Activity Monitor to identify what processes are running, which user owns the process, and how much CPU capacity and memory the process is using. You can even use this feature to quit or force-quit a process that you think might be causing problems for you.

Messing around in Activity Monitor isn't a good idea for most users. If you're having problems with an application or with OS X, try quitting open applications; force-quitting applications (press ⌘+Option+Esc — the Mac "three-finger salute"); or logging out and then logging back in again before you start mucking around with processes.

AirPort Utility

You use AirPort Utility to set up an AirPort Base Station, AirPort Extreme, AirPort Express, or TimeCapsule, and configure its individual settings, such as base-station and wireless-network passwords, network name, Internet connection type, and so on.

When you first open AirPort Utility, select the AirPort Base Station you want to work with by clicking its icon on the left side of the window.

If you want assistance with setting up your base station, just click the Continue button in the bottom-right corner of the AirPort Utility window. You're asked a series of questions, and your base station is configured accordingly. If you know what you're doing and want to change your base station's settings manually, choose Base Station⇨Manual Setup (⌘+L) instead.

ColorSync Utility

ColorSync helps ensure color consistency when you're scanning, printing, and working with color images. This package includes ColorSync software as well as premade ColorSync profiles for a variety of monitors, scanners, and printers. And the ColorSync Utility has a bunch of tools designed to make working with ColorSync profiles and devices easier. You'll probably never need it, but I wanted to let you know it's there, just in case.

A *ColorSync profile* is a set of instructions for a monitor, scanner, or printer, which tells the device how to deal with colors and white so the device's output is consistent with that of other devices, as determined by the ColorSync profiles of the other devices. In theory, if two devices have ColorSync profiles, their output (on-screen, on a printed page, or in a scanned image) should match. Put another way, the color that you see on-screen should be exactly the same shade of color that you see on a printed page or in a scanned image.

If you're not a graphic artist working with color files and calibrating monitors and printers to achieve accurate color matching, you probably don't need the ColorSync Utility (unless you've gotten hooked on iPhoto and want your printed inkjet color pictures to match up correctly).

If you're compelled to do whatever it takes to get accurate color on your monitor and printer, check out *Color Management For Digital Photographers For Dummies,* by Ted Padova and Don Mason (Wiley).

DigitalColor Meter

The DigitalColor Meter program displays what's on your screen as numerical color values, according to two different systems: RGB (red-green-blue) or CIE (the abbreviation for a chromaticity coordinate system developed by the Commission Internationale de l'Eclairage, the international commission on illumination). If you're not a graphic artist or otherwise involved in the production of high-end color documents, or working in HTML, you'll probably never need it.

Disk Utility

If you're having problems with your hard drive or need to make changes to it, Disk Utility is a good place to start. Start by clicking a disk or volume in the column on the left and then click one of the five tabs described in the following sections.

First Aid tab

If you suspect that something's not quite right with your Mac, the First Aid portion of Disk Utility should be among your first stops. Use First Aid to verify and (if necessary) repair an ailing drive. To use it, click the First Aid button on the left side of the Disk Utility window. Click a volume's icon, and then click Verify. You get information about any problems that the software finds. If First Aid doesn't find any problems, you can go on your merry way, secure in the knowledge that your Mac is A-okay. If verification turns up trouble, click Repair to have the problem fixed. You can also use First Aid to fix disk-permission problems.

You won't be able to use the copy of Disk Utility in your `Applications/Utilities` folder to repair your OS X boot disk. To do that, you must reboot from Mountain Lion's Recovery Disk or another bootable disk.

You can't use Disk Utility First Aid to fix a CD or DVD, nor can you use it to fix most disk image files. These disks are read-only and can't be altered.

Erase tab

Use Erase to format (completely erase) any disk except the current startup disk.

Of partitions and volumes

Partitioning a drive lets you create multiple volumes. A *volume* is a storage space that (from the Mac's point of view) looks and acts just like a hard drive; a *partition* is simply a designated volume on a drive, completely separate from all other partitions (volumes). You can create any number of partitions, but it's a good idea to limit yourself to no more than a small handful.

You can create drive partitions only on a newly formatted drive. So to partition a drive, first format it in Drive Setup, and then create partitions. Before you do that, give some thought to how large a partition you want to create. You won't be able to change your mind about it later.

By the same token, it's absolutely not necessary to use partitions unless you are running Boot Camp. Many users never partition a hard drive and get along just fine. If you do choose to partition, you should probably limit the number of partitions you create. An iMac with a 500GB drive will do just fine with one or two (or maybe three) partitions; there's no need to create more.

When you format a disk, you erase all information on it permanently. Formatting can't be undone — so unless you're *absolutely sure* this is what you want to do, don't do it. Unless you have no use for whatever's currently on the disk, make a complete backup of the disk before you format it. If the data is critical, you should have at least two (or even three) known-to-be-valid backup copies of that disk before you reformat.

Partition tab

Use this tab to create disk partitions (multiple volumes on a single disk). OS X treats each partition as a separate disk. When you select an item in the column on the left, you see only a partition tab when you select a disk, such as the 500.11GB Hitachi and Seagate or 16.01GB Verbatim drives in Figure 19-3.

Be careful here. While some adjustments can be made to partitions without loss of data, not all adjustments can. You'll be warned if what you're about to do will permanently erase your data, but I thought I'd give you fair warning first.

By the way, you won't see a Partition tab if you select a volume or partition — PussInBootsMBP, Lion HD, Fast 'n' Small, and Tuff 'n' Tiny in Figure 19-3, instead of a disk (500.11GB Hitachi, 500GB Seagate, and 16.01GB Verbatim in Figure 19-3). Makes sense when you think about it.

Figure 19-3: Select a disk (500.11GB Hitachi, 500GB Seagate, or 16.01GB Verbatim), and the Partition tab makes itself available.

RAID tab

By using Redundant Array of Individual (or Independent) Disks (RAID), you can treat multiple disks as a single volume, which is sort of the opposite of partitioning.

Restore tab

Use the Restore tab to restore your Mac to factory-fresh condition from a CD-ROM or disk-image file. In most cases, you install new software on your Mac from the Mac App Store, a CD or DVD or the Internet. Software vendors typically use an installer program that decompresses and copies files to their proper places on your hard drive. After you've installed the software, you're back in business.

Apple's variation on this theme is a humongous file called the *disk image* — everything you'd normally find on a disk, without the disk. These days, more developers are adopting the disk-image format for their downloadable installers and updaters. When mounted on your Desktop (more on what *mounting* means in a minute), a disk image looks and acts just like a real disk. You can open it and see its contents in a Finder window, copy files from its window to another disk, drag it to the Eject button to remove it from your Desktop — go wild. To make a disk image appear on your Desktop, you double-click the image file. At that point, the Disk Utility application takes over and puts an icon (which for all intents and purposes looks like a disk) on your Desktop.

Disk Utility not only mounts images when you double-click them, but also lets you create your own disk-image files and burn them onto CD-ROMs and DVD-ROMs.

Because you can transfer disk images via the Internet — and because they act just like disks — they're great substitutes for CD-ROMs and other disk-based software installers. A software maker can create both a CD version of an installer and a disk image that can be downloaded.

By the way, you find out more about Disk Utility (mostly how to use it for troubleshooting) in Chapter 20.

Grab

Want to take a picture of your screen? You can use Grab to take a picture of all or part of the screen and save that file for printing or sending around (say, to all your screaming fans who want to see your Desktop pattern or how you've organized your windows).

For the first edition of this book, I used Grab to create the screen shots, but I've used the superb Snapz Pro X utility (Ambrosia Software; `www.ambrosia sw.com`) for the figures in subsequent editions. In addition to offering many useful screen shot options not available in Grab, it also does full-motion screen recording.

Grab's best feature is its capability to do a timed screen capture. Like those cameras that let you start the timer and then run to get into the shot, Grab gives you 10 seconds to bring the window you want to the front, pull down a menu, and get the cursor out of the way or whatever you need to do to get the screen just right.

Grab's default behavior is to display no cursor. If you want to show a cursor in your screen shots, choose Grab➪Preferences and then select a pointer from the ten choices in the Preference dialog. To have no cursor, click the topmost, leftmost item, which is an empty box that indicates *no cursor*.

Grapher

Grapher is a venerable piece of eye candy that shows off your CPU's computational power. A quick, visual math instructor, Grapher can graph equations in two or three dimensions and speaks hexadecimal, octal, base ten (decimal), and binary to boot. You can even graph curves, surfaces, inequalities, differential equations, discrete series, and vector and scalar fields . . . whatever that means. (I found all that information in Apple Help.)

Keychain Access

A *keychain* is a way to consolidate your passwords — the one you use to log into your Mac, your e-mail password, and passwords required by any websites. Here's how it works: You use a single password to unlock your keychain (which holds your various passwords), and then you don't have to remember all your other passwords. Rest assured that your passwords are secure because only a user who has your keychain password can reach the other password-protected applications.

The Keychain Access utility is particularly cool if you have multiple e-mail accounts, and each one has a different password. Just add them all to your keychain, and you can get all your mail at the same time with one password.

A special "master" keychain called the Login Keychain is created automatically for every OS X Mountain Lion user.

Here's how to add passwords to your login keychain:

- **To add passwords for applications,** just open Mail or another application that supports the keychain. When the program asks for your password, supply it and choose Yes to add the password to the keychain.

    How do you know which programs support the Keychain Access utility? You don't until you're prompted to save your password in a keychain in that Open dialog, connect window, or so forth. If a program supports Keychain Access, it offers a check box for it in the user ID/password dialog or window.

- **To add a website password to a keychain,** open the Keychain Access application and click the Password button. In the New Password Item window that opens, type the URL of the page (or copy and paste it) in the Keychain Item Name text field; type your username in the Account Name field; and then type your password in the Password text field, as shown in Figure 19-4.

To use the new URL password, use Safari to open the URL. If the account name and password aren't filled in for you automatically, choose Edit⇨ AutoFill Form (⌘+Shift+A), and they will be. Now just click the appropriate button on the web page to log in.

Keychain Item Name:

http://www.macworld.com

Enter a name for this keychain item. If you are adding an Internet password item, enter its URL (for example: http://www.apple.com)

Account Name:

DoctorMac

Enter the account name associated with this keychain item.

Password:

•••••••••••

Enter the password to be stored in the keychain.

Password Strength: Weak

☐ Show Typing

Cancel   Add

Figure 19-4: Add a URL to the keychain manually by using Keychain Access.

If you select the User Names and Passwords check box on the AutoFill tab of Safari's Preferences window (Safari⇨Preferences or ⌘+,), you don't have to add sites, accounts, or passwords manually. Instead, the first time you visit a site that requires an account name and password, when you log in, Safari asks whether you would like to save your password, as shown in Figure 19-5.

Would you like to save this password?
To review or remove passwords you have saved, open Safari preferences, and then click AutoFill.

Never for this Website   Not Now   Yes

Figure 19-5: The easy way to add to your keychain in Safari.

Migration Assistant

Migration Assistant is pretty much a one-trick pony, but that pony is a prize winner. You use the Migration Assistant to transfer your account and other user information from another Mac or another volume on the current Mac to this one. You need to authenticate as an administrator to use it, but it's a pretty handy way to transfer an account without having to re-create all the preferences and other settings. When you first installed Mountain Lion (or when you booted your nice new Mountain Lion-based Mac for the first time), the setup utility asked you whether you wanted to transfer your information from another Mac. If you answered in the affirmative, it ran the Migration Assistant.

It's not just for new Mountain Lions. You can launch this puppy any time to transfer all or some user accounts, applications, settings, and files from another Mac or PC to this one. Or use it after replacing a hard drive or reinstalling OS X (see the Appendix). Last but not least, Migration Assistant can import user accounts, applications, settings, and files from Windows PCs as well as Macs.

System Information

System Information (the App Formerly Known as System Profiler) is a little program that is launched when you click the More Info button in the About This Mac window (➚About This Mac). It provides information about your Mac. (What a concept!) If you're curious about arcane questions such as what processor your Mac has or what devices are stashed inside it or are connected to it, give this baby a try. Click various items in the Contents list on the left side of the window, and information about the item appears on the right side of the window. Feel free to poke around this little puppy as much as you like; it's benign and can't hurt anything.

If you ever have occasion to call for technical support for your Mac, software, or peripherals, you're probably going to be asked to provide information from System Information, so don't get rid of it just because you don't care about this kind of stuff.

Terminal

OS X is based on Unix. If you need proof — or if you actually want to operate your Mac as the Unix machine that it is — Terminal is the place to start.

Because Unix is a command-line-based operating system, you use Terminal to type your commands. You can issue commands that show a directory listing, copy and move files, search for filenames or contents, or establish or change passwords. In short, if you know what you're doing, you can do everything on the command line that you can do in OS X. For most folks, that's not a desirable alternative to the windows-and-icons of the Finder window. But take my word for it; true geeks who are also Mac lovers get all misty-eyed about the combination of a command line *and* a graphical user interface.

You can wreck havoc upon your poor operating system with Terminal. You can harm your Mountain Lion in many ways that just aren't possible using mere windows and icons and clicks. So — before you type a single command in Terminal — think seriously about what I just said. And if you're not 100 percent certain about the command you've just typed, don't even think about pressing Return or Enter.

Troubleshooting OS X

In This Chapter

▶ Facing the ol' "My Mac Won't Boot" blues

▶ Dealing with the prohibitory sign

▶ Recovering from startup crashes

As a bleeding-edge Mac enthusiast with over a quarter century of Mac experience under my belt, I've had more than my share of Mac troubles. Over those years, I've developed an arsenal of mostly surefire tips and tricks that I believe can resolve more than 90 percent of Mac issues without a trip to the repair shop.

Alas, if your hardware is dead, then, sadly, neither you nor I can do anything about it because it is now a job for your friendly Mac repairman — and your fat checkbook or high-limit credit card. But if your hardware is okay, you have a fighting chance of using the suggestions in this chapter to get your machine up and running.

About Startup Disks and Booting

Although you usually see a stylish Apple logo when you turn on your computer, once in a blue moon, you might not. You might instead see a solid blue screen, a solid gray screen, a solid black screen, or something else entirely, as described in the next section.

The point is that your Mac isn't starting up as it should. When this happens, it usually indicates that something bad has happened to your Mac. Sometimes, it's a hardware component that has bitten the dust; at other times, OS X itself has somehow been damaged.

Rest assured that these occurrences are rather uncommon — many Macs and Mac users go an entire lifetime without seeing one. If you ever have a Mac that won't boot, don't despair. Before you declare your Mac terminally ill, try out the advice in this chapter.

Finding or creating a startup disk

When I talk about *booting*, I mean using a particular disk or disk partition as your startup disk. I bet you have a copy of the ultimate startup disk right there on your computer table — the installation DVD (or the first disc if you received more than one) that came with your computer.

For the entire history of OS X, I've advised my readers to keep their OS X installation disc close at hand . . . the one that came in the boxed retail copy they bought. At the time I'm writing this chapter, I can't repeat that advice for Mountain Lion. Apple has announced that only App Store purchases will be available for people upgrading to Mountain Lion. In other words, unless Apple changes its policy between now and the time you read this, you won't have a Mountain Lion Install DVD from which to work. So whatever else you do, make backup copies of the Mountain Lion Installer file that you receive from the App Store. The lack of a bootable installer disc solution should do wonders for the sale of external hard drives and high-capacity flash drives.

With Mountain Lion, however, because there is no bootable DVD, the Installer creates a bootable partition named Recovery HD on that disk when you first install Mountain Lion.

Explaining how to create a bootable recovery disk is beyond the purview of this book, but I hope you'll take it upon yourself to figure it out and make one. The Recovery HD partition is a good concept, but if your hard disk dies, the Recovery HD partition dies too. Which is why I recommend making a bootable clone of your startup disk as soon as possible, just in case.

Apple offers a free program called Recovery Disk Assistant (`http://support.apple.com/kb/DL1433`), which can create a bootable Mountain Lion installer disk for you. Another option is Carbon Copy Cloner (`www.bombich.com`), a donationware app that lets you create a clone of your boot disk with a minimum of fuss. Or try my favorite SuperDuper! (shareware from `www.shirt-pocket.com`), Just add a hard disk as large as or larger than your boot disk, and you'll be good to go.

They call it a prohibitory sign for a reason

When you turn on your Mac, the first thing it does (after the hardware tests) is check for a startup disk that has OS X on it. If your system doesn't find such a disk on your internal hard drive, it begins looking elsewhere — on a FireWire, Thunderbolt, Universal Serial Bus (USB) disk or thumb drive, or on DVD.

If you have more than one startup disk attached to your Mac, as many users do, you can choose which one your Mac boots from in the Startup Disk System Preferences pane.

At this point, your Mac usually finds your hard drive, which contains your operating system, and the startup process continues on its merry way with the subtle Apple logo and all the rest. If your Mac can't find your hard drive (or doesn't find on it what it needs to boot OS X), you encounter the dreaded prohibitory sign. Think of the prohibitory sign as your Mac's way of saying, "Please provide me a startup disk."

If Apple can figure out a way to put a prohibitory sign on the screen, why the heck can't the software engineers find a way to put the words *I need a startup disk* on the screen as well? The curtness of these icons is one of my pet peeves about the Macintosh. I know — you're clever and smart (because, of course, you're smart enough to find help reading *OS X Mountain Lion For Dummies*), so *you* know that a prohibitory sign means you should insert a startup disk. But what about everyone else?

If you encounter any of these warning icons, shown in Figure 20-1, go through the steps I outline later in this chapter. You can try different options, such as using Disk Tools and First Aid, zapping the parameter RAM (PRAM), and performing a Safe Boot. Try them in the order listed, starting with Step 1. Then, if one doesn't work, move on to the next.

Figure 20-1: Any of these means it's trouble-shooting time.

Recovering with Recovery HD

If you see a prohibitory sign (top left in Figure 20-1), spinning-disc cursor (top right), or kernel panic alert (the text in four languages that appears below the other two images) that doesn't go away when you start up your Mac, the first thing to do is attempt to repair hidden damage to your hard drive with the Disk Utility program's First Aid feature. And to do that, you'll have to boot from the Recovery HD partition. That's because you can't run Disk Utility's First Aid feature on the current startup disk.

To start up from this magical disk (actually, a disk partition), here's what to do:

1. **Restart your Mac.**

2. **Press and hold ⌘+R until you see the Apple logo.**

If your Mac doesn't boot from the Recovery HD after Step 2, hold down the Option key while booting to display the built-in Startup Manager (see Figure 20-2).

If you press Option after the startup chime instead of ⌘+R, the built-in Startup Manager appears. From this screen, you can click the Recovery HD icon (see Figure 20-2), and then click the arrow below it or press Enter or Return to boot from it. Or, if you're going to boot from a disk other than the Recovery HD, you can select it here.

Figure 20-2: The built-in Startup Manager.

Pressing Option during startup displays icons for all bootable volumes it sees and allows you to select one (including the Recovery HD partition).

Click the disk you want to start up from (Mountain Lion HD in Figure 20-2), and then click the arrow below it or press Return or Enter to start up your Mac from it.

This technique is quite useful if your usual startup disk is damaged or having an identity crisis during startup and the ⌘+R trick isn't working to boot from the Recovery HD partition.

If you can boot from the Recovery HD partition (or a, external startup drive, clone, DVD-ROM, or other disk): If you see the OS X Utilities window after booting from the Recovery HD partition, hope flickers for your Mac. The fact that you can boot from another volume indicates that the problem lies in one of two places: your startup volume and/or the OS X installation on that volume.

Regardless of what the cause is, your Mac will probably respond to one of the techniques I discuss throughout the rest of this chapter.

Please skip to Step 1.

If you can't boot from the Recovery HD partition, (or an external startup drive, clone, DVD-ROM, or other disk): If you can't get your Mac to boot from the Recovery HD partition or another bootable disk, please skip to Step 5.

Step 1: Run First Aid

In most cases, after you've booted successfully from the Recovery HD or another bootable disk, the first logical troubleshooting step is to use the First Aid option in the Disk Utility application.

Every drive has several strangely named components such as B-trees, extent files, catalog files, and other creatively named invisible files. They're all involved in managing the data on your drives. Disk Utility's First Aid feature checks all those files and repairs the damaged ones.

One last thing: If you booted from a disk other than the Recovery HD partition, you'll have to find and launch Disk Utility on that disk before you can follow these instructions:

1. **Boot from the Recovery HD volume by restarting your Mac while pressing the ⌘ and R keys.**

   The OS X Utilities window appears.

2. **Select Disk Utility and click Continue (Recovery HD).**

3. **When the Disk Utility window appears, click the First Aid tab to select that function of Disk Utility.**

4. **Click the icon for your boot hard drive at the left of the Disk Utility window (Mountain Lion HD in Figure 20-3).**

    Your boot drive is the one with OS X and your Home folder on it; mine is called *Mountain Lion HD.*

5. **Click the Repair Disk button.**

    Your Mac whirs and hums for a few minutes, and the results window tells you what's going on. Ultimately, First Aid tells you (you hope) that the drive has been repaired and is now okay, as shown in Figure 20-3. If so, go back to work.

Figure 20-3: First Aid has repaired the disk and gives it a clean bill of health.

6. **Quit Disk Utility by choosing Disk Utility⇨Quit Disk Utility or by pressing ⌘+Q.**

7. **Reboot without holding any keys down.**

If First Aid finds damage that it can't fix, a commercial disk-recovery tool, such as Alsoft's DiskWarrior (my personal favorite) or Prosoft's also-excellent Drive Genius, might be able to repair the damage. And even if First Aid gave you a clean bill of health, you might want to run DiskWarrior or another third-party utility anyway, just to have a second opinion. Make sure you're running a current version; older versions might not be compatible with OS X Mountain Lion boot disks.

DiskWarrior has resurrected more dead and dying hard drives for me than any other disk-repair utility I've ever tried — more than all of them combined. If you're going to buy only one utility, make sure that it's DiskWarrior. It's almost like magic.

If everything checks out with First Aid, restart and try to boot from your hard drive again. If you still get the prohibitory sign, proceed to the next section to try a dance called booting into Safe Mode.

Step 2: Safe Boot into Safe Mode

Booting your Mac in Safe Mode might help you resolve your startup issue by not loading nonessential (and non–OS X) software at boot time. You do it by holding down the Shift key during startup.

If your Mac is set up so you don't have to log in, keep pressing the Shift key until the Finder loads completely. If you do log in to your Mac, type your password as usual, but before clicking the Log In button, press the Shift key again and hold it until the Finder loads completely.

You know you held the Shift key long enough if your Login Items don't load (assuming that you have Login Items; you can designate them in the Users & Groups System Preferences pane, although some programs create them for you).

Booting in Safe Mode does three things to help you with troubleshooting:

- ✏ It forces a directory check of the startup (boot) volume.

- ✏ It loads only required kernel extensions (some of the items in `/System/Library/Extensions`).

- ✏ It runs only Apple-installed essential startup items (some of the items in `/Library/StartupItems` and `/System/Library/StartupItems`). Note that the startup items in the Library folders are different from the Login Items in the Users & Groups System Preferences pane.

Taken together, these changes often work around issues caused by software or directory damage on the startup volume.

Some features don't work in Safe Mode. Among them are DVD Player, capturing video (in iMovie or other video-editing software), using an AirPort card, using some audio input or output devices, or using a USB modem. Use Safe Mode only if you need to troubleshoot a startup issue.

If your Mac boots in Safe Mode, you might be able to determine what's causing the issue by moving the contents of your Preferences folder (in Home/Library, which you can make visible by pressing the Option key when opening the Go menu) to the Desktop temporarily or by disabling Login Items (in the Users & Groups System Preferences pane). If either of these things resolves the issue, you can put preferences files back in `Home/Library/Preferences` a few at a time, or you can re-enable login items one at a time until you figure out which preferences file or login item is causing your problems. If your Mac still has problems, try Step 3.

Step 3: Zapping the PRAM/NVRAM

Sometimes your *parameter RAM* (PRAM) or *Non-Volatile RAM* (NVRAM) becomes scrambled and needs to be reset. Both of these are small pieces of memory that aren't erased or forgotten when you shut down. They keep track of things such as

- Time-zone setting
- Startup volume choice
- Speaker volume
- Any recent kernel-panic information
- DVD region setting

To reset (a process often called *zapping*) your PRAM/NVRAM, restart your Mac and press ⌘+Option+P+R (that's four keys — good luck; it's okay to use your nose) until your Mac restarts itself. It's kind of like a hiccup. You might see the spinning-disc cursor for a minute or two while your Mac thinks about it — then the icon disappears, and your Mac chimes again and restarts. Most power users believe you should zap it more than once, letting it chime two, three, or even four times before releasing the keys and allowing the startup process to proceed.

Now restart your Mac without holding down any keys. If the PRAM/NVRAM zap didn't fix your Mac, move on to "Step 4: Reinstalling OS X."

Remember that your chosen startup disk, time zone, and sound volume are reset to their default values when you zap your PRAM. So after zapping, open the System Preferences application to reselect your usual startup disk and time zone, and set the sound volume the way you like it.

Unlike previous versions of the Mac OS, OS X doesn't store display or network settings in PRAM. If you're having problems with video or networking, resetting PRAM probably won't help.

Step 4: Reinstalling OS X

I present the procedure to reinstall the system software as a second-to-last resort when your Mac won't boot correctly because it takes the longest and is the biggest hassle. I detail this procedure at length in the Appendix.

Read the Appendix, and follow the instructions. If you're still unsuccessful after that point, you have no choice but to consider Step 5. . . .

Step 5: Things to try before taking your Mac in for repair

To get your Mac up and running again, you can try any of the following:

- **Call the tech-support hotline.** Before you drag it down to the shop, try calling 1-800-SOS-APPL, the Apple Tech Support hotline. The service representatives there may be able to suggest something else that you can try. If your Mac is still under warranty, it's even free.

- **Ask a local user group for help.** Another thing you might consider is contacting your local Macintosh user group. You can find a group of Mac users near you by visiting Apple's User Group web pages at www. apple.com/usergroups.

- **Try Dr. Mac Consulting.** Shameless plug alert! You can check out my consulting services at www.boblevitus.com or call 408-627-7577. My team of expert troubleshooters does nothing but provide technical help and training to Mac users, via telephone, e-mail, and/or our unique Internet-enabled remote-control software, which allows us to see and control your Mac no matter where in the world you are. Best of all, if we don't fix it, you pay nothing!

- **Check whether you have RAM issues.** Here's a common problem: If you have problems immediately after installing random-access memory (RAM) — or any new hardware, for that matter — double-check that the RAM chips are properly seated in their sockets. (*Warning:* Don't forget to shut down your Mac first.) With the power off and your Mac unplugged, remove and reinsert the RAM chips to make sure they're seated properly. If you still have problems, remove the RAM chips temporarily and see whether the problem still exists.

  Follow the installation instructions that came with the RAM chips — or the ones in the booklet that came with your Mac. But even if they don't say to get rid of the static spark, you should — either by using an anti-static strap (available from most RAM sellers) or by touching an appropriate surface (such as the power-supply case inside your Mac) *before you handle RAM chips.*

If none of my suggestions works for you, and you're still seeing anything you shouldn't when you start up your Mac, you have big trouble. You could have any one of the following problems:

- Your hard drive is dead.

- You have some other type of hardware failure.

- All your startup disks and your system software DVDs are defective (unlikely).

The bottom line: If you still can't start up normally after trying all the cures I list in this chapter, you almost certainly need to have your Mac serviced by a qualified technician.

If Your Mac Crashes at Startup

Startup crashes are another bad thing that can happen to your Mac. These crashes can be more of a hassle to resolve than prohibitory-sign problems, but they are rarely fatal.

You know that a *crash* has happened when you see a Quit Unexpectedly dialog, a frozen cursor, a frozen screen, or any other disabling event. A *startup crash* happens when your system shows a crash symptom any time between the moment you flick the power key or switch (or restarting) and the moment you have full use of the Desktop.

Try all the steps in the previous sections *before* you panic. The easiest way to fix startup crashes (in most cases) is to just reinstall OS X from the Recovery HD partition. I detail this procedure at great length in the Appendix. Read the Appendix, and follow the instructions. If you're still unsuccessful after that point, come back and reread the "Step 5: Things to try before taking your Mac in for repair" section.

Part VI
The Part of Tens

The 5th Wave   By Rich Tennant

TEACHERS LOUNGE

"Fortunately, at this grade level the Mac is very intuitive for them to use. Unfortunately, so is sailing mousepads across the classroom."

In this part . . .

These last chapters are a little different — they're kind of like long top-ten lists. Although I'd like for you to believe I included them because I'm a big fan of Dave Letterman, the truth is that Wiley always includes The Part of Tens section in its *For Dummies* books. This book continues the tradition. And because Wiley pays me, I do these chapters how I'm asked. (The truth is, I think it's fun.)

First, I tell you how to speed up your Mac experience. I then move on to a subject near and dear to my heart — awesome things for your Mac that are worth spending money on. Last but not least is a collection of great Mac-related websites.

Almost Ten Ways to Speed Up Your Mac Experience

*T*his chapter is for speed demons only. At some time in their Mac lives, most users have wished that their machines would work faster — even if their Macs have multiple cores or processors. I can't help you make your processors any faster, but here's where I cover some ways to make your Mac at least *seem* faster. Better still, at least some of these tips won't cost you one red cent.

Because this is the infamous Part of Tens, the powers that be require the word *ten* in the chapter title. But try as I might, I couldn't come up with ten ways to speed up your Mac. The nine tips that follow were the best I could do. So if you think of another one (or two) great ways to speed up your Mac, please send them to me at MountainLion4Dummies@boblevitus. com. If your suggestion is really good, I'll include it in the next edition and give you full credit for thinking of it!

Use Those Keyboard Shortcuts

Keyboard shortcuts (see Table 21-1 for a nice little list of the most useful ones) can make navigating your Mac a much faster experience compared with constantly using the mouse, offering these benefits:

- ✔ If you use keyboard shortcuts, your hands stay focused on the keyboard, reducing the amount of time that you remove your hand from the keyboard to fiddle with the mouse or trackpad.

- ✔ If you memorize keyboard shortcuts with your head, your fingers will memorize them too.

- ✔ The more keyboard shortcuts you use, the faster you can do what you're doing.

Trust me when I say that using the keyboard shortcuts for commands you use often can save you a ton of effort and hours upon hours of time.

Make a list of keyboard shortcuts you want to memorize, and tape it to your monitor or somewhere where you'll see it all the time when using your Mac. (Heck, make a photocopy of Table 21-1!)

Table 21-1	Great Keyboard Shortcuts	
Keyboard Shortcut	*What It's Called*	*What It Does*
⌘+O	Open	Opens the selected item.
⌘+. (period)	Cancel	Cancels the current operation in many programs, including the Finder. The Esc key often does the same thing as Cancel.
⌘+P	Print	Brings up a dialog that enables you to print the active window's contents. (See Chapter 15 for info on printing.)
⌘+X	Cut	Cuts whatever you select and places it on the Clipboard. (I cover the Clipboard in Chapter 6.)
⌘+C	Copy	Copies whatever you select and places it on the Clipboard.
⌘+V	Paste	Pastes the contents of the Clipboard at the spot where your cursor is.
⌘+F	Find	Brings up a Find window in the Finder; brings up a Find dialog in most programs.
⌘+A	Select All	Selects the entire contents of the active window in many programs, including the Finder.
⌘+Z	Undo	Undoes the last thing you did in many programs, including the Finder.
⌘+Shift+?	Help	Brings up the Mac Help window in the Finder; usually, the shortcut to summon Help in other programs.

Keyboard Shortcut	What It's Called	What It Does
⌘+Q	Quit	Perhaps the most useful keyboard shortcut of all — quits the current application (but not the Finder because the Finder is always running).
⌘+Shift+Q	Log Out	Logs out the current user. The login window appears on-screen until a user logs in.
⌘+Delete	Move to Trash	Moves the selected item to the Trash.
⌘+Shift+Delete	Empty Trash	Empties the Trash.

Improve Your Typing Skills

One way to make your Mac seem faster is to make your fingers move faster. The quicker you finish a task, the quicker you're on to something else. Keyboard shortcuts are nifty tools, and improving your typing speed and accuracy *will* save you time, plus you'll get stuff done faster if you're not always looking down at the keys when you type.

As your typing skills improve, you also spend less time correcting errors or editing your work.

The speed and accuracy that you gain has an added bonus: When you're a decent touch typist, your fingers fly even faster when you use those nifty keyboard shortcuts. (I list a gaggle of these in the preceding section, in Table 21-1.)

An easy way to improve your keyboarding skills is by using a typing tutor program such as Ten Thumbs Typing Tutor ($25.95 at `www.tenthumbs typingtutor.com`) or any of the myriads of typing instruction apps you'll find in the Mac App Store (search for **typing**.)

Resolution: It's Not Just for New Year's Anymore

A setting that you can change to potentially improve your Mac's performance is the resolution of your monitor. Most modern monitors and video cards (or onboard video circuitry, depending on which Mac model you use) can display multiple degrees of screen resolution. You change your monitor's display resolution in the same place where you choose the number of colors you want: the Display System Preferences pane. Select your resolution choice from the Resolutions list on the left side of this tab.

In Displays System Preferences, select the Show Displays in Menu Bar check box to change resolutions and color depth without opening System Preferences. You can then select your resolution from the Displays menu that appears near the right end of your menu bar, as shown in Figure 21-1.

Figure 21-1: The handy Displays menu.

Here's the deal on display resolution: The first number is the number of pixels (color dots) that run horizontally, and the second number is the number of lines running vertically. It used to be that fewer pixels refreshed faster. But with LCD and LED (flat-panel) monitors and notebooks, this isn't always true. I have to admit that the speed difference between resolutions these days is a lot less important than it used to be. In fact, I can almost never tell the difference between one and the other. Furthermore, because you can see more on-screen at higher resolutions, a higher resolution reduces the amount of scrolling that you have to do and lets you have more open windows on the screen. Finally, the highest resolution is almost always the "native" resolution of that display, which means it will usually look the sharpest. So you could just as easily say that higher resolutions can speed up your Mac experience as well.

Bottom line: Choose a resolution based on what looks best and works best for you. That said, if your Mac seems slow at its current resolution, try a lower resolution, and see whether it feels faster.

Although you can use OS X at resolutions of less than 1,024 x 768, Apple has designed the OS X windows and dialogs on the assumption that your resolution will be *at least* 1,280 x 800. So if you choose a resolution lower than that, some interface elements in some windows or programs may be drawn partially (or completely) off-screen. Just keep that in mind if you choose a resolution below 1,280 x 800.

A Mac with a View — and Preferences, Too

The type of icon display and the Desktop background that you choose affect how quickly your screen updates in the Finder. You can set and change these choices in the View Options window. From the Finder, choose View➪Show View Options (or use the keyboard shortcut ⌘+J).

The View Options window, like your old friend the contextual menu, is . . . well, contextual: Depending on what's active when you choose it from the View menu, you see one of five similar versions (shown in Figure 21-2). From left to right, the figure shows the options for folders in icon view, folders in list view, folders in column view, folders in Cover Flow view, and the Desktop.

Figure 21-2: Your choices in the View Options windows for icon view, list view, column view, Cover Flow view, and the Desktop.

A handful of settings can affect the speed of your Mac or your ability to see what you want quickly:

✔ **Icon size:** The smaller the icon, the faster the screen updates, especially if the folder has many graphic files with *thumbnails* (those little icon pictures that represent the big picture the file contains).

In the icon view of the View Options window, moving the Icon Size slider to the left makes icons smaller and faster; moving it to the right makes them bigger and slower. In list view, select one of the two Icon Size radio buttons to choose smaller (faster) or larger (slower) icons. The difference is greater if you have a slower Mac.

✔ **Calculate All Sizes:** I recommend that you deselect the Calculate All Sizes check box in the View Options window for list view. If you activate this option, the Finder calculates the size of every folder of every open window in list view and displays that number in the Size column. At least to me, the screen feels as though it redraws faster with this feature turned off.

If you want to know how big a folder is, you can always just click it and choose File⇨Get Info (or use the keyboard shortcut, ⌘+I).

✔ **Show Columns:** When it comes to speed, don't worry about the Show Columns check boxes in the View Options window for list view — Date Modified, Date Created, Size, Kind, Version, and Comments. The effect of these items on screen updating is pretty small these days, so your choice should probably be made according to the specific information you want to see in Finder windows, not on whether choosing them slows down your Mac.

The Use As Defaults buttons at the bottom of the icon and list View Options windows set the default appearance for *all* Finder windows of that type. If you don't click the Use As Defaults button, any changes you make apply only to the active window (bobl in Figure 21-2). Note that column view windows and the Desktop don't have a Use As Defaults button; in both cases, any changes you make automatically become the defaults.

Get a New, Faster Model

Apple keeps putting out faster and faster Macs at lower and lower prices. But some Mac models still ship with a paltry 2GB of RAM. Yes, it's officially enough RAM to run Mountain Lion, but I say it's not enough to run it at its best.

Check out the latest iMacs and Mac minis — they're excellent values. Or if you crave portability, MacBook Airs and MacBook Pros are rocking good computers and have never been less expensive. You might even consider a used Mac that's faster than yours. eBay (www.ebay.com) has hundreds of used Macs up for auction at any given time. Shopping on eBay might just get you a better Mac at an outstanding price. Give it a try!

Another excellent option is to visit the Apple website and search for refurbished equipment. You can frequently save hundreds of dollars by purchasing a slightly used Mac that has been refurbished to factory specifications by Apple. Another advantage to refurbs is that they come with an Apple warranty. If you're on a tight budget, definitely check it out.

You Can Never Have Too Much RAM!

You get a lot of bang for your buck when you upgrade your Mac's RAM. Get an additional 2GB or 4GB; you can never have too much. Your Mac will run better with at least 4GB of RAM, which will cost you under $100 in most cases and can be installed by anyone. Yes, anyone — the instructions are right there in your User Guide booklet, or you can find them at the Apple Technical Support pages (www.apple.com/support; search for *RAM upgrade* and your Mac model).

Unless, that is, you own a MacBook Air. The MacBook Air is exceedingly difficult to open, and Apple frowns upon users opening their MacBook Air. You might want to opt for the services of an authorized, certified Mac cracker-opener to perform your MacBook Air RAM upgrade. Or not.

Get an Accelerated Graphics Card

An accelerated graphics card is designed to speed up one thing: the screen-update rate. They're extremely popular with graphic-arts professionals and with gamers. Accelerated graphics cards blast pixels onto your screen at amazing speeds. And because the OS X Quartz Extreme imaging architecture hands off part of its load to the processor on an accelerated graphics card, it might even make your Mac's other tasks faster because it does some of the work that your Mac's main processor (CPU) used to do. That's the good news.

The bad news is that you can use a graphics accelerator only if your Mac has an *accelerated PCI slot* for it, which is where you install these suckers. Currently, only the Mac Pro models are capable of graphics-card upgrades.

Again, visit www.macworld.com for information on the various graphics cards available and how they compare with one another. Cards start at around $100 and go up from there. And remember, the older your Mac, the greater the performance boost you'll see.

Consider ordering your next Mac with an upgraded video subsystem. Most Macs today are available with at least two video subsystems; consider ordering the higher-performance model. Let's put it this way — if you are thinking about upgrading the video in your current Mac, you'll probably be happier if your next one has the fastest video you can afford.

Get a New Hard Drive

Depending on how old your Mac is, a faster hard drive could provide a substantial speedup. Because you have a Mac with an Intel processor ('cause Macs with older PowerPC processors can't run Mountain Lion), the internal hard drive that came with your Mac is probably pretty fast already. Unless you also need more storage space, a new hard drive is probably not the best way to spend your bucks.

On the other hand, if you have an older model, a faster (and larger) hard drive — whether FireWire, USB, or Thunderbolt — could be just the ticket. FireWire and Thunderbolt are the fastest *busses* (data pathways) you can use for external devices on most Macs.

FireWire, considered (until quite recently) the state of the art in connecting devices that need fast transfer speeds, is used to connect devices that require high-speed communication with your Mac — hard drives, CD burners, scanners, camcorders, and such. It's also the fastest bus that many Macs support natively.

Note that all current Mac models that *do* have FireWire have a type called FireWire 800. It uses a different type of cable from FireWire 400, which was found on older Macs. If you get a device that has FireWire 400, and your Mac has only FireWire 800 (or vice versa), it'll work as long as you get a FireWire 400-to-FireWire-800 adapter cable, available at the Apple Store and many other places.

Thunderbolt, which is available only on the newest Mac models, is the fastest bus around by far. That said, there are few Thunderbolt peripherals at this writing, and I've yet to see a single device with Thunderbolt cross my desk for testing. And the few devices that are out are significantly more expensive than their FireWire or USB counterparts. So while Thunderbolt shows much promise, I can't tell you much more about it at this juncture.

If you must use USB, make sure you get USB 2 and not plain old USB (Universal Serial Bus). Plain ol' USB might work, but it's as slow as molasses by comparison. (Plain ol' USB runs at about 3 percent of the speed of FireWire.)

USB 2, on the other hand, transfers data at roughly the same speed as FireWire. So if you have the need for speed, be sure you opt for a FireWire, USB 2 or Thunderbolt-equipped external hard drive and not an old, stale, plain ol' USB model.

The good news is that whatever you choose, you can usually just plug it in and start using it. 99 percent of the time, there's nothing more to it!

Get a Solid State Drive (SSD)

The latest and greatest storage device is called a Solid State Drive or SSD. It uses flash memory in place of a mechanical hard drive's spinning platters, which means, among other things, that there are no moving parts.

Another benefit is that they perform most operations at up to twice the speed of mechanical drives.

The bad news is that they're expensive — five or more times more than a mechanical hard drive with the same capacity. That said, many users report it's the best money they've ever spent on an upgrade. I'm definitely getting one in my next Mac.

Ten Ways to Make Your Mac Better by Throwing Money at It

*T*his is one of my favorite chapters. I love souping up my Macs. I live to find ways of working smarter, saving time or hand motion, and coaxing my Mac to do more work in less time. So it gives me great pleasure to share in this chapter my favorite top ten things that you can buy for your Mac to tweak it and make it faster, easier to use, and (I hope) more fun.

The items listed in this chapter are things I have, use every day, love dearly, and would (and probably will!) buy again.

RAM

RAM, or *random-access memory,* is your computer's primary working memory. The more you have, the smoother your Mac runs — period. If you have only 2GB in your Mac, you'll like your Mac *a lot* better if you upgrade to 4GB or more. If you like to do more than a few things at the same time, more RAM will make you a much happier camper. (For what it's worth, RAM has never been cheaper than it is today — and it's worth every penny.)

I know I mention it in the previous chapter, but in addition to speeding up your Mac, more RAM makes using your Mac better in other ways. For example, when you have plenty of RAM, you can open many programs at the same time without a performance penalty. I have 16GB in my Mac Pro. I almost always have the 15 or 20 programs I use most open at all times. Then all my favorite applications are available instantly, and I don't have to wait while a program launches.

Right this moment, for example, I have 14 programs running, as shown in Figure 22-1. And even so, Activity Monitor tells me I've still got almost 7GB of RAM available (out of a total of 16GB), and my Mac is still quite fast and responsive.

Figure 22-1: Here's what my Dock looked like a few seconds ago (left side on top; right side on bottom).

It's also easy as pie to install RAM in most Macs made this decade. Chances are good that the manual for your Mac includes step-by-step instructions simple enough for a 9-year-old to follow. I know, because I once asked my (then) 9-year-old son to do it. Which he did — and with no trouble, either.

Backup Software and/or Hardware

Only two kinds of Mac users exist: Those who have lost data and those who are going to. If your work means anything to you, you had better back it up before it's too late. If you have a spare hard drive, by all means use the cool (and free) Time Machine software that comes with Mac OS X Lion. If you want to create multiple backups to several different devices or types of media (DVD-R, CD-R, tape, and so on), invest in the appropriate hardware and software.

In case you missed it, you can find a lot of info about backup software and hardware in Chapter 18.

A Better Monitor (Or a Second One)

If you have a tiny monitor, get a bigger one. With a larger monitor, you spend less time scrolling and rearranging windows, and more time getting actual work done — which is a good thing, right?

The best thing about it is that current Macs let you use two monitors as though they were a single display. For example, my main computer setup is a Mac Pro with one 30-inch and one 24-inch flat-panel LCD displays. It's an awesome setup — one that I highly recommend. With two monitors, I keep the menu bar and most windows I'm working with on the big display. Then, with programs like Adobe Photoshop (which has lots of floating palettes), I put some (or all) of the palettes on smaller monitor so I can see more of the document I'm working on. And so on.

Another thing Macs can do with two monitors is mirror what's on one display on the second one. So you can work with one display facing you and point the other one (or a projector) at the audience so they can see what you're doing, too.

Flat-panel LCD displays have come down dramatically in price over the past few years. If you can afford a bigger display, or a second one, I promise you'll love it.

A Fast Internet Connection

Not all DSL and cable Internet connections are equal. In my opinion, a faster Internet connection equals a better experience. Check the prices for higher-speed digital subscriber line (DSL) or cable modem connections. Or threaten to switch and see what kind of deal you can wrangle for a faster connection.

Once you do, web pages that took a while to load appear on-screen almost instantly. And streaming audio and video play with few, if any, hiccups.

If you can afford a faster tier of cable/DSL (from around \$30–40/month in most places) and live in an area where you can get faster cable modem or DSL (not all places can yet), it will change the way you use the Internet. For more on setting up an Internet connection, see Chapter 10.

I pay a bit more for the fastest premium cable Internet access offered by my cable operator. It's up to twice as fast as the "standard" speed package — and it's worth every penny.

Games

Gaming on the Mac has never been better, and the game developers are getting better and better at coaxing even more performance out of OS X.

Some of the games I love include *Bejeweled 3, Angry Birds,* and every pinball game LittleWing (`www.littlewingpinball.com`) has ever created. Try one — you'll be amazed at how far computer gaming has come.

Multimedia Titles

Many great games, references, and educational titles come on CD-ROM or DVD-ROM these days. My favorite is still *World Book,* which makes use of many Mac features to deliver an encyclopedia that's both authoritative and fun to use. You'll love it, and so will your kids. Remember, your Mac is more than just a computer — it's a full-blown multimedia player. Enjoy it.

Don't forget that all Macs (but the MacBook Air and Mac mini) can also play video DVDs like those you rent at Blockbuster or NetFlix.

Some Big Honking Speakers with a Subwoofer

Face it: Macs have crummy speakers (or, worse, only *one* crummy speaker). With a decent set of speakers, games are more fun, music sounds like music instead of AM radio, and the voiceovers in your multimedia titles suddenly become intelligible. If you're into sound, you'll enjoy your Mac much more if you add a set of window-rattling speakers, preferably with a massive sub-woofer to provide that booming bass that sound lovers crave. So crank it up! I'm partial to Audioengine A5 speakers (www.audioengineusa.com), which are totally awesome but not cheap (around $400). But any good speakers kick the stuffing out of the speakers built into any Mac.

A killer set of speakers makes watching movies on your Mac a zillion times better.

A New Mouse and/or Keyboard

If you don't really love the mouse or keyboard you're using, do yourself a favor, and beat them to death with a hammer. Then buy a mouse or keyboard that suits you. You'll be so much happier if you upgrade to a mouse that's easier to move around, more comfortable to use, and maybe even has extra buttons and/or a scroll wheel. Or consider Apple's Magic Trackpad so you can enjoy gestures like your laptop brethren and sisteren.

You'll be amazed at how much easier it is to work with a mouse, trackpad, or keyboard that fits your hand size and needs.

Most third-party mice and keyboards work flawlessly on a Mac. Also consider ditching the silly little keyboard that came with your iMac, Mac Pro, or what-ever. Third-party Mac keyboards on the market today are a huge improve-ment over what came with your Mac.

I'm partial to third-party keyboards and mice because I can't stand any of the bundled Apple mice or keyboards. They're aesthetically pleasing but not very good compared with almost all third-party mice and keyboards.

I'm partial to so-called ergonomic keyboards, which I find more comfortable for prolonged writing sessions. I also think I type faster with this kind of keyboard. My current axe is a Microsoft Natural Ergonomic Keyboard 4000. It's big and strangely shaped, but no other keyboard is as comfortable for my fat fingers. Even though it's a Windows keyboard and the modifier keys are mislabeled (the ⌘ key says *Alt,* and the Option key says *Start* and has a Windows logo on it), Microsoft offers excellent OS X drivers for it.

Finally, my mouse is a Logitech Performance MX (`www.logitech.com`). Like my speakers, it's somewhat expensive (around $90) but well worth it.

A MacBook Air or MacBook Pro

You need a laptop because one Mac is never enough. With a portable Mac, you can go anywhere and continue to compute. And MacBook Airs and MacBook Pros come with Apple AirPort Extreme wireless networking, so you can surf the Net, print, and share files from the couch, the pool, the airport (the kind with airplanes and a lowercase *a* and *p)* — or Starbucks, for that matter.

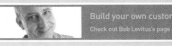

23

Ten (Or So) Great Websites for Mac Freaks

*A*s much as I would love to think that this book tells you everything you need to know about using your Mac, I know better. You have a lot more to discover about using your Mac, and new tools and products come out every single day.

The best way to gather more information than you could ever possibly soak up about all things Macintosh is to hop onto the web. There, you can find news, *freeware* and *shareware* (try-before-you-buy software) to download, troubleshooting sites, tons of news and information about your new favorite OS, and lots of places to shop.

The sites in this chapter are the best, most chock-full-o'-stuff places on the web for Mac users. By the time you finish checking out these websites, you'll know so much about your Mac and OS X Mountain Lion that you'll feel like your brain is in danger of exploding. On the other hand, you might just feel a whole lot smarter. Happy surfing!

MacFixIt

www.macfixit.com

Long ago, on an Internet you'd hardly recognize today, troubleshooting guru Ted Landau created an excellent troubleshooting site to help Mac users solve common problems and keep current on compatibility issues with new system software and third-party products.

It's now an arm of web behemoth CNET, but it's still a good resource when you have a problem with your Mac. Chances are pretty good that you'll find a solution at MacFixIt.

Fortunately, though no longer affiliated with MacFixIt, Ted still writes regularly for *Macworld* and *The Mac Observer,* which are both on my Top Ten list. Read on.

Macworld

www.macworld.com

This site describes itself thusly: "News, info, and opinion by Mac users, for Mac users."

And it's true. Macworld is perhaps the best and most comprehensive source of product information for Mac (and other Apple device) users. It's especially strong for comparative reviews of Mac and iPhone/iPad products. For example, when you want to know which inkjet printer or digital camera is the best in its price class, Macworld.com can almost certainly offer guidance. And, you won't merely find product information here; you'll find it accompanied by expert opinions and professional fact-checking.

Put another way, I trust the writers and editors at Macworld more than I trust the writers and editors of any other Mac-oriented website. Any other Mac-oriented site, that is, except for. . . .

The Mac Observer

www.macobserver.com

The Mac Observer gives you Mac news, views, reviews, and much more.

Disclosure: I write a column — "Dr. Mac's Rants & Raves" — whenever the mood strikes me. I'm also a reviews editor and contribute the occasional review. But I loved The Mac Observer long before I wrote a word for it.

What I love is that The Mac Observer offers thoughtful opinion pieces in addition to tons of news and product reviews. The quality of the most writing by The Mac Observer staff is a cut above what you'll find at most other sites.

CNET Downloads (formerly VersionTracker)

www.versiontracker.com or http://download.cnet.com/mac/

For free software or shareware, check out the CNET Downloads Mac Download section. It's one of the best sites in the world for software to use with Mountain Lion (or any version of Mac OS, for that matter). It's also terrific for getting the latest version of any kind of software: commercial, shareware, and/or freeware. VersionTracker is a virtual treasure trove of software and updates, and it's worth visiting even when you aren't looking for anything in particular.

I love this site and try to visit it several times a week. (I know — I should get a life.)

MacInTouch

www.macintouch.com

For the latest in Mac news, updated every single day, check out MacInTouch. Authored by longtime *MacWeek* columnist Ric Ford and his staff of news-hounds, along with a legion of knowledgeable readers, this site keeps you on the bleeding edge of Mac news — including software updates, virus alerts, and Apple happenings. It also offers extensive and unbiased reviews of most Apple hardware and software soon after its release.

I consider MacInTouch essential for keeping up with what's new and cool for your Mac, and have since its inception in 1994.

Alltop

http://mac.alltop.com

Alltop aggregates news from a variety of websites and serves them up in an appealing format that allows you to scan a large number of headlines and summaries from a wide variety of sources in a very short time. This is a case where a picture is worth 1,000 words, so check out Figure 23-1.

Figure 23-1 shows the custom Alltop page I created at http://my.alltop.com/levitus so I could scan the headlines of my favorite websites quickly and easily. My cursor is hovering over a story ("Rumor: Siri coming to iPad in iOS 6"), which is one of those Mac Observer opinion pieces I mention earlier in this chapter.

Figure 23-1: Hover the cursor over any headline, and Alltop provides a concise summary of the story.

Notice the little summary, which appears only when I hover my cursor over that story, which is in the little box with "4 June 2012 | 8:39 am" as its headline in Figure 23-1. That's Alltop's killer feature, at least in my humble opinion.

You can build your own customized Alltop page at `http://my.alltop.com`.

Alltop isn't just for Mac news. There are Alltop pages for a plethora of subjects, including

> Marketing: `http://marketing.alltop.com`
>
> Science: `http://science.alltop.com`
>
> Gadgets: `http://gadgets.alltop.com`
>
> Filmmaking: `http://filmmaking.alltop.com`

. . . and literally hundreds more. Alltop has become one of my favorite places to get the information I need quickly and easily.

Apple Support and Knowledge Base

www.apple.com/support

Do you have a technical question about any version of Mac OS or any Apple product — including OS X Mountain Lion? March your question right over to the Apple Support and Knowledge Base page, where you can find searchable archives of tech notes, software update information, and documentation. The Knowledge Base is especially useful if you need info about your old Mac; Apple archives all its info here. Choose among a preset list of topics or products, and type a keyword to research. You're rewarded with a list of helpful documents. Clicking any one of these entries (they're all links) takes you right to the info you seek. The site even has tools that can help narrow your search.

The site also offers a section with user discussions of Apple-related topics. Although not "officially" sanctioned or monitored by Apple, it's often the best place to gain insights, especially on slightly esoteric or obscure issues not covered in the Knowledge Base.

Ramseeker

www.ramseeker.com

One of the best ways to make your Mac better is to buy more random-access memory (RAM). RAM is the readily available memory that your computer uses; the more you have, the smoother programs run. Although OS X might run on a Mac with less than 2GB of RAM, it works much better and faster with more than that — at least 1GB, in my opinion. As cheap as RAM is today, the price that you pay for it can still vary quite a bit. The best way I know to get the lowdown on RAM prices is to use the Ramseeker feature of this site, which surveys multiple vendors daily and then organizes current memory prices by Mac type.

Figure 23-2 shows how it works.

Figure 23-2: Ramseeker serves up prices for RAM
upgrades from 7 vendors, including The Apple Store.

Other World Computing

www.macsales.com

Other World Computing has become the "go to" place for Mac peripherals.
Whether you need RAM, hard drives, optical drives, video cards, processor upgrades, cables, discs, or anything else you can think of, Other World
Computing probably has it at a reasonable price. Because of its inexpensive
and reliable delivery and a solid guarantee of every item, you can't go wrong
buying from OWC.

EveryMac.com

www.everymac.com

The author of this site claims that it's "the complete guide" to every
Macintosh, Mac-compatible, and upgrade card "in the world." You can't
argue with that (unless you've done a staggering amount of research). Check
out the Forum and Q&A sections (recently updated for Mountain Lion) for
answers to Mac-related questions.

dealmac

www.dealmac.com

Shopping for Mac stuff? Go to dealmac ("How to go broke saving money," this site boasts) first to find out about sale prices, rebates, and other bargain opportunities on upgrades, software, peripherals, and more.

Dr. Mac Consulting

www.boblevitus.com

Dr. Mac Consulting is (in all due modesty) my troubleshooting, training, and technical-support site. Our only goal is to help you with whatever is ailing your Mac (or iPhone or iPad or other Apple device). With expert technicians on staff, Dr. Mac Consulting provides jargon-free expert technical help at a fair price, regardless of your physical location — and usually on the same day. Let one of our experts (or even me) provide high-quality Macintosh troubleshooting, technical support, software or system training, prepurchase advice, and more! We do our thing via phone; e-mail; iChat/Messages; and/or our unique web-enabled, remote-control software (or Mountain Lion Screen Sharing), which lets us fix many common Mac ailments in less than an hour, controlling your mouse and keyboard remotely as we explain everything we're doing to you on the phone. Best of all, if we don't fix it, you don't pay!

The next time you need help, and none of the aforementioned sites does the trick, why not let Dr. Mac Consulting make the mouse call? (So to squeak.)

Note: This crass commercial message is one of two places in the whole book where I blather on about my day job. So if there's something you want to know about your Mac or something you would like examined or fixed, we can probably help you in less than an hour. I hope you'll give it a try.

And now, back to your regularly scheduled programming.

Appendix

Installing or Reinstalling
OS X Mountain Lion
(Only If You Have To)

· ·

*I*f OS X Mountain Lion came preinstalled on your new Mac, you'll probably never need this Appendix.

If you're thinking about reinstalling because something has gone wrong with your Mac, know that an OS X reinstallation should be your last resort. Be sure you've tried all the stuff in Chapter 20 before even *thinking* about reinstalling OS X. If nothing else fixes your Mac, reinstalling OS X could well be your final option before invasive surgery (that is, trundling your Mac to a repair shop). You don't *want* to reinstall OS X if something easier can correct the problem. So if you have to do a reinstallation, realize that this is more or less your last hope (this side of the dreaded screwdriver, anyway).

In this Appendix, you discover all you need to know to install or reinstall OS X, if you should have to. I say reinstalling is a hassle because although you won't lose the contents of your Home folder, applications you've installed, or the stuff in your Documents folder (unless something goes horribly wrong or you have to reformat your hard drive), you might lose the settings for some System Preferences, which means you'll have to manually reconfigure those panes after you reinstall. And you might have to reinstall drivers for third-party hardware such as mice, keyboards, printers, tablets, and the like. Finally, you might have to reregister or reinstall some of your software.

It's not the end of the world, but it's almost always inconvenient. That said, reinstalling OS X almost always corrects all but the most horrifying and malignant of problems. And as you soon see, the process in Mountain Lion is (compared with root-canal work, income taxes, or previous versions of OS X) relatively painless. I stay with you through it all, though; don't you worry about a thing.

How to Install (or Reinstall) OS X

In theory, you should have to install Mountain Lion only once, or never if your Mac came with Mountain Lion preinstalled. And in a perfect world, that would be the case. But you might find occasions when you have to install/ reinstall it, such as

- If you get a Mac that didn't come with OS X Mountain Lion preinstalled
- If you have a catastrophic hard-drive crash that requires you to initialize (format) or replace your boot drive
- If you buy an external hard drive and want it to be capable of being your Mac's startup disk (that is, a bootable disk)
- If you replace your internal hard drive with a larger, faster, or solid state drive
- If any essential OS X files become damaged or corrupted, or are deleted or renamed

The following instructions do double duty: They're what you do to install OS X for the first time on a Mac, and they're also what you do if something really bad happens to the copy of OS X that you boot your Mac from. The instructions offered here describe both the process for installing and the process for reinstalling OS X.

Here's how to install (or reinstall) OS X, step by step:

1. **Boot from your Recovery HD partition by restarting your Mac while holding down the ⌘+R keys.**

   The OS X Utilities window appears. Select Reinstall OS X, and click Continue. The OS X Mountain Lion splash screen appears. Click Continue.

   A sheet appears informing you that your computer's eligibility needs to be verified by Apple. Click Continue to begin the process of installing or reinstalling OS X.

   If you're not connected to the Internet, you'll be asked to choose a Wi-Fi network from the AirPort menu in the top-right corner.

2. **The Mountain Lion software license agreement screen appears. Read it and click Agree.**

   A sheet drops down, asking whether you agree to the terms of the license agreement. Yes, you did just click Agree; this time you're being asked to confirm that you indeed clicked the Agree button.

   If you don't click Agree you can't go any farther, so I advise you to click Agree now.

3. **Choose the disk on which you want to reinstall OS X by clicking its icon once in the pane where you select a disk.**

   If only one suitable disk is available you won't have to choose; it will be selected for you automatically.

   Click the Install button.

4. **A sheet asks for your Apple ID and password. Type them in the appropriate fields; click Sign In, and your Mountain Lion installation (or reinstallation) begins.**

   The operating system takes 30 to 60 minutes to install, so now might be a good time to take a coffee break. When the install is finished, your Mac restarts itself. If you were reinstalling OS X on a hard disk that it had been installed on previously, you're done. Your Mac will reboot and you can begin using your new, freshly installed (and ideally trouble-free) copy of OS X Mountain Lion.

   If you're installing Mountain Lion on a hard disk for the first time, however, you still have one last step to complete. After your Mac reboots, the Setup Assistant window appears. You need to work your way through the Setup Assistant's screens as described in the following section.

Getting Set Up with Setup Assistant

Assuming that your installation (or reinstallation) process goes well and your Mac restarts itself, the next thing you should see (and hear) is a short, colorful movie that ends by transforming into the first Setup Assistant screen (Apple Assistants such as this are like wizards in Windows, only smarter), fetchingly named *Welcome*.

To tiptoe through the Setup Assistant, follow these steps:

1. **When the Welcome screen appears, choose your country from the list by clicking it once, and then click the Continue button.**

   If your country doesn't appear in the list, select the Show All check box, which causes a bunch of additional countries to appear.

   After you click Continue, the Select Your Keyboard screen appears.

2. **Choose a keyboard layout from the list by clicking it once; then click Continue.**

   If you're an American (or want to use an American keyboard setup), click the U.S. listing. If you prefer a different country's keyboard layout, select the Show All check box, and a bunch of additional countries' keyboards (as well as a pair of Dvorak keyboard layouts) appear in the list. Choose the one you prefer by clicking it — and *then* click Continue.

The Select a Wireless Network screen appears.

3. **Click the name of the wireless network you use to connect to the Internet; then click Continue.**

   If you don't see the network you want to use, click Rescan. If you don't use a wireless network, click Other Network Setup, and then choose one of the available options, or choose My Computer Does Not Connect to the Internet. Click Continue.

   The Migration Assistant (also known as the Transfer Information to This Mac) screen appears.

4. **Choose to transfer data or not and then click Continue.**

   If this is a brand-new Mac or you're installing OS X Mountain Lion on a Mac and have another Mac or Time Machine backup disk nearby, you can transfer all of your important files and settings by following the on-screen instructions and connecting the new and old Macs via FireWire or Ethernet cable.

   The Enable Location Services screen appears.

5. **Select or deselect the Enable Location Services on This Mac check box and click Continue.**

   If you want to allow your Mac and its apps to gather and use data indicating your approximate location, select the check box. If you don't, deselect the check box. To learn more about Location Services, click the blue, "Learn More" link.

   The Enter Your Apple ID screen appears.

6. **If you have an Apple ID, type it (such as** tcook@me.com) **and your password in the appropriate fields, and then click Continue.**

   To learn more about getting an Apple ID, click the blue, "Learn More" link. In a nutshell, it lets you make one-click purchases at the iTunes Store, iPhoto, or the Apple Store, and includes free iCloud membership.

   The Terms and Conditions screen appears.

7. **Read the Terms and Conditions and click Agree. A dialog confirms your agreement. Click Agree again.**

   The Set Up iCloud screen appears.

8. **Select or deselect the Set Up iCloud On This Mac check box and click Continue.**

   To learn more about iCloud, click the blue, "Learn More" link.

   The Use iCloud for Find My Mac screen appears.

9. **Select or deselect the Use iCloud for Find My Mac check box and click Continue. A dialog confirms your desire. Click the Allow button.**

   To learn more about Find My Mac, click where it says "Learn More" in blue text.

   The Create Your Computer Account screen appears.

10. **Fill in the Full Name, Account Name (sometimes called Short Name), Password, and Verify Password fields, and then click Continue.**

   This first account that you create will automatically have administrator privileges for this Mac. You can't easily delete or change the name you choose for this account, so think it through before you click Continue.

   You can't click the Continue button until you've filled in the first two fields. Because a password is optional, you can choose to leave both password fields blank if you like. If you do, your Mac warns you that without a password, your Mac won't be secure. If that's okay, click OK. If you change your mind and want to have a password, click Cancel.

   Click on the little picture next to your name if you want to choose a different picture or take a picture of yourself with your Mac's built-in camera.

   If you choose to take a picture, click the Take Photo Snapshot button. When the picture appears, you can change its size by using the slider control directly below the image and/or move it around in the frame by clicking your face and dragging. If you're not happy with this snapshot, click Retake a Video Snapshot. When you're happy with it, click Continue.

   If you choose a select a picture from the picture library, click the picture you want to represent you — the butterfly, dog, parrot, flower, or whatever — and then click Continue.

   The Select Your Time Zone screen appears.

11. **Click the map to set this Mac's time zone. Select the Set Time Automatically Using Current Location check box if you want your Mac to do that, or deselect it if you don't. Click Continue.**

   The Thank You screen appears. Click the Start Using Your Mac button to start using your Mac.

   The OS X Finder's Desktop appears.

And that's all there is to it. You're done.

Index

• A •

About Finder command, 105
About This Mac option, 42
accelerated graphics cards, 417–418
accelerated PCI slot, 417
access
  folders shared by default, 328–329
  groups, 320–321
  guests, 320–321
  overview, 320
  permissions, overview of, 329–330
  permissions, types of, 330–332
  permissions, useful settings for, 334–336
  sharing folders, 332–334
  unsharing folders, 336
  users, changing, 325–326
  users, limiting capabilities of, 326–328
  users, overview of, 320–325
  users, removing, 326
Accessibility System Preferences pane
  Hearing section, 362
  Interacting section, 362–363
  overview, 361
  Seeing section, 361–362
accounts, Mail, 235–236
Action button
  Desktop, 29
  toolbar, 91
activating firewall, 380–381
active windows, 32–33
Activity Monitor, 388–390
Add Rule button, 243
Add to iPhoto button, 249
Add to Library option, 261
Add to Sidebar check box, 154
Adjust Keyboard Brightness in Low Light
    check box, 61
Administrator users
  folders created for, 329
  overview, 320–321

Advanced pane, Finder preferences, 114
Advanced Search button, 223
Advanced searches, 222–223
AFP (Apple File Protocol), 319
Agree button, 300
AirDrop command, 109
AirDrop feature, 316
AirDrop option, 165
AirPlay Mirroring feature, 366–367
AirPort Extreme base station, 315, 318
AirPort Utility, 390
AirPort wireless cards, building networks
    with, 317
alerts, Calendar, 201
aliases
  creating, 97–98
  deleting, 98
  icons for, 94
  overview, 95–97
  parent files, finding, 98
All Controls radio button, 63–64
All Desktops option, 179
All My Files command, 109
Alltop website, 429–430
Alsoft's DiskWarrior tool, 404, 405
Always Open Folders in a New Window
    check box, 113
Animate Opening apps option, 85
antivirus software, 379, 380
App Store
  app updates, 382
  general discussion, 361
  icon for, 361
app Support folder, 131
Appearance pop-up menu, 58
Apple File Protocol (AFP), 319
Apple key, 44
Apple menu, 42–43
Apple Support and Knowledge Base web
    page, 431
Apple Tech Support hotline, 407

Apple Time Capsule, 373
Apple TV
  AirPlay Mirroring, 366
  general discussion, 367
AppleScript commands, 349, 351
AppleScript Editor app, 358
AppleScript programming, 356–358
Apply to Enclosed Items feature for
    permissions, 336
apps. *See also* Finder; System
    Preferences app
  AppleScript Editor, 358
  assigning file type to, 145–146
  bundled, 193
  Calculator, 387–388
  Calendar, 194–201
  Contacts, 71, 227–235, 328
  DigitalColor Meter, 391
  DVD Player, 273–276
  DVD Sharing, 346
  FaceTime, 72, 224–226
  FileVault, 383–384
  Font Book, 293–294
  Grab, 394
  Grapher, 394–395
  iCloud, 215, 233–234
  icons for, 70, 93
  Ink, 364
  iTunes, 72, 257–271
  Mail, 71, 235–249
  Messages, 72, 249–255
  Migration Assistant, 396–397
  Notes, 72, 206–208
  opening files with, 145–147
  opening menus in Dock, 75–77
  other than default, opening files with,
    146–147
  Parallels Desktop, 366
  Parental Controls for, 328
  Photo Booth, 72, 277–279
  Preview, 82, 279–280, 309–311
  Recovery Disk Assistant, 400
  Reminders, 72, 202–206
  Safari, 71, 215–224, 396
  SuperDuper!, 377, 400
  System Information, 15, 397
  Terminal, 397–398
  TextEdit, 285–291, 308
  updates, 382
  VirtualBox, 366
  word-processing, 82
apps command, 109
apps folder, 125
Are You Sure You Want To Shut Down
    Your Computer Now? dialog, 16–17
Arrange button, 91
Arrange By command, 102
Arrange menu, 29
As Icons option, 100
Ask to Keep Changes when Closing
    Documents check box, 59
Attach option, 237
audio accessibility options, 362
audio chats, Messages, 252–253
Audioengine A5 speakers, 424
Auto Save feature, 134
automatic login
  disabling, 384
  overview, 365
automatic visual help cues, 23
Automatically Hide and Show the Dock
    option, 85
automation
  AppleScript, 357–358
  Automator, 358–360
  overview, 356–357
Automator, 357, 358–360
Availability panel, Calendar, 201

• B •

Back button
  Go menu, 108
  toolbar, 91
  in windows, 29, 30
backup disks, 373–374
backups
  commercial backup software, 376
  manual, 375–376
  of Mountain Lion Installer file, 400
  restoring files, 374–375
  software and hardware for, 422
  with Time Machine, 372–375
  two sets of, 376–378
Balance slider, 68
Base Stations, AirPort Extreme, 315, 318

black screen of death, 14
blocking or limiting connections, 383
blue screen of death, 14
Bluetooth technology
  general discussion, 364
  preferences, 65
  sharing, 346
Bonjour network protocol, 316
bookmarking favorite pages, Safari,
    217–219
Boot Camp technology, 365–366
bootable installer discs, 400
bootable recovery disks, 400
booting
  computer, 12–16
  defined, 14
Border option, 308
Bring All to Front command, 37
Browse All Versions option, 140
build number, 42
burn folders, creating, 191
Burn Speed pop-up menu, 190
burning CDs and DVDs
  creating burn folder, 191
  on fly, 187–190
  overview, 186–187
burning playlists to CDs, 268–269
buttons
  customizing, 57–60
  on top of windows, 30
Buy Album button, 262
Buy Song buttons, 262
By Time option, 206

• C •

cable modem connections, 423
Calculate All Sizes check box, View
    Options window, 416
Calculator app, 387–388
Calendar app
  alerts, 201
  Availability panel, 201
  creating, 195–197
  deleting group or, 198
  events, 199–201
  grouping, 197–198
  invitations, 200

  overview, 194
  views, 194–195
Calendar icon, 71
camcorder, downloading DV video from,
    283–284
camera, downloading photos from,
    281–283
Cancel keyboard shortcut, 412
Carbon Copy Cloner, 400
Card Only view, 232
CD Sharing feature, 346
CDs
  backups on, 375–376
  burn folder, creating, 191
  burning, overview, 186–187
  burning on fly, 187–190
  burning playlists to, 268–269
Change All button, 146
chatting
  audio chats, 252–253
  iMessage, 250
  overview, 249–251
  remote screen sharing, 253–255
  video chats, 252–253
check boxes, 34
Check Document Now option, 290
checking mail, 241
Choose app button, 144
Clean Up By command, 102
Clean Up command, 101–102
Click in the Scroll Bar To radio buttons, 58
clicking and dragging, 20
clicks, 19
Clipboard feature
  commands for, 156
  overview, 155–156
  pasting from, 157
Close button, 29, 30
Close Windows when Quitting an app
    check box, 59
closing windows, 35
CNET Downloads website, 429
Color Matching feature, 308
ColorSync Utility, 390–391
Column view, 99–100
Command key, 44
command line, 397–398

commands
About Finder, 105
AirDrop, 109
All My Files, 109
AppleScript, 349, 351
apps, 109
Arrange By, 102
Bring All to Front, 37
Clean Up, 101–102
Clean Up By, 102
for Clipboard feature, 156
Computer, 109
Connect to Server, 110
Copy, 45
Cycle Through Windows, 37
Desktop, 109
Documents, 109
Downloads, 109
Duplicate, 45, 138–141, 185
Empty Trash, 74, 161
Enclosing Folder, 109
Get Info, 45, 264
Go to Folder, 110
Hide Finder, 107
Hide Others, 107
Home, 109
keyboard shortcut, 44–46
Log Out, 43
Network, 109
New Finder Window, 35, 45
New Folder, 45, 137
Open, 35, 45
Other items, 37
Preferences, 105
Quick Look, 143–144, 163–166
Recent Folders, 110
Restart, 43
Save a Version, 134
Secure Empty Trash, 162
Select All, 45
Show All, 107
Shut Down, 43
Sleep, 43
Special Characters, 288
Speech Commands window, 352, 353
Zoom, 29, 30, 37

commercial backup software, 376
composing new messages, Mail, 236–238
compressing files, 161
Computer command, 109
Computer folder, 124–125
computers
Microsoft versus Mac, 11
sleep settings for, 363
Connect dialog, 338, 339, 342
Connect to Server command, 110
connecting printers
overview, 298–299
printer sharing, 302
setting up printer for first time, 300–302
connection settings, Internet, 213–215
Contacts app
adding contacts, 228–230
e-mailing contacts or groups, 234–235
groups, creating, 230–231
iCloud, using with, 233–234
icon for, 71
importing contacts from other
programs, 230
overview, 227–228
Parental Controls for, 328
Smart Groups, setting up, 231–232
views, 232–233
Contains pop-up menu, 243
contextual menus, 19, 39–40
contiguous photos, 282
control-clicks, 19, 39
Convert menu, Calculator, 388
converting images and PDFs in Preview,
279–280
Copies option, 307
Copy command, 45
Copy keyboard shortcut, 412
copying
contents of disks, 185
files and folders, 156–157
Cover Flow feature, 104–105
Cover Page feature, 308
CPU Monitor windows, 389
crashes at startup, 408
CrashPlan server, 377
Create New Account button, 262

Create Quick Event button, 199
current folder pop-up menu, 107–108
custom settings, Print sheet
  choosing, 306–308
  saving, 309
customization
  Bluetooth, 65
  buttons, 57–60
  keyboard, 60–64
  Launchpad, 182
  menus, 57–60
  mouse, 64–65
  overview, 47, 60
  pictures on Desktop, 50–51
  screen saver, 51–53
  System Preferences, 47–49
  trackpad, 66–67
  windows, 57–60
customizing Dock
  adding icons, 78–80
  folder and disk icon menu preferences,
    85–86
  global Dock preferences, 83–85
  items to add to, 82–83
  overview, 78
  preferences, 83–86
  removing icons, 81
  resizing, 82
customizing Finder windows
  adding folders to Sidebar, 111
  Advanced preferences, 114
  General preferences, 112–113
  Labels preferences, 113
  overview, 111
  preferences, 112–114
  Sidebar preferences, 114
customizing sound
  changing sound effects, 68
  choosing output and input options, 68
  overview, 67–68
customizing widgets on Dashboard
  Flight Tracker, 56–57
  overview, 53–55
  Translation, 56

Cut keyboard shortcut, 412
Cycle Through Windows command, 37

Dashboard widgets
  Flight Tracker, 56–57
  overview, 53–55
  Translation, 56
data CDs, 268
dealmac website, 433
default icons on Dock, 70–73
Default Paper Size menu, 301
Default Printer pop-up menu, 301
Delay until Repeat slider, 60
Delete Group option, 232
Delete messages button, 238
deleting
  aliases, 98
  Calendars or groups, 198
  icons, 161–162
Desktop & Screen Saver icon, 50
Desktop command, 109
desktop computers, sleep settings for, 363
Desktop feature
  general discussion, 26–27, 88–90
  pictures on, 50–51
  screen savers, 51–53
Desktop folder, 129
detail pane, 141
Developer ID program, 385
diagnostic data, sending to Apple, 385
dialogs
  Are You Sure You Want To Shut Down
    Your Computer Now?, 16–17
  Connect, 338, 339, 342
  overview, 33–34
Dial-Up Networking (DUN) Profile
    feature, 312
Dictation feature, 348–349
digital subscriber line (DSL), 423
DigitalColor Meter app, 391
disabled options in menus, 40–41
disabling fonts, 293–294

disclosure triangles, 102
disconnecting from remote Macs, 340
discs
  backups on, 375–376
  burning, 187
  disks versus, 184
disk icons
  on dock, 70
  overview, 94
  preferences for, 85–86
disk images
  of deleted users Home folders, 326
  restoring Macs with, 393–394
Disk Utility
  Erase tab, 391–392
  First Aid feature, 403–404
  First Aid tab, 391
  overview, 391
  Partition tab, 392–393
  RAID tab, 393
  Restore tab, 393–394
Disk Utility program, 184
disks
  burn folder, creating, 191
  burning CDs and DVDs on fly, 187–190
  burning CDs and DVDs, overview,
      186–187
  discs versus, 184
  ejecting, 191–192
  formatting, 184, 391–392
  moving and copying between, 185
  overview, 183–184
  PC, compatibility with Macs, 185–186
  shared, connecting to on remote Macs,
      337–340
DiskWarrior, Alsoft's, 404, 405
display accessibility options, 361
Display As option, 86
Display System Preferences pane, 414
Divider icon, 72
DJ feature, 270–271
Dock feature
  adding icons, 78–80
  default icons, 70–73
  folder and disk icon menu preferences,
      85–86

global Dock preferences, 83–85
icon movements, 77
icons, 69
items to add to, 82–83
opening app menus in, 75–77
opening files from, 78
overview, 27, 69–70, 78
preferences, 83–86
removing icons, 81
resizing, 82
trash, 73–75
Dock option, 43
documents
  creating and composing, 286–288
  graphics, adding to, 290–291
  icons for, 70, 93
  printing, 304–305
  selecting and formatting text, 288–290
  sharing on web, 344
Documents command, 109
Documents folder, 129
.docx format, 287
Double-Click a Window's Title Bar to
    Minimize option, 84
Double-Click Speed setting, 64, 65
double-clicks, 19
downloading
  DV video from camcorder, 283–284
  photos from camera, 281–283
Downloads button, 216
Downloads command, 109
Downloads folder, 73
Dr. Mac Consulting website, 407, 433
drag-and-drop technique, 143
dragging, 20
Drive Genius, Prosoft's, 404
drive partitions, 392
drivers, for printers, 302
DriveSavers Data Recovery Service, 371
Drop Box folder, 329
Drop Box (Write Only) permission, 334
drop folder permissions, 335–336
Dropbox service, 377
DSL (digital subscriber line), 423
DUN (Dial-Up Networking) Profile
    feature, 312

duplex printing, 308
Duplicate command
    keyboard shortcut for, 45
    Save As versus, 138–141
    using between disks, 185
DV video, downloading from camcorder,
        283–284
DVD Player app
    overview, 273–276
    troubleshooting, 276
DVD Sharing app, 346
DVDs
    backups on, 375–376
    burn folder, creating, 191
    burning, overview, 186–187
    burning on fly, 187–190

• E •

eBay website, 417
ejecting disks, 191–192
e-mail
    checking mail, 241
    composing new messages, 236–238
    mailboxes, 244–246
    overview, 235
    preferences, 242
    Quick Look Slideshow feature, 247–249
    rules, 243–244
    sending to contacts or groups, 234–235
    setting up account, 235–236
    signatures, 246–247
    smart mailboxes, 245–246
    spam, 241–242
    stationery, 240–241
    toolbar, 238–239
E-mail option, 165
Empty Trash command, 74, 161
Empty Trash keyboard shortcut, 413
Empty Trash Securely check box, 114
Enclosing Folder command, 109
encryption of files, 383
energy-saving features, 17, 363–364
Erase tab, Disk Utility, 391–392
ergonomic keyboards, 425

Ethernet
    building networks with, 317–318
    defined, 314
    sleep settings for networks, 363
Ethernet ports, defined, 314
events, Calendar
    alerts, 201
    invitations, 200
    overview, 199–200
EveryMac website, 432
Everyone's permissions, 331–332, 334, 335
.exe extension, 186
Export option, 280
external DVD drives, 276

• F •

FaceTime app
    icon for, 72
    overview, 224–226
Fax PDF option, 312
faxing, 311–312
File Format pop-up menu, 137
files
    assigning type to apps, 145–146
    Clipboard, 155–156
    compressing, 161
    copying, 156–157
    versus folders, 147–148
    getting rid of icons, 161–162
    inability to open, 144–145
    moving, 158–159
    new folders, creating, 150–151
    opening, overview, 141–143
    opening from Dock, 78
    opening with apps, 145–147
    opening with drag-and-drop, 143
    opening with Quick Look, 143–144
    pasting from Clipboard, 157
    renaming icons, 160–161
    Save As versus Duplicate, 138–141
    saving, basic process of, 133–138
    saving, overview, 132–133
    selecting multiple icons, 159–160
    sharing, overview, 314–315

files *(continued)*
  sharing, setting up, 318–319
  smart folders, 152–155
  spring-loaded folders, 151–152
  subfolders, 148–150
FileVault app, 383–384
Find keyboard shortcut, 412
Finder app
  aliases, creating, 97–98
  aliases, deleting, 98
  aliases, overview, 95–97
  Column view, 99–100
  Cover Flow view, 104–105
  current folder pop-up menu, 107–108
  customizing windows, 111–114
  Desktop, 88–90
  Finder menu, items on, 105–107
  folders, adding to Sidebar, 111
  general discussion, 26–27
  Go menu, 108–110
  Icon view, 100–102
  icons, 71, 93–95
  Info window, 114–117
  List view, 102–104
  overview, 87
  parent files, finding, 98
  preferences, 112–114
  search boxes in windows, 167–169
  toolbar, 90–92
  views, 99–105
Finder menu
  current folder pop-up menu, 107–108
  Go menu, 108–110
  items on, 105–107
  overview, 105
Finder preferences
  Advanced pane, 114
  General pane, 112–113
  Labels pane, 113
  overview, 112
  Sidebar pane, 114
firewalls, 380–381
FireWire connections, 418
First Aid feature, 402
First Aid tab, Disk Utility, 391, 403–405
fixed-width fonts, 288

Flag/Unflag drop-down menu, 239
Flashbacks, 379
flashing-question-mark disk, 14–15
Flickr option, 166
Flight Tracker widget, 56–57
Flip Horizontally check box, 308
folders
  adding to Sidebar, 111
  app Support, 131
  apps, 125
  burn, creating, 191
  Clipboard, 155–156
  compressing files, 161
  Computer, 124–125
  copying, 156–157
  creating new, 150–151
  Desktop, 129
  Dock preferences for, 85–86
  Documents, 129
  Downloads, 73
  Drop Box, 329
  drop folder permissions, 335–336
  Enclosing Folder command, 109
  files versus, 147–148
  Fonts, 131–132
  getting rid of icons, 161–162
  Go to Folder command, 110
  hierarchy created with user
    accounts, 329
  Home, 128–130, 326, 329, 332, 337–340
  icons for, 69, 70, 94
  Library, 125–127, 129
  Library subfolder, 130–132
  moving, 158–159
  nested, 123–124
  New Folder command, 45, 137
  overview, 121–122
  pasting from Clipboard, 157
  permissions for, 332
  renaming icons, 160–161
  selecting multiple icons, 159–160
  shared, connecting to on remote Macs,
    337–340
  shared by default, 328–329
  sharing, 332–334
  smart, 152–155

spring-loaded, 151–152
structure of, 122–123
subfolders, 148–150
System, 127–128
unsharing, 336
Users, 122, 128
Font Book app, 293–294
fonts
Font Book app, 293–294
installing manually, 294
overview, 292
types of, 292–293
Fonts folder, 131–132
Force Quit option, 43
Format For option, 303–304
Format option, 238
formatting
disks, 184, 391–392
text, 288–290
Forward button, 29, 30, 91
freeware, 429
Full Screen button, 249
full-screen (Slideshow) mode, 166, 275

• **G** •

games, 423
Gatekeeper feature, 384–385
General pane, Finder preferences, 112–113
General section, 116
Genius playlist, 269–270
Get Episode button, 263, 264
Get Info command, 45, 264
Get Mail button, 238
global Dock preferences, 83–85
Go menu, 108–110, 275
Go to Folder command, 110
Go to Today button, 194
Google searches, 222–224
Grab app, 394
Grapher app, 394–395
graphics
adding to documents, 290–291
files, 279

gray screen of death, 14
grayscale display, 361
groups
Calendar, 197–198
creating in Contacts, 230–231
permissions, 320–321, 331, 334–335
Groups view, 232
Guest accounts, Parental Controls on, 328
guests, 320–321

• **H** •

handwriting recognition program, 364
hard drives
backing up data with Time Machine on, 373–374
buying, 418–419
care of, 18
sleep settings, 363
hardware, setting preferences for, 60–67
hardware zoom feature, 362
Hearing section, Accessibility System Preferences pane, 362
Help Center, Safari, 224
Help keyboard shortcut, 412
help system, 20–23
Hide Extension check box, 137
Hide Finder command, 107
Hide Others command, 107
Highlight Color pop-up menu, 58
Home command, 109
Home folders
accessing from remote Macs, 337–340
of deleted users, options for, 326
hierarchy created with user accounts, 329
overview, 128–130
sharing only folders in, 332
home-office networking, 315–317
Hot Corners button, 52, 175
hotline, Apple Tech Support, 407
hubs, 317, 318

• *I* •

iCloud app
  button for, 215
  using with Contacts, 233–234
Icon Resizer slider, 29
Icon view, 100–102, 416
icons
  Dock, adding, 78–80
  Dock, movements, 77
  Dock, overview, 70
  Dock, preferences for, 85–86
  Dock, removing, 81
  getting rid of, 161–162
  overview, 27, 77
  renaming, 160–161
  selecting multiple, 159–160
Ignore option, 188
iLife bundle, 284
Image Capture window, 281
images
  on Desktop, 50–51
  downloading from camera, 281–283
  previewing, 279–280
  user account, changing, 326
  user account, setting, 325
iMessage, 250
Import All option, 281
importing contacts from other
    programs, 230
importing media
  downloading DV video from camcorder,
      283–284
  downloading photos from camera,
      281–283
  overview, 281
In Menu check box, 171
inactive window, 33
incremental backups, 376
Index Sheet button, 248
Info window, 114–117
Ink app, 364
input sound options, 68
Input Sources button, 61
Install button, 300

installation disc, 400
Installer file, 400
installing fonts manually, 294
installing OS X
  overview, 435
  process, 436–437
  Setup Assistant, 437–439
installing recommended software updates,
    381–382
installing Windows on Macs, 366
Interacting section, Accessibility System
    Preferences pane, 362–363
Internet
  connection settings, 213–215
  Dictation feature, 349
  fast connections, 423
  ISPs, 213
  modem setup, 212–213
  overview, 211–212
  sharing on network connections, 316
  video calls with FaceTime, 224–226
  Web Sharing feature, 344
Internet browser, Safari
  bookmarking favorite pages, 217–219
  Help Center, 224
  navigating with toolbar buttons, 215–217
  overview, 215
  Reading List, 219–220
  searching with Google, 222–224
  Top Sites page, 220–221
Internet radio, 265–266
Internet Service Providers (ISPs), 213
Internet Sharing, 345
invitations, Calendar, 200
items to add to Dock, 82–83
iTunes app
  DJ feature, 270–271
  Genius playlists, 269–270
  icon for, 72
  Internet radio, 265–266
  iTunes DJ, 270–271
  iTunes U, 264
  movies and videos, adding, 263
  overview, 257–260
  playlists, burning to CD, 268–269
  playlists, creating, 266–267

playlists, overview, 266
podcasts, adding, 263–264
smart playlists, 267–268
songs, adding, 261–262
iTunes DJ, 270–271
iTunes Store option, 262
iTunes U, 264

• *J* •

Jump to the Spot That's Clicked radio
   button, 58
Junk button, 238

• *K* •

Keep in Dock option, 80
kernel panic, defined, 15
Key Repeat Rate slider, 60
keyboard accessibility options, 362–363
keyboard shortcut commands, 44–46
keyboard shortcuts, 411–413
Keyboard shortcuts tab, Keyboard System
   Preferences pane, 63–64
Keyboard System Preferences pane
   Keyboard shortcuts tab, 63–64
   Keyboard tab, 60–62
   overview, 60
Keyboard tab, Keyboard System
   Preferences pane, 60–62
keyboards, buying, 424–425
Keychain Access, 395–396

• *L* •

Labels pane, Finder preferences, 113
landscape-oriented option, 304
Launchpad feature
   icon for, 71
   overview, 181–182
Layout Direction option, 308
Layout feature, 308
Left margin marker, 290
Library folder, 125–127, 129
Library subfolder, 130–132

lightning, effect of, 18
limiting capabilities of users, 326–328
List and Card view, 232
List view, 102–104, 416
Listening Continuously with Keyword
   method, 350–351
Listening Key method, 350
listening methods, 350
Lists, Reminders, 202–203
local devices, defined, 314
local user groups, getting help from, 407
location services, 385
locations, defined, 214
Locked check box, 116
Log Out command, 43
Log out keyboard shortcut, 413
login, disabling automatic, 384
Login Items, discovering problem-causing
   items, 406
Login Keychain feature, 395
login screens, disabling, 365
Logitech Performance MX, 425

• *M* •

Mac App Store
   icon for, 72
   running only apps downloaded from, 384
Mac computers
   PC disks, compatibility with, 185–186
   remote, changing account passwords
      from, 342–343
   remote, disconnecting from, 340
   screen sharing, 343–344
   shared disks, connecting to on, 337–340
   shared folders, connecting to on, 337–340
   Windows computers versus, 11
Mac Developers Program, 385
Mac Help, 20–23
Mac Observer website, 428
MacBook Air, 417, 425
MacBook Pro, 425
MacFixIt website, 427–428
MacInTouch website, 429
macro viruses, 378–379
Macworld website, 428

Magnification slider, 84
Mail app
    checking mail, 241
    composing new messages, 236–238
    icon for, 71
    mailboxes, 244–245
    overview, 235
    preferences, 242
    Quick Look Slideshow feature, 247–249
    rules, 243–244
    setting up account, 235–236
    signatures, 246–247
    smart mailboxes, 245–246
    spam, 241–242
    stationery, 240–241
    toolbar, 238–239
mailboxes, Mail
    overview, 244
    plain, 244–245
    smart, 245–246
malware, 378–380
Manage Widgets button, 54
Managed accounts
    folders created for, 329
    Parental Controls on, 328
manual backups, 375–376
manually installing fonts, 294
Manually option, 206
margin markers, 290
master password, 383
media
    downloading DV video from camcorder,
        283–284
    downloading photos from camera,
        281–283
    DVD Player, 273–276
    importing, 281–284
    overview, 273
    Photo Booth, 277–279
    Preview, 279–280
    QuickTime Player, 276–277
menu bar, 38–39
Menu Extras menu, 46
menus
    Appearance pop-up, 58
    Apple, 42–43

Arrange, 29
    Burn Speed pop-up, 190
    Contains pop-up, 243
    contextual, 19, 39–40
    Convert, Calculator, 388
    current folder pop-up, 107–108
    customizing, 57–60
    Default Paper Size, 301
    Default Printer pop-up, 301
    disabled options, 40–41
    File Format pop-up, 137
    Finder, items on, 105–107
    Finder, overview, 105
    Flag/Unflag drop-down, 239
    Go, 108–110, 275
    Highlight Color pop-up, 58
    keyboard shortcut commands, 44–46
    menu bar, 38–39
    Menu Extras, 46
    Minimize Windows Using pop-up, 84
    New Finder Windows Open pop-up, 112
    News drop-down, 217
    The Options submenu, 86
    overview, 27, 38
    Paper Size pop-up, 304
    Popular drop-down, 217
    pop-up, 34, 107–108
    pull-down, 38
    Services, 105–106
    Share, 165–166, 277
    shortcut, 39–40
    Sidebar Icon Size pop-up, 58
    Sort Notification Center pop-up, 206
    submenus, 41
    View, 275
    When Performing a Search pop-up, 114
    Where pop-up, 138
Message option, 165
Messages app
    audio chats, 252–253
    icon for, 72
    iMessage, 250
    overview, 249–250
    remote screen sharing, 253–255
    using, 250–251
    video chats, 252–253

mice, third-party, 424–425
Microsoft Natural Ergonomic Keyboard
    4000, 425
Microsoft Windows
  disks, compatibility with Macs, 185–186
  enabling file sharing with, 319
  Mac versus, 11
  macro viruses, 378–379
  using Boot Camp to run on Macs, 365–366
Microsoft Word program, 287
Migration Assistant app, 396–397
Minimize button, 29, 30, 37
Minimize Windows into app Icon option,
    84–85
Minimize Windows Using pop-up menu, 84
Mirroring feature, 366–367
Mission Control tool
  Hot Corners button, 175
  icon for, 71
  overview, 172–175
  spaces, general discussion, 175–178
  spaces, navigating, 179–181
modem setup, 212–213
Modifier Keys button, 61
monitors
  overview, 422–423
  resolution of, 413–414
More Info section, 117
mouse
  buying, 424–425
  learning to use, 19–20
  preferences, 64–65
Move to Trash keyboard shortcut, 413
Movie Inspector window, 277
movies
  adding in iTunes, 263
  DVD Player, 273–276
  QuickTime Player, 276–277
moving
  files and folders, 158–159
  files between disks, 185
  windows, 36
MP3 CD format, 268
multimedia titles, 424
music, QuickTime Player, 276–277
Mute check box, 68

• *N* •

Name & Extension section, 117
nested folders, 123–124
Network command, 109
network connections, 214
network printers, 315, 316
Network Setup Assistant feature, 215
networks
  defined, 314
  home-office networking, 315–317
  overview, 314–315
  three ways to build, 317–318
New Calendar button, 194
New Finder Window command, 35, 45
New Finder Windows Open pop-up
    menu, 112
New Folder command, 45, 137
New Message button, 238
New Smart Playlist option, 267
News drop-down menu, 217
Next button, 248
No Access permission, 334
noncontiguous photos, 282
Non-Volatile RAM (NVRAM), 406
Not in Notification Center section, 206
Not Junk button, 242
notebook computers
  power settings for, 364
  sleep settings for, 363
Notes app
  icon for, 72
  overview, 206–208
Notification Center feature, 205–206
NVRAM (Non-Volatile RAM), 406

• *O* •

Open command, 35, 45
Open Disk Utility option, 188
Open Finder option, 188
Open iDVD option, 188
Open in 32-bit mode check box, 116
Open iTunes option, 188
Open keyboard shortcut, 412

Open Other app option, 188
Open Stream option, 266
Open with Preview button, 249
Open/Close Control Drawer option, 274
opened icons, 70
opening files
  with apps, 145–147
  from Dock, 78
  with drag-and-drop, 143
  inability to, 144–145
  overview, 141–143
  with Quick Look, 143–144
OpenType fonts, 293
operating system, general discussion of,
  10–11
optical discs, backups on, 375–376
Option-key symbol, 44
Organize by Categories option, 49
organizing files in folders
  creating new folders, 150–151
  files versus folder, 147–148
  overview, 147
  smart folders, 152–155
  spring-loaded folders, 151–152
  with subfolders, 148–150
Orientation option, 304, 307
Other items command, 37
Other World Computing website, 432
output sound options, 68
Output Volume slider, 68
owner permissions, 330–331, 334, 335

packages, 147
Page keys, 32
Page Setup sheet, 298, 302–304
Pages option, 307
Pages per Sheet option, 308
panes, 28
Paper Handling feature, 308
Paper Size option, 307
Paper Size pop-up menu, 304
Parallels Desktop app, 366
parameter RAM (PRAM), 406
parent files of aliases, finding, 98

parent icon, 97–98
Parental controls, Users & Groups System
  Preferences pane, 326–328
Partition tab, Disk Utility, 392–393
partitions, 392
Party Shuffle feature, 269
Password Assistant feature, 324
passwords
  changing, of any account on Macs,
    341–342
  changing on other Macs, 342–343
  changing on personal Macs, 341
  Keychain Access utility, 395
  master, 383
  settings for, 384
  user account, setting, 324, 326
Paste keyboard shortcut, 412
pasting from Clipboard, 157
path bar, 89–90
PC disks, compatibility with Macs, 185–186
PDFs
  Preview, 279–280
  viewing documents as, 309–311
peripherals
  dealmac website, 433
  Other World Computing website, 432
permissions
  overview, 329–330
  setting for folders, 332
  sharing folders, 332–334
  types of, 330–332
  useful settings for, 334–336
personal account passwords
  changing on other Macs, 342–343
  changing on personal Macs, 341
Photo Booth app
  icon for, 72
  overview, 277–279
Photo Browser option, 238
photos
  on Desktop, 50–51
  downloading from camera, 281–283
  previewing, 279–280
  user account, changing, 326
  user account, setting, 325

plain mailboxes, 244–245
Play Sound when Receiving Notifications
    check box, 206
Play User Interface Sound Effects check
    box, 68
playlists, iTunes
    burning to CD, 268–269
    creating, 266–267
    Genius, 269–270
    iTunes DJ, 270–271
    overview, 266
    smart, 267–268
Play/Pause button, 249
podcasts, adding in iTunes, 263–264
point-and-click techniques, 19–20
pointing, defined, 19
Point-to-Point Protocol over Ethernet
    (PPPoE), 214
Point-to-Point Protocol (PPP), 214
Popular drop-down menu, 217
pop-up menus
    for current folders, 107–108
    overview, 34
portrait-oriented option, 304
ports, Ethernet, 314
Position on Screen option, 84
PostScript Type 1 fonts, 292
power button
    overview, 12
    sleep settings for, 364
PPP (Point-to-Point Protocol), 214
PPPoE (Point-to-Point Protocol over
    Ethernet), 214
PRAM (parameter RAM), 406
preferences
    Dock, 83–86
    folder and disk icon menu, 85–86
    global Dock, 83–85
    Mail, 242
Preferences command, 105
Preferences folder
    contents of, 132
    discovering problem-causing files in, 406
presets, 309
Preview app, 82, 279–280, 309–311
Preview section, 117

Previous button, 248
Primary Mouse Button radio buttons, 64
Print & Scan icon, 300
Print & Scan System Preferences pane, 300
Print keyboard shortcut, 412
Print option, 279
Print Settings option, 308
Print sheet
    choosing among different printers,
        305–306
    custom settings, 306–308
    overview, 304
    printing document, 304–305
    saving custom settings, 309
printer font, 293
Printer Sharing, 346
printers
    choosing, on Print sheet, 305–306
    connecting, 298–299
    in networks, 315, 316
    setting up for first time, 300–302
    sharing, 302
printing
    choosing among different printers,
        305–306
    connecting printers, 298–299
    custom settings, 306–308
    document, 304–305
    faxing, 311–312
    overview, 297–298
    Page Setup sheet, 302–304
    PDFs, viewing documents as, 309–311
    Preview, 309–311
    Print sheet, 304–309
    printer sharing, 302
    saving custom settings, 309
    setting up for first time, 300–302
    sharing, 298–302
    wireless, 299
processes, 388–390
programmer calculator, 388
prohibitory signs, 14–15, 400–401
Prosoft's Drive Genius tool, 404
protecting data
    blocking or limiting connections, 383
    locking down files with FileVault, 383–384

protecting data *(continued)*
  other security options, 384–385
  overview, 382
protocols, defined, 314–315
proxy servers, 214
Public folder, 130, 319–322, 329
pull-down menus, 38
punctuation, dictating, 348

Quick Look command
  opening files with, 143–144
  overview, 163–165
  Share menu, 165–166
  Slideshow (full-screen) mode, 166
Quick Look Slideshow feature, 247–249
QuickLook button, 248
QuickTime Player, 276–277
Quit keyboard shortcut, 413

Radio buttons, 33
RAID tab, Disk Utility, 393
RAM (random-access memory)
  Ramseeker website, 431–432
  troubleshooting, 407
  upgrading, 417
Ramseeker website, 431–432
Read & Write permission, 334
Read Only permission, 334
Reader button, 216
Reading List, Safari, 219–220
read-only bulletin boards, 336
Recent Folders command, 110
Recent Items option, 43
recommended software updates, installing, 381–382
Recovery Disk Assistant app, 400
Recovery HD partition
  booting into Safe Mode, 405–406
  overview, 400, 402–403
  reinstalling OS X, 407
  repair options, 407–408
  running First Aid, 403–405
  zapping PRAM/NVRAM, 406

refurbished computers, 417
reinstalling OS X
  overview, 435
  process, 436–437
  Setup Assistant, 437–439
  when troubleshooting, 407
Reminders app
  creating Reminders, 203–204
  icon for, 72
  Lists, 202–203
  Notification Center, 205–206
  overview, 202
remote devices, defined, 314
remote Macs
  account passwords, changing from, 342–343
  disconnecting from, 340
  screen sharing, 343–344
  shared disks, connecting to on, 337–340
  shared folders, connecting to on, 337–340
remote screen sharing, 253–255
Remove from Dock option, 81, 86
removing
  icons from Dock, 81
  users, 326
renaming icons, 160–161
renewing models, 416–417
repair options, 407–408
Reply All button, 239
Reply button, 239
resetting PRAM/NVRAM, 406
resizing
  Dock, 82
  windows, 36
resolution, screen, 413–414
Restart command, 43
restarts, automatic, 363
Restore tab, Disk Utility, 393–394
restoring files, 374–375
Reverse Page Orientation check box, 308
Right margin marker, 290
right-clicks, 39
routers, 317, 318
rules, Mail, 243–244
Run Script option, 188

• S •

Safari app
  bookmarking favorite pages, 217–219
  Help Center, 224
  icon for, 71
  navigating with toolbar buttons, 215–217
  overview, 215
  Reading List, 219–220
  saving passwords in, 396
  searching with Google, 222–224
  Top Sites page, 220–221
Safe Mode, booting in, 405–406
Save a Version command, 134
Save As option, 138–141
Save Burn Folder To check box, 190
Save sheet, 135
saving documents
  basic process, 133–138
  overview, 132–133
  Save As versus Duplicate, 138–141
saving Print sheet custom settings,
    305–306
scalable fonts, 292
Scale option, 304
Scanner Sharing feature, 346
scientific calculator, 388
Screen Flash feature, 278
screen of death, 14
screen resolution, 413–414
screen savers
  overview, 51–53
  password requirement after start of, 384
Screen Sharing feature, 343–344
screen shots, 394
scroll bars
  overview, 29
  in windows, 31–32
Scrolling Speed slider, 64
search attributes, 170–172
Search box
  in Finder windows, 167–169
  in toolbar, 92
Search field, 29
second monitors, 422–423

Secure Empty Trash command, 162
security
  backups, manual, 375–376
  backups, two sets of, 376–378
  backups, with commercial software, 376
  backups with Time Machine, 372–375
  blocking or limiting connections, 383
  firewall, 380–381
  installing recommended software
    updates, 381–382
  locking down files with FileVault, 383–384
  malware, 378–380
  other options, 384–385
  overview, 371–372
  protecting data, 382–385
  viruses, 378–380
Security and Privacy icon, 53
Seeing section, Accessibility System
    Preferences pane, 361–362
Select All command, 45
Select All keyboard shortcut, 412
Select the Badge App Icon check box, 206
selected icons, 70
selecting multiple icons, 159–160
selecting text, 288–290
Send button, 237
Server Message Block (SMB), 319
Services menu, 105–106
Settings option, 303
Share menu, 165–166, 277
Share My Screen option, 253
shared disks, connecting to on remote
    Mac, 337–340
Shared folder check box, 116
shared folders
  connecting to on remote Mac, 337–340
  overview, 128
  shared by default, 329
shareware, 429
sharing. *See also* access
  connecting to shared disk or folder on
    remote Mac, 337–340
  files, overview, 314–315
  files, setting up, 318–319
  Internet Sharing, 345
  networks, building, 317–318

sharing *(continued)*
  networks, home-office networking, 315–317
  networks, overview, 314–315
  other types of, 346
  overview, 313–314
  passwords, changing, 341–343
  passwords of any account on Macs, changing, 341–342
  personal account password on other Macs, changing, 342–343
  personal account password on personal Macs, changing, 341
  printers, 302
  Screen Sharing, 343–344
  Web Sharing, 344
Sharing & Permissions section, 117
Sharing Accounts, creating, 321–322
Sharing System Preferences pane, 318–319, 332–336
shortcut menus, 39–40
Show Alerts and Banners switch, 206
Show All command, 107
Show All Filename Extensions check box, 114
Show All in Finder item, 170
Show Columns check boxes, 416
Show Controller option, 274
Show in Finder option, 75, 86
Show in Notification Center check box, 206
Show in Notification Center pop-up menu, 206
Show Indicator Lights for Open apps option, 85
Show Keyboard & Character Viewers in the Menu Bar check box, 61
Show Path Bar option, 122
Show Scroll Bars radio buttons, 58
Show Stationery option, 238
Show These Items on the Desktop check boxes, 112
Show Top Sites option, 221
Show Volume in Menu Bar check box, 68
Show Warning before Changing an Extension check box, 114
Show Warning before Emptying the Trash check box, 114

Show with Clock check box, 52
Show/Hide Calendar option, 202
Show/Hide Sidebar option, 203
shuffling windows, 37
Shut Down command, 43
shutting down computer
  options for, 43
  overview, 16–17
Sidebar
  adding folders to, 111
  buttons in, 29
Sidebar Icon Size pop-up menu, 58
Sidebar pane, Finder preferences, 114
Sign in button, 262
signatures, Mail, 246–247
single clicks, 19
Size preferences, 83
Sleep command, 43
sleep settings
  password required upon waking, 384
  saving energy with, 363
Slideshow (full-screen) mode, 166, 275
Slideshow feature, Quick Look, 247–249
Slideshow option, 247
Slow Keys, 362
smart folders, 152–155
Smart Groups, setting up in Contacts, 231–232
smart mailboxes, 245–246
Smart Playlist window, 268
smart playlists, 267–268
SMB (Server Message Block), 319
Snapz Pro X utility, 394
Snooze button, 206
software
  firewalls, 380–381
  installing recommended updates, 381–382
  typing instruction, 413
  virus-detection, 379
Software Update option, 42
Software Update System Preferences pane, 382
Software Update window, 300
Solid State Drive (SSD), 419
songs, adding in iTunes, 261–262
Sort By option, 86

Sort Notification Center pop-up menu, 206
sound
  changing sound effects, 68
  choosing output and input options, 68
  overview, 67–68
spaces
  general discussion, 175–178
  navigating, 179–181
spam, 241–242
speakers, 424
Special Characters command, 288
Speech Commands window, 352, 353
Speech Recognition feature
  overview, 349
  setting up, 350–351
  using, 351–354
Speech System Preferences pane, 355–356
speeding up user experience
  accelerated graphics cards, 417–418
  hard drives, 418–419
  keyboard shortcuts, 411–413
  overview, 411
  RAM, upgrading, 417
  renewing models, 416–417
  resolution, 413–414
  SSD, 419
  typing skills, improving, 413
  view options, 415–416
Spotlight Comments section, 116
Spotlight feature
  overview, 167
  search attributes, 170–172
  using search box in Finder windows,
    167–169
  using Spotlight menu and window,
    169–170
spring-loaded folders, 151–152
SSD (Solid State Drive), 419
stacks, 69
Start Genius button, 269
startup
  crashes at, 408
  general discussion, 12–16
startup disks
  finding or creating, 400
  prohibitory signs, 400–401

troubleshooting, 399–402
  using with permissions, 330
Startup Manager feature, 402
stationery, Mail, 240–241
Stationery Pad check box, 116
status bar, 89–90
Sticky Keys, 362
streaming audio, 265
subfolders, 147, 148–150
submailboxes, 244–245
submenus, 41
Subscribe button, 263, 264
subwoofers, 424
suitcase file, 293
SuperDuper! app, 377, 400
switches, 317, 318
System folder, 127–128
System Information app, 15, 397
System Preferences app
  Accessibility pane, 361–363
  Display pane, 414
  general discussion, 47–49
  icon for, 72
  Keyboard pane, 60–64
  Print & Scan pane, 300
  Sharing pane, 318–319, 332–336
  Software Update pane, 382
  Speech pane, 355–356
  Users & Groups pane, 321–328, 341–342

• *T* •

tabs, 33
TCP/IP network connection, 214
Tech Support hotline, Apple, 407
Ten Thumbs Typing Tutor, 413
Terminal app, 397–398
text. *See also* TextEdit app
  Font Book, 293–294
  fonts, installing manually, 294
  fonts, overview, 292
  fonts, types of, 292–293
  formatting, 288–290
  overview, 285
  selecting, 288–290

Text Boxes and Lists Only radio button, 63
Text to Speech feature, 355–356
TextEdit app
  creating and composing documents, 286–288
  custom settings for, 308
  graphics, adding to documents, 290–291
  overview, 285–286
  selecting and formatting text, 288–290
text-entry fields, 34
The Options submenu, 86
third-party backup programs, 376
third-party keyboards, 424–425
third-party mice, 424–425
This Desktop option, 179–180
thumbnails, 416
Thunderbolt bus, 418
Time Capsule device, 315, 373
time limits, Parental Controls for, 328
Time Machine system
  overview, 372–375
  recommendations for, 377
timed screen captures, 394
timesaving tools
  Hot Corners button, 175
  Launchpad, 181–182
  Mission Control, 172–181
  overview, 163
  Quick Look, 163–166
  search box in Finder windows, using, 167–169
  spaces, general discussion, 175–178
  spaces, navigating, 179–181
  Spotlight, overview, 167
  Spotlight, search attributes, 170–172
  Spotlight menu and window, using, 169–170
toolbar
  buttons in, 29
  Finder, 90–92
  Mail, 238–239
  Safari, 215–217
Top Sites page, Safari, 220–221
Tracking Speed slider, 64, 67
trackpad preferences, 66–67
transferring files, 251

Translation widget, 56
Trash container
  icon for, 73
  overview, 73–75
Trim control, 277
tri-state check boxes, 34
troubleshooting
  booting, 399–401
  crashes at startup, 408
  overview, 399
  recovery from Recovery HD partition, 402–408
  reinstalling OS X, 407
  repair options, 407–408
  running First Aid, 403–405
  Safe Mode, booting into, 405–406
  startup disks, 399–401
  zapping PRAM/NVRAM, 406
TrueType fonts, 292
Turn Off When Computer Is Not Used For slider, 61
turning on computer, 12
two-finger swipes, 32
Two-Sided option, 308
two-sided printing, 308
Type 1 fonts, 292–293
typefaces, 285
typing skills, improving, 413

• U •

Undo keyboard shortcut, 412
Undo option, 73–74, 146
unsharing folders, 336
updates
  for apps, 361
  automatically installing as security measure, 379
  installing recommended software, 381–382
USB 2, 419
Use all F1, F2 Keys as Standard Function Keys check box, 61
Use Cover page check box, 312

user accounts
  creating, 321–325
  editing information, 325–326
  transferring with Migration Assistant, 396–397
user experience, speeding up
  accelerated graphics cards, 417–418
  hard drives, 418–419
  keyboard shortcuts, 411–413
  overview, 411
  RAM, upgrading, 417
  renewing models, 416–417
  resolution, 413–414
  SSD, 419
  typing skills, improving, 413
  view options, 415–416
users
  changing, 325–326
  limiting capabilities of, 326–328
  overview, 320–325
  removing, 326
Users & Groups System Preferences pane
  account passwords, changing, 341–342
  administrative use of, 321
  creating user accounts, 322–325
  editing user accounts, 325–327
  Parental Controls, 326–328
Users folder, 122, 128
utilities
  Activity Monitor, 388–390
  AirPort Utility, 390
  Calculator, 387–388
  ColorSync Utility, 390–391
  DigitalColor Meter, 391
  Disk Utility, 391–394
  Grab, 394
  Grapher, 394–395
  Keychain Access, 395–396
  Migration Assistant, 396–397
  overview, 387
  System Information, 397
  Terminal, 397–398

• **V** •

vCard (virtual business card), 235
Versions feature, 134
video subsystems, 418
videos
  adding in iTunes, 263
  calling with FaceTime, 224–226
  chatting with Messages, 252–253
  DV, downloading from camcorder, 283–284
View buttons, 29, 91
View Contents As option, 86
View menu, 275
View options, 415–416
views
  Calendar, 194–195
  Column, 99–100
  Contacts, 232–233
  Cover Flow, 104–105
  Icon, 100–102
  List, 102–104
  overview, 99
virtual business card (vCard), 235
virtual mailboxes, 245
VirtualBox app, 366
virus-detection software, 379, 380
viruses, 378–380
VMWare Fusion, 366
voice features
  Dictation, 348–349
  overview, 347–348
  Speech Recognition, overview, 349
  Speech Recognition, setting up, 350–351
  Speech Recognition, using, 351–354
  Text to Speech, 355–356
  VoiceOver technology, 354–355
  VoiceOver Utility, 355
VoiceOver technology, 354–355
VoiceOver Utility, 355
volume
  level for dictation, 348
  storage space as, 392

• W •

Web Sharing, 344
websites
  adding passwords to keychains, 395–396
  Alltop, 429–430
  Apple Support and Knowledge Base, 431
  CNET Downloads, 429
  dealmac, 433
  Dr. Mac Consulting, 433
  EveryMac.com, 432
  Mac Observer, 428
  MacFixIt, 427–428
  MacInTouch, 429
  Macworld, 428
  Other World Computing, 432
  Parental Controls for, 328
  Ramseeker, 431–432
What You See Is What You Get (WYSIWYG)
    software, 290
When Performing a Search pop-up
    menu, 114
Where pop-up menu, 138
Widget Selection Screen, 54–55
widgets on Dashboard
  Flight Tracker, 56–57
  overview, 53–55
  Translation, 56
Wi-Fi
  printing using, 299
  sharing, 345
Window title, 29

windows
  active, 32–33
  buttons on top of, 30
  closing, 35
  customizing, 57–60
  dialogs, 33–34
  moving, 36
  opening, 35
  overview, 27–30, 35
  resizing, 36
  scroll bars, 31–32
  shuffling, 37
Windows, Microsoft
  disks, compatibility with Macs, 185–186
  enabling file sharing with, 319
  Mac versus, 11
  macro viruses, 378–379
  using Boot Camp to run on Macs, 365–366
wireless Base Stations, AirPort Extreme,
    315, 318
wireless printing, 299
Word program, 287
word-processing apps, placing in dock, 82
workflow, Automator, 359
Write Only (Drop Box) permission, 334
WYSIWYG (What You See Is What You Get)
    software, 290

• Z •

zapping PRAM/NVRAM, 406
zoom accessibility options, 362
Zoom command, 29, 30, 37